Esther van Eijk is a postdoctoral researcher in the Faculty of Law at Maastricht University and holds a PhD from Leiden University. Her work has appeared in the books *Sharia Incorporated: A Comparative Overview of the Legal Systems of Twelve Muslim Countries in Past and Present* (2010) and *Family Law in Islam: Divorce, Marriage and Women in the Muslim World* (I.B.Tauris, 2012). She has also published in the journals *Electronic Journal of Islamic and Middle Eastern Law* and *Erasmus Law Review*. She is Board Member and Secretary of the Dutch Association for the Study of the Law of Islam and the Middle East.

'This is an excellent piece of work in a poorly researched topic. Indeed, while the personal status of Muslims has attracted much attention, family law of non-Muslim communities in Muslim-majority societies has been neglected. However, this study provides a wonderful entry into the legal and social evolutions of contemporary multi-confessional societies in which co-existence and tolerance have become especially problematic recently.'

Baudouin Dupret, Director of Research at the National Centre for Scientific Research (CNRS), France, and Associate Professor for Law, Political Science and Anthropology at Leiden University, Netherlands and the University of Louvain, Belgium

'This book is a significant addition to the literature on contemporary family law in the Middle East, with valuable research material on Syrian law and court practice presented within the frames of emerging scholarly themes.'

Lynn Welchman, Professor of Law, School of Oriental and African Studies (SOAS), University of London

FAMILY LAW IN SYRIA

Patriarchy, Pluralism and Personal Status Laws

Esther van Eijk

I.B. TAURIS
LONDON · NEW YORK

Published in 2016 by
I.B.Tauris & Co. Ltd
London • New York
www.ibtauris.com

Library of Islamic Law 7

ISBN: 978 1 78453 334 2
eISBN: 978 1 78672 019 1
ePDF: 978 1 78673 019 0

A full CIP record for this book is available from the British Library
A full CIP record is available from the Library of Congress

Library of Congress Catalog Card Number: available

Typeset in Garamond Three by OKS Prepress Services, Chennai, India

Calligraphy on dedication page by Chafik Jeddou

There is a crack, a crack in everything
That's how the light gets in.

Anthem, Leonard Cohen (1992)

إلى أهلي وأصحابي وأحبابي في سوريا بلاد الشام

CONTENTS

NOTE ON TRANSLITERATION

In this book both Modern Standard Arabic and Syrian colloquial Arabic terms and expressions (with the exception of proper names and geographic names) are presented and transliterated into English. A simplified system is used without diacritical marks, except for the *'ayn* (') and *hamza* ('), the latter only in the middle or at the end of a word. Long vowels have also been omitted.

Arabic	Transliterated English
ء	'
ب	b
ت	t
ث	th
ج	j
ح	h
خ	kh
د	d
ذ	dh
ر	r
ز	z
س	s
ش	sh
ص	s
ض	d
ط	t
ظ	z

ع	‘
غ	gh
ف	f
ق	q
ك	k
ل	l
م	m
ن	n
ه	h
و	w / u
ي	y / i / iyy

LIST OF ABBREVIATIONS

ASI	Association for the Social Initiative
CCEO	*Codex Canonum Ecclesiarum Orientalium*; Code of Canons of the Eastern Churches
CEDAW	Convention of Elimination of All Forms of Discrimination Against Women
CLPS	Catholic Law of Personal Status
CRC	Convention on the Rights of the Child
LR	*Lois et Réglements*
OLFR	Ottoman Law of Family Rights
SCFA	Syrian Commission for Family Affairs
SLPS	Syrian Law of Personal Status

ACKNOWLEDGEMENTS

I am indebted to many people who contributed and supported me in various ways in the completion of this book. My utmost thanks go out to the people I met in Syria, who made it possible for me to conduct my research, both professionally and personally. In particular, I would like to express my deepest and most profound gratitude to Catherine and Muhanned, who have assisted me in my research in countless ways and who became dear and wonderful friends. I hope and pray that you will soon be able to return to your beloved country.

My thanks also goes out to my 'Syrian family' who generously looked after me and, by sharing their lives and thoughts with me, have taught me invaluable lessons about Syrian history, family life, politics and culture. Also, I would like to extend my earnest appreciation and gratitude to judge Ibrahim and his clerk; judges Antoun and Eliyas and other staff members of the Catholic court of Damascus; staff members of the Greek Orthodox court of Damascus; and lawyers Ahmed, Hanan, Nawal, Rania, and Yusuf. My thanks are also due to other persons who I have interviewed and/or interacted with in various ways whilst in Syria.

My fieldwork stays in Syria were made possible by funding from the Leiden University Fund (LUF) and funding from the Leiden University Institute for Area Studies (LIAS), previously known as the CNWS. I would like to thank the now-dissolved Netherlands Institute for Academic Studies in Damascus (NIASD) and the (former) staff of LIAS/CNWS for their assistance during my time in Damascus and Leiden, respectively.

My sincere appreciation goes out to Léon Buskens for his support and constructive comments on earlier versions of this book. I would also like to thank Ton Meijers and Johan Meijer for their comments and suggestions on the sections on Eastern Catholic Law.

I also thank my (former) editor at I.B.Tauris, Maria Marsh, and her successor, Sophie Rudland, for guiding me through the publishing process, and Dan Shutt, production editor at I.B.Tauris, for the very pleasant and smooth co-operation in realising this book. A warm thank you goes out to Louise Massara, who did a great job copy-editing the manuscript.

I would like to extend my appreciation and thanks to the many colleagues in the field (in its broadest sense) whose valuable suggestions, thoughts, and work have contributed to the successful completion of this work, including, amongst others, Mohammed Al-Sulami, Mary Davies, Pauline Kruiniger, Iva Peša, Iris Sportel, and Maaike Voorhoeve. A special thanks goes out to Nadia Sonneveld for her encouragement and many valuable comments on my work. And to many others, unmentioned here but not forgotten – I thank you.

INTRODUCTION

In April 2009 I attended a court hearing in the Greek Orthodox court of Damascus. A young couple seeking divorce appeared in the court for a cross-examination session. The plaintiff was a strong-willed woman who claimed that the marriage was never consummated and that she was still a virgin because her husband was not 'manly' enough. The husband, for his part, was clearly annoyed and embarrassed by her allegations. In his defence he presented a little plastic bag to the court, which he said contained the proof that she had lost her virginity: the blood-stained cloth of the wedding night.

This case particularly struck me because, according to my prior assumptions, I associated the importance of physical proof of a bride's virginity as typical of Muslim societies rather than of Christian societies. The case proved these assumptions to be false. During my fieldwork I increasingly realised that the Christian and Muslim communities of Syria shared many common normative values and practices, in particular views on marriage, family, gender and sexual propriety. Examples like this confirmed my growing conviction that statutory laws were not the only normative force in the field of family law.

This book is an account of research undertaken between the years 2007 and 2012 into the legal plurality of Syria's family law. It might seem trivial to write a study on family law in Syria while the country has fallen into a full-scale civil war. At the moment of finalising the manuscript of this book (2015), there is no way of knowing in which direction Syria will go, which leaves us with numerous questions: when will this conflict end, who will stay or come to power, what type of government will emerge from the turmoil, and what will become of the state institutions, including the legal system? Despite the tragic, ongoing conflict in Syria and the country's bleak prospects, this book will nevertheless make a very valuable contribution to understanding the historical, socio-political and religious complexities that still mark today's Syria. Not only did the multi-religious composition of Syrian society feed into the formulation and application of family law and thus have an impact on inter-communal relationships and the daily lives of individual Syrians, but the country's sectarian composition also shaped the socio-political context that underpinned the origins and development of the current conflict. Whatever the future holds for the country and its people, the way in which a (future) government deals with the plurality of Syria's personal status law will be significant, in particular for the (future) position of religious minorities in Syria.

As the legal system of Syria has not been disbanded and still appears to function, at least in the government-controlled areas, this book will consider the official legal system, its laws and institutions as currently in force.[1]

Family law in Syria

> Syria is located on the Mediterranean Sea and borders Turkey, Lebanon, Israel, Jordan and Iraq. Before the outbreak of the conflict in March 2011, the Syrian Arab Republic had a population of well over 22 million people. At that time, about 90 per cent of the Syrians were of Arab ethnicity, the rest being mainly Kurdish and Armenian. There were never any official statistics available on religion, but according to (pre-conflict) estimates about 74 per cent of all Syrians were Sunni Muslims, and around 16 per cent were non-Sunni Muslims, such as Druze, Shi'a and 'Alawi. About 10 per cent of the population belonged to various Christian denominations. In addition, a few Jewish and Yazidi families lived in Syria.[2]

Syria has always been a multi-religious and multi-ethnic country, with a Muslim majority and several religious minorities, most notably various Christian denominations. Since Ottoman times, the different religious communities have enjoyed the right to regulate and administer their family relations according to their respective religious laws. The main law in Syria that currently regulates family relations, the 1953 Syrian Law of Personal Status[3] (*qanun al-ahwal al-shakhsiyya*) (hereafter SLPS), amended in 1975, 2003 and 2010, is predominately based on Islamic legal sources, particularly Hanafi *fiqh* (i.e. Islamic jurisprudence). The SLPS is the general law because it applies to all Syrians, irrespective of their religion. This means, for example, that non-Muslims also have to refer to a *shar'iyya*[4] court (i.e. the competent courts to hear cases under the SLPS) for matters related to, most notably, the determination of paternity and legal capacity and representation. That said, conversely – or perhaps more importantly – the SLPS grants the Druze, Jewish and Christian communities limited legislative and judicial autonomy in personal status matters, most importantly marriage and divorce. Family relations in Syria are thus governed by a multiplicity of personal status (or family) laws that regulate matters of personal status, including marriage, dower, dissolution of marriage, maintenance, child custody and succession.

Manifestations of legal plurality

Family law in Syria as such is pluralistic, as a multiplicity of personal status laws and courts operate within the legal framework of the state. This situation of legal plurality is further complicated by the fact that the various laws are generally religion-based: Islamic, Christian and Jewish, although in varying degrees. What's more, the courts that implement these laws are either civil (i.e. non-religious) courts or religious courts: a situation which can lead to interesting and complex intersections of jurisdictions and communal relations.[5] This situation of legal plurality does not, however, imply equality of laws and jurisdictions, as the general law that regulates family relations (i.e. the SLPS) and the courts that implement this law, that is, the *shar'iyya* courts, clearly have supremacy over the other (i.e. non-Muslim) laws and courts. This asymmetrical plurality will be discussed in further detail in Chapter 2.

A variety of statutory personal status laws and courts thus organises and regulates matters of personal status through legislation and courts – but only to a certain degree. In this study I will maintain that besides the inherent pluralism of Syria's personal status law, other (i.e. non-state) 'forms of normative ordering'[6] are at work within and in conjunction with this legal field.[7] First of all, the SLPS itself accommodates legal enforcement of extra-judicial customary practices, by allowing retroactive registration of (customary) marriage, unilateral divorce and proof of paternity. Accordingly, the state recognises and incorporates customary practices into its legal framework and thereby enhances legal plurality in the field of family law.[8] Furthermore, state law does not exclude the existence of norms acknowledged and upheld by other (i.e. non-state or lay) actors engaging in the legal arena. Litigants and witnesses, as participants of the legal process, expressed or emphasised (intentionally or unintentionally) the importance or prevalence of communal, religious or moral norms and values about marriage, divorce, gender relations and family relations, in their statements and testimonies. These expressions then, to a certain extent, found their way into legal proceedings and rulings, as judges and lawyers working in the personal status courts had to direct or translate these narratives to accommodate them within the framework of the law.

This book will examine how legal or normative plurality was manifested in Syria's family law between the years 2007 and 2012, taking into account a variety of levels, including statutory, political, communal and individual. First of all, it will describe and analyse a number of historical, legal and political aspects of Syria's plural family law system. Whereas the different aspects of Syria's plural legal landscape are the focus of Part I, Part II aims to demonstrate that, despite this plurality, Syrian personal status law was also characterised by the prevalence of shared norms and views on marriage, gender relations, sexual propriety and family relations. One of the main arguments of this work is that these communal norms were shared amongst the diverse – primarily Muslim and Christian – communities and found their expression in both statutory family law provisions and the legal proceedings of the personal status courts. Part II also provides an analysis of the actual content of the various personal status laws, in addition to an examination of legal practices as observed by the author in a *shar'iyya*, a Catholic and a Greek-Orthodox personal status court in Damascus. Other (i.e. non-state) 'forms of normative ordering' that played a role in the domain of family law, such as patriarchal norms and values[9] regarding marriage and gender roles, will be included in these latter analyses. In doing so, the influence and interactions of various players, that is, the state, the judiciary, legal professionals, women and civil society groups, 'religious men' and individuals (e.g. litigants, witnesses) will be taken into account, as they all contributed to the legal plurality of Syria's personal status law.

Family law in the Middle East and North Africa

This work is informed and inspired by the work of others on family or personal status laws in the Middle East and North Africa. Numerous studies have been conducted about various countries and societies, from a variety of disciplinary angles, including anthropology, gender studies, law, history and religious studies. As Syria is geographically situated in the Middle East, I primarily focused on contemporary studies of other Middle Eastern countries, most notably Egypt, Palestine, Lebanon and Yemen, but also two *Maghrib* (North African) countries, Morocco and Tunisia. For this study a few well-known legal-anthropological studies on family law written by established scholars in the field were selected, including: Buskens (1999) (Morocco), Mir-Hosseini (2000) (Morocco and Iran), Moors (1995) and Welchman (2000) (West Bank, Palestine), Shehada (2005) (Gaza, Palestine).[10] However, inspiration was also drawn from the work of some more junior, upcoming scholars, most notably Carlisle (2007) (Syria), Sonneveld (2012) (Egypt) and Voorhoeve 2014 (Tunisia).[11] These studies focus on the practical (social) implications and/or the application of the personal status laws by courts in the respective countries. Furthermore, some of these scholars have written about debates around personal status laws, see, most importantly, Moors (2003), Buskens (2003) (on Morocco) and Sonneveld (2012) (on Egypt), which is also one of the subjects under study in this book.[12]

Studies on family law in societies and countries in the Middle East and North Africa often focus specifically on Islamic law or Islamic family law. This is understandable to a certain degree, as most statutory family or personal status laws are based on or inspired by Islamic law. Baudouin Dupret in his article 'What is Islamic Law?', however, asserts that scholars regularly claim that Arab personal status laws are Islamic personal status laws. He maintains that such assumptions have to be challenged, for 'these claims fall short of any satisfactory definition of what is specifically Islamic that would make this [or these] law[s] an Islamic law and its provisions something better characterized by their Islamic rather than their national [. . .] dimension'.[13] I agree with Dupret when he asserts that personal status laws should not be made 'an instance of' the general

Islamic law model,[14] but that we have to take into account the specific national (or local) and temporal context of the different laws, which are not necessarily Islamic.[15] Lynn Welchman adopts a similar approach in her book *Women and Muslim Family Laws in Arab States*. She points out that state legislatures, judiciaries and women's movements invoke *shari'a* in relation to Muslim family law in a variety of ways, for example to inform the legislative choices governments make concerning the codification of their statutory family laws.[16]

Before turning to Syrian family law, it is necessary to reflect briefly on the question of what Islamic law is. Islamic law or *shari'a* carries various meanings and connotations: it has been described as 'the expression of God's will for mankind'[17] or 'the sacred Law of Islam'.[18] Calder writes in the entry on *shari'a* of the second edition of the *Encyclopedia of Islam*: 'Within Muslim discourse, *sharīʿa* designates the rules and regulations governing the lives of Muslims, in principal from the Ḳur'ān and ḥadīth.'[19] According to the Islamic faith, God revealed his will and guidance to mankind in the Qur'an through the Prophet Muhammad (*c*.570–632 CE). The Qur'an and the sayings and exemplary actions of the Prophet, the *Sunna*, are the two main sources for Muslims to understand 'God's will for mankind'. Efforts to expound God's will and guidance were traditionally undertaken by religious jurists (*fuqaha'*) and laid down in writing in so-called *fiqh* works. The word *shari'a* is therefore also closely associated with *fiqh*, that is, legal doctrine or the outcome of legal reasoning (Islamic jurisprudence) or, to quote Dupret again: 'Islamic law can be the mere reference to Islam in a legal setting or it can be a legal system identified with the classical body of *fiqh*.'[20] Thus, since there is plurality of definitions and understandings of Islamic law or *shari'a*, we have to be cautious when we use the term Islamic law or *shari'a*, bearing in mind the nuances and sensitivities of this term. For example, I chose to leave the adjective *shar'iyya* in relation to the courts untranslated because I do not want to use the term 'Muslim' or 'Islamic' to denote this type of court. Moreover, to add to the confusion, the adjective *shar'iyya* can also mean 'legal' or 'legitimate'. Besides, they cannot be labelled as religious courts; *shar'iyya* judges are civil servants trained at secular law faculties, unlike the Christian courts, where priests act as judges (see Chapter 6). It is important to note here that the *shar'iyya* courts are regarded as the general personal status courts because, even though the majority of their cases involve Muslims, they also have (limited) jurisdiction over non-Muslims.

It is necessary to provide the reader with a historical context of Islam and Islamic law in order to understand the position of family law within Syria's legal system, the religious minorities–majority relations in the legal context and to understand in which (*fiqh*) tradition concepts and provisions of the SLPS find their origin. That is why, for example, in the description of the historical development of family law in Syria (Chapter 1), the changing position and role of Islamic law or *shari'a* in relation to the state is discussed. In Syria's case, it would, however, be wrong to focus solely on Muslim personal status law because Syrian family law consists of more than the SLPS alone: Druze, Christian and Jewish laws and courts are also part of the picture. Mariz Tadros opens her article on the 'othering' of non-Muslims in relation to personal status law in Egypt as follows:

> There has been a conspicuous tendency in literature on family law in the Arab world to deal separately with Muslim and non-Muslim family legislation as if it affects two communities who inhabit two completely separate and isolated worlds where there is no convergence, engagement or interaction.[21]

I agree with Tadros' observation that family law in the Middle East has too often been regarded from a purely Islamic point of view, thereby ignoring the legal and practical implications of the asymmetrical plurality for non-Muslims, in particular non-Muslim women. Syrian Muslims, Christians, Jews and Druze might belong to different religious communities, with their respective laws and courts, but that does not mean that they confine themselves to their own group (i.e. personal status). They occasionally move up and down these legal-religious categories: they engage with each other, possibly marry and divorce one another, convert to another religion, go to a different (not their own) court to achieve a particular, personal goal. This mobility is not always advantageous though; it can have negative consequences, particularly for non-Muslim women (see Chapter 2).

What do we know about Syrian family law?

Syria is a white spot on the map in many respects: empirical knowledge about the country's socio-political and religious make-up is limited, as has become evident in the current crisis. During the last decades, access to Syria for researchers (and journalists, for that matter) has been difficult due to the political situation. Especially since the 1970s, during the Hafez al-Asad years, Syria was considered an impenetrable country for (in particular) social scientists and anthropologists. Contemporary studies on Syria are written by scholars coming from predominantly archeological, historical (pre-Asad), agricultural and political sciences. Sociological or anthropological studies based on empirical research are scant. Apart from the work of Annika Rabo (1986 and onwards), hardly any empirical studies on Syria have been published since the 1970s. With the coming to power of the son, Bashar al-Asad, in 2000, the country cautiously opened up, and so became more accessible to academic researchers. From the 2000s, more sociological research has been conducted, resulting in academic publications, such as those by Böttcher, Khatib, Pierret and Pinto, who have written on Islam and the state in Syria.

When we look at the field of contemporary family law, however, we find only a small selection of publications. Botiveau, Cardinal and el-Hakim, for example, have written about Syria's legal system and the judiciary, and Dupret and Maktabi about debates on Syrian family law. But when we consider the laws themselves, apart from the articles written by Anderson and Berger,[22] respectively, there is barely any (especially non-Arabic)[23] literature available on the contents of Syria's main family law: the SLPS of 1953. The latest addition, important from a socio-legal perspective, is the work of Jessica Carlisle; she wrote her PhD thesis (SOAS, University of London, 2007) on 'judicial discretion in a Damascus shari'a court'. Apart from her publications, studies on family law practices or practices of the Syrian personal status courts are (to my knowledge) non-existent. More importantly, I have not yet come across any studies dealing with contemporary legal or court practices in Christian family courts in the Middle East. With this work I therefore seek to contribute to filling a gap in the existing body of literature on contemporary laws of personal status in the Middle East.

Methodology and fieldwork

It is important to understand how the various family laws operate in their – inextricably intertwined – legal, socio-political, religious and cultural contexts. The plural nature of Syrian family law requires a multi-disciplinary research approach, including legal studies, historical and anthropological studies. Because family law and religion in Syria are inherently intertwined, a study of the subject requires an appreciation of the historical, religious dimension of the legislation and its implementation. Studying family law from a merely formalistic, legal angle would give us an incomplete and perhaps even false picture. I therefore employed a socio-legal approach to address the question of plurality in Syria's family law. This entails both an analysis of legal texts (e.g. statutory laws and law commentaries), as well as analyses of debates on Syrian family law reform, observations of the law in practice (including court observations), interviews with legal practitioners and other experts, and informal conversations with lawyers.

From March to April 2008 and between October 2008 and July 2009, I conducted fieldwork in Syria, primarily in the city of Damascus. In this period, Syria was already a politically unstable country, which limited research possibilities and my fieldwork. During my two field visits to Damascus I took Arabic language classes, not only to improve my Arabic language skills in order to conduct interviews effectively, engage in participant observation and interact with people, but also because of the lack of an official research permit. I was unable to file for a research permit due to the political situation and, consequently, always stayed in Syria on a tourist or student visa.[24] In spring 2011, I had planned to go back to Syria for a two to three months field visit to follow up on unanswered questions (which were numerous) and other outstanding issues. Unfortunately, due to the developments following the Syrian revolution, which started in mid-March 2011, I had to postpone my travel plans indefinitely, meaning that I have not been back to Syria since I left in the summer of 2009. Instead, I obtained additional information with the help of some befriended Syrian lawyers via email correspondence but this proved difficult, as they themselves had left the country and were preoccupied with other, more pressing issues.

Sources and data collection

The material for this study consists of in-depth, semi-structured interviews, informal interactions and court observations, as well as primary and secondary written sources. These interviews were conducted during the two field visits to Damascus, with the purpose of identifying the different actors in the field and gaining better insight into the Syrian legal system and family law in particular. A total of 28 individuals were interviewed, some of whom (11) were interviewed more than once. The group of respondents consisted of a wide variety of people, including lawyers, judges (two Catholic, a *shar'iyya*, a Protestant and a Druze judge), members of Parliament, diplomats, representatives of religious organisations and governmental bodies, women's rights activists and representatives of civil society groups, who had been active in seeking to change personal status laws and other laws related to women and family issues. The selection process of respondents was rather informal; selections were made on the recommendation of scholars who (had) worked in Syria and through personal contacts in Syria but mostly via other interviewees. The information provided by the experts in the field gave me insight into the legal system in general, the position of family law in the legal system, legal proceedings at the court and more. In addition, I was able to identify the issues at stake in the public debates about reforming family law and subjects related to women and family relations, which included opinions about gender roles and the role of religion in society.

Besides interviews, an important source of information was the recurrent informal interactions I had with (legal) experts, particularly lawyers. Working with lawyers provided me with many insights, and familiarised me with legal procedures, laws and customs.[25] Furthermore, it provided me with an interesting perspective on Syrian legal practice. Through my interactions with them, I got the opportunity to take a closer look behind the scenes of the personal status courts. Whereas I found that judges took on a more formal attitude in their interactions with me, that is using 'official rhetoric', lawyers were often more straightforward. In my experience, most lawyers were generally not hampered by formalities and therefore less inclined to give desirable but 'honest' answers.[26] They pointed out that the 'theory' often did not correspond with what happened in actual practice.

Besides, interactions with Syrian friends, including lawyers, my Arabic teacher and 'family members' provided a much-needed insight into Syrian society. In particular the role of my Syrian 'family members' has been instrumental in my fieldwork and analyses. My ideas and perceptions about family and gender roles – in particular those with regard to women – in Syrian society were influenced by frequent interactions with them. 'My family' was from a predominantly Christian town close to Damascus; they were Christian by birth, but not necessarily by conviction. It was particularly my interactions with the two daughters of this family that taught me much about gender relations in Syrian society and made me realise that many gender norms and values apply equally to all Syrian women, regardless of religion.

Syria's political climate posed challenges in gaining access to the courts, court records and other relevant material. The possibility of conducting frequent court observations in the *shar'iyya* courts of Damascus was limited due to various reasons, most importantly because I did not have the required clearance from the authorities.[27] However, through my network of lawyers, I gained access to three types of personal status courts: a *shar'iyya* court, a Catholic court and a Greek Orthodox court.[28] In the period from February until July 2009, I observed court cases in these three courts in Damascus. It proved to be a challenge to work out the different court schedules, which often collided with each other, and to distribute my time wisely so that I could attend as many sessions as possible in the different personal status courts.

Although the possibility of conducting frequent court observations in the *shar'iyya* courts of Damascus was limited, due to my lacking clearance, I managed to get permission from one *shar'iyya* judge presiding over one of the six *shar'iyya* courts of Damascus proper, to sit in on his court sessions as of late February 2009 (see Chapter 5). I gained access in the first instance to a Catholic court in Damascus through a friend. After two interviews with a Catholic judge in the autumn of 2008, I got the judge's permission to attend his court sessions in March 2009 (see Chapter 6). The same befriended lawyer also opened the door to the Greek Orthodox court. This meant that, around the same time (April 2009), I also got permission to observe court cases in the Greek Orthodox court in Damascus. However, due to a variety of reasons,[29] I attended a limited number of hearings in this court.[30] Therefore, these latter court observations are only used in passing in this study.

The court visits, observations and interactions with the judges, court personnel and lawyers, at all the above-mentioned courts, produced ample and valuable data for my research. The court sessions, that is to say, the interactions between the judges, other court personnel, litigants, lawyers and witnesses, were generally conducted in colloquial Arabic.

Testimonies of litigants, witnesses and/or experts, and all other verbal exchanges were heard in colloquial Arabic. However, court hearings and proceedings were not transcribed verbatim. In all the personal status courts, the presiding judge summarised and dictated what had to be written in the case file in Modern Standard Arabic to his clerk.

Because of the sensitivity of the political situation, I had decided to refrain from asking for permission to record the interviews I conducted and the court sessions I was permitted to attend. Instead, I asked for permission to take notes during the interviews and the court observations and I was never denied permission.[31] All the names used, including the name of the *shar'iyya* judge, in the case studies are fictitious. With regard to my interviewees and informants, when I feared that using their real names could harm them, I used pseudonyms to protect their identity.

Finally, in addition to empirical material collected during my fieldwork in Syria, this work is also based on a variety of textual sources, including primary and secondary written resources. It has to be noted however that, as mentioned earlier, comprehensive published studies about contemporary family law in Syria are scarce. Besides, much of the available material, both in European languages as well as in Arabic, dates from a much earlier period, generally from the 1950s and 1960s. In addition to existing literature, I purchased or received a significant part of the (primary) written material during my visits to Damascus. This includes statutory laws, law commentaries, draft law projects and publications written by women's organisations, legal and religious experts. The available written sources, supplemented with interviews with legal scholars, judges and lawyers, provided a base of material to write about the legal-historical development of Syrian law and Syria's contemporary legal system in general.

Research obstacles

In addition to the obvious practical challenges caused by the political climate in Syria, the 'culture of fear' also had an impact on my data collection and my stay in Syria in general. I agree with the observation of Panagiotis Geros, who has done extensive fieldwork in Syria on Christian identities that 'the academic literature that deals with Syria has underestimated the culture of fear disseminated by Asad's regime and its ramifications for all kinds of social relations'.[32] This culture of fear was cultivated and sustained by the regime with its (allegedly) vast and omnipresent secret police force (*mukhabarat*). The prevailing view that anyone could potentially be a *mukhabarat* agent or be willing to pass on information to the *mukhabarat*, including neighbours, colleagues, family members and friends, contributed to this culture of fear and created a general sense of distrust amongst many Syrians.[33] Furthermore, there were numerous stories going around about foreigners living and working in Syria who had had some sort of encounter with the *mukhabarat*. The general perception that was popular amongst foreigners was that they (foreigners) were considered Western spies by the Syrian government. This culture of fear, whether real or perceived, also had an effect on my experiences and working strategies and, most importantly, limited my data collection. My presence in the court was, however, never the subject of serious concern for the authorities or the court personnel, lawyers or litigants, at least not to my knowledge, but of course my presence did not go unnoticed. Towards the end of my fieldwork, one of the Catholic judges asked for a copy of my passport because the authorities had requested it. In addition, the *shar'iyya* judge asked me a few times if I intended to apply for official permission from the Minister of Justice,[34] despite his explicit approval of my presence in his courtroom.

During my stay in Syria, I also struggled with the question of how to conduct research in a non-transparent, corrupt legal community. My research contacts frequently pointed out to me that corruption had permeated all levels of the judiciary and that bribery, political interference and backroom deals were part of day-to-day reality. Being aware of this fact, I realised even more that what I was able to observe, with regard to legal proceedings and legal practices in the personal status courts of Damascus, was only a small part of a much bigger picture.

Organisation of the book

This book consists of eight chapters and is divided into two parts. In Part I ('The Plural Legal Landscape') a sketch is drawn of the plural legal landscape of Syria, starting with a description of the historical development of the (religious) family law. This inherited plurality founded the fabric of Syria's current mosaic of family law, with all its complexities and contestations. Part II, entitled 'Unity in Multiplicity', focuses on the content of the various personal status laws and on judicial practices in and around various personal status courts in Damascus. In addition, the argument that the diverse personal status courts were united in their shared communal, cultural understandings of marriage, gender and family relations, will run as a connecting thread through this second part of the book.

Chapter 1 discusses the historical development of the position of religion, most notably Islam and Islamic (family) law in relation to the central state authority in Syria's past and present. I will argue that the religious legal plurality in personal status matters was maintained by the Syrian governments and the religious communities.

Chapter 2 will map out the different laws and courts of personal status that we find in Syria today; particular attention will be given to the general law of personal status, the SLPS. Furthermore, the difference in position of personal status for Muslims and non-Muslims will be examined, thereby also addressing the complexities that arise out of the intersection of the different jurisdictions.

Chapter 3 describes attempts that were made, some more successful than others, to change the SLPS and other personal status laws during the last decade (2000–10), including the debates that surrounded those proposed reforms. I will conclude the chapter with an analysis of why reform in family law has remained a political sensitive issue in the recent past.

Chapter 4 focuses on the intersection of law and culture; it will describe the cultural context in which Syrian family law operates. It will first introduce some key concepts in relation to family relations in Syria in order to provide an understanding of how they relate to and interact with the content of, and legal discourses and practices around, the various laws of personal status. Secondly, this chapter will analyse the legal regulation of marriage and divorce, according to the provisions of the SLPS and the major Christian laws of personal status.

Chapter 5 is concerned with the practical implementation of the SLPS, focusing on legal procedures and practices in the *shar'iyya* courts in Damascus. It will describe and analyse the merits and demerits of the versatility of the SLPS and the legal system. In addition, I will address the subject of (legal and non-legal) shared norms and views on morality, social propriety, marriage and gender relations.

Chapter 6 will expound the Catholic Law of Personal Status (CLPS) of 2006 and the workings of a Catholic court in Damascus. I will address the particularities of this court, in addition to similarities with other personal status courts. The latter issue manifested itself particularly in the presence of, and importance attached to, patriarchal norms and values on marriage and family relations.

The Conclusion draws together the main arguments of the book and ends with some reflections on one of the major challenges that any future government of Syria will have to address: what should they do with Syria's plural family law system?

The content of this study, including any error, (mis)interpretation or presentation of the data, is solely my responsibility and does not represent the views and opinions of my informants.

PART I

THE PLURAL LEGAL LANDSCAPE

CHAPTER 1

LAW, POLITICS AND RELIGION IN SYRIA: PAST AND PRESENT

Syria's legal system is a mix of Ottoman, French, Egyptian and religious law; the latter is predominantly found in the field of family law. The different religious communities have long since enjoyed the right to regulate and administer their family relations according to their respective religious laws. Consequently, family relations in Syria are governed by a multiplicity of religion-based personal status (or family) laws. This chapter will examine how this system of legal plurality, in particular with regard to personal status law, came about. Starting from the Ottoman era, I will concentrate on important historical and legal developments in Syria in general, as well as on developments relevant to Syria's legal system, especially those in the area of (religious) family law. The subsequent two chapters will elaborate in detail on the developments in the field of personal status law from the 1950s to recent times.

As Syrian family law is, for the most part, based on religious law, it is important to take into account how the position of religion, especially Islam, in relation to the central state authority, developed over time. Some key moments in history that had a long-lasting effect on the relationship between *shari'a*, Islam and the state, in addition to events or episodes that affected the position of non-Muslim minorities vis-à-vis the Muslim majority in the area of personal status law, will be discussed. The final sections of this chapter are devoted to an analysis of the contemporary relationship between Islam and the state, including the Constitution and the position of the President. This chapter will conclude with a discussion of contemporary state policies concerning (religious) legal plurality in personal status law, in particular in relation to its non-Muslim minorities.

Syria in the Ottoman era

The country that is today's Syria became part of the Ottoman Empire in 1516, when the Ottoman Turks defeated the Mamluk Sultanate and conquered Syria. The Ottoman Empire had started to gain ground from the early fourteenth century onwards; at the height of its reign (sixteenth to seventeenth century), the Empire stretched from North Africa to Persia, deep into Europe and all the way down to the Gulf of Aden. Ottoman rule over Syria lasted until 1918, when the Ottoman Empire ceased to exist.[1]

From the start, Ottoman rule from Istanbul was challenged from outside and inside the Empire. Istanbul's control over its provinces was never all-encompassing, yet its attempts to centralise and control the administration of its territories, including taxation, education and the legal system, proved seminal. The Ottoman political and legal heritage is significant to all contemporary countries in the Middle East, including Syria. Syria's legal system is similar to those found in other former Ottoman provinces: Egypt, Lebanon, Iraq and Jordan.

The Ottoman legacy is not only evident in the legal system in general but also in the field of family law. The reason that the Hanafi school of law is the preferred doctrine in matters of personal status in Syria today is that the official rite of the Empire was the Hanafi school of law. Consequently, the Hanafi doctrine spread throughout the Empire, often superseding other schools of law in the conquered areas.[2] Customary law, sultan's law (*qanun*) and *shari'a* were all recognised sources of law in the Ottoman state. Over the course of time, however, sultan's or state law became the dominant force; *shari'a* and the traditional *shari'a* (or *qadi*) courts, who had general jurisdiction to adjudicate in all civil and criminal disputes, eventually lost out to the reform policies of the Ottomans which were put in place from the mid-nineteenth century onwards.[3]

Non-Muslims under Ottoman rule: the millet system

Like Syria today, the Ottoman Empire was also multi-religious; in addition to its Muslim subjects, the Empire had a significant number of non-Muslim subjects, that is, *dhimmi*s – a *dhimmi* is a non-Muslim living under Islamic rule. Beginning in early Islamic history, non-Muslims living in conquered Islamic lands were offered a contract of protection (*dhimma*) in exchange for acceptance to live under Islamic rule.[4] Due to this protected status, Christian and Jewish subjects were guaranteed certain privileges.

Under Ottoman rule, non-Muslims were guaranteed these privileges under the so-called *millet* system.[5] The religious or confessional communities (*millet*s) enjoyed the right to retain and apply their own religious laws, in liturgy and church affairs but also in matters related to a person's status, such as marriage and inheritance. However, this protected position came with certain conditions, meaning that *dhimmi*s had to pay the poll-tax (*jizya*), they were prohibited from carrying arms, they had to live in segregated areas and they were required to dress in a distinctive style. In addition, *dhimmi*s could not testify against Muslims in court and they were excluded from high public offices.[6]

The recognised *millet*s had their own *milla* courts, where each *millet* applied its own religious law, most importantly in matters of marriage and divorce. Various studies on Ottoman history have, however, demonstrated that non-Muslims frequently appealed to *qadi* courts instead of to their own communal courts, also in matters concerning marriage, divorce and inheritance.[7] Al-Qattan explains in a study on the legal status of *dhimmi*s in Muslim courts that the Ottoman records (*sijill*s) of the eighteenth and nineteenth centuries reveal that Jews and Christians in Damascus regularly made their appearance at the Muslim courts: either because they were obliged to, for example in the case of an inter-communal dispute, capital crime or cases which threatened public order and security; or voluntarily, for example to record their property and commercial transactions. The latter can be explained by the fact that the *qadi* courts, being the general 'state' courts, were the only official courts with the authority of enforcement. Nevertheless, *dhimmi*s also came to the *qadi* courts because they preferred these courts over their own communal courts, because the former were considered more efficient and had stronger enforcement powers, or because *dhimmi* litigants believed that their 'personal and financial interests were better served by shari'a law'.[8] Al-Qattan provides examples of Christians who went to *qadi* courts to get their marriage validated or notarised in conformity with *shari'a* rules to secure matrimonial financial rights, to obtain a divorce or because of more favourable *shari'a* inheritance law regulations.[9]

Ottoman reforms: Tanzimat *and the millet system*

In the nineteenth century, the sultans of Istanbul, under European influence, introduced a series of far-reaching administrative, military, economic and legal reforms to meet the challenges of a rapidly changing society. The *Tanzimat* period (1839–76) started with the proclamation of the Edict of Gülhane in 1839 by Sultan Abdulmecid. The Edict of Gülhane emphasised equal rights for Muslims and non-Muslims alike. The Edict of Humayun, issued in 1856, took it a step further and stated that all Ottoman citizens were regarded equal before the law, in taxes, government positions and military service, regardless of their religion. The restrictions imposed on non-Muslim Ottomans were officially lifted; they could now be admitted to political and military posts. In addition, the poll-tax and the distinction between Muslim and non-Muslim testimony in court were abolished.[10]

Hence, the Ottoman state introduced the concept of 'citizenship'[11] and with that the *millet* regime was – at least on a national level – abolished.[12] However, the separate status of Muslims and non-Muslims in family law matters continued to exist, for the Edict of Humayun reaffirmed that the privileges granted to all the non-Muslim communities would be maintained.[13] This meant that they could continue to apply their own religious laws in personal status matters. This plurality in legal status or national citizenship, on the one hand, and denominational membership as the decisive feature in personal status matters, on the other hand, created a complexity in the legal system – a complexity which not only Syrians but also Egyptians and Jordanians continue to grapple with today.

The 1856 Edict, however, also required each denomination to reach consensus on inheritance law: if they failed to do so, then this area of law would fall under the state's jurisdiction, the *qadi* courts. Since many of them failed to reach such a consensus, the patriarchs and rabbis lost this part of their jurisdiction to the state, as a result of which Christians (and Jews) were governed by the Islamic inheritance rules.[14] As a matter of fact, Christian denominations in contemporary Syria were governed by *shari'a* inheritance law until 2010: it was only then that Christian communities regained this lost jurisdiction (see Chapter 3).

The *Tanzimat* reforms were not accepted and implemented in all parts of the Empire; a large segment of the Sunni Muslim majority did not welcome the reforms. In combination with a general deteriorating economic situation, the newly obtained rights of, in particular, Christians stirred up violent sectarian clashes in Mount Lebanon (1840 and 1860), Aleppo (1850) and Damascus (1860). Massacres of Christians at the hands of Muslims in Aleppo and Damascus followed from Muslim resentment against the reforms, particularly because they were perceived as the outcome of European interference for the benefit and protection of the Christian populations.[15]

In spite of the official abolishment of the *dhimmi* status and, perhaps, because of the emotionally charged responses, the *millet* system was never completely erased in all parts of the Empire. Remnants of the Ottoman *millet* system can still be found to varying degrees in Egypt, Lebanon, Israel and Syria today, as will become evident in the subsequent sections and chapters.

Ottoman codifications of Islamic (family) law

The Western-inspired *Tanzimat* reforms not only overhauled the legal system but also fundamentally altered the status of *shari'a* and of its authorised interpreters, the religious scholars (*'ulama'*). The Ottoman sultans introduced European-style law codes[16] which were presented as additional to *shari'a* law, but, in fact, these (secular) laws came to dominate *shari'a* law in the nineteenth century.[17] This meant that Islamic law now had to compete with these new laws and saw its scope reduced to the domain of family law.

Before the *Tanzimat* reforms, the *qadi* courts had general jurisdiction over all matters of civil, criminal, commercial and other areas of law. From the 1860s, the Ottoman government set up 'regular' (*nizamiyya*) courts to apply the new legislation. This meant that the jurisdiction of the already existing *qadi* courts became limited to matters related to Islamic endowment (*waqf*) and what was now called personal status matters, most importantly, matters of marriage, divorce and inheritance.[18] This created a dichotomy in the legal system: *qadi* courts applying *shari'a*-based personal status law on the one hand, and 'regular' or European-style courts[19] applying European-based law codes on the other. This dichotomy remains a typical feature of today's legal systems of the former Ottoman provinces.

Another significant reform of the *Tanzimat* project was the codification of *shari'a* law in the Ottoman Civil Code, the *Mecelle* (1869–76). For the first time in history an Islamic state codified *shari'a* rules and principles in a statutory law code.[20] This process of codification was an apparent break with the Islamic legal tradition, a process in which scholars and traditional judges gradually lost their legal authority to the state.[21]

The *Mecelle* was arranged as a Western-style law code and was a codification of Hanafi opinions on matters of contract, tort and civil procedures, combined with general established principles of law. It did not, however, contain rules and regulations pertaining to family matters, such as marriage, divorce and inheritance.[22] Its enactment was a break with Islamic legal tradition for it abandoned the doctrine of *taqlid*, the practice of following the authoritative opinions of one's school of law. The *Mecelle* was compiled differently; it consisted of an eclectic selection of opinions (*takhayyur*) of Hanafi jurists.

The *Mecelle* was enacted between 1870 and 1877. The civil code applied to both Muslim and non-Muslim subjects of the Ottoman Empire. It was intended to be applied in the *nizamiyya* courts as well as in the *qadi* courts, but in the end only the judges of the *nizamiyya* courts resorted to the *Mecelle* in civil law cases.[23] The judges in the *qadi* courts, on the other hand, continued to resort to the various *fiqh* books for personal status matters and Islamic *waqf*.[24]

In the early twentieth century, the Ottoman authorities again took it a step further and drafted a law code that was composed of a variety of legal rules and juristic opinions, modelled on a Western-style law code. In 1917, the Ottoman Law of Family Rights (hereafter OLFR) was enacted; it governed the family relations of Muslims and also included special sections for Jews and Christians.[25] The OLFR contained not only Islamic legal provisions derived from the Hanafi tradition but also drew on rules from other schools of law. Furthermore, in addition to *shari'a* provisions, the OLFR included European notions of marriage and family.[26] The OLFR was the first state-promulgated codification of Muslim family law.[27] After the collapse of the Ottoman Empire, the OLFR remained in place in several Middle Eastern countries, for example in Jordan until 1951 and in Syria until 1953. The personal status laws of many modern Arab states, promulgated from the 1920s onwards, were commonly based on the Ottoman Civil Code, the *Mecelle* and the OLFR of 1917.[28]

Amira Sonbol argues that from the late nineteenth century the Ottomans, in addition to several other Middle Eastern states (in particular Egypt), incorporated European patriarchal notions into their personal status and nationality laws. Consequently, 'personal status laws handling gender-specific issues or family relations confined the social structure within the parameters of patriarchal power.' It is thus important to recognise, Sonbol continues:

> that the personal status laws of today are the result of modern laws introduced by the modern state. The outlook and parameters of these laws may stem from the Shari'ah, but the formulation, codification and the laws themselves are, in part, borrowed from European codes of the late nineteenth and early twentieth centuries.[29]

Decline of the Ottoman Empire and the Arab Kingdom of Syria

In the early twentieth century the Ottoman government sought to restrict the role of religious authorities. The introduction of European-style law codes, the *Mecelle*, the OLFR and the newly created *nizamiyya* courts had already affected the position of the religious scholars (*'ulama'*) and the *qadi* courts. In 1917, the *qadi* courts were placed under the authority of the Ministry of Justice and a special section for *shari'a* cases was created in the Court of Cassation in Istanbul.[30] Eventually, the *qadi* courts disappeared altogether in the new state of Turkey, which abolished them in 1924.

Although the Ottomans undertook serious efforts to reform the Empire to keep up with the increasing economic and technical advancement of Europe, its fate was doomed. In November 1914, the already crumbling Ottoman Empire allied with Germany and Austria-Hungary against the Allied forces: Great Britain, France and Russia. Around the same time, an independent group of Arabs had sided with the Allied forces and fought with them against the Ottomans. The Arab Revolt was supported by Great Britain; the British had promised the Arabs that their leader, Sharif Husayn of Mecca, would get his own Arab state with Damascus as its capital, once the Ottomans were defeated. From 1916 until 1918, Arab forces under the command of

Amir Faysal, the son of Sharif Husayn, assisted by the British officer T.E. Lawrence (also known as Lawrence of Arabia), fought a guerrilla war against the Ottomans. They were successful in their campaign: in October 1918 Amir Faysal and his troops paraded into the city of Damascus.

The fragile independent Arab state headed by Amir Faysal lasted from October 1918 until July 1920. On 8 March 1920, the Syrian National Congress proclaimed Amir Faysal as the king of Greater Syria (*bilad ash-sham*),[31] the new independent Syrian Arab Kingdom.[32] His reign as king only lasted four months as French troops occupied Damascus and unseated Faysal's government in July 1920. King Faysal was expelled from the country and was later made king of the new country Iraq (r. 1921–33) by Great Britain. During the short existence of the Arab state of Syria, King Faysal initiated and implemented some substantial legal and judicial reform policies, including the establishment of a Law Faculty and a Syrian Court of Cassation in Damascus in 1919.[33]

In 1916, France and Great Britain had already divided the Ottoman Empire into zones of permanent influence according to the Sykes–Picot Agreement. Consequently, in 1919, after the end of the World War I, it was decided, as stipulated in the Treaty of Versailles, that 'the Arab countries formerly under Ottoman rule could be provisionally recognised as independent, subject to the rendering of assistance and advice by a state charged with the "mandate" for them'.[34] The secret agreement of 1916 between France and Britain was reaffirmed at the San Remo Conference in April 1920. As a result, France received the mandate for Syria and Lebanon: Greater Lebanon; it was placed under the authority of High Commissioner Henri Gourand in 1921. In 1922, the League of Nations officially awarded the mandate over Greater Lebanon to France.

Syria under the French Mandate

The French administration policy over Greater Lebanon was based on a policy of divide and rule, which emphasised and reinforced the already existing religious, ethnic and regional differences in Syria and Lebanon. France and Great Britain re-drew the borders of the former Ottoman provinces and the new countries Syria and Lebanon were established, adding some of Syria's land to Lebanon, which created political claims and tensions that continue to exist in present times.

In an attempt to repress the rise of nationalistic aspirations in Syria, the French implemented several geographical policies. For instance, they allowed the 'Alawis in the mountains on the Mediterranean coast and the Druze community in the South to create their own state in 1922. Except for a short intermission from 1936 to 1939, these two states or territories were able to retain their independent status until 1942.[35] French mandatory policy, however, was met with strong resistance: Syrians organised several nationwide revolts against the French in the years 1925 to 1927, initiated by the Druze in July 1925.[36] At the same time, several national movements were formed, united in one central political organisation: the National Bloc (established 1931). The majority of the founders and leaders of the National Bloc belonged to the Sunni urban and landowning elites and many of them had gone to Istanbul or Europe for their higher education.[37] The French authorities co-operated with the National Bloc, hoping that it would temper further nationalistic aspirations. The leaders of the National Bloc, in turn, hoped to take over the country's administration, as soon as the French left.

France considered itself to be the protector of the Christians of the Levant, particularly the Catholics, but also of other minorities, such as the 'Alawi's and the Druze. The French tried to emancipate the various religious minorities and 'to denigrate the influence of Islam by relegating it to the status of one religion among many'.[38] The Sunni religious establishment saw its authority and influence decline under the French and for that reason the Muslim leaders supported nationalist resistance to French rule.

In 1928, elections were held for a Constituent Assembly, whose task it was to draw up a constitution. The Assembly, comprised of predominantly deputies of the Nationalist Bloc, drafted a constitution that was inspired by European democratic principles. It included a provision which reaffirmed 'the equality of all citizens of all religious persuasions' but it also stipulated that the executive power was to be vested in a Muslim president. According to Khoury, the nationalists included the latter provision to safeguard the support of the religious establishment and the Muslim Syrian masses, 'who were still very much attached to and guided by their religious beliefs and practices and who regarded the nationalists as defenders of the faith and guardians of culture'.[39] The French administration opposed the draft because it assigned far-reaching powers to the Syrian president and thus contravened the international accords of the mandate. A year later, the French enacted a different constitution, in which the French Mandate was firmly secured.[40]

In 1922, in addition to the establishment of separate Druze and 'Alawi states, the French administration authorised the establishment of separate courts for both communities. Thus, whereas the Ottomans had made no judicial divisions between different Muslim groups, so all Muslims fell under the competence of the Ottoman *qadi* courts, the French did make such a distinction. According to Botiveau, the French also made efforts to grant the Shi'ite, Yazidi and Isma'ili communities legal autonomy in matters of personal status, but apparently these plans never materialised.[41]

Under Ottoman rule, the Druze and 'Alawi communities were generally governed by the rules of the Hanafi school of law; the judges of the newly established 'Alawi courts were expected to rule in accordance with the Twelver Shi'i (i.e. Ja'fari) school of law in matters of personal status. According to Kramer, this school of law 'was as remote from Alawi custom as any other'.[42] In Syria, there were no 'Alawi religious scholars available who were versed in Ja'fari jurisprudence and therefore Shi'i judges had to come from Lebanon to serve in the courts. In time, 'Alawi shaykhs accustomed themselves with Ja'fari *fiqh* books and these religious men were soon appointed as judges to the 'Alawi courts. After Syrian independence, the 'Alawi courts were abolished and 'Alawis were brought back into the realm of the general personal status (i.e. *shar'iyya*) courts.[43]

French-initiated personal status law reforms: religious and secular protests

The 1922 Mandate Charter divided the legal authority 'between state's jurisdiction over civil law and religious patriarchs' supervision of religious law';[44] it thus limited the administration's authority over religious affairs. However, this was not the case on all levels, for the High Commissioner assumed control of the *awqaf* (Islamic endowments), which was a remarkable development; or as Grafton writes: '[t]he fact that a non-Muslim was in control of a primary Muslim institution was unprecedented'.[45]

The Charter explicitly required the French authorities to respect the laws of personal status, including the religious authorities responsible for the implementation and reforms of these laws.[46] The religious clergy thereby regained some of the authority they had lost under the Ottoman rule. The French, unlike the Ottomans, did not promote unification but diversification.[47] Consequently, this plurality in the legal system, in which various religious laws and courts operated next to the general state laws and courts, continued to exist: first created by the Ottomans and now reinforced and expanded by the French authorities.[48]

According to Thompson, this duality in the legal system 'posed religious patriarchs as autonomous legal authorities in competition with the state', which caused particular problems in the more ambiguous legal areas over which the state and religious leaders competed for jurisdiction. Members of the emerging nationalist movement opposed the mere existence of religious laws and courts, which ran counter to their ideal of creating a secular, national and republican community. The Islamic populists, on the other hand, favoured the elimination of all forms of civil law and, alternatively, the reintroduction of Islamic law as the common law for the entire community.[49] Although the two groups differed significantly in their views on religion and its role in the state, they joined forces in their opposition against French rule.

The French administration sought to replace the Ottoman *millet* system and the various independent communal laws with a secular civil structure.[50] Stemming from a desire to equalise the status of Muslims and non-Muslims, the French proposed some reforms with regard to personal status affairs. Christian authorities had called upon the French to make uniform, in particular, marriage laws but also requested that the Christian communities would be safeguarded from the influence of Islamic law in matters such as inheritance.[51] In response to these requests, the French High Commissioner, Damien de Martel, enacted Law no. 60/LR (*Lois et Réglements*, hereafter LR) on 13 March 1936. This law gave the 17 recognised religious communities the right to 'devise their own family laws and to establish religious sectarian courts to adjudicate matters of family law',[52] meaning that everyone was expected to follow the law of his or her own community. However, the central government retained the final say in the ratification of all personal status laws.[53]

Muslims opposed the Law because it placed them on an equal footing with non-Muslims; in other words, they would lose their privileged position. To meet the objections of the Muslim opposition, a new law was enacted by the then new High Commissioner, Gabriel Puaux, namely Law no. 146/LR of 18 November 1938.[54] However, Muslim clergy did not approve of this law as it included the option to recognise civil marriages contracted abroad and 'created a high jurisdiction in charge of arbitrating conflicts between civil law and the personal status law of each religious community'.[55] The 1938 Law required citizens to follow civil law in cases not explicitly regulated by the applicable religious law of one's community, that is, 'it proposed the standardization of citizens' civil rights that were heretofore so varied under differing religious laws and even permitted, for the first time, citizens to claim their status solely under civil law'. Thompson argues that this, in effect, meant an abolition of Islamic law as the common law of the land.[56]

Muslims all over Syria and Lebanon fiercely opposed the two issued laws, claiming their issuance was an illegal intervention into religious affairs. In February 1939, leading Syrian religious scholars (*'ulama'*) from Homs and Damascus took collective action against the laws. In a petition addressed to, respectively, the Prime Minister and the Minister of Interior, they articulated their objections to specific provisions, which included, most importantly, the provision which allowed an adult Muslim to change his or her religion and the fact that it would be made possible for a Muslim woman to marry a non-Muslim man.[57] The National Bloc sided with the protesters and the Prime Minister resigned as an act of solidarity. In the end, the French acknowledged that the personal status reforms were bound to fall through. Consequently, the 1938 Law was retracted by High Commissioner Puaux in March 1939. However, Legislative Decree no. 60/1936, which defines the recognised religious communities with (partial) legislative and judicial authority in personal status matters, continued to stay in force, and continues today.[58]

Since no new laws on civil law or family affairs had been enacted, the Ottoman Civil Code, the *Mecelle* (1870–7) and the 1917 Ottoman Law of Family Rights remained in force during the French Mandate, until they were replaced by, respectively, the 1949 Syrian Civil Code and the 1953 Syrian Law of Personal Status.

Syria (and Lebanon) gained independence from France on 12 April 1946. Although Syria was now independent, it had little knowledge or experience in how to govern a country. Due to the French policy of direct rule, Syria's new leaders were not equipped to rule the country; the French had left behind a divided and unstable country.[59]

Post-independence: military dictatorships (1949–54) and the United Arab Republic (1958–61)

Following independence from France, Syria was subjected to a string of military coups, starting with the coup of Colonel Husni al-Za'im in March 1949. Colonel al-Za'im was a great admirer of the secular achievements of the Turkish statesman Mustafa Kemal Atatürk. He found inspiration in Atatürk's separation of religion and state, such as the reform of the *waqf* and the introduction of secular legislation, recorded in the new Turkish Civil Code (1926) modelled after the Swiss Civil Code. Seeking to follow his example, al-Za'im allegedly planned to introduce 'a new personal status law to replace the *shari'a*'.[60] However, there was little opportunity for him to execute his secular policies since his rule lasted only four months. Nevertheless, during this short rule, three secular codes were promulgated: a Civil Code, a Penal Code and a Commercial Code, which are, with amendments, still in force today. Also in 1949, private and family Islamic endowments (*waqf*, pl. *awqaf*) were prohibited – all existing *awqaf* of this nature could therefore be liquidated.[61]

During the rule of Colonel al-Za'im, in 1949, Syria enacted its first self-written civil code. Actually, that does not hold true completely, because the 1949 civil code was a 'rather faithful copy' of the 1948 Egyptian Civil Code, which was a mix of *shari'a* principles and Western legal concepts.[62] The Explanatory Memorandum to the Syrian Civil Code explains why the Egyptian code served as a model: it is because of 'the common traditions, similar customs and closely related social conditions prevailing in both countries, thus permitting the application of the Egyptian code in Syria'.[63]

Egypt served as an example to other Arab states in its introduction of legal reforms, starting from the late 1940s. In fact, the famous Egyptian jurist, Abd al-Razzaq al-Sanhuri (1895–1971), responsible for the Egyptian version, drafted or assisted in the drafting process of the civil codes of Syria (1949), Iraq (1951), Jordan (1952, replaced in 1976), Libya (1953), Yemen (1979) and Kuwait (1981).[64] The adoption of Egyptian laws by other Arab states was also explained in light of the then popular Arab nationalist ideology. The Explanatory Memorandum of the Syrian Civil Code continues by stating that:

> the modelling of the Syrian Code along the pattern of the Egyptian Code fulfils an important purpose aimed at by the Arabs at present, i.e. the unification of the laws of the Arab countries. Arab lawyers have been trying hard to reach this goal, and the present Code is indeed a practical step forward on the way to legal unity among the Arab countries.[65]

In August 1949, Al-Za'im's rule ended by a counter-coup by Colonel Hannawi, followed by another counter-coup in December by another officer, Adib Shishakli. Shishakli's rule ended in February 1954, due to a successful military revolt which forced him into exile in Brazil.[66] During his rule, the Code of Penal Procedure (1950), the Nationality Law (1951) and the Code of Civil Procedure (1953) were promulgated, as well as the law that is of great importance to this study, that is, the 1953 SLPS. In this period of successive military regimes many laws were promulgated, which are, for the most part, still in force today.

The years following this string of military dictatorships (1949–54) were characterised by nationalist rapprochement and Arab unity, notably manifested in the union between Egypt and Syria. On 1 February 1958, Syria and Egypt established the United Arab Republic (UAR), under leadership of the charismatic Egyptian president, Gamal Abdul Nasser. Syria and Egypt became, respectively, the 'northern region' and 'southern region' of the UAR. The UAR was the materialisation of the nationalist dream of Arab unity and social equality for all. However, the Syrian–Egyptian marriage lasted only three and a half years. Syrians, especially members of the socialist Ba'th Party, were disappointed with the union, mostly because of Egypt's political dominance in the UAR. On 18 September 1961, a group of army officers staged a coup d'état, which led to Syria's secession from the UAR and the Syrian Arab Republic was reinstated. However, it did not take long before Syria was, again, subjected to a string of coups.

Ba'th Party rule

The Arab socialist *Ba'th* ('resurrection') movement was an intellectual movement, founded by two Syrians in the early 1940s: Michel 'Aflaq, a Greek Orthodox Christian, and Salahadin al-Bitar, a Sunni Muslim.[67] The movement advocated a social revolution which would lead to one Arab nation, free from Western imperialism, in which Arab and social values would be guaranteed. As pan-Arab nationalism and socialism were the dominant ideologies, any form of religious, sectarian, regional or tribal factionalism had to be resisted for the sake of national unity.[68] Although the Ba'th ideology was secular, its founding father, Michel 'Aflaq, maintained that 'the Arab movement was inseparably connected with Islam and that Muhammad's life was a perfect picture and symbol of "the nature of the Arab soul and its rich possibilities"'. Moreover, God had revealed the Islamic faith to the Arabs and therefore Arabs 'had a universal duty to create an "Arab humanism"'.[69] According to Ba'thist doctrine, Arab nationalism could therefore not be completely separated from Islam, meaning Islam as an 'Arab' or 'humanist' ideology,[70] as opposed to the European ideal of separation of church and state.[71]

The Ba'th movement attracted young followers from the middle and lower classes, rural minority groups in particular, such as 'Alawis from the mountainous coastal area. In the 1950s, after the overthrow of General Shishakli, the Ba'thists gradually gained ground in the political arena. However, it took until 1963 before the Arab Socialist Ba'th Party actually came to power. A month after the Ba'th Party had come to power in Iraq, a group of Ba'thist officers seized power in Syria on 8 March 1963.[72]

During their first few years in power, the Ba'th Party struggled with internal contesting forces, including early Ba'thists versus the new generation, civilians versus the military, Ba'thists versus Nasserists. These conflicts were partly settled by a bloody intra-party coup by a group of army officers, led by Salah Jadid and Hafez al-Asad on 23 February 1966, which forced the Party's founding fathers and civilian Ba'thists to leave the country. Salah Jadid became the effective new ruler and Hafez al-Asad was appointed Minister of Defence of the new government.[73] Following Syria's defeat against Israel in the Six-Day War of 1967, a power struggle between 'Alawi generals Jadid and al-Asad eventually led to a final intra-party coup (referred to as 'the corrective movement') led by al-Asad, on 16 November 1970. Hafez al-Asad took over the presidency, arrested his former comrade Salah Jadid and incarcerated him in Mezze prison in Damascus, where he died in 1993.[74]

Syria under Hafez al-Asad

With Hafez al-Asad's ascension to power, Syria entered a period of relative political stability. The new regime established itself as a strong authoritarian power; it controlled the country by creating a strong state apparatus dominated by Ba'th Party members, aided by a vast omnipresent secret police force. The rule of the al-Asad family, past and present, is often described as being based on a system of patronage, formed by tribal (or familial), regional and sectarian loyalties.[75] Furthermore, from its inception, the Islamic legitimacy of the 'Alawi-dominated Ba'th regime was questioned and challenged by the country's Sunni Muslim majority.

In the 1970s and 1980s, Sunni Muslim opposition groups mounted a violent struggle against the Ba'th regime. The Syrian government responded by ruthlessly suppressing any opposition to its rule, either Islamic or secular. Thousands of people were arrested, imprisoned or disappeared, especially those who were associated with the Muslim Brotherhood. The Brotherhood was the state's number one enemy and for that reason membership of the Brotherhood was punishable by death according to Law no. 49/1980.[76] The climax of the regime's confrontation with the Brotherhood was the bloody suppression of the insurrection in the city of Hama, which was considered a traditional stronghold of the Muslim Brotherhood, in February 1982. It remains unclear how many people died in the Hama massacre; numbers vary from 5,000 to 25,000 and more.[77]

Following the events of the late 1970s and early 1980s, the regime changed its policy towards Islam; what is more, the President 'started to cultivate a public air of Sunni religiosity'.[78] For example, on major Muslim religious holidays he, together with other high-ranking members of the government and the Ba'th Party, would pray in the Umayyad mosque in Damascus. Besides, the 'Islamic character of public space', particularly in cities like Aleppo and Damascus, increased over the last few decades, most notably epitomised by an increase in female veiling.[79] It should be noted that veiling was a sensitive issue in Syria. Before the 1990s, veiling was officially forbidden in many public places; there had been incidents where veiled women were attacked (i.e. unveiled) by Ba'thi youth groups. According to Rabo, 'veiling may be regarded as a clear political demonstration against the state and the Ba'th party'.[80]

The Ba'th ideology became a dominant force in Syrian society: it constituted an integral part of the curriculum in all Syrian schools and universities; numerous popular organisations, such as trade unions, youth, student and women's organisations were administered by the Party. For many years, membership of the Party was a requirement for employment in most state sectors.

More importantly, the Ba'th ideology was institutionalised in the Constitution of 1973, which was in force until February 2012, when a new Constitution was adopted (see below: 'Islam and the state'). The 1973 Constitution firmly consolidated the leading political role of the Ba'th Party in the Syrian society and the state. The Explanatory Memorandum of the Constitution stated that the Arab socialist Ba'th Party advocated and aspired unity and freedom for all (Arab) people, which includes equality of all its citizens before the law (Art. 25.3) and equality between men and women (Art. 45).

In line with the aspirations laid down in the 1973 Constitution, the government, in the early al-Asad years, worked to improve the status of Syrian women; also in the field of family law. According to Rabo, '[t]he Ba'th Party leadership intermittently tried to put forward a secular personal status law [. . .] Such a law would [. . .] make polygamy illegal and give equal inheritance to men and women. However, opposition to such reforms has been strong, even within the Ba'th Party.'[81] Nevertheless, some significant amendments to the Law of Personal Status were adopted in 1975 but the core of the SLPS has basically remained intact since its promulgation in 1953, as will be explained in the following chapters.

Syria under Bashar al-Asad

After 30 years in power, Hafez al-Asad died on 10 June 2000. A month later he was succeeded by his son Bashar al-Asad, who was elected President by referendum with 97.2 per cent of the votes.[82] In June 2014, amid a raging civil war, he was re-elected as President for a third seven-year term with 88.7 per cent of the votes.[83] When Bashar al-Asad came to power in 2000, he promised to implement political and democratic reforms. There was hope that the country would change under Bashar. He had worked as a British-trained ophthalmologist in London until 1994 when he was called back, after the death of his brother Basil (the heir apparent), to be prepared for the presidency. Many hoped that with his efforts to reform the economy and curb corruption, the introduction of the internet, changes in the Ba'th Party hierarchy and the release of hundreds of political prisoners, Bashar's promises to reform would materialise. Unfortunately, that was not the case.

During the so-called 'Damascus Spring' of 2000, various civil society and opposition groups emerged and publicly debated on a wide range of political and social topics, but the spring turned out to be short-lived. In the autumn of 2001, the regime tightened the authoritarian strings again and the 'Damascus Winter' followed.[84] However, not all social initiatives were wiped out completely. Women activists were able to keep women's issues on the public agenda, one of which eventually led to a minor reform in the SLPS in 2003. In addition, different laws in relation to family law issues were drafted during this last decade; for the most part these came from reformed-minded groups but also some more controversial proposals issued by religious conservative groups were put to the fore. In Chapter 3 these developments with regard to draft law projects and amendments concerning personal status law will be discussed in more detail.

From revolution to civil war

In mid-March 2011, inspired by the popular protests in other Arab countries and the subsequent overthrow of presidents in Tunisia and Egypt, the 'Arab Spring' gained ground in Syria. Demonstrations sprang up in different parts of the country, most notably in Deraa in the south, Baniyas and Lattakia at the coast, Hama and Homs in the central west, Idlib and Aleppo in the north, and in several Damascus suburbs. In the succeeding months, the protests spread and grew in size and strength, as did the regime's brutal suppression of the uprising. As the uprising became more widespread, both sides also became more violent.

In April 2011, one of the first actions of the government, in an effort to appease the anti-government protesters, was to lift the state of emergency, which had been in place since 1962.[85] In the same month, the government also granted Syrian citizenship to thousands of stateless

Kurds.[86] A special census held in the Hassakeh province in 1962 had left thousands of Kurds stateless;[87] consequently, this amounted to approximately – according to estimates – 300,000 stateless Kurds living in Syria in 2011.[88] In the early months of the uprising, the government also released several hundred politicial prisoners and promised to take steps towards political reforms, including a new constitution and parliamentary elections.

The government commissioned a committee to draft a new constitution, which was approved by constitutional referendum on 26 February 2012, with 89.4 per cent of the votes, despite a boycott by opposition groups.[89] The Constitution came into effect the following day, by order of Presidential Decree no. 94. Whereas the preceding 1973 Constitution assigned and firmly consolidated the leading political role of the Ba'th Party in the Syrian society and the state, in the new constitution this contested article (Art. 8 of the 1973 Constitution) had been omitted.

In alignment with a new constitution was the endorsement of a multi-party system, as laid down in Article 8 of the 2012 Constitution. However, Article 8.4 also states that '[c]arrying out any political activity or forming any political parties or groupings on the basis of religious, sectarian, tribal, regional, class-based, professional, or on discrimination based on gender, origin, race or color may not be undertaken',[90] meaning that Islamic political parties and organisations such as the Muslim Brotherhood continued to be banned.[91] On 7 May 2012, amid the growing popular unrest and calls to boycott the elections, parliamentary elections were held, with the Ba'th Party winning 134 out of the 250 seats.[92] The new constitution also allowed for multiple candidates to run for presidency.[93] On 3 June 2014, presidential elections were held in the government-controlled areas, despite the fact that by then the country had fallen into a full-scale civil war. Bashar al-Asad had to face two other candidates in the race for presidency, but they posed no threat to his re-election: al-Asad collected 88.7 per cent of the votes and, thus, he became the president of Syria for another seven years.

Despite the political measures taken to appease the protesters, the 2011 uprising gradually escalated into a full-scale civil war, with different factions fighting against the al-Asad government and each other. These factions included, amongst others, the Free Syrian Army (mainly composed of defected Syrian soldiers), the Islamic Front, the al-Qa'ida-linked Jabhat al-Nusra and Islamic State (IS).[94] The situation became even more complicated due to active involvement from outside insurgents, such as IS and Hezbollah, but also due to financial and military support by foreign governments such as Iran and Russia (supporting the Syrian government) and, on the other side (supporting anti-government forces), countries like Qatar, Saudi Arabia and Turkey. Adding a new twist to the already complicated situation, was the bombing of IS targets in Syria and Nothern Iraq, which started in September 2014, by the US air force together with coalition forces, including – again – Saudi Arabia and Qatar.[95] At the moment of finalising this book (autumn 2015), more than four years into the conflict, the situation does not look promising. There is no way of telling what this conflict entails for the future of Syria: the country, its people, the role of religion, the composition of the government and the executive branch or the legal system.

However, despite the ongoing, disturbing events taking place in Syria and not knowing what the future will hold for Syria, the following sections will proceed with the subject at hand, that is the relationship between state and religion, particularly Islam, and the position of religious family law, since Syria's independence in 1946. It is necessary to examine the relation between Islam and the state, and the effects this changing and contested relationship had on family law, in order to understand the role of religion in Syrian society at large.

Islam and the state

Islam and the Constitution

Article 1 of the 2012 Constitution reads as follows:

> The Syrian Arab Republic is a democratic state with full sovereignty, indivisible, and may not waive any part of its territory, and is part of the Arab homeland; The people of Syria are part of the Arab nation.[96]

The Republic prides itself on being a secular nation where the various religious communities co-exist peacefully. The major Muslim and Christian holidays, for example, such as *'id al-adha* (Sacrifice Feast), Birthday of the Prophet Muhammad, Easter (both Catholic and

Orthodox) and Christmas are officially observed because Syria is, officially, a secular state and it therefore has no state religion. That said, Islam remains the prevailing religion and maintains the upper hand in all strata of society, including the Constitution. It should be noted that the content of the articles of the 2012 Constitution that relate to religion and personal status law is very similar to the previous constitution of 1973, notwithstanding the important constitutional changes mentioned above.

Article 3, paragraph 1 of the 2012 Constitution states that: 'the religion of the president of the republic is Islam', the following paragraph of the same article reads 'the Islamic jurisprudence [*fiqh*] is a main source of law'.[97] At present, Islamic legal principles are most obviously and predominantly present in the 1953 Syrian Law of Personal Status. Traces of Islamic law can also be found in other statutory laws, for example in the 1949 Civil Code, as demonstrated by the wording of its Explanatory Memorandum, which states that Islamic law is 'a fundamental and flexible source from which an important part of any deficiency which may exist in the Code may be supplied'.[98] Paragraph 3 of Article 3 of the 2012 Constitution stipulates that 'the state respects all religions and it guarantees the freedom to hold any religious rites, provided they do not disturb the public order'.[99] The last paragraph (Art. 3.4) is 'new', that is to say no similar provision existed in the 1973 Constitution;[100] it states that 'the personal status of the religious groups shall be protected and respected'.

The religion of the President is Islam

Since the 1930s, all constitutions included a provision stipulating that the religion of the head of state had to be Islam.[101] Traditionally, before and during the Ottoman Era, political power belonged to the Sunni urban establishment. In 1971, Hafez al-Asad became the first non-Sunni president; he belonged to the 'Alawi community, a heterodox Shi'i sect founded in Iraq in the ninth century. It is important to note that many Sunnis do not regard 'Alawis as Muslims 'because of the particularities of the 'Alawi religious doctrine'.[102] Because of their esoteric and other dissenting beliefs, 'Alawis (also referred to as Nusayris) were often denounced by Sunni scholars as infidels and heretics. In the past, they were regularly oppressed and prosecuted: that is why they had retreated to the rugged, mountain areas of the Mediterranean coast.

In January 1973, when the government put forward a new constitution, the document omitted to stipulate a provision that the President of the Syrian Republic should be a Muslim. This omission was not well received by many Sunni Muslims and led to protests in different parts of the country, especially in Hama. The problem was ironed out by adopting an amendment which re-introduced the desired clause into the Constitution. Nonetheless, another issue was still on the table: the claim that the President should be a Sunni Muslim. To solve this problem, President al-Asad turned to Imam Musa al-Sadr, director of the Supreme Shi'i Council in Lebanon. Imam Musa issued a *fatwa* in 1973 stating that 'Alawis and Twelver Shi'a were brothers in faith and that both sects follow the Ja'fari school of law.[103] Despite the fact that some groups still demanded that Islam should be acknowledged as the state religion – a demand that was never acknowledged – the Constitution was adopted by popular referendum on 12 March 1973.[104]

'Official Islam'

From the late 1970s, the Syrian regime started to develop its own version of Islam and with that moved away from its original promotion of secularism.[105] Syria's 'official Islam' is a Sufi Islam, according to Böttcher; Sufi *shaykh*s were considered attractive co-operation partners for the regime in its attempt to polish its Islamic image. For example, both the late Grand Mufti, Shaykh Ahmad Kaftaru (d. 2004) and the present Grand Mufti Shaykh Ahmad Hassun belong to the Naqshbandi Sufi order.[106] Furthermore, Sunni Kurds dominated the official Islam; according to Böttcher, this decision was made by Hafez al-Asad 'in response to the refusal on the part of the *'ulamâ* to co-operate with the authorities. Asad favored a "confessional minority, that is Sufis over Salafis, and an ethnic minority, the Kurds, over the Arabs"'.[107] As will be discussed in Chapter 3, political co-optation with the religious establishment of particular minority groups (e.g. the Kurdish religious elite, but also church leaders) was part and parcel of Syria's domestic politics under the al-Asads.

Despite the regime's efforts to establish an 'official Islam' or 'societal Islam',[108] Islam in Syria was never fully institutionalised or, at least, to a lesser degree when compared to, for example, Egypt. The regime never tried to educate or appoint their own brand of religious scholars; instead, they preferred to manage the Sunni establishment by co-optation of personalities with a genuine social base for support.[109] Pinto argues that with the appointment of Shaykh Ahmad Kaftaru as the Grand Mufti of Syria in 1964, the regime was able, with his help, to 'consolidate its control over the Sunni Muslim religious establishment'.[110] In addition to Grand Mufti Kaftaru, certain religious key figures, like (the late) Shaykh Muhammad Sa'id al-Buti, the independent member of Parliament Dr Muhammad al-Habash,[111] and the current Grand Mufti Ahmad Hassun, who preach a moderate Islam, were given easy access to the media and were allowed to set up Islamic schools, educational and charitable institutions.[112]

The recognition of Islam started under Hafez al-Asad from the mid-1990s but became more apparent in public political discourse under his son Bashar. Since his ascension to the presidency, the regime has 'increased its use of Islamic symbols and vocabulary in an attempt to gain legitimacy and popularity among pious Sunni Muslims'.[113] The President lifted the ban on headscarves in schools and allowed for prayer-rooms in universities to be opened. Islamic references were fused with nationalistic discourse; the use of Islamic symbols and discourse 'allowed for the expression of a multiplicity of meanings and claims by the various social actors who dialogued, disputed and negotiated through them'.[114] Pinto states that this 'use of Islam as a cultural idiom' allows for the expression of different cultural understandings and dynamics,[115] for example, power struggles over religious identity and influence. A good example of the use of Islam as a cultural idiom by different actors, including the state, are the efforts made to reform Syrian family law and the debates around it (see Chapter 3).

State-sponsored religious legal plurality

Syria's legal system, similar to most Middle Eastern states, cannot be characterised as entirely civil or secular. Following independence from France in 1946, the successive Syrian governments of the late 1940s until the late 1960s, in line with the then popular ideologies of secularism and nationalism, sought to uplift and unify the nation and eradicate all remnants of the feudal and colonial past. The wish for unification also affected the field of family law but this ideal was never fully achieved, as was shown earlier in this chapter.

From the late 1940s onwards, a series of statutory laws were promulgated, including Syria's first codified Law of Personal Status, the

1953 SLPS. An important goal of the promulgation of this law was the government's wish to subsume all Syrian nationals under one law. Before 1953, religious scholars and clergymen were authorised to determine which laws applied in matters of personal status to their respective communities. With this uniform or 'standardised' law, the state took control over the legal system and thus, the religious men essentially lost their interpretive authority in matters of religious law to the state. Botiveau, when writing on similar legal reforms in Egypt, states that 'this "standardization" was facilitated by the fact that the legal culture of the religious groups differed less than is often claimed, if one admits that they were influenced more by "patriarchal" than "religious" solidarity'.[116]

However, the religious men did not lose their judicial authority completely; the SLPS stipulates in Article 306 that the law applies to *all Syrians* but it also stipulates that, following the subsequent two articles, the Druze community, the various Christian communities and the Jewish community are exempted from several provisions of the law and are allowed to apply their own laws.[117] Thus, these latter three articles of the SLPS undo the aim of unification by allowing a continuation of separate, though limited, jurisdictions for the three singled-out communities.

It is evident that in the field of personal status law the Syrian government has adopted or maintained a plurality of laws and jurisdictions. However, this state-sponsored legal plurality does not entail equality between the different religious communities. Rather, it is an imbalanced plurality – imbalanced because of the supremacy of the SLPS and the *shar'iyya* courts.[118] This affects especially the non-Muslim minorities, whose status as a minority in the legal system is accentuated by the above-mentioned stipulations of the SLPS. Examples of complex legal realities that can arise from this intersection of jurisdictions in relation to the supremacy of the SLPS will be described in the next chapter.

Thus, on the one hand, the post-independence Syrian governments sought to unify the legal system inspired by principles of nationalism and citizenship, but on the other hand they preserved the *millet* system or an adapted version thereof. Mainly due to conservative religious opposition, both Muslim and Christian, religious legal plurality in personal status matters has been maintained up to the present time.[119]

Rabo states that plurality in family law may be intended to protect religious 'minorities' and respect the differences between religious groups, 'but also perpetuates the legal distinction between Muslims and Christians'.[120] Maktabi argues along the same lines and states that:

> Legal pluralism within family law serves not only as a means of maintaining and regulating the internal affairs of religious groups. Family law also defines the dividing lines *between* the different religious groups, with state authorities as gatekeepers who maintain and monitor intra-group boundaries through the state's personal status registries.[121]

Father Antoun Mouslih, a senior Catholic judge and the driving force behind the new Catholic law of 2006 (see below), admitted that this legal plurality constitutes a structural problem and divides Syrian citizens. He was therefore in favour of the promulgation of a more unified family law, especially since all the different communities share so many similarities, for example the financial and social hardship that women and children face in the event of a troublesome marriage. A more unified law, in particular more cohesive administrative procedures, based on civil law, could improve the status of women and children and decrease the current religious inequality between the Muslim majority and other religious minorities.[122]

According to Rowe, the secular policies of the post-colonial governments did not gain mainstream acceptance, which led to 'the development of parallel institutions and regulations for religious minorities that accept the secular system so long as they can retain a measure of internal autonomy'. He describes this situation as a 'neo-millet system'.[123] In this modernised version of the Ottoman *millet* system, the state and the Churches entered into a neo-*millet* partnership:

> Churches thereby provide support and legitimization to the state and the state confers importance and legitimacy to the church. But these systems are challenged when the regime liberalizes, differentiates from a communitarian focus, or the civil society presents challenges to the received wisdom of identity politics.[124]

The church leaders[125] and Christian communities in Syria are generally perceived as loyal to the al-Asad regime, for it is alleged that the 'secular', minority government offers the best possible protection for religious minorities against Sunni dominance. Since the start of the uprising in 2011, the regime continued to propagate this discourse, enforcing the assumption 'that the authoritarian status quo was preferable to democratic uncertainties'.[126] Accordingly, a modernised version of the *millet* system remained in place due to the partnership between the religious communities and the state.

In the recent past, the foundations of Syria's religious legal plural system were put to the test, partly due to legislative developments in the Christian communities. As this study shows, Christian clergy, in particular, strongly adhered to their specified areas of legislative and judicial autonomy, especially being a minority in a Muslim majority country. In this context, Tadros' article on non-Muslims in Egypt's framework of personal status law is interesting. She argues in her article that '[t]he political context in which legislation is mediated is crucial', especially in countries with sectarian tensions, like Egypt and Syria. When a religious minority feels it is facing pressure from the religious majority, it is more likely 'to first, cling on to the idea of its religious distinctiveness, and the personal status law is one manifestation thereof'.[127] Tadros refers here to the Coptic Orthodox Church in Egypt, more specifically to the power struggle between the government and the Church, which was played out in the family law arena. The same holds true for Syria, where tensions between the different Christian groups emerged when the Catholics managed to obtain a new independent personal status law in 2006, by which they placed themselves outside the scope of the SLPS as well as outside the jurisdiction of the *shar'iyya* courts. This exceptional position of the Catholics created ill-feeling between non-Catholic and Catholic Christian groups, for the former did not attain full jurisdiction over all their personal status affairs. The government had to respond to this precarious situation and did so by accepting an amendment to the SLPS in 2010, which equalised the inheritance rights of all Christians and abrogated a large part of the Catholic personal status law. The above-mentioned changes in the respective personal status laws will be addressed in more detail in Chapter 3.

Conclusion

This chapter described the historical development of the position of religion, most importantly Islam and Islamic (family) law in relation to the central state authority in Syria's past and present. Significant historical developments concerning this relationship took place in the Ottoman era, during the French Mandate, the early years of independence and in more recent times under the al-Asad rule.

The Ottomans developed the so-called *millet* system in which non-Muslim communities – Jews and Christians – enjoyed the right to retain and apply their own religious laws, particularly with regard to matters of personal status. The legal plurality that stemmed from the *millet* system created a plural legal system, in which civil and various religious laws and courts operated simultaneously. This legal plurality in family law has never ceased to exist. It not only survived the Ottomans, the French and the secular al-Asad regime but it was, in fact, reinforced time and again, often dictated by political motives.

Changes or reforms in the domain of personal status law were generally controversial. This chapter described examples of such controversial reforms undertaken during the Ottoman and the French administrations. In the post-Independence period the relationship between the Syrian state and religion, most importantly Islam, became increasingly problematic. In particular the al-Asad regime, which has been in power since the 1970s, has always had a difficult relationship with Islam. Syria is officially a secular, socialist state and has no state religion. The state recognises all religions and guarantees freedom of religion, which also comprises the guarantee to respect non-Muslim communities' legal and judicial autonomy in personal status. That being said, Islam nevertheless remains the prevailing religion and retains the upper hand in all strata of society, including the Constitution and perhaps even more so in the plurality of Syria's personal status law.

CHAPTER 2

MAPPING THE PLURALITY OF JURISDICTIONS: THE LAWS OF PERSONAL STATUS

The previous chapter outlined the historical development of the position of Syria's family law in the legal system. It explained why legal plurality in family law, as elaborated by the Ottomans and expanded by the French, continues to exist in Syria today. This plurality in family law entails that specific religious communities retain their legislative and judicial autonomy in the field of family law, parallel to the general state law on family relations, namely the 1953 SLPS. The organisation of personal status law in Syria is similar to that of Egypt. Berger speaks about 'interreligious duality or bi-polarity' when referring to the plurality of personal status laws in Egypt, meaning that a distinction is made between Islamic law, on the one hand, and the collective of non-Muslim laws on the other. Another similarity between Syria and Egypt is the position of the Muslim personal status law vis-à-vis non-Muslim laws, for the Egyptian personal status law 'enjoys the status of *primus inter pares* by being the general law'.[1] The same applies to the SLPS, which is upheld as the general, overriding law in matters of personal status.

The purpose of this chapter is to present the mosaic of the laws of personal status that we find in Syria today. Once the legal map is outlined, it will help us to understand some of the complexities that arise from this legal plurality. I will first map out the different effective family laws and courts that operate in Syria's contemporary legal system.

The first part of this chapter is devoted to an analysis of the development, the contents and the scope of application of the SLPS. Following this general discussion of the SLPS, I will consider the personal status courts and its judiciary, most importantly the *shar'iyya* judges. The SLPS is analysed in more detail than the other personal status laws, because of its particular position vis-à-vis the other laws, that is, those pertaining to the Druze community and the different Christian communities. The religious regulations regarding matters of personal status of the Jewish community will, however, be left aside, since there are very few Jewish families in Syria.[2] The final section of this chapter will discuss the issue of competing jurisdictions, addressing questions and issues such as 'Which jurisdiction applies in an interreligious marriage?' and 'What if a Christian man converts to Islam – who will get paternal authority over the children when the Christian mother adheres to her original faith?'

The 1953 Syrian Law of Personal Status

In the 1950s many 'new' – that is post-independence – Arab governments, like Jordan (1951), Tunisia (1956), Morocco (1958) and Iraq (1959) issued their first national codifications of Muslim family law. On 17 September 1953 the Shishakli regime promulgated the Law of Personal Status (*qanun al-ahwal al-shakhsiyya*) as Legislative Decree no. 59. It came into force on 1 November in the same year and was considered one of the most progressive family law codes in the Middle East at the time.[3] The Jordanian government had promulgated a personal status code two years earlier, in 1951, which served as an example to the drafting committee of the SLPS.[4] The Syrian legislators, for their part, took it a step further and introduced some bold, unprecedented reforms to the corpus of Arab personal status law.

The Explanatory Memorandum to the SLPS elaborates on the motives and reasoning behind the text. According to the Explanatory Memorandum, there was a need in Syria for a single comprehensive law code containing the *shari'a* regulations regarding matters of personal status. The SLPS is 'based on an eclectic choice of those juristic opinions which most closely accord with local custom and modern needs'.[5]

As explained in the previous chapter, the codification of personal status law was initiated by the Ottoman government, which eventually led to the promulgation of the Ottoman Law of Family Rights (OLFR) in 1917. The OLFR not only contained provisions derived from the Hanafi *fiqh*, but also drew on rules from other schools of law. This method of lawmaking, known as *takhayyur* (eclectic selection) or *talfiq* (lit. amalgation),[6] was continued by the drafters of the various Arab personal status codes of the 1950s. In the Explanatory Memorandum, the Syrian lawmakers regularly refer to principles that are taken from Maliki, Shafi'i or Hanbali *fiqh*, so as to explain why certain provisions deviate from established Hanafi jurisprudence or to provide an explanation for an 'innovation' which has no direct ground in established Sunni doctrine.[7] The divergence from traditional Hanafi *fiqh* is most obvious in the expansion of divorce grounds (mainly taken from Maliki doctrine) and the possibility of including various stipulations in the marriage contract (inspired by Hanbali doctrine).

A specially appointed committee drafted the code, based on five different sources:

(1) the 1917 Ottoman Law of Family Rights (OLFR), which had been in force and to which the people and the courts had already become accustomed;
(2) Egyptian legislation, with some amendments, in accordance with local needs (*al-maslahat al-mahalli*);
(3) the unofficial, that is, never formally enacted, personal status code compiled by the Egyptian jurist Qadri Pasha;
(4) non-Hanafi opinions and provisions which the committee considered 'not contrary to *shari'a* regulations'; and
(5) a draft code written by a Damascus judge, al-Shaykh 'Ali al-Tantawi.[8]

According to Anderson, the inclusion of the phrase 'not contrary to *shari'a* regulations' (*la tunafi al-hukm al-shar'i*) is significant, because it opened 'the door extremely wide'.[9] He marked this as a perfect example of how the legal reformers of the mid-twentieth century sought to combine the demands of modern life with the wish to ground their legal interpretations in religious authority. He stated that '[t]here can be no manner of doubt, [. . .] that the motive behind these reforms was the pressure of modern life, social change, and social conscience; that the inspiration was, in origin, Western; and that only the form was Islamic.'[10] To some scholars, the legal-religious foundations of some of the innovations in the personal status laws were rather narrow.

According to Layish, drafters of statutory legislation in countries such as Egypt and Syria founded such innovations by referring to the principle of *maslaha* (public interest), to the extent that 'social need became a source of law in its own right'.[11] Indeed, the Explanatory Memorandum does refer to the *maslaha* principle a number of times. For example in its introduction to the section pertaining to 'divorce' (*talaq*), it states that *shari'a* itself opens the 'door of grace' (*bab al-rahma*) through the principle of *siyasa shar'iyya*,[12] to return to the origins of the rules of divorce, which also include opinions other than the four (Sunni) schools of law, as long as they conduce to the public interest (*maslaha 'amma*).[13]

A concrete example of how the *maslaha* principle was invoked to legitimise an innovative provision can be found in the explanation on Article 117 SLPS. This article stipulates that a woman can claim a payment of compensation (*ta'wid*) to be paid by her husband when he has misused his unilateral divorce rights and divorced her arbitrarily and she has suffered hardship as a result. Syria was the first Arab country to introduce the possibility of a woman seeking compensation from her former husband in the case of an arbitrary divorce.[14] The Explanatory Memorandum explains that when a ruler regulates to comply with something that is recommended (*mandub*) or permitted (*mubah*), the regulation becomes binding (*wajib*), according to the Hanafi doctrine, provided that there is benefit in accordance with *shari'a* (*maslaha shar'iyya*) in it.[15] Anderson and Layish each call this, respectively, a bold or revolutionary innovation for which the legislator only provided general *shari'a* principles as a base, as in the prohibition to cause damage.[16] Yet while the SLPS was considered progressive or revolutionary in the Arab world in the early 1950s, this no longer holds true today, especially when compared to the current family laws of, for example, Egypt, Morocco and Tunisia.

The SLPS is schematically organised as a classical *fiqh* treatise;[17] it consists of 308 articles, divided into six books. The first book deals with marriage, more specifically: betrothal, the marriage contract, types of marriage and the legal effects of marriage. Book Two covers the dissolution of marriage, in which different types of divorce and their legal effects are discussed. Book Three deals with paternity, nursing, suckling and the maintenance of relatives. Book Four concerns legal capacity and legal representation, or more specifically: legal guardianship, custodianship and curatorship. Book Five provides the regulations regarding bequests. The final book deals with the rules governing inheritance. The final four provisions (Arts 305–8) are part of the latter book, but are not exclusively related to 'inheritance'. They are, in fact, applicable to the SLPS as a whole.

Article 305 states that for matters that are not specified in the SLPS, one shall resort to the most authoritative doctrine of the Hanafi school. The Hanafi doctrine thus remains not only the point of departure of the SLPS, but also the final resort. Similar provisions, incidentally, can be found in other Muslim personal status laws, including those of Egypt, Jordan, Kuwait, Mauritania, Morocco, Somalia and Qatar.[18] According to Carlisle, this article is regularly quoted in court rulings by *shar'iyya* judges in Damascus, but not explained. Carlisle notes that the inclusion of Article 305 in a ruling seems in part to serve a legitimising function.[19]

For the practical application of this provision, judges and lawyers today still consult and refer to the Personal Status Code compiled by the Egyptian jurist Muhammad Qadri Pasha in 1875.[20] The edition of the SLPS issued by the Syrian Bar Association, for example, consists of two parts: first, the substantive text itself, followed by the complete text of the Qadri Pasha code (647 articles). In comparison, in the Gaza Strip (Palestine) *shar'iyya* courts also rely on the Qadri Pasha Code, in addition to the 1954 Law of Family Rights issued by the Egyptian Governor-General for the Gaza Strip.[21] Shehada asserts that Gaza judges are more reliant on the Qadri Pasha Code for their rulings since the Law of Family Rights provides fewer details than the Qadri Pasha Code.[22] Similarly, in Syria, the provisions of the SLPS are not narrowly defined and are not exhaustive in their treatment of issues, which provides ample room for application of sources other than the SLPS, such as the Qadri Pasha Code. In fact, with Article 305, the Syrian legislator facilitated resort to references outside the SLPS. This inherent flexibility of the SLPS and its open norms or lacunae allows judges broad discretion in deciding personal status cases.[23] In Chapter 5, I will elaborate in more detail on how judges and other legal practitioners work with(in) this flexibility of the Syrian law.

The final three articles (Arts 306–8) set out the exceptions for the Druze, Christians and the Jewish communities, which will be discussed below.

Amendments to the SLPS

In 1953, the SLPS was considered to be one of the most comprehensive of law codes in terms of scope, content and application, including some innovations that had not been incorporated in any other family code in the Middle East.[24] Other countries followed suit and proceeded with the introduction of more sweeping reforms in family law. The personal status code promulgated by Tunisian President Habib Bourguiba in 1956 is generally considered to be the most progressive family law code, both inside and outside Tunisia.[25] The Tunisian law introduced some important, unprecedented reforms, such as the prohibition of polygamy and the legislation of adoption. The Tunisian law was considered to be a shining example for many Syrian women activists, with whom I interacted during my fieldwork. Several activists seeking to change the SLPS often referred to the Tunisian law as a guiding paradigm for family law reform.

Syria never made their changes as far-reaching as those of Tunisia, but since the promulgation in 1953, some amendments were made to the SLPS, such as those in 1975, 2003 and 2010. In 1975, the regime introduced a series of amendments by Law no. 34/1975, intended to improve the position of women. The provisions relating to polygamy, dower, maintenance, divorce, nursing, legal guardianship and custodianship were changed by this amendment.[26] After the changes of 1975 it was not until 2003 that any further changes in the SLPS were implemented and that was not more than a minor amendment. Following a petition action by a collection of women's groups, the nursing rights of divorced mothers were slightly improved. The most recent change dates back to September 2010, when an amendment was made to Article 308 SLPS. With this latter amendment the special jurisdiction of the Christian and Jewish communities over personal status matters was extended to include inheritance and bequests. The events and circumstances leading up to the 2003 and 2010 amendments will be discussed in the next chapter in more detail, in addition to other amendments and draft law projects related to family law.

Articles 306–8: application of the SLPS

Article 306 provides that '[t]he provisions of this law apply to all Syrians except for what is stated in the following two articles': Articles 307 and 308. Pursuant to Article 306, the SLPS is considered the general law (*qanun 'amm*); the Jewish law and the various Christian laws are special laws (*qawanin khassa*);[27] or in Latin, the SLPS is the *lex generalis* and the Jewish and Christian laws the *leges speciali*. This supremacy of the SLPS over other personal status laws can lead to situations of intersection of jurisdictions. This already complex situation becomes even more complicated in cases of interdenominational or interreligious relations or when one of the spouses converts to another religion, as will be discussed later.

Article 307 provides that the Druze community is explicitly exempted from those provisions that run counter to their beliefs.[28] Article 308 provides that Christians and Jews will apply their own religious regulations in matters of betrothal, conditions of marriage, marriage conclusion, wife's obedience, wife's and children's maintenance, annulment and dissolution of marriage, the bride's dowry (*dutta* or *ba'ina*), nursing and, since 2010, inheritance and bequests. Interestingly, depending on which edition of the SLPS you obtain, the text of Article 308 varies. The edition published by publishing house Al-Nuri ('Atari 2006) omitted the Jewish communities from the text. I consulted other, recently published, editions of the SLPS, which, likewise, made no reference to the Jewish communities. On the other hand, the edition published by the Damascus Bar Association, which is generally used by lawyers, does include the Jewish communities (*al-tawa'if al-yahudiyya*) in Article 308 (Damascus Bar Association 2006). One can only guess at the reason why the Jewish communities are omitted in some editions of the SLPS; one possible explanation could be that the phrase was omitted due to censorship. Because Syria has been at war with Israel since 1948, the relationship between the two states is sensitive, to say the least. During my time in Damascus, I noticed that Syrians were generally very negative about Israel and anything Jewish. It is possible that the Al-Nuri edition for sale in the bookshop, which can be considered as the public SLPS edition, omitted the reference to the Jewish communities for that reason, owing to state censorship.

It is important to note that the SLPS does not make a distinction between Sunni (estimated at 74 per cent of the population) and Twelver Shi'i, Isma'ili or 'Alawi (together estimated at 13 per cent) Muslims. Interestingly, the situation is different in Lebanon, where such a distinction is made. In Lebanon, each religious group has its own personal status law and courts, including the different Muslim communities, such as Sunni, Shi'a and 'Alawi. There is no 'general' personal status law applicable to all Lebanese, as in Syria. In other words, in Lebanon each religious community is equal to the other and the personal status law for Sunni Muslims is just one of the 14 laws.[29] Finally, the SLPS also applies when one spouse has Syrian nationality (Art. 15 Civil Code) and it applies to non-Syrian Muslims who are subjected to Islamic personal status laws in their home country.[30]

Personal status courts

In Egypt, unification of the legal system in 1955 led to the abolition of the different religious (Muslim, Christian, Jewish) courts and the establishment of national courts with designated family sections.[31] During the United Arab Republic period (1958 to 1961), the Egyptians tried to get Syria to adopt the Egyptian judicial reforms of 1955, but to no avail.[32] In Syria, the Christian, Jewish and Druze communities retained their respective jurisdictions in family affairs. Due to pressure of Sunni *'ulama'*, the government did not push for a comprehensive unification of the judicial system or an abolition of the religious courts.[33]

The Judicial Authority Law (*qanun al-sultat al-qada'iyya*), Law No. 98/1961 with amendments, regulates the judicial system, which consists of civil and criminal courts, state security courts and personal status courts. The general personal status courts, those that apply the SLPS, are the *shar'iyya* courts.

Article 306 SLPS states that its provisions apply to all Syrians, which implies that the *shar'iyya* courts have general jurisdiction in all matters of personal status. However, this is not the case. Article 33 of the Judicial Authority Law states that the courts that have jurisdiction to hear matters of personal status are the following:

(1) the *shar'iyya* courts;
(2) a doctrinal court (*al-mahkama al-madhhabiyya*) for the Druze community;
(3) the denominational courts (*al-mahakim al-ruhiyya*) for the various recognised Christian and Jewish communities.

The Druze doctrinal court and the various Christian denominational courts will be addressed later: in this and the following section I will focus on the *shar'iyya* courts.

In Syria there are 24 *shar'iyya* courts in total, the majority of which are in Damascus proper, that is, six courts.[34] *Shar'iyya* courts are first-instance courts, presided over by a single judge (Art. 34.1 Judicial Authority Law). There are no *shar'iyya* courts of appeal; SLPS appeals cases are heard by the *shar'iyya* chamber of the Court of Cassation (Art. 48 Judicial Authority Law). Cases of conflicts of competence between the different personal status courts are heard by the Civil Chamber of the Court of Cassation (Art. 46.3 Judicial Authority Law).

Articles 535–47 of the Law of Judicial Procedures (*qanun usul al-mahakimat*), Law No. 84/1953 with amendments, sets out the jurisdiction of the *shar'iyya* courts. Article 535 stipulates that the *shar'iyya* courts have exclusive jurisdiction (*hukm niha'iyyan*) in matters involving:

(1) legal guardianship (*wilaya*), trusteeship (*wisaya*) and legal representation (*niyaba shar'iyya*);
(2) registration of deaths;
(3) interdiction (*hajr*) and legal capacity/mental maturity (*rushd*);
(4) missing persons;
(5) descent (*nasab*); and
(6) maintenance of relatives.

The exclusive jurisdiction of the *shar'iyya* courts in matters of inheritance and bequests involving non-Muslims changed with the amendment of September 2010; jurisdiction in these matters now rests with the communities themselves. That being said, any Syrian, regardless of his or her religion, still has to refer to a *shar'iyya* court for matters related to, for example, the determination of paternity and legal guardianship (*wilaya*).

The *shar'iyya* courts have full jurisdiction over all personal status cases involving Muslims, including: marriage; dissolution of marriage; dower and trousseau; nursing; fosterage; maintenance of spouses and children; judgements concerning charitable endowments (*al-waqf al-khayri*) (Art. 536).[35] According to Article 542 of the Law of Judicial Procedures, *shar'iyya* courts have no jurisdiction over foreigners who are subject to civil law in their home country.[36]

The judiciary

Similar to Egypt in its desire for unification, the Syrian government sought to place the laws, jurisdictions and the judiciary of the different religious groups under state control. Judges serving in the *shar'iyya* courts are appointed, transferred and dismissed by the High Judicial Council, under the supervision of the Minister of Justice (Art. 66 Judicial Authority Law). The judicial appointments of the Christian denominational courts, on the other hand, are made by the church authorities, in conjunction with Article 36 Judicial Authority Law, but do require retroactive government approval.[37]

The traditional religious scholars and judges lost their authority to the state because they were no longer able to base their rulings on classical *fiqh* texts. The state now decided by which regulations personal status matters were to be adjudicated, by codification of Islamic substantive law, as laid down in the SLPS. In addition, the judges responsible for its implementation could no longer be traditional legal scholars. On the contrary, they were required to attend state law schools, controlled by the Ministry of Justice. Since 1947, judges working in the *shar'iyya* courts have had to be graduates from the regular faculties of law,[38] who, like all law students, receive legal training in all areas of law. There are no programmes for specific fields of law and for that reason every law graduate can work in any field, be it criminal, civil or personal status. Thus, graduates from the *shari'a* faculties of the universities of Damascus and Aleppo cannot work as judges in the *shar'iyya* courts. They share the same fate as women and non-Sunni Muslims, who are also excluded from the office of *shar'iyya* judge.[39] There is no explicit legislation or official directive which prohibits women being appointed as *shar'iyya* judges. Cardinal conducted interviews with judges and other legal professionals in Syria about this issue. She writes that the majority of respondents quoted Article 24 SLPS as the reason why women cannot become *shar'iyya* judges. The article stipulates that a (*shar'iyya*) judge will act as the guardian of whoever has no guardian; based on this provision the respondents argued: '[s]ince a woman cannot serve as the guardian of a minor or as a marriage guardian, she cannot exercise the functions of a sharī'a court judge.'[40]

Shar'iyya judges are not religion-trained; they do not receive specific *shari'a* or *fiqh* training. The law school curricula include a course on personal status law, which is commonly taught by professors from the *shari'a* faculties.[41] The classes only focus on the contents of the SLPS and not on the historical sources on which this law is based.[42] Even though they administer, for the most part, *shari'a*-based law, *shar'iyya* judges function as civil law judges.[43] Whereas the Judicial Authority Law states that the judge of the Druze court has to belong to the Druze community (Art. 35), it is silent on the religious background of *shar'iyya* judges. However, this does not exclude the fact that most *shar'iyya* judges appeared, in my observation, to be faithful Muslims. Cardinal writes that 'piety and circumspect behaviour are qualities demanded of a *shar'iyya* court judge' in Syria.[44] For example, just like Cardinal's experience in the *shar'iyya* courts, the judges I met in the Damascus courts would not shake my hand in greeting. Cardinal sums up the qualities a *shar'iyya* judge should have as follows:

> it takes a special type of person to be a judge in the special courts of the sharīʿa jurisdiction. In the eyes of the public and the legal community, a sharīʿa court judge must be a pious man who respects religious norms and values in order to live up to the high moral standards expected of him as a judge. He must also refer to the classical Islamic treaties whenever the odd case requires him to do so [...] Religious and judicial duties come together in the person of the sharīʿa court judge.[45]

Whereas the *shar'iyya* judges are considered civil servants, working full time in the courts, the judges in the Christian courts are not – they are clergymen. This is also how they view themselves, as, for example, minister (*qassis*) and judge of the Protestant court of Damascus, Boutrus Zaʿour, put it 'First I am a priest, second a judge!'[46] Holding the position of judge in an ecclesiastical court is for a clerical judge merely a secondary job, in addition to, for example, instruction and guidance in matters of faith and the administration of the sacraments, such as the Eucharist, baptism and marriage.

To my knowledge, Syrian law students are trained only in the SLPS, the other personal status laws are not part of the university law curricula. Cardinal asserts in her article on Syrian *shar'iyya* court judges that law school students study the Muslim, Christian and Jewish personal status laws.[47] However, during the frequent interactions I had with various junior lawyers (trainees), I noticed that their knowledge of Christian (and Druze) family law was very limited and often almost non-existent.[48] My observation was confirmed by a statement from the senior lawyer Mr Mulhim that law students are trained only in the SLPS.[49]

For that reason, Mr Mulhim asked his (only) Christian trainee and me to give a series of mini-lectures on Christian family law, based on visits we made to the Greek Orthodox and Catholic courts. He considered it essential that his trainees gained knowledge of the other (i.e. not SLPS) family laws and their procedures, and the Christian community in general.[50] He acknowledged that many Muslims were ignorant about the beliefs and practices of their fellow Christian citizens. During the first mini-lecture, one of the trainees asked a question which seemed to confirm Mr Mulhim's statement. The trainee asked his Christian colleague whether it was true that Christians baptise their babies in wine. According to the Christian trainee this was a widespread misconception in Syria. Next to Mr Mulhim's wish for mutual understanding between Muslims and Christians, he pressed his trainees to educate themselves in the Christian court procedures. He did not want them to have to turn down a potential client just because they did not have any knowledge of Christian family law.[51]

Other personal status laws and courts

The Druze community

According to estimates, about 400–500,000 Druze live in Syria, which is the lion's share of the entire Druze population worldwide (estimated at 1 million).[52] They live predominantly in the rugged, mountainous region of Jabal al-Druz, in the southern governorate of Suwayda.

The Druze call themselves 'unitarians' (*muwahhidun*), meaning they believe in the unity of God. The Druze religion originated from Isma'ili Shi'i faith and was founded in the eleventh century in Egypt.[53] Druzism is generally considered a blend of various beliefs and rituals, influenced by particularly Isma'ilism, Neo-Platonic philosophy, Sufism and Gnosticism. For that reason, many Syrian Muslims do not consider the Druze to be part of the Muslim faith.[54] Their religious beliefs and practices are shrouded in mystery, even to the majority of the Druze people. Only a small group of initiates (*al-'uqqal*, 'the knowledgeable ones'), either men or women, has access to the secret texts and are fully initiated into the Druze doctrine. The vast majority of the Druze community, the uninitiated (*al-juhhal*, 'the ignorant ones'), are not trained in the religious teachings and only know what is handed down to them through tradition.

Article 307 SLPS states that the Druze community is explicitly exempted from those provisions that run counter to their beliefs. The article excludes the application of the SLPS for the Druze community on nine points, most importantly: impediments to marriage, dissolution of marriage, return of the dower or trousseau, intestate and testate succession. The most salient feature of the Druze stance towards Islamic law is the prohibition of polygamy, outlined in Article 307 paragraph B.

The Druze generally follow the Hanafi school of law, though not in matters specifically regulated by the Druze law and customs, such as those related to marriage, divorce and bequests. The Druze community has its own law of personal status (*qanun al-ahwal al-shakhsiyyat li-l-ta'ifat al-druziyya*). The Druze personal status law was issued in Lebanon on 24 February 1948 and amended on 2 July 1959, again in Lebanon. This law applies, for the most part, to Druze communities in Syria, Lebanon and Israel.[55]

The Ottomans did not recognise the Druze as a religious community: for personal status matters they had to refer to the 'general', *shar'iyya*, courts handling such matters.[56] However, the French granted the Druze their own denominational court (*al-mahkama al-madhhabiyya*) in Suwayda. Syria became independent in 1946: the Syrian government officially recognised the court in 1948.[57]

The Druze first-instance court is housed in the general court building of Suwayda, next door to the *shar'iyya* court. There is only one Druze court with a single judge in the entire country, thus there is only one Druze judge presiding over all Druze personal status affairs. In case of appeal, parties have to refer to the *shar'iyya* chamber of the Court of Cassation in Damascus. There once was a special court of appeal for the Druze, which consisted of a group of shaykhs, but this court was abolished in the 1950s.[58]

In May 2009, I travelled to Suwayda. I visited the Druze court and talked to the then Druze judge, Ma'moun Barjas al-'Afif. According to Judge al-'Afif, the majority of the cases presented to the court involved legal validation of bequests (*tathbit al-wisaya*). The Druze have a different stance on testate succession from that of the Hanafi school of law, that is, the Druze recognise absolute freedom in testation, without any restriction, whereas the Hanafi doctrine does not accept exclusion of legal heirs by a bequest.[59] Other cases that were presented to the Druze court mostly concerned divorce cases. The divorce rate among the Druze, similar to other communities (see Chapters 5 and 6), increased rapidly in recent times, although, according to Judge al-'Afif, divorce cases constituted only 5 per cent of all the court cases, mostly judicial divorce (*tafriq*) cases.[60]

Christian communities in Syria

During the first centuries of Christianity, five cities emerged as important centres of Christianity: Jerusalem, Antioch, Alexandria, Constantinople and Rome. These five original Patriarchates essentially form the stem from which the abundance of present-day churches derive. The first four Patriarchates or Churches are clustered together under the banner of 'Eastern Christianity'. In plain words one could say that each 'Eastern' rite has an Orthodox Church and a Catholic counterpart ('rite' meaning an ecclesiastical tradition about how the sacraments are to be celebrated). For example, in Syria we find a Syriac[61] Catholic Church and Syriac Orthodox Church. Generally, the Orthodox churches are not united under a single authority; they have their own synods and bishops. The Eastern Catholic Churches, on the other hand, are united in communion with the Bishop of Rome, which means they acknowledge the Pope's authority.

Understanding Christianity in the Middle East, especially understanding the history, divisions and relations between the Eastern churches, is an arduous task. For the historical schisms, doctrinal and organisational differences and varieties of the Eastern Christian denominations, I refer to the numerous publications on Eastern Christianity.[62] Following the division made by the Middle East Council of Churches, we see that the Eastern churches can be divided into four 'families': the Oriental Orthodox (non-Chalcedonian) Churches, the Eastern Orthodox (Chalcedonian) Churches, the Catholic Churches and the Evangelical (or Protestant) Churches.[63] The Assyrian Church of the East can be considered a fifth 'family'; however, it is not listed as such by the Middle East Council of Churches. It would be beyond the scope and topic of this study to try to summarise or explain how these 'families' differ from one another or how they relate to one another. I will therefore only deal with the churches that are found in Syria, particularly the churches and courts I was able to include in my research.

Syria is part of the cradle of early Christianity and continues to house the earliest churches until this day. In addition, as a result of the

Crusades' campaigns in the Levant, the settlement of Christian missionaries and more recently, of Iraqi refugees and foreign domestic workers in Syria, various Western, mainly Protestant, churches emerged in the country. Allegedly, just before the outbreak of conflict in March 2011, the various Christian denominations made up around 10 per cent of Syria's estimated 22 million population.[64] Since there are no official statistics available on religion in Syria, one can only guess how many Christians citizens there really were. It has been reported that the number of Christians had dropped to 8 per cent, due to immigration following the nationalisation projects of the Syrian economy and education system in the 1960s.[65] On the other hand, after the American invasion of Iraq in 2003, Syria took in about 1.5 million Iraqi refugees, many of whom were Christians. Most Christians live in urban areas in and around the cities of Damascus, Homs, Hama, Aleppo, Lattakia and in the far north-east governorate of Hassaka.

I and II. The Orthodox Churches (Oriental and Eastern Orthodox)

The largest group of Christians belongs to the Greek Orthodox (*rum urthudhuks*)[66] church; the number is estimated at 503,000 souls.[67] The Patriarch of Antioch and All the East, His Beatitude John X (Yazigi), is their spiritual leader and has had his seat in Damascus since 1342. Other Orthodox churches are the Armenian Orthodox (est. 111,800 members) and the Syriac Orthodox (est. 89,400 members). The Patriarch of the Syriac Orthodox Church, His Holiness Ignatius Ephrem II, has had his seat in Damascus since 1959.[68]

III. The Catholic Churches

In Syria there are six Catholic denominations that recognise the authority of the Pope; these are Melkite Greek (est. 111,800 members), Maronite (est. 28,000), Armenian Catholic (est. 24,600), Syriac Catholic (est. 22,400), Latin[69] (est. 11,100) and Chaldean Catholic (est. 6,700). The Patriarch of the Melkite Greek Catholic church, His Beatitude George III Laham, has his seat in Damascus.

IV. The Evangelical or Protestant Churches

The third recognised Christian 'group' are the Evangelical communities or Protestants, commonly referred to in Arabic as *injili,* in total estimated at 20,100 adherents. The Evangelical churches include

Baptist, Presbyterian, Alliance Church, Church of Nazarene, Reformed, Episcopal (Anglican)[70] and Armenian Evangelicals. Most churches are associated with the National Evangelical Synod of Syria and Lebanon, which has its headquarters in Beirut.

V. The Assyrian Church of the East

From an historic perspective, one could group the Assyrian Church of the East (est. 16,800)[71] and the Chaldean Catholics together into a 'fifth' family group of Eastern Christian churches. I have no information on the legal situation of the Assyrian Church of the East, but I assume its members are governed by a separate personal status code as they are recognised as a religious community with legislative and judicial autonomy in the field of personal status (see below). The Chaldean Catholics are the Catholic counterpart of the Assyrian Church; because the Chaldean Catholics recognise the authority of the Bishop of Rome, they are considered to be part of the Catholic 'family group'.

Christian personal status laws and courts

Article 36 of the Judicial Authority Law stipulates that the denominational courts (*al-mahakim al-ruhiyya*) remain the competent courts for non-Muslim denominations, as defined in Law no. 60/LR enacted by the French High Commissioner de Martel on 13 March 1936. The 1936 Resolution lists the following communities: Maronite, Greek Orthodox, Greek Catholic Melkite, Armenian Orthodox, Armenian Catholic, Syriac Orthodox, Syriac Catholic, Assyrian Chaldean, Chaldean (Catholic), Latin, Protestant.[72] Only these officially recognised religious communities are permitted to draft and apply their legislation internally, however, within the national legal framework, meaning that they still require official government approval by law if they wish to change their legislation.[73] The most recent example (in 2006), is the promulgation of a new personal status law for the Catholic communities; this was authorised by Presidential Decree.

Orthodox laws of personal status and courts

The three Orthodox churches each have their own recognised Orthodox law of personal status; these are the Greek Orthodox Personal Status Law (Law no. 23, 27 June 2004), the Syriac Orthodox Personal Status

Law (Law no. 10, 6 April 2004) and Armenian Orthodox Personal Status Law (number and date unknown). The Syriac as well as the Armenian Orthodox laws are applicable to the respective communities in Syria *and* Lebanon. During my time in Syria, various sources hinted that the Orthodox churches recently attempted to draft new personal status laws, but as far as I know none of these drafts have ever been submitted to Parliament.

There is an Orthodox denominational (*ruhiyya*) court in every diocese, which includes Damascus, Homs, Hama, Lattakia and Aleppo. Cardinal writes that, since 2004, lay judges, in other words non-clergy, have the right to preside over Greek Orthodox courts. What is more, contrary to the *shar'iyya* courts, women can serve as judges in the Greek Orthodox courts.[74]

Catholic Law of Personal Status and courts

On 13 June 2006, the People's Assembly (*majlis ash-sha'b*) approved a new law for the Catholic communities in Syria: the Catholic Law of Personal Status (hereafter CLPS); on 18 June 2006 it was promulgated by Presidential Decree as Law no. 31.[75] The CLPS is, for the most part, based on the Code of Canons of the Eastern Churches, issued by the late Pope John Paul II in 1990. In addition to the CLPS, the Catholic courts also resort to Chapter VII 'Marriage' of the Code of Canons of the Eastern Churches in its entirety, that is, Canons 776–866. These canons are added as a supplement (in Arabic) to the CLPS and have direct legal effect. The Catholics have a first-instance court in every diocese and, in addition, Damascus has a court of appeal.

Evangelical Law of Personal Status and courts

The Evangelical Law of Personal Status was drafted by the National Evangelical Synod of Syria and Lebanon, which has its headquarters in Beirut, Lebanon, and dates back to 1949. The Syrian government accepted the Law in 1952, subsequently amending it in 1962.[76] In the spring of 2009, I was told that a new draft law was before the government waiting for approval. However, as far as I know, it was never approved.

The Evangelical personal status courts can hear cases of the following four denominations: Baptist, Presbyterian, Alliance Church and Church of Nazarene. In total there are four denominational courts – in Damascus, Homs, Lattakia and Aleppo.[77]

The Jewish community

Following Syria's longstanding state of war with Israel, the Jewish communities in Syria diminished. From 1947 until 1992, Jews were travel-restricted, both in and outside the country, until President Hafez al-Asad lifted the travel restrictions in 1992. As a result, in the 1990s, thousands of Jews left the country and emigrated to the United States, Brazil and Mexico. Until recently, fewer than 100 Jews remained in the cities of Damascus, Aleppo and Qamishli.[78]

The Jewish community is governed by the Jewish Book of Rulings concerning Personal Status (*kitab al-ahkam al-shar'iyyat fi al-ahwal al-shakhsiyyat li-l-musawiyyin*). If, how and by whom the law is applied is unknown; because of the sensitivity of anything to do with the Jewish community in Syria, during my fieldwork I did not make any inquiries into the position of the Jewish community.

Other applicable laws

The Law of Judicial Procedures and the Judicial Authority Law have been mentioned already. These national laws set out the organisation of the judiciary and the basic judicial proceedings to be followed by all courts, including the various personal status courts.[79] Furthermore, the courts are required to follow the rules of evidence as prescribed by the Law of Evidence (*qanun al-bayyinat*), Law no. 359/1947. The law is inspired by Egyptian law, which, in turn, has been inspired by French law and contains a few rules inherited from *shari'a*. However, the SLPS diverts from the Law of Evidence when it comes to rules regarding testimonies and oaths. The SLPS differentiates between men and women: women need to testify and pronounce an oath in unison, pursuant to Article 12 concerning marriage witnesses.[80] The Law of Evidence, on the other hand, does not make a distinction between the testimony of a man and that of a woman; their individual testimonies are equally valid in a civil or criminal court.[81] All personal status courts are also bound by the procedures laid down in the Civil Status Law (*qanun al-ahwal al-madaniyya*), Law no. 26/2007, amended in 2011.[82] The law stipulates that all marriages, divorces, children and deaths have to be registered at the Civil Registry.[83]

Complex realities of the intersection of jurisdictions

Religion (*din*) or denomination (*ta'ifiyya*) is the determining feature in choosing which personal status law applies. The religion into which one is born determines which jurisdiction in matters of personal status apply. A person's religious identity is not registered on one's identity card[84] but has to be registered in the Civil Registries. It is not possible to have 'no religion'; atheists do not exist in Syria, at least not according to the Civil Registry. For that reason it is not possible, for example, to contract a civil marriage; one has to marry either according to the provisions of the SLPS or one of the canonical laws. But what happens when persons belonging to different religions or denominations want to get married or divorced? Which jurisdiction applies when one of the parties (or both) seeks to exercise his or her rights or when a legal dispute arises?

To call to mind what was described earlier, in line with Berger's study on Egyptian family law, one could say that there are two legal systems in the field of family law, one for Muslims and one for non-Muslims.[85] This duality or legal plurality does not, however, entail equality between the different religious communities, but rather an imbalanced or asymmetrical plurality, because the SLPS and the courts that apply the law, the *shar'iyya* courts, clearly have the upper hand, as will be explained below.

The supremacy of the SLPS and the *shar'iyya* courts is explained by the concept of public order (*al-nizam al-'amm*).[86] The SLPS is the general law in matters of personal status and only exempts Druze and non-Muslims in specified cases. As we saw earlier, this asymmetric duality is reinforced by various laws, such as the SLPS (Arts 306–8), the Law of Judicial Procedures (Arts 535–47) and the Judicial Authority Law (Arts 33–6).

Mixed marriages and conversions

The supremacy of the SLPS becomes especially apparent when the jurisdictions of different religions intersect.[87] When a non-Muslim woman marries a Muslim man, the SLPS will be applicable; when a Druze woman marries a Sunni Muslim man, again the SLPS will be applicable. A Christian or Jewish woman, that is, a woman who belongs to the *ahl al-kitab* (the recognised monotheistic religions), can marry a Muslim man, but it is not possible for a non-Muslim man to marry a

Muslim woman, for Article 48.2 SLPS states that a marriage between a Muslim woman and a non-Muslim man is considered invalid (*batil*).[88] If a non-Muslim man wants to marry a Muslim woman, he needs to convert to Islam. A Christian or Jewish woman who marries a Muslim man is not required to change her religion, but the children will be automatically Muslim and the wife cannot inherit from her husband, for Article 264 sub B SLPS states that a non-Muslim cannot inherit from a Muslim. However, when a woman converts to Islam and the husband does not, the marriage will be considered invalid and will be dissolved due to Article 48 paragraph 2. Interestingly, in Lebanon, following the equality in personal status laws, mixed marriages across all religions and denomination are legally possible, which means that a non-Muslim Lebanese man can marry a Lebanese Muslim woman.[89] It should be noted, however, that legally impossible (such as a marriage between a Muslim woman and a Christian man) or socially unacceptable marriages can be circumvented by contracting a civil marriage abroad, for example on Cyprus; a practice that is also common among mixed couples from Israel and Lebanon.[90]

Various studies, both historical and contemporary, on legal practices in the Middle East demonstrated that non-Muslims frequently took their case to a *shar'iyya* court.[91] Either because they had to, for example because it concerned a mixed religion case (e.g. Muslim vs non-Muslim) or they resorted to a Muslim court, instead of turning to their own denominational court, in order to obtain a more favourable ruling. In the present time, Christians in Muslim-majority countries, such as Egypt and Syria, occasionally still turn to *shar'iyya* or family state courts because they believe their personal or financial interests are better served by personal status laws that apply to Muslims. The most common reason, however, is to obtain a divorce under the SLPS.

It is very difficult for Christians to divorce, so men and women sometimes turn to drastic measures, such as converting to Islam, in order to obtain a divorce. Maktabi maintains that these 'conversions of convenience' by Christian men occur with the intention of avoiding the long divorce proceedings of the Christian courts, and because the Islamic divorce rules 'are more lenient'.[92] Judges in the Christian courts are aware that this can happen. As a result of this, according to one of my interviewees, Christian court rulings are sometimes intentionally more favourable to the husband, for example, by awarding the wife only a small amount of alimony after dissolution (or nullification) of the marriage. When a wife objects to such a ruling, the judges commonly tell her to accept the ruling because otherwise she runs the risk of her ex-husband converting to Islam and taking the children from her.[93]

Through my contacts with lawyers and other legal practitioners, I learned of some of these conversion cases. When I enquired further with some, mostly Christian, legal professionals, the response was generally cautious; most of them nervously dismissed the issue. The reactions to my enquiries made it very clear it was a highly sensitive subject, particularly among Christians. During my time in the Catholic court of Damascus, a few cases were presented to the court involving a spouse, usually the wife, filing a petition for nullification of the marriage because the other spouse had converted to Islam. This was because even if the marriage had been dissolved by a *shar'iyya* court, it does not mean that the marriage is thereby considered dissolved by a Christian court. The Christian courts will not recognise the 'Muslim' divorce, for the marriage will continue to exist according to Christian doctrine. The 'divorced' Christian spouse will need to resort to his/her denomination court to ask for a separation or nullification of the marriage according to his/her canonical law, if he/she wants to remarry. This will be explained later.

What is important here is that, in the case of conversion to Islam, the SLPS becomes the applicable law and the *shar'iyya* courts are considered the competent courts.[94] In this context, an interesting Court of Cassation ruling of 1998 cited by Georges in his study on the rights of Christians in the Middle East is worth mentioning. It concerned a case in which two brothers of a Muslim wife who was married (out of court) to a Christian man, had stated in a *shar'iyya* court that they witnessed the husband's pronunciation of the *shahada*, the Muslim declaration of faith. The brothers' testimony was accepted by the court and the man was considered Muslim, despite the fact that the husband denied he had converted to Islam; he claimed he never pronounced the *shahada*. The husband appealed to the Court of Cassation, but it denied his claim and confirmed the ruling of the *shar'iyya* court. The man was considered Muslim even though he considered himself Christian.[95]

Children and interreligious marriages

Conversion also affects the issue of child custody. When one of the parents converts to Islam, the SLPS can also be invoked by the converted parent in order to claim full child custody. In order to understand the complexities that arise from claims over child custody in an interreligious marriage or parenthood, the different aspects of child custody as regulated by the SLPS need to be elaborated upon and analysed in more detail.

Child custody can be divided into legal guardianship (*wilaya*) and nursing (*hadana*). The parents have shared custody of their children, but the father will always have sole legal guardianship (*wilaya*) of his children until they reach the age of 18 (Art. 162 SLPS), also when the parents divorce. Guardianship is divided into two categories: guardianship over the person (*al-wilaya al-nafsiyya*) and guardianship over the minor's property (*al-wilayat 'ala al-mal*). Guardianship over the person implies authority over education, medical treatment, instruction, careers guidance, consent to marriage and any other affairs concerning a minor's interests (Art. 170.3). Both types of guardianship devolve upon the father or the paternal grandfather (Art. 172). In the absence of a father or paternal grandfather, the second paragraph of the latter provision refers to Article 21, which deals with guardianship in marriage (*al-wilayat fi al-zawaj*). Guardianship over the minor's person, and not guardianship over the minor's property, can be awarded to a male agnate, in the order of inheritance, provided that he is in a degree of consanguinity precluding marriage (*mahram*) (Art. 170.2 in conjunction with Art. 21). Furthermore, the court can appoint a female, for example the mother, as a custodian (*wasi*) to manage the minor's property (Art. 173). However, a mother cannot act as a guardian of her minor son/daughter's person, which means that she cannot, for example, act as his or her guardian in marriage.[96]

The other component of child custody, besides legal guardianship (*wilaya*), is physical custody or nursing (*hadana*). The right to nurse a child is the prerogative of the mother (Art. 139). In the event of divorce, the mother may ask for the court to give her the right to nurse her children until the age of 15 for girls and 13 for boys (Art. 146). However, Article 138 stipulates that a woman loses her nursing right when she (re)marries someone outside the child's immediate family, that is, to a non-*mahram* man.

It is important to bear in mind that the SLPS rules pertaining to legal guardianship (*wilaya*) are applicable to Muslims as well as non-Muslims (Art. 535 Law of Judicial Procedures). Physical custody (*hadana*), on the other hand, is one of the matters in which Christian and Jewish communities are competent to apply their own laws (Art. 308 SLPS). This intersection of different jurisdictional aspects of child custody can lead to complicated and often distressing situations.

'Islam is the better religion'

Some of my informants told me about cases where Christian men had converted to Islam and subsequently went to a *shar'iyya* court to demand full custody over their children – physical custody in addition to legal guardianship. I heard of at least three court rulings, one of which I read myself, in which a *shar'iyya* judge had awarded the father the exclusive nursing right. In this particular case the father had obtained the nursing right over his children, who were still in the age of *hadana*, as he was considered more suitable because he was a Muslim. The ruling said in so many words that his religion, Islam, is the better religion and for that reason he should raise the children (*dinuhu huwa al-din al-aslah li-tarbiyyat al-awlad*). In other words, the Muslim father was given preference over the non-Muslim mother.[97]

In another case, a Christian married man had begotten a child by another woman – a Muslim woman. The woman wanted the father to recognise the child as his own, which he did. However, legal guardianship over his child was taken from him because he was a Christian and the mother insisted on raising the child as a Muslim. I do not know, however, who was appointed as the legal guardian of this child, instead of the father. According to Article 170.1 SLPS, the paternal grandfather would have been first in line to be appointed as the legal guardian, but since he was probably a Christian too, it is more likely that one of the mother's male relatives was appointed legal guardian.

The SLPS remains silent on the issue of custody and the upbringing of children of an interreligious marriage. Georges explains that the judiciary of several Arab countries, including Syria (in line with Art. 305 SLPS), therefore refer to the work of Qadri Pasha.[98] The argumentation that the Muslim parent belongs to the better religion refers to Article 381 of the Qadri Pasha Code. This article states that a non-Muslim parent, holding the nursing right, can take care of the child until he/she can understand religion (*hatta ya'qila dinan*), but this right can be taken from the non-Muslim parent if the court establishes that he/she has a negative influence on the child's religion: Islam.[99]

Another article that is of importance here is Article 129 of the Qadri Pasha Code. This provision states that when a non-Muslim spouse converts to Islam, the children born (and those not yet born), that is, minors, from this marriage will follow the religion of the Muslim parent.[100] The Court of Cassation, however, ruled on 12 February 1970 that a child may return to the Christian faith when he/she has reached the age of discernment (*rushd*), if he/she chooses not to recognise Islam as his/her religion.[101] Interestingly, Berger refers to another Court of Cassation ruling, dated 23 May 1970, concerning a case in which this right was not recognised by the highest court of Syria. In the latter case, a father had converted to Islam when his son was still a minor. When the son attained the age of majority he wanted to return to his original faith – Christianity – but the Court of Cassation ruled that 'it could not interfere in the freedom and competence of the Civil Registrar', who had refused to register this change in religion.[102] Georges, on the other hand, describes the case of a Christian son who, at the age of 23, discovered that his father, before marrying his mother, converted to Islam in order to divorce his first wife. The 'Muslim' father remarried another Christian woman and the children born from this marriage were registered as Muslims by the Civil Registry, because, after all, children follow the religion of the father, in this case, Islam. For the sake of completeness, it should be mentioned that a converted adult cannot return to his/her original faith. The now adult son was raised a Christian by his parents and for that reason the court accepted the son's request to be registered as a Christian in the Civil Registry. Nevertheless, the difference in religion between this father and his children exclude the latter from inheritance from their father, who was considered Muslim.[103]

Finally, some people contract an interfaith marriage, even though it is legally invalid. What happens to these types of marriages and, more importantly, what about the status of the children born of these marriages? An invalid interfaith marriage can lead to sad legal realities for all family members, both spouses and children, as the following example demonstrates. In his study on the rights of Christian minorities in the Middle East *Le droit des minorities*, Georges cites a case in which, although legally impossible following Article 48.2, a Muslim woman had married a Christian man.[104] When they wanted to register their two children at the Civil Registry, they were told they could not because the children were born of an invalid marriage. Following the advice of a judge, the woman claimed before a *shar'iyya* court that the husband had lied about his religion. The court declared the marriage irregular and ordered the immediate separation of the spouses. The children were recognised as belonging to the father and were registered as Muslims, because 'la religion la plus honnête des parents'.[105] Thus, the couple was forced to divorce because the SLPS did not recognise their union. Furthermore, they were forced to lie in order to obtain proof of paternity. Here too, the children followed the Muslim parent, in this case the mother, because Islam was considered the righteous religion.

The examples above demonstrate how the Muslim faith is given preference over other faiths. When a non-Muslim father or mother converts to Islam, the religious identity of the converted parent automatically devolves upon the children. Here we see that, using Tadros' words, 'the application of the content of the Muslim Personal Status Law is not gender specific, rather religion-specific'.[106] The supremacy of Islam is particularly evident when a non-Muslim woman converts to Islam. Whereas the provisions of the SLPS, similar to Egypt's personal status law, normally privilege men over women, in the event of conversion of the wife or mother, the husband or father loses out to his Muslim (former) spouse. Thus, as an exception to the rule, when a non-Muslim woman converts to Islam, the woman is privileged over the man. Here we see how the 'laws of patriarchy' are superseded by 'the laws of religious affiliation',[107] in this case to the advantage of Islam and the SLPS.

Conclusion

This chapter presented the mosaic of personal status laws and courts that are found in contemporary Syria. The most important law of personal status, the SLPS, enjoys the status of being the general, overriding law, which applies to all Syrians, regardless of their religion or denomination. That being said, the Druze, Jewish and various Christian communities are exempted from certain provisions of the SLPS and are allowed to apply their own laws within the framework of the national legal system. Still, the SLPS and the courts applying the SLPS, the *shar'iyya* courts, clearly hold a privileged position in the field of personal status. This creates an asymmetrical duality in Syria's family law, where the SLPS and the *shar'iyya* courts enjoy the upper hand over the other laws and courts.

Consequently, because the SLPS is based primarily on Islamic jurisprudence, non-Muslims sometimes find themselves in a position where Islamic law is applicable to them too. The supremacy of the SLPS thus has significant implications for non-Muslims, especially when different jurisdictions intersect, for example, in cases of interdenominational or interreligious relations or when one of the spouses converts to another religion. The asymmetrical duality in Syria's family law becomes especially apparent in interreligious relations, which can have detrimental effects on spousal as well as parent–child relationships, as a converted Muslim spouse or parent is generally privileged over the non-Muslim spouse or parent. The privileged position of Muslim affiliation over non-Muslim can lead to, for example, a forced dissolution of the marriage, due to the provisions of the SLPS, or child custody being taken from the non-Muslim parent in favour of the Muslim parent.

CHAPTER 3

DEBATING AND CHANGING FAMILY LAW

'[L]e moment le plus dangereux pour un mauvais gouvernement est d'ordinaire celui où il commence à se réformer.'

A. de Tocqueville, *L'Ancien Régime et la Révolution*[1]

The previous two chapters described the historical and contemporary development of Syria's family law and its current plural legal landscape, in which we find an array of personal status laws and courts. History shows that changes or reforms in the domain of family law in the Middle East were often controversial and, as will be explained in this chapter, remain a sensitive issue today. During the last decade (2000 to 2010), several efforts were made by the Syrian government and civil society groups to introduce changes to the personal status laws, most importantly the SLPS; some of these recent developments will be discussed in this chapter. It will become clear that (proposed) changes in the field of family law of late were often accompanied by political and social turbulence. While the government always retained final decision-making authority, it was nevertheless susceptible to demands of various – sometimes opposing – groups, including secular, civil society and religious groups.

Buskens contends in his article on family law reform in Morocco that the content of the Moroccan family law 'is a social construction, shaped by political considerations'.[2] Similarly, the content of the SLPS is a product of its time, influenced and shaped by socio-political developments. Although its contents are, for the most part, nearly 60 years old, today's SLPS can still be regarded as a compromise or result of a delicate balancing act between patriarchal family values, religious claims and progressive demands. The recent developments concerning personal status reforms in Syria, as I will argue below, confirmed this observation.

In Chapter 1, I discussed Pinto's 'use of Islam as a cultural idiom' by different actors, including the state, as a political instrument. In his article, Buskens points to the important symbolic role of Islam in society, in relation to Moroccan family law. He maintains that '[f]amily law has become a symbol of the place of Islam in society and of the right to participate in politics.'[3] He explains that 'family law and gender serve as powerful political symbols in the modern Muslim world'.[4] I will contend that the role that family law plays in Morocco is similar to that in Syria. In Syria too, family law and gender policies are of great symbolic value, and indicative of the role religion and the various religious communities (are allowed to) play in Syrian society. Of course, like any comparison, the comparison of the role of family law in Morocco and Syria does not hold true completely, as the countries come from different historical, political and religious backgrounds. For example, the current Moroccan King Muhammad VI played a decisive role in reforming and proclaiming the new family law in 2004; President Bashar al-Asad's role regarding law reform, on the other hand, was not as decisive. Rather, al-Asad's stance bears more resemblance to the strategy employed by the late Moroccan King Hassan II who, in 1993, took firm control over the reforms and accepted only extremely modest reforms, so as to avoid social upheaval in the country.[5] Similarly, the government of al-Asad has attempted to avoid social and religious unrest and has instead sought to preserve the status quo.

This chapter embarks on an examination of the government's secular ideology in relation to its contested relationship with Islam. In line with this ideology, the Syrian government advocated state feminism and equality between the sexes. Gender equality and religious diversity are important ideologies for the regime to support, yet difficult to uphold due to its contested political legitimacy, as will be explained in the course of this chapter.

The year 2003 was a year that marked the start of various social initiatives in the field of family law, including proposals to reform the

SLPS and other proposals to amend existing laws. The second and longest section of this chapter will describe several such proposals and activities, in addition to a number of civil society organisations and individuals who were active in this domain. Furthermore, some noteworthy changes in the field of family law will be discussed, including the new Catholic personal status law of 2006, two controversial drafts for a new SLPS in 2009, and finally, a minor but significant amendment to the SLPS that was made in 2010. This chapter will be concluded with an analysis as to why reform in family law has remained a politically sensitive issue in the recent past.[6]

The challenge of secularism

The Ba'th Party has always, in line with the ideology of Arab nationalism, espoused a secular ideology. The Party envisioned 'a society in which all Arabs would be equal, irrespective of their religion',[7] a vision which would minimise the role of religion in society and guarantee equality for all citizens, including religious minorities. However, the secular nationalist ideals did not touch a chord with all Syrians.

Since coming to power in 1963, Syria's Ba'th Party has had a troublesome relationship with Islam, in particular with some segments of the Sunni population. The Party's secular ideology, with regard to family law, proved difficult to uphold. As explained earlier, history showed that both the Sunni majority and the various Christian minorities were often ill-disposed towards far-reaching government interference in the domain of family affairs. An initiative by the early Ba'th government to introduce a secular family law was staunchly rejected and no attempt to introduce a civil family law has been undertaken since. Christian leaders feared they would lose their privileges, whereas many Sunnis perceived any secular-oriented reform in family law by the secular, non-Sunni government as interference in religious affairs – a matter in which, according to many Sunnis, the 'Alawi-dominated government has no legitimate say, because of its lack of, or at least shaky, religious legitimacy. Due to this sensitivity, the government remained reluctant to push for reforms in family law.[8]

In response to challenges to its political and religious legitimacy, the regime felt 'compelled to allow some room for controlled religious activity and discourse'.[9] It did so by allowing the 'Islamic character of public space' to increase over the last few decades. According to Rabo, this increased public display of Islam is a source of great concern to many Christians, who fear that it may infringe upon the 'secular, minority' character of the regime, which is considered a safeguard against increased Islamic public dominance.[10] Rabo's observation corresponds with some of my own experiences in Damascus; during my fieldwork I met several Christians who longingly recalled the times when women were able to wear miniskirts and interact more freely with the opposite sex. Besides allowing public display of Islam, the regime also tried to reaffirm and expand its control of religious activities and Islamic discourse. In his article about the relationship of the Ba'th regime with Islam, Paulo Pinto cites President Bashar al-Asad from an interview (with al-Asad) by an American journalist in May 2010, in which he stated 'that the biggest challenge he faced was "[h]ow can we keep our society as secular as it is today"'.[11]

State feminism

The Ba'th Party in Syria, similar to other secular-oriented governments in the region, such as Turkey and Tunisia, used and mobilised women as symbols of development and modernisation of the nation. At the same time, the government fostered the ideal of a sound and stable family as the mainstay of society.[12] Ba'thist socialist ideology stressed the importance of women's participation in public life and encouraged women to contribute to the progress of Syrian society. According to official Party rhetoric, women had to be liberated from 'feudal and backward' family and kin-group bonds in order for them to contribute to building a new and better nation.[13] To this end, gender equality and equal access to education and employment for both men and women were important ideologies for the Ba'thi government.

During the 1970s, the Syrian government had invested heavily in education and employment, which led to a significantly higher literacy rate, a dramatically increased number of people working in the public sector, as well as a considerably higher number of male and female students enrolled in basic and higher education.[14] The state's investments and development of a large state apparatus and welfare programme were crucial in gaining control over political and economic resources and, at the same time, generating support from the nation. The increased employment opportunities were also open to women; that is why the number of women working outside the house increased noticeably, with the public sector as the main employer of women.[15] The Labour Law also made it easier for women to work outside the house, as its provisions stipulate that women employees are entitled to at least 75 days (depending on whether it is a first, second or third child) paid maternity leave, and additionally, the state provides for state-funded day care centres.[16]

Since the late 1980s, due to high unemployment rates, increased inflation, and enormous population growth, the need for educated women in the public workforce has withered away and, consequently, the number of women workers has decreased dramatically. The state has therefore encouraged women to take on the role of wives and mothers at home. Sparre argues that there is another explanation for the state's changed policy towards women's participation in society, which she attributes to 'the increased role of Islam in both the public and private sectors'. She writes that 'in Islamic discourses women most often are presented as mothers and housewives'[17] and for that reason 'the idea of women as the nurturers and educators of the nation's future citizens' has become common place in Syria of late.[18] In this context it is interesting to point out the recently released documentary *The Light in Her Eyes* (2011), directed by Julia Meltzer and Laura Nix, which portrays a conservative Muslim preacher, Huda al-Habash. She founded a (non-state) all girls' Qur'an school in Damascus where she teaches girls and women about the Qur'an and Islam. Mrs al-Habash propagates exactly this message, namely that women have a duty to be(come) nurturers and educators of the nation.

Equality for all citizens?

Syria has often portrayed itself as one of the leading Arab countries in promoting gender equality and women's full participation in Syrian society. Similar to the previous Constitution of 1973, the current Constitution also guarantees equal citizens' rights. Article 33, paragraph 3 of the 2012 Constitution reads that 'citizens shall be equal in rights and duties without discrimination among them on grounds of sex, origin, language, religion or creed'.[19] In addition, Article 23 reads '[t]he state shall provide women with all opportunities enabling them to effectively and fully contribute to the political, economic, social and cultural life, and the state shall work on removing the restrictions that prevent their development and participation in building society.' However, whether the Syrian government takes its own constitutional guarantees of equality for all seriously is debatable.

The Syrian government officially promotes state feminism and equality for all, but legal realities are sometimes very different, in particular in family relations. The contents of the different personal status laws, the Nationality Law, and the Penal Code clearly prevent the equal enjoyment of rights by men and women. These laws contain numerous provisions that conflict with principles of gender equality and non-discrimination,[20] as laid down not only in the Constitution but also in international conventions, such as the Convention of Elimination of All Forms of Discrimination Against Women (CEDAW), to which Syria is a party.

When we look at personal status law, it is evident that the SLPS does not assert equal rights and responsibilities to both men and women in marital and family life. Inequality in marriage, divorce, child custody, inheritance and so on between men and women is manifestly present in the provisions of the general Syrian family law. A woman's status is determined by her relationship to her male family members: until she marries she is connected to her paternal family and, after marriage, her status is connected to that of her husband. Nor is she regarded as a full Syrian citizen. For example, a *married* mother cannot pass on her nationality to her children under the Nationality Law, because that law, in principle, only allows the father to confer the Syrian nationality upon his children.[21]

In fact, an influential female Ba'th Party member, Bouthaina Sha'aban,[22] admitted that, despite the constitutional gender equality before the law:

> [i]n practice, however, none of the leaders of the Baath party seem to be great supporters of women's rights. Although they are members of a secular party, Baath Party members support traditional morality (Christian or Muslim) when it comes to women's issues. Any demands for establishing more equal laws for women are often met with the argument that we are a religious society and we cannot anger the fundamentalists of both religions.[23]

Sha'aban's observation hits the nail on the head. It reflects the government's quandary in trying to balance its official secular discourse and policies, on the one hand, *and* accommodate the demands of a significant segment of its conservative Muslim and Christian citizens, on the other.[24] Recent examples of how the government tried to manage this difficult balancing act in the field of family law will be discussed in more detail below.

Syria is, obviously, not unique in its gendered laws of personal status and nationality; laws of other Arab countries bear, although in varying degrees, a resemblance to Syria. Mayer points out in her article on personal status reforms in North Africa that:

> [b]oth in their movement toward accepting women's equality and their resistance to this same norm, societies on the northern and southern shores of the Mediterranean are involved in a common dynamic. In this clash of systems, patriarchal norms sanctified by religion and tradition contend with the impact of profound social and economic transformations and the influence of prevailing international norms of equality between the sexes. Although religion and tradition may seem to be potent forces militating against change, countervailing forces have been set in motion that should undermine discriminatory laws in the Maghrib, just as they have done already in Europe.[25]

As mentioned earlier, the ascension to the presidency of Bashar al-Asad in 2000 ushered in an era of hope, hope for reform and social and political change in the country, but within a few years this hope faded away. The cautiously emerging civil society in the early years of Bashar's presidency was nipped in the bud by the regime. Initially it seemed that the government was willing to consider (modest) legal reforms in family and gender relations. Although some social reforms were accepted, most notably in 2003, the door to reform was securely closed in 2007. From that time onwards it became clear that the Syrian government would not accept changes that would upset the conservative segments of society; in fact, the conservative forces gained the upper hand in the struggle for change in the family law.

In the following sections, several recent proposals for reform of the family law, in particular the SLPS, will be discussed, including draft laws that were put forward by the state and non-state actors.

Mending family law: who wants change?

As explained earlier, the 1953 SLPS was, at the time, considered to be one of the most progressive family law codes in the Middle East, but later it lost its significance in this respect. The last major amendments to the 1953 Personal Status Code were made in 1975 (by Law no. 34), with the aim of improving the position of women. The annotation to the 1975 amendment law states that the state has a constitutional obligation to 'lift the bonds that restrain the development of women' and 'their participation in the development of society'.[26] To that end, the amendments aimed to restrict the practice of polygamous marriages and traditional divorce rights of men.[27] In addition to polygamy and divorce, the amendments also changed SLPS provisions related to the dower, maintenance, nursing, legal guardianship and custodianship. After 1975, it took another 28 years before any further changes to the SLPS were made in 2003, and this time it concerned merely a minor amendment (see below). It is important to note that the amendments to the SLPS never profoundly affected or changed the substantive contents of the law, but that they were mostly procedural. For example, polygamy and a man's unilateral right to divorce (*talaq*) were not proscribed, but merely restricted by imposing procedural limitations on them. This type of legislative reform policy is, incidentally, common in many Arab Muslim countries.[28]

Those seeking change to the existing personal status law(s) in Syria come in all shapes and sizes: women rights' activists, members of Parliament, religious figures, lawyers, union members, and so on. When we focus on the last decade, we can distinguish various individuals, several organisations, either state-funded, affiliated or semi-independent from the state, who were actively involved in efforts to reform the laws. It is beyond the scope of this book to discuss all the different actors, I will therefore only mention those whom I interviewed personally. I interviewed a number of people, either acting in their individual capacity or as (former) representatives of organisations, who were active in the field of family law and/or gender-based law reforms.

2003: Syria's accession to CEDAW – a catalyst for social and legal action

On 28 March 2003, Syria acceded to the international human rights agreement, the CEDAW, with reservations referring to *shari'a*.

The reservations made by Syria exclude the application of certain CEDAW provisions, most notably those that guarantee equal rights of men and women pertaining to marriage and family life.[29] The accession to the Women's Convention worked as a catalyst for civil society groups to discuss and develop plans for legal reforms. Women's organisations arranged seminars and established working groups to discuss the need to lift the reservations the Syrian government made to the Convention, as well as the possibilities of changing the personal status law and other laws that discriminate on the basis of gender.

A government body that played an instrumental role in the campaign for review of the options around lifting the reservations to CEDAW was the Syrian Commission for Family Affairs (SCFA). The SCFA was established by Law no. 42/2003, following Syria's ratification of the CEDAW; it was officially assigned to review discriminatory legislation and to propose new legislation and amendments to existing laws. In addition, the SCFA was responsible for raising awareness on family issues, advising the government in policies and national plans related to family affairs, as well as coordination of the reporting process to international human rights bodies.

In the years following Syria's accession to CEDAW, the SCFA coordinated various projects. Under its auspices, several laws in relation to personal status issues were drafted, including a so-called Children's Rights Law,[30] and various drafts to reform the SLPS and the Nationality Law. In 2004 and 2005, the SCFA organised workshops and seminars in which a wide range of individuals debated the possibilities of lifting the CEDAW reservations that the Syrian government had made.[31] The SCFA had asked Dr Muhammad al-Habash, member of Parliament and an expert in Qur'anic studies and Islamic jurisprudence (*fiqh*),[32] to examine the (in)compatibility of the provisions of CEDAW with *shari'a*. In his study he concluded that all reservations could be lifted – all but one – namely the reservation to Article 16 paragraph 1 pertaining to marriage and family law (cf. al-Habash 2005, 2006). According to al-Habash, men and women cannot have equal right in divorce and marriage, because of what is ordained by *shari'a*. In the same line of argument, he argued that the concept of adoption is not acceptable under Islamic law and thus, for those reasons, the reservation to Article 16 paragraph 1 was justified.[33]

Al-Habash's study was discussed in Parliament, in mosques, and in the media, but to no avail. In May 2007 the Syrian government met with the CEDAW Committee in New York to discuss Syria's initial periodic report. Following this meeting, several civil society groups drew up a draft law proposing to abolish the reservations to the Convention; the draft law was submitted to Parliament. Earlier the government had promised to lift the reservations, at least partially, but the draft was nevertheless rejected by Parliament in November 2008.[34] Several of my interviewees believed that the reason for this inaction on the part of the government was the preservation of the delicate power balance between the government and conservative Muslim clerics who generally oppose any 'progressive' changes to the family law. This argument of maintaining the status quo or preserving the balance of power is a recurring argument, as will become clear below.

Syria's accession to the Women's Convention also sparked off debates about reform of the family law and other laws that discriminate on the basis of gender. The government and civil society groups studied and drafted proposals for amendments to the family law, which were fervently discussed in Parliament and wider society. Women's organisations, together with influential individuals, such as women's rights activist and former member of Parliament, Hanaan Najmeh, had worked on proposals to change the SLPS since the 1980s.[35] In 2003, the time was finally ripe for a public debate on the reform of family law.

In the early 2000s, several proposals were drafted. According to Sabah Hallaq, a women's rights activist, there were two drafts for a new SLPS that were put forward to the government. One draft was prepared by a group that was more closely affiliated with the government, this included Mrs Najmeh; and a more 'independent' group of women activists and NGOs submitted a second, slightly different, draft.[36] The family laws of Tunisia and Morocco, in particular, served as examples of inspiration to the different groups working on family law reform. The two drafts included the following proposals, that with regard to marriage:

- the marriageable age for girls should be raised from 17 to 18 years;
- girls should be allowed to marry without the consent of their legal guardian;
- polygamy should be limited further (government draft);
- polygamy should be forbidden (NGO draft).

The changes concerning divorce included the following:

- the standard marriage contract should provide the option to include a stipulation that, in the event of divorce, the marital community of property will be divided equally between the two spouses;
- when such a stipulation is not recorded in the marriage contract, the wife should receive compensation;[37]
- men and women should receive equal divorce rights; for example, following the example of Egypt, a revised SLPS should include the option for a woman to initiate divorce without her husband's consent[38] (NGO draft);
- a state-regulated maintenance (*nafaqa*) fund should be established, which would supervise and ensure that divorced mothers and children receive their maintenance fees.

With regard to custody of children, the guiding principle should be 'the best interest of the child', and with that in mind, the following proposals were made:

- a divorced mother has a right to nurse (*hadana*) her children until a certain age, the age for both sons and daughters should be raised to 15 years;[39]
- when the children turn 15, they should be able to choose whether they want to stay with their father or mother;
- when the parents divorce and the children stay with their mother, she should be able to stay in the marital home with the children.

Finally, also following Egypt's example, general family courts should be established, instead of different denominational courts.[40]

Petitioning for change: the 2003 SLPS amendment

In 2003, in line with the above-mentioned proposals, the women's organisations staged a petition calling for amendments to the family law. The petition asked for four changes to the SLPS:

(1) the age for nursing (*hadana*) should be the same for boys and girls;
(2) a divorced mother with the nursing right should be provided with a house;

(3) when a divorced mother with the nursing right remarries, she should not lose her *hadana*-rights;
(4) the amount of maintenance (*nafaqa*) should be raised.[41]

The petitioners collected 15,000 signatures, which was enough to induce the Parliament to study the proposed amendments: the proposed reforms were vehemently debated in the Parliament and wider society. Some religious conservatives accused women's rights activists of seeking to tarnish the Qur'an and religious laws by calling for equality between men and women, which they considered an imitation of the West. The women activists claimed that the current law was a male law, not necessarily Islamic; they questioned the patriarchal interpretation of the existing laws.[42]

In the end, only one amendment, in adjusted form, made it into the SLPS. Article 146 was modified and now gives a divorced mother the right to nurse her children until the age of 15 for girls and 13 for boys, an increase of two years respectively. The original proposal intended to abolish the age distinction between boys and girls, and leave them both in the *hadana* care of their mother until the age of 15.[43] Interestingly, the amendment was not issued by Parliament, the People's Assembly, but promulgated by Presidential Decree as Law no. 18/2003. According to Rabo, the President intervened by personally reforming the family law, in order to settle the debate between the conservative clerics and the civil society groups.[44]

Baudouin Dupret made an ethnomethodological analysis of the debate in the Syrian Parliament on raising the age for *hadana*, which took place on 19 October 2003. Dupret's analysis focuses on the form or context of the debates (i.e. performance of the participants, form of speech, procedural rules, etc.) and not so much on the contents of the arguments employed by the members of Parliament. Nevertheless, it is interesting to note that, when looking at the quoted excerpts of the debates in Dupret's article, the independent Member of Parliament, Dr Muhammad al-Habash, played an instrumental role in the realisation of the rise in age for *hadana*-care. In the debate he based his argumentation on Article 3 of the Constitution, which states that Islamic jurisprudence (*fiqh*) is a main source of law. According to al-Habash, this article opens the door to a wide range of legal interpretations on the subject.[45]

Let me devote a few words to the person of Dr Muhammad al-Habash. In an interview I had with al-Habash, he introduced himself as an advocate for a liberal Islam. According to al-Habash, about 80 per cent of Muslims are conservative and the remaining 20 per cent belong to the renewal movement.[46] He explained that, with regard to Islam and the reform of family law, the conservatives believe that Muslims today do not have the right to change the rules; instead 'we' (Muslims) have to go back to the time of the Prophet. In addition, the same conservative Muslims believe that there is only one way to God, that is one truth, one interpretation. Reformers like al-Habash, on the other hand, believe that Muslims can adjust the rules, within limits, to the needs of the present time. He therefore supported plurality and rejected a static, monolithic interpretation of Islam.[47]

Al-Habash believed that the SLPS needed to be adjusted for the present time, but, at the same time, must conform with *shari'a*. He said that one of his goals, as a Member of Parliament, was to change 'old' laws, especially those that affect women negatively. For that reason he supported several activities undertaken by civil society groups, such as the projects against honour crimes, and the establishment of a maintenance fund to support divorced mothers and children.[48]

The Association for the Social Initiative (ASI) was one of the main driving forces behind the 2003 petition calling for changes to the SLPS.[49] The ASI was a non-governmental group created in 2001 and in 2003, was officially recognised by the government to work as a civil society organisation. After the successful, though minor, change to the law in 2003, the ASI continued its activities asking for additional changes to the SLPS. In 2005, for example, it conducted a nation-wide survey called 'Survey on the need to change laws prejudicial to women'.[50] The questionnaire was filled out by 2,855 Syrians (male and female) from seven of the country's 14 governorates.[51] The survey included questions such as 'Do you support an adult woman's right to conclude her own marriage?', 'Does polygamy have a negative impact on the family?', 'Do you support equality in inheritance for men and women?', and 'Do you support making an honor crime a criminal, punishable offence?'[52] According to Maktabi, the publication of the survey in 2006 caused quite a stir in Syria, with conservative clerics accusing the ASI and other women activists of seeking the abrogation of *shari'a* based law and creating tumult by imitating Western countries in their demand for changes to the family law.[53] Soon after, in January 2007, the licence of the ASI was withdrawn by the Ministry of Labour and Social Affairs under the pretext of public interest,[54] and the collaborating researchers from Damascus University were banned from proceeding with the analyses of the survey results.

Other law reform projects concerning family and gender

During the last decade, considerable attention has been given to the problem of Violence Against Women (VAW), in particular domestic violence and honour crimes. Several activities were employed; for example, the largest women's organisation in Syria, the General Union of Syrian Women,[55] conducted a study on violence and discrimination against women in co-operation with United Nations Development Fund for Women (UNIFEM).[56] In subsequent years, other governmental organisations, in co-operation with the Ministry of Justice and the Ministry of Religious Endowments, recommended to abrogate and amend some highly disputed articles of the Penal Code[57] pertaining to honour crimes.[58] For example, Article 548 which stipulates that a man can be exempted from punishment or receive a reduced punishment when he kills or hurts a female relative because he saw her committing adultery or engaged in an illegitimate sexual relation. In the end, in 2009 and 2011, this article was amended and a man found guilty of an honour crime now faces five to seven years' imprisonment.[59]

Another important law that was subject to criticism was the Nationality Law of 1969. The Syrian Women League (est. 1948), in origin a communist organisation, was instrumental in proposing amendments to change the Nationality Law, so as to make it possible for all Syrian mothers to pass their nationality on to their children.[60] In March 2004, a proposal to change Article 3 of the Nationality Law, which stipulates that a child acquires nationality through the father, was submitted to Parliament.[61] The proposal, which would also make it possible for all Syrian mothers to pass on her nationality to her children, was discussed in Parliament. A number of members of Parliament put forward some proposals requesting a change of the law to the Cabinet of Ministers, but it came to nothing. A number of interviewees mentioned that the official explanation for the unwillingness to change the Nationality Law was that it could not be changed because of the

'Palestinian issue'.[62] The reasoning was as follows: Palestinians have a right to return to Palestine and if 'we', that is the Syrian government, gave them Syrian nationality, they would not return to Palestine when they were able. Several persons told me that they questioned whether this was the real reason for the rejection; most likely the 'Kurdish issue' also played a role. At the time (spring 2008), there were an estimated 300,000 stateless Kurds living in Syria, according to a special census held in the Hassakeh province in 1962.[63] In response to the Syrian uprising, which started in March 2011, the government granted stateless Kurds citizenship in April 2011. However, the Nationality Law remained unchanged, so married mothers are still unable to pass on their citizenship to their children.[64]

The 2006 Catholic Law of Personal Status

Against the background of these proposed law reforms, a new law in the field of personal status was issued. In 2006, the Catholic Churches in Syria managed to obtain a new, and some say revolutionary, law, namely the Catholic Law of Personal Status (CLPS).

In October 2004, the drafting process started under leadership of Archimandrite,[65] Antoun Mousleh, assisted by two experienced lawyers working in the Catholic denominational courts. The main source of legislation for the draft was the Code of Canons of the Eastern Churches (the CCEO; in Arabic: *majmu'at qawanin al-kana'is al-sharqiyya*).[66] In addition to the CCEO, other sources were used; most importantly, international conventions pertaining to women's and children's rights, such as CEDAW and the Convention on the Rights of the Child (CRC), and provisions from the previous Catholic personal status law.[67] A few months later the draft was presented to the council of the heads of the Catholic Churches in Syria, who, after approval, submitted it to the Council of Ministers. After some additional revisions it was eventually send to the People's Assembly, who approved it on 13 June 2006 and five days later, on 18 June 2006, it was promulgated by Presidential Decree as Law no. 31.[68]

Novelties in the CLPS, compared to the old Catholic Law and other Syrian personal status laws, were, most importantly: Catholics were allowed to adopt a child,[69] men and women were guaranteed equal inheritance rights, and fathers and mothers were given equal custody rights over their children in the event of separation. The major legal consequence of the law however, was that with the coming into force of the law, all Catholics of Syria were solely governed by the provisions of the CLPS, and thus excluded from application of the SLPS.[70] Moreover, the Catholic courts had full jurisdiction over all personal status matters pertaining to Catholics. I deliberately use the past tense because this situation lasted only four years; in 2010 the position of the Catholics in the field of family law changed significantly, as will be explained below.

The promulgation of the Catholic law happened quickly and quietly, and came as a great surprise to many, including the Catholic communities themselves. The exceptional position of Catholics vis-à-vis the other Christian groups following the issuance of the CLPS was subject to criticism. Non-Catholic Christians particularly were discontented that they were put in a false position in relation to the Catholic Churches with regard to the SLPS and the *shar'iyya* courts. Instead of working towards harmonisation or unification of a Christian family law, the Catholics 'underlined Christian sectarian divisions thus weakening the minority as a whole, some argued.'[71] Others, striving for a secular or civil family law devoid of any religious references, feared that Law no. 31/2006 would open the door wide to demands for religiously inspired family law reforms from other religious groups. Rabo remarks that 'some Christian lawyers and lay people [repeatedly, according to Rabo] claimed that the law was so easily changed in order to pave the way for Muslims to demand a more patriarchal and "religious" personal status law'.[72] Interestingly enough, this is in fact what happened in 2009, as we will see below.

Rabo writes that the Church only started to educate its clergy and lay members about the new law after its promulgation (in June 2006). She attended such educational seminars in Aleppo and observed that reactions to the new law varied greatly. Women were generally happy with the new law as it improved their legal position as wives and mothers; some men, on the other hand, were less pleased with the content of the law or complained about its immediate enforcement.[73] Most of the Catholics I met during my fieldwork told me that they were very pleased with their new law, while several Orthodox Christians admitted being slightly jealous of, or disgruntled with, their Catholic counterparts and they expressed the wish to have a similar law. The reason why the Catholics managed to be granted this special position vis-à-vis the other Christian groups is unclear and remains a subject for further study.

As mentioned above, this situation only lasted for four years; in the meantime new attempts to change the SLPS came to light in 2009.

The 2009 SLPS drafts

In May 2009, various lawyers, judges, representatives of churches and civil society organisations and others were taken by surprise when they received a copy of a draft for a new personal status law, that is, a new SLPS. They were given one week to study and comment on the draft, which was significantly more elaborate than the current SLPS – 665 Articles compared to 308 Articles respectively. From June 2007, a committee of five anonymous Islamic legal scholars appointed by the Council of Ministers had worked on the draft in secret.[74] The draft was heavily criticised by members of Parliament, religious figures, lawyers and intellectuals, in national newspapers and on the internet, the latter including media forums such as Facebook, at the time still officially banned in Syria.[75] Opponents accused the committee of imposing extremist Islamic views 'similar to those of the Taliban'.[76] In their view, the proposal was regressive instead of progressive; it swept aside all the attempts of the last decades to reform family law and improve the position of women and children.

The draft contained a number of strongly controversial issues. One highly contested issue concerned the proposal to create a body called the *shar'iyya* public prosecutor (*al-niyaba al-'amma*), which would be authorised to raise and investigate certain personal status claims related to public policy (*al-nizam al-'amm*), such as claims regarding impediments to marriage, annulment of marriage, claims related to descent, endowments and bequests.[77] The public prosecutor would have the authority to initiate actions against unlawful marriages, for example if one of the spouses was deemed to be an apostate (*murtadd*; someone who had renounced his or her faith – Islam).[78] The draft retained the inequality of rights between men and women already laid down in the current SLPS, such as the duty of the husband to pay maintenance of the wife in return for the wife's obedience, unequal divorce rights, a divorced mother's limited custody rights over her children, and so on. More than that, it reintroduced classical Islamic legal divorce grounds that were generally considered outdated, that is 'denial of paternity' (*li'an*) and two types of oaths of sexual abstention (*ila'* and *zihar*),[79] and it used religious-sensitive language, such as the term *dhimmi* to designate non-Muslims.[80] In early July, following a successful nationwide campaign against it, the draft law was withdrawn by the President. A few months later a revised draft was published. The second draft omitted most of the contested provisions of its predecessor, but the reform-minded critics also disregarded this second draft since its content closely mirrored that of the current SLPS. It appears that this second draft also never made it out of the ministries' offices, and ended where most draft legislation of late ended up – on a shelf collecting dust. Due to the strong opposition against the two drafts, it seemed the government abandoned, at least for the time being, the idea of introducing a new comprehensive family law. Instead it introduced a minor but significant modification of Article 308 of the SLPS, which was intended to grant all Christian communities autonomy in testate and intestate inheritance, as will be explained below.

It has been argued that the Ministry of Justice and the Ministry of Religious Endowments (*awqaf*) played a significant role in the recent attempts to change the personal status laws.[81] Apparently, both played an instrumental role in the drafting process of the two government-issued (2009) draft laws and in blocking recent 'more progressive' proposals put forward by civil society groups, together with the Syrian Commission for Family Affairs (SCFA).[82] That being said, the role of the SCFA and the Ministry of Labour and Social Affairs, for their part, was also questionable.[83] According to several of my interviewees, both the Ministry and the SCFA had failed in their duty to promote family and women's interests. The Ministry has the mandate to actively seek to modify or abolish any laws that are discriminatory against women and children; yet the Minister did not appear to be in favour of any of the activities or proposals put forward by the SCFA or other organisations. In fact, the Minister only seemed to frustrate any progress or development. Some people were of the opinion that the Minister's attitude was the reason why, since 2007, legislative progress had come to a standstill.[84] Interestingly, instead of the draft proposals being put into law, the year 2007, as we saw above, witnessed the establishment of the above-mentioned secret committee, composed of religious scholars, which was responsible for the two controversial SLPS drafts.

SLPS amendment no. 76/2010

The Catholics' *status aparte* in family law was changed in September 2010, when an amendment was made to Article 308 SLPS. Presidential Decree no. 76, issued on 29 September 2010, amended Article 308 to such an extent that the special jurisdiction of the Christian and Jewish communities over personal status matters now also extends to inheritance and bequests. Before the 2010 amendment, these matters belonged to the competence of the *shar'iyya* courts.

It should be noted that, according to Rabo, '[s]ome Christians claim that their clergy were given the option of adopting Christian inheritance rules at the time when the law [i.e. the SLPS] was made in the early 1950s, but that they were happy to follow the misogynist state law.' Others, however, stressed that being governed by the inheritance rules of the SLPS was an improvement for many Christian women, who, especially those from rural areas, often did not inherit anything.[85]

Whereas the first article of the amendment expanded the jurisdiction of all Christian communities, the second article limited their jurisdiction. This article was of particular interest to the Catholics of Syria, but at their expense. The article states that provisions of the Syriac Orthodox Personal Status Law, the Greek Orthodox Personal Status Law, and the Catholic Personal Status Law, pertaining to matters of personal status other than those listed in the revised Article 308, are abrogated by the amendment. Seeing that from June 2006 until September 2010, the Catholics of Syria were governed solely by the provisions of the 2006 Law (i.e. the CLPS), which allowed them to apply provisions which before 2006 were not able to be implemented by the Catholic personal status courts. The 2010 amendment of Article 308 SLPS, however, ended this exceptional legal position for the Catholics, for it stipulated that matters of personal status other than those listed in the revised Article 308 were abrogated by the amendment. As a result, the amendment rendered a substantial part of the CLPS inoperative, and thus its regulations regarding, for example, adoption, legal guardianship, paternity (or descent), were no longer applicable. Due to this amendment, the Catholics again fell under the scope of Article 308, and thus back within the competence of the *shar'iyya* courts.[86] At the time of writing, it was unclear what the consequences of this change were for, in particular, the Catholic communities.[87]

Balancing legitimacy

The relationship between patriarchy, religion and the state is a complex one, in Syria and elsewhere in the Arab world. The dynamics of gender relations, patriarchy and religion have influenced Syria's pluralistic family law system. The state delegated its legislative power in the area of family law to conservative clerics and with that the state, Suad Joseph argues, 'throws family matters into the domain of non-negotiable sacred religion and into the hands of patriarchal religious clerics'.[88] Moreover, the clerics generally support patriarchal kinship structures, which also 'limits the manoeuvring space in which women's groups can pressure for changes in family law'.[89] Although Joseph refers here to the Lebanese state, I argue, together with Maktabi, that the same accounts for Syria.

The Syrian government kept the legal plurality in family law in place by granting (relative) autonomy to the religious establishments. The religious establishments, for their part, supported this legal plurality because it allowed them (within the boundaries of the state) to administer their own affairs in their respective communities. According to Maktabi, the Christian minorities of Syria (and Egypt and Lebanon) 'see the persistence of group-based citizenship rights as vital to their survival as religious communites'.[90] She furthermore argues that the existence of a multiple court system in particular, instead of a unitary court system, allows for 'clerical resilience' and the ability of religious authorities 'to muster sufficient leverage among political authorities to oppose reform'.[91]

Hence, on the one hand, conservative religious authorities often resisted reforms to preserve their (partial though significant) legislative and judicial authority in matters of personal status. The Syrian government, on the other hand, also resisted any profound legal changes which might endanger the status quo. According to *Muñoz*, authoritarian Arab states fear that allowing 'progressive' reform in the domain of family law and thereby 'extending freedoms and developing individual autonomy within the family – and so weakening patriarchal authority – could lead to a questioning in the public arena of the ideological basis of state power'. Arab governments have often invoked religious norms and made references to 'tradition and custom' so as to 'legitimize the continuation of patriarchal rule'.[92] That is why projects or ideologies such as state feminism and participation of women in the political arena were often merely symbolic; it is 'more a demonstration of rhetoric or political symbolism, concerned primarily with projecting a progressive image internationally, than it is a real motor for change'.[93] Therefore, if change threatens to disrupt established patriarchal structures, a government will consider it more opportune to keep these structures in place.

Furthermore, it is the nature of the state itself, which can be defined as 'neopatriarchal' that reinforces patriarchal structures and social control in a modernising context.[94] In a neopatriarchal state, according to Moghadam, 'religion is bound to power and state authority; moreover, the family, rather than the individual, constitutes the universal building block of the community. The neopatriarchal state and the patriarchal family reflect and reinforce each other.'[95] In Syria too, the complex, reciprocal relation between state authority, religion and family patriarchy fostered a woman's subordinate status as a citizen and in society. In this regard, personal status law, because of its religious imprint and its plural composition, is a convenient tool for the state to use for its own political objectives, in particular to maintain or strengthen its political legitimacy.[96]

Manea argues in her book *The Arab State and Women's Rights* that 'lack of legitimacy' has shaped the gender policies of the Arab authoritarian states of Syria, Yemen, and Kuwait. The preservation of patriarchal structures benefits these states in their 'politics of survival'. In Syria, according to Manea, the regime's reluctance to change the family law system can be explained by its politics of survival, '[b]ecause of its sectarian character it has been afraid of antagonizing the Sunni majority, which resents Alawite control.'[97] Secondly, according to Manea, the religious foundation of the family law system was never changed because family law was never considered a relevant issue for the Ba'th Party.[98] The third explanation that Manea provides is that the family law system suited the Asad regime's divide and rule tactic: 'It must keep the sectarian and religious division intact in order to continue this survival policy, and the Syrian family law system, based on legal pluralism, is the instrument that preserves this division.'[99]

Warrick follows the same line of argument and maintains in her book about gender and politics in Jordan that the duality of many Arab legal systems, that is, secular and Islamic law, is the outcome of a purposive political choice by the state, in particular to serve the need for legitimacy.

According to Warrick, '[d]ual legal systems provide a flexible framework for social regulation, the exercise of state power and the maintenance of popular legitimacy in various sectors of society.'[100] This observation corresponds with the situation described in Chapter 1, where I argued that the Syrian government maintained a plurality of family laws and jurisdictions as a result of a partnership between the state and the various religious communities.

To counter-balance this challenge of legitimacy, the government employed various strategies. First of all, it continued to play the secular card; the Syrian government, being a 'secular' minority regime, presented itself as the best (or only) possible safeguard for the various religious minorities against Sunni dominance. Connected to this was the preservation of the plural family law system, which allows the Druze and Christian communities the authority to regulate their own affairs in personal status matters. This led to the remarkable decision of the Syrian government to promulgate a new Catholic law of personal status, the CLPS, in 2006. The CLPS was remarkable in many ways; first of all because it granted the Catholic communities full jurisdiction in all matters of personal status, and with that allowed the Catholics to break away from the supremacy of the SLPS and the *shar'iyya* courts. How and why it happened as it happened remained unclear but it was clear that it was not favourably received by other Christian groups and some conservative Muslim groups.

Another significant event that marked a fundamental shift in government policy on family law reform happened in 2007. In June 2007 (one month after the CEDAW meeting in New York), the government installed a secret committee of Islamic legal scholars, responsible for two conservative and controversial SLPS drafts. A plausible explanation for the establishment of this committee is that the government took a step too far with the promulgation of the CLPS and in response to protests of, most importantly, conservative Muslims, it allowed the formation of this committee. It is remarkable that conservative Muslim scholars were given ample opportunity to put forward family law proposals based on strict interpretations of Islamic law. Al-Aws explains this leeway for conservative Sunni scholars as an attempt by the government to channel religious opinions through state organs, and with that to circumvent public debates about family law and prevent strong religious opposition to law reforms.[101] The year 2007 appears to be a watershed year for Syrian family law, as the government clearly redrew the boundaries of its religious plural legal system, most importantly by providing a platform for conservative Muslim scholars to voice their opinions on personal status law. According to Pierret, the flirtatious episode (in particular 2005 to 2006) between the Syrian regime and the clergy came to an end in early 2009, in favour of secularism.[102] In addition, the government reinforced the old system by the 2010 amendment to the SLPS, by retracting the privileges extended to the Catholic communities in 2006 and, at the same time, expanding the jurisdiction over inheritance matters to all Christian communities.

Here we see an example of 'the use of Islam [or religion] as a cultural idiom' (cf. Pinto). When we understand personal status law as 'a symbol of the place of Islam in society' (cf. Buskens), we can see how the SLPS and the other personal status laws were used as a political instrument by the Syrian government and other stakeholders to serve several political purposes. The amendment of 2003, for example, was a good example of a compromise in the delicate balancing act between patriarchal family values, religious claims, and progressive demands. The recent developments should be understood in the light of the government's 'politics of survival', as an attempt to preserve the balance between social change and maintaining the status quo.

Conclusion

This chapter has demonstrated that (proposed) changes or reforms of the first decade of the twenty-first century in the domain of family law in Syria were controversial, mostly because of the regime's difficult relationship with religion, in particular Islam. The political and religious legitimacy of the 'Alawi-dominated minority regime has been challenged from the very beginning of its coming to power and forced the regime to continuously try to find a balance between religion and politics. Recent modifications to the SLPS (2003, 2010) and introduction of controversial family (draft) laws (2006, 2009) caused quite a stir in the heterogeneous Syrian society and reverberated on the already tense relations between the Sunni majority population and the religious minority groups, and within these communities themselves. From the early 2000s, the government was engaged in a balancing act in which maintaining religious differentiation and patriarchal family structures played an important role. It was a delicate balancing act of, on the one hand, upholding its official secular discourse and the wish to improve the position of women and minorities, and on the other hand, maintaining the status quo and appeasing, most importantly, a significant segment of its conservative Sunni Muslim citizens.

In the introduction to this chapter, reference was made to recent reforms in Morocco's family law. The current King Muhammad VI played a decisive role in the promulgation of the new family law of 2004. Conversely, the Syrian President, Bashar al-Asad, did not play such a decisive role in implementing personal status law reforms. Only through the personal intervention of the President, minor legal amendments were enacted to existing legislation concerning personal status and gender equality. This strategy bears more resemblance to the government style of the former Moroccan King, Hassan II, who only accepted extremely modest reforms, so as to avoid social upheaval in the country.

For many years, the government appeared to be unwilling to undertake any serious large-scale reforms, not just regarding personal status laws, but regarding any law in general. Instead, the government employed a 'patchwork approach', which consisted of minor modifications to various laws without really improving the existing situation.[103] The reason for this reluctance was, most likely, as was suggested to me by several people during my time in Syria, that the government feared that any serious family law reform, or law reform in general, might incite calls for other legal and political reforms. Tocqueville wrote in 1856 that the most critical moment for a bad government is when it witnesses its first steps toward reform, for then they run the risk of being destroyed by a revolution. That said, it appears that for the al-Asad regime that critical moment has already passed, as the ongoing Syrian uprising seriously threatens its survival.

PART II

UNITY IN MULTIPLICITY

CHAPTER 4

PATRIARCHY, RELIGION AND LEGAL RULES

Laws do not operate in a vacuum and have to be understood in context, not only in their historical and socio-political context but also in their cultural context. This chapter will, therefore, focus on the intersection of law and culture. More precisely, it will describe the cultural context in which Syrian family law operates. The first part of the chapter analyses some key concepts in relation to family relations in the Middle East (including Syria), namely (in order of analysis): patriarchal family, morality and propriety, family honour and women's sexuality, and marriage ideals. It is important to introduce these cultural concepts in order to understand how they relate to and interact with the contents of and discourse around the various personal status laws.

The second part of this chapter focuses on the legal regulation of marriage and divorce. The provisions related to marriage and divorce in the SLPS and Christian laws of personal status will be discussed; because the SLPS is the dominant and default law in the field of family law, an extensive analysis of the substantial contents of this law will be presented first. Besides, since studies on the contents of the SLPS are scant, a detailed discussion of this law is indispensable. Secondly, some general observations about legal regulation of Christian marriage and the dissolution of a Christian marriage, with reference to the various Christian laws of personal status, will be made. This latter section, however, will not be as elaborate as the first. After all, the SLPS is considered the general law; the Druze, Jewish, and various Christian personal status laws, on the other hand, are considered special laws.

The chapter will function as a conceptual framework for the following two chapters, which deal with legal practices within a *shar'iyya* court and a Catholic court, respectively. It will be demonstrated, among other things, that shared norms and views on social propriety, marriage and gender relations were emphasised and reinforced by all participants in the family law arena. During my time in the *shar'iyya*, Catholic, and Greek Orthodox courts, I noticed that the same themes were constantly addressed: the ideal of marriage, the proper role of women, wives in particular, the husband as the provider and head of the household, and so on. Regardless of their legal and religious differences, the personal status courts were united in their shared cultural understandings of gender, family relations, social norms and behaviour. I contend that in the Syrian family context, the patriarchal family model was preserved and reinforced by the various personal status laws and by the various actors which operated in the field of family law. It is this family model which determined the gender roles in society; it was more powerful than legal or religious norms, specific to the different ethnic and religious communities.

Patriarchal family: family as the nucleus of society

Syria's Constitution, similar to most Middle Eastern constitutions, defines 'the family' as 'the nucleus of society' and guarantees that 'the law protects its existence and strengthens its ties' (Art. 20 Syrian Constitution 2012).[1] The fact that 'the family' and not the individual is considered the mainstay of society is not surprising; researchers from different disciplines regard family as the basic unit in Middle Eastern societies.[2] The concept of 'family' in the Middle East has been an object of study for many researchers from different disciplines, including anthropology, gender studies, history, law, religion, and economics. Studies on family in the Middle East focused on its many different aspects and manifestations, including kinship and marriage, family law, patriarchy, nuclear families, rural or urban family relations, family as an ideological project of the state or as an economic unit.[3]

In Syria, as elsewhere in the Middle East, families[4] are commonly patriarchal, meaning that (senior) men are the heads of families, with women and younger family members in a more subordinate role. In a common Arab nuclear family, the father traditionally has authority and is the breadwinner or provider; the mother, on the other hand, usually takes on the role of housewife and takes care of the children. This male dominance within the family manifests itself on several levels. In this regard, I would like to refer to the definition of the term 'patriarchal family model' given by Léon Buskens, who describes it as follows:

> [a] model for family life in which senior men are entitled to a dominant position over subordinate women and children. This male dominance, grounded in their position as husbands and fathers, is expressed in norms about gender, descent, obedience, sexuality, the use of space and freedom of movement, as well as the economy of the household.[5]

Kinship or descent through the father's lineage is a key feature of patriarchal Arab families; in Syria too, 'kinship remains a central organizing institution'.[6] One's patrilineal descent group is decisive for one's economic security, religious affiliation, citizenship, social life, and identity. Kinship determines one's religion and with that also one's status in family law. In other words, a son or daughter does not only inherit his or her father's religion, but kinship also determines his or her future family relations. Thus, when a man or woman wants to marry and start a family, it is not Syrian citizenship that is the determining factor but one's religious denomination and gender.

Syria's personal status laws, as with many other Arab family laws, in varying degrees, reflect the patriarchal family model. The laws privilege men, in particular men from the patrilineal line, in numerous ways: in child custody, inheritance, divorce, choice of marriage partner, passing on religious identity to children (and with that, citizenship), household division of labour, and authority and obedience in marriage. It should be noted, however, that as of late, several of these 'patriarchal' notions, such as the maintenance–obedience equation, have been successfully challenged by women activists in several Arab states, such as Morocco and Algeria. In Syria, however, the patriarchal family model is, by and large, enshrined in all laws of personal status, Muslim and Christian. Certain matters are typically associated with Muslim family law or, on the contrary, Christian family law, but the underlying structures are generally the same. All laws oblige the husband to provide for his wife and children, the wife, in return, is obliged to take care of the household and the children and obey her husband. Hence, in Syria, the 'patriarchal gender contract' (Moghadam 1998) or 'patriarchal bargain' (Kandiyoti 1988) is realised within the family and laid down in the laws of personal status.[7]

Family patriarchy can also not be separated from 'religious patriarchy' in the field of family law.[8] As mentioned earlier, the various personal status laws are written and applied by men, often religious men. Regardless whether they are 'official' religious men (i.e. appointed by a religious or state authority) or not, the drafters of the laws and the ones who apply them (i.e. judges) are selected on their religious merits and knowledge of the religious sources. Besides, Syria's personal status laws not only embrace and solidify the patriarchal family model, but they also bear a religious imprint: the SLPS carries an Islamic legal imprint; the various Christian family laws carry, obviously, a Christian imprint. The religious imprint, that is, its symbolic (most importantly Islamic) value, of personal status law also holds great political weight in the government's delicate relationship with the various religious communities, as demonstrated in the previous chapter.

Before analysing the different aspects of the patriarchal family model, as laid down in the various family laws, I will first discuss some key issues that are important to Syrian gender relations in general. As explained earlier, the Syrian laws of personal status cannot be analysed solely from a formalistic legal angle, they need to be understood in their cultural context. The normative order developed and imposed by the state, through state laws and courts, aims to organise and regulate family relations, but is only able to do so to a certain degree, as there are other, not necessarily legal, norms at work. The interaction between various social, legal, and religious norms (codified and uncodified) in the field of family law cannot be underestimated, as was also demonstrated by other studies on Middle Eastern family law.[9] It is therefore important to understand against which cultural and moral setting these norms are expressed, endorsed and enforced.

In this light I will analyse the following concepts: 'morality and propriety' (in particular gender behaviour), 'family honour and women's sexuality' and 'marriage ideals', for they shape and influence legal discourses and practices. Ideas about proper gender comportment, family and marriage are continuously expressed by individuals in the courtrooms and they play a role in, most importantly, the assessment of spousal or parental behaviour of the parties involved. The narratives presented to the court by the litigants, their lawyers and witnesses influence the outcome of a case, as judges take social (and not necessarily legal) norms and values into account.

Morality and propriety

Dahlgren maintains in her book *Contesting Realities*, which discusses the versatile and changing gender and family relations in contemporary Adeni society (Southern Yemen), that cultural understandings of family and family relations are continuously communicated in the field of personal status law. Men and women 'as gendered subjects', as husbands, wives, fathers, mothers, sons, and daughters are confronted with and subjected to 'dominant familial ideologies'; Dahlgren defines 'familial ideology' as 'a set of norms, values, and assumptions about the way in which the family life is expected to be organised in a normative way'.[10] In the context of a marriage we should think of the rights and obligations of the husband and the wife. A wife ought to obey her husband and fulfil her marital duties, a husband, for his part, is expected to provide for his family. Dahlgren states that a wife's 'moral value is constructed in her fulfilling her marital duties, and thus it is only as a dutiful wife that she safeguards her moral dignity and legal rights'.[11] This latter aspect of the 'familial ideology' (the dutiful wife) made its way into the different personal status laws, as we shall see below and in the following chapters.

Dahlgren describes in her study how morality and propriety or proper comportment (*adab*) affect gender and family relations in Adeni society. She emphasises that propriety in everyday life 'is not a fixed entity but instead has a variety of manifestations'.[12] With that in mind, I use the term 'morality' in a broad sense.[13] I will not link 'morality' directly to Islam or Christianity, that is, denoting norms as 'typically' Muslim or Christian, unless people themselves denoted it as such. My argument aims to demonstrate that many familial norms and values were shared amongst the diverse (in this case primarily Muslim and Christian) Syrian communities.

Morality and propriety are also gendered concepts, with different expectations for men and women. The proper comportment for wives and husbands differs; each is expected to take on a different role. In the event of a family dispute, and particularly those disputes that make it to court, these expectations are clearly articulated and publicly assessed by, first of all, the spouses themselves and others involved in the dispute, most importantly judges, lawyers, witnesses. During divorce proceedings, participants in the process express whether or not one spouse (or both) lived up to or fell short of expectations as a wife or husband. A negative assessment can be made based on seemingly simple acts such as serving coffee for guests, cooking or idling about at home.

Similar to Dahlgren, I observed that when people talked about others, be it in court or elsewhere, they often made moral comments on the behaviour and character of others. A person of high moral character (*akhlaq*) is generally highly appreciated by people from all walks of life, across the various Syrian communities. The assessment of a person's character and/or behaviour is usually based on daily interactions. Syrian families commonly live in tightly knit communities, many of which may have lived in the same village, town or quarter for generations. People usually keep a close eye on each other's lives, families and social relations. Living close together and being a part of each other's life also means that people talk, either good or bad. Gossip, positive or negative, is a way to communicate and reinforce dominant social norms and/or denounce behaviour that contravenes familial or gender ideals.

The reputation of an individual or a family can be damaged, improved or reinforced through the gossip of neighbours, family or other community members.[14] Gossip about, in particular, women's behaviour, marital or other family disputes, can make or break a marriage and affect a family's reputation. Through gossip, social codes or norms are communicated, upheld, and used to exert social control on, particularly, the female and younger members of the community. Rumours about improper behaviour of a girl can ruin her chances of a good marriage, for example. Or worse, it may put her at risk of becoming a victim of an honour killing, a practice which does occur in Syria, in Muslim, Christian, and Druze communities alike.[15]

Women are in a more vulnerable position than men when it comes to harmful gossip, that is why 'most women maintain consciousness about how any dress, behavior, interaction or location can result in people talking and lead to serious harm to their social position and well-being'.[16] To give an example, non-related men and women are not expected to interact unsupervised in public. For that reason, family members often control and restrict, especially unmarried, women's behaviour and mobility. Gender segregation is often regarded as something typical for Muslim communities but, following my observations in Christian courts and my interactions with Christian informants, it became clear to me that the same conventions apply to Christian youth. Fear of gossip can be a powerful tool to ensure that men and women adhere to their expected gender roles. Under the watchful eye of family and community, individuals are expected to keep in line with social decorum: 'both men and women should behave with constraint and modesty'.[17]

Preserving the honour of the family – control of women's sexuality

Upholding the family's reputation or good name is of great importance in the various Syrian communities, similar to most Arab societies. The honour of a family is usually centred on the sexuality of the female family members. The reputation of a wife, daughter or other female family member, particularly a girl's virginity, is important and should be protected. Compromising her reputation or sexual honour would not only reflect upon and endanger her reputation but also that of her family as a whole.[18] The male family members have the responsibility of controlling and protecting the family honour, by monitoring a woman's behaviour and, possibly, disciplining the transgressors.[19] In this light, I would like to share a personal anecdote.

> During my fieldwork (2008–2009) a (Christian) Syrian family had generously taken me into their care and helped me in countless ways, including assisting me in finding an apartment. I lived with this Syrian family for some time and then visited them regularly; once I had moved into my own place, the daughters of the family stayed in my house on a regular basis. When I was looking for a place to live, the father of the house was visiting relatives abroad and therefore one of his daughters did the honours. She negotiated the rent, arranged all the necessary paperwork with the real estate agent, the authorities, and, at the insistence of the mother, made sure the lock of the front door was replaced. The family had a family friend, George, who was a locksmith. But as George did not have time to replace the lock himself, he sent a colleague to my

> house to change the lock. The man came to my house (I was alone), he replaced the lock and asked me to try to see if it worked, which I did. Whilst testing the key he rubbed my knee and told me how beautiful he thought I was. It was all rather harmless, nevertheless I was shocked and insulted; I started yelling at him and told him to leave my house. He was surprised by my reaction and started pleading with me not to tell anyone. In the evening I went to the family's house and told the daughter what had happened. She was shocked and called George immediately. George rushed over and apologised numerous times for what had happened; interestingly enough he also exclaimed 'but he is a Christian!', as if it was unthinkable that a Christian could do something like that. George conferred with the daughter and one of her brothers what would be proper course of action. George suggested that he, with the help of others, would teach the man a lesson, by delivering a few blows. I was invited to come and watch, if I wanted. I told George that I thought beating the man up was not really necessary and that I would prefer it if he refrained from doing so. A week later I was told some blows were delivered, but since the man cried and pleaded not to be touched, George had dropped the matter. I asked the daughter why George had taken up the matter so seriously. She explained that because her father was not at home to take care of things, George had felt responsible to defend her father's name. The father, however, when hearing what had happened, disapproved of George's chosen course of action because he denounced all forms of violence. As the family had taken me into their care, I was also considered part of the (extended) family, and therefore my encounter with the transgressor had to be avenged.

Whether it was truly about the family's honour or possibly George's own honour (or a combination of both), I do not know. Whatever the case may be, I want to pay some attention to George's comment 'but he is a Christian!'. His comment is an illustrative example of the (mis) conceptions Christians often have of Muslims and vice versa, especially with regard to gender relations and sexuality. It is often claimed by Christians that Christian women have more freedom than Muslim women, and that they can interact more freely with the opposite sex, because Christians are not as obsessed with sexuality as Muslims are. Christian or Muslim, a woman's sexual virtue is closely connected to a man's masculinity, but there is a difference. Rabo sums it up as follows:

> To generalize, the ideal for Christian men is to be able to protect their womenfolk and enable them to mix and mingle in public space. The ideal for Muslim men is to be able to protect their womenfolk from mixing and mingling in public space. The ability to both protect and control one's own womenfolk is a crucial aspect of Syrian masculinity.[20]

Even though Christian men generally allow and enable 'their women' to mix and mingle in public, some Christian female friends informed me that, in all honesty, they could not really mingle freely with unrelated men, even if they were Christian, for the eyes of the community were always watching (i.e. they feared it may lead to gossip).

As stated earlier, a woman's sexual conduct is connected to her reputation and honour, and that of her family; this counts for most Syrians, regardless of their ethnicity or religion. For example, it is important for a woman to enter her marriage as a virgin. Sato, who conducted fieldwork among Syriac Orthodox Christians in Aleppo and the al-Jazira region (northeast Syria) in the late 1990s, writes that in the past a Christian bride was expected 'to show the sign of her purity' (virginal blood on a cloth), to her mother-in-law and other female in-laws on the morning after the wedding night. The blood-stained cloth was public proof of the wife's purity and 'also demonstrated the groom's masculinity'; it proved the bride's modesty, good character, obedience to her parents, and also corroborated her family's successful upbringing and preservation of the family honour.[21] My Christian friends told me, just as Sato observed, that this practice of public display of proof of the bride's virginity was no longer common amongst Christians, as it was generally believed that a couple's sexual intimacy was a private matter.[22]

That being said, the importance that is attached to a wife's sexual virtue and a husband's masculinity has not changed, especially when a husband's masculinity is challenged. The introductory chapter of this book started with the following divorce case, in which this subject was raised.

A young couple seeking divorce appeared in the Greek Orthodox court in Damascus for a cross-examination session. Before the court started the interrogation, the judge spoke to the couple in a serious tone, reminding them of the importance of a good marriage and telling them to continue to strive for reconciliation.

The wife (the plaintiff) told the judge that they got married when she was 17 years old and they had now been married for two years, whilst living with the husband's family. She claimed that her husband and his family beat her and that her husband did not support her in any way. She also claimed that the marriage had not been consummated. The claims made by the wife made the husband very nervous and he denied all allegations. The wife was a strong-willed woman, making the husband taste defeat on several accounts during the interrogation by the court.

The judge concluded the session by announcing that in a next session the claims would be discussed in the presence of their lawyers. Yet, the wife remained agitated and kept on repeating that she was still a virgin because her husband was not 'manly' enough. She claimed that she and her lawyer went to see a doctor who confirmed that she had not yet lost her virginity. The husband was clearly annoyed and embarrassed. Before leaving the court, he turned to the judge and his clerk to assure them that the marriage was consummated; he said that he could prove it. He presented a little plastic bag which he said contained the proof that she had lost her virginity, i.e. the blood-stained cloth of the wedding night.[23]

Marriage ideals: marriage as a 'safety-valve'

To control and prevent any improper behaviour of, in particular, young individuals, it is generally believed that it is better that people get married, preferably when young. For that same reason, long engagements are not desirable, Sato argues.[24] Her observation corresponds with what I observed in the different personal status courts, namely that couples generally married quickly, after an engagement period of a few months. Rabo mentions that her informants talked of early marriages 'as a "safety-valve" for young people's sexuality'.[25] It should be noted though that the average age of marriage, reportedly, has risen in the last decades. One of the reasons for this is that the costs of a wedding feast and furnishing a house or apartment have increased considerably, making it difficult for men, in particular, to marry young.[26]

Tucker asserts that in seventeenth to eighteenth-century Ottoman Syria 'marriage was central to social relations'; it reinforced social ties within the community and promoted harmony and stability.[27] I would argue that marriage in Syria today is still central to social and familial life, as it is in most Middle Eastern societies. Marriage is not just a union between a man and a woman but it is considered a family affair. More than that, a good marriage is favourable, not only to the parties and families involved but to the community as whole.[28] But what makes a good marriage?

This will depend on the families' background and position in their community. Factors that are considered important in the choice of a potential marriage candidate are: religion, denomination or sect, wealth, moral character, level of education, age difference, 'the family name'.[29] These qualifications are not only valued when assessing the candidate as an individual, but they also apply to the candidate's family members. As Rabo writes: 'The more that is known about the family of the groom or the bride, the more one is able to vouch for the character of the individual'.[30]

Troublesome unions, on the other hand, may become a source of social conflict and should therefore be avoided. For this reason, the role of the marriage guardian, as protector of the bride's and the family's interest, is crucial. In most cases, the bride's legal guardian, usually her father or grandfather, will be consulted before a marriage contract is signed. For who is better to serve and preserve the interests of the family and the wider community than the senior male family members? Besides, a marriage union without the approval of the families of both sides will be extremely difficult to sustain, especially for women, because, if the marriage failed, where would she go? Since there is no national social security system available in Syria, most individuals rely completely on their family's support for socio-economic security and protection. So, if an 'objectionable' marriage fails, who will support the divorcée? In her article 'Mother Love', Carlisle describes a striking example of a couple who were forced to divorce under the pressure of the wife's family. The mother of the wife, who insisted she would agree to a divorce, stressed exactly this point: that if the marriage failed, she (the bride) would have no-one to fall back on, because her family declared that they would ostracise her if she did not listen to them.[31]

Unsuitable marriages

Another complicating factor is when one falls in love with someone who belongs to a different religious community. According to my sources, interreligious marriages were rare in Syria, for various reasons.[32] Since civil marriage does not exist in Syria, a wife has to follow her husband's religion in marriage. A Muslim man can marry a Christian or Jewish woman, but a non-Muslim man cannot marry a Muslim woman, unless he converts to Islam. In Chapter 2, we saw that mixed marriages and conversions can lead to complicated and sad legal realities, due to conflicting jurisdictions of the different personal status laws and courts. Even so, interfaith unions do exist, but they are usually contracted in secret or are not officially registered because of social condemnation. During my fieldwork I heard of examples of engagements and marriages between Sunni–ʿAlawi, Druze–Sunni, and Shiʿi–Sunni. Christian interdenominational marriages, however, were usually not considered problematic. In fact, according to the minister (*qassis*) and judge of the Protestant court of Damascus, Boutrus Zaʿour, such marriages were concluded on a regular basis.[33]

Under the SLPS, a Christian woman can marry a Muslim man, but whether these unions are socially acceptable or not is another matter. I was told that such unions are strongly condemned within the Christian communities. Christians in Syria are a minority and that fact alone can be sufficient reason to encourage endogamy, that is, to marry within one's own group. One of my Christian informants told me that when a Christian woman marries a Muslim man she is considered a prostitute, for she brings shame on the entire town/village/community, not just her own family.

> During my fieldwork period in Damascus, I got to know a couple who wanted to get married, but her family strongly opposed the match. It concerned a Christian woman who wanted to marry an ʿAlawi man; they had been together for years and considered a civil marriage abroad. The family was against the marriage, irrespective of where it would be contracted, in Syria or abroad. The family was not against the marriage because of religious reasons, as her family

> was not religious in any way, but because it was socially unacceptable in their [Christian] community. The father of the girl was a respected man in the town, where the family had lived for many generations. The fact that the family had close connections with the family of the husband-to-be, due to a shared political past, did not make a difference. The girl's father was known for his secular, liberal-egalitarian convictions, yet, he vehemently opposed the intended marriage, as did the rest of her family. The girl repeatedly expressed her disappointment about her father's attitude to me; she could not understand how her father (whom she adored and admired) could act against his own convictions, the same convictions he raised her with. The father's explanation for his objection was that he did not want to bring shame on the family. If she married this man, their whole family would be looked down upon and it would make life difficult for them.

This case illustrates the importance of the social implications that come with marriage. It chimes with Tucker's finding that marriage functions to reinforce social ties within the community. With that in mind, the consequences of a good or, on the contrary, socially unacceptable marriage for the family of both spouses have to be thoroughly considered before an intended engagement of marriage can be declared. In the case described above, the marriage between the Christian woman and the 'Alawi man would have such a negative impact on her family, that all her nuclear family members vehemently opposed it (including those who lived abroad). The girl pleaded with her family, and promised that they would live in a neighbourhood in Damascus where their interfaith background would not stand out.[34] But it made no difference to their kin; they put the interest of the family first.[35]

This brings us to the end of the first part of this chapter. Now that I have sketched the contours of the cultural context in which Syrian family laws operate, we will move on to the contents of the various laws. First of all, Syria's most important personal status law, the SLPS, will be discussed; I will particularly analyse the (Muslim) notions of marriage and divorce as set out in the SLPS. Finally, in the latter sections of this chapter, I will briefly discuss some key aspects of Christian marriage and divorce, as set out in the most important Christian laws of personal status.

Muslim marriage: a contractual relationship

The purpose of marriage in Muslim societies is commonly designated as being legalisation of sexual relations and preservation of paternal lineage.[36] According to Tucker, Islamic jurists of the past agreed that the first and foremost purpose of the marriage contract is 'the establishment of licit sexual relations between a man and a woman'.[37] The confinement of sexual relations within the realm of a marriage also served the larger society, for with the institution of marriage, the primary cause of social discord, that is, illicit sexual behaviour (*zina'*), could be eradicated. That is why the vast majority of classical jurists deemed it commendable (*mandub, mustahabb*) for a Muslim to marry.[38] In this regard a famous *hadith* narrated by Malik ibn Anas is often quoted: the Prophet Muhammad reportedly said that 'when a man marries he has fulfilled half of the religion; so let him fear God regarding the remaining half'.

A Muslim marriage is generally depicted along the lines of the maintenance–obedience divide:[39] a husband is obliged to support (maintain) his wife and children and in exchange she will be obliged to co-habit and obey him. Earlier we saw that this divide has been described as the 'patriarchal gender contract' (Moghadam 1998) and the 'patriarchal bargain' (Kandiyoti 1988), and that this maintenance–obedience divide continued to exist in the contemporary family law codes, despite attempts by many Arab states to reform this law (from the early twentieth century onwards). Abu-Odeh maintains that the Arab states tried to use the reforms to 'chip away at the most cruel aspects of gendered reciprocity by first, limiting the scope of the wife's obedience; second, expanding the scope of the husband's financial duties'.[40] It should be noted that indeed some states, as of late, have left out the wife's duty of obedience to her husband, including Algeria (2005), Libya (1984), Morocco (2004), Tunisia (1993), and (South) Yemen (1974); but, at the same time, maintained the husband's obligation to provide maintenance for the wife.[41] Syria, however, always retained the maintenance–obedience divide: in the following paragraphs I will describe how it was translated into the provisions of the SLPS.

As mentioned earlier, the SLPS is predominately based on Islamic legal sources, particularly on the Hanafi *fiqh*. For that reason, the provisions of the SLPS pertaining to marriage and divorce, discussed in the following paragraphs, strongly relate to classical Hanafi *fiqh* rules and interpretations. On some (generally minor) points, however, the authors of the SLPS diverted from the classical Hanafi *fiqh* and incorporated interpretations from other schools of law or minority opinions. Besides, the 'residual' Article 305, stating '[i]n every matter in regard to which there is no relevant provision in this Law reference shall be made to the most authoritative doctrine in Ḥanafī school',[42] opens the door wide to the rich collection of jurisprudence of the Hanafi school of law. This is a welcome option for legal practitioners as the substantive text of the SLPS is rather brief in many areas. For the practical application of Article 305, judges and lawyers still consulted and referred to the personal status code compiled by the Egyptian jurist Qadri Pasha in 1875, which is much more detailed than the SLPS. For that reason I will occasionally refer to the 'Qadri Pasha Code' in my analysis of the provisions of the SLPS, especially where the text of the SLPS is ambiguous or insufficiently detailed.

Marriage according to the SLPS

The SLPS starts with the definition of marriage. Article 1 reads as follows:

> Marriage is a contract between a man and a woman, who is lawfully permitted to him, with the aim to establish a bond for a joint life and procreation.[43]

The marriage contract is an essential element in a Muslim marriage, for only a valid (*sahih*) marriage can generate legal effects, most importantly rights and duties for the two contracting parties. For a marriage to produce legal effects, it has to meet certain requirements. These requirements include, amongst others, legal capacity, a marriage contract, a dower, and social parity between the spouses.

A detailed analysis of these central legal elements pertaining to marriage (and divorce), as defined and regulated by the SLPS, is given in the Appendix. In the following sections I will focus on those aspects that are relevant to the subjects under study in this chapter and the next: the marriage guardian, dower, marital rights and duties, dissolution of the marriage, and its consequences.

The role of the marriage guardian

I have already explained that marriage is a family affair – approval of the family for the union is therefore imperative. As marriages are socially considered to be the mainstay of society and communal harmony, contracting a 'good' marriage is of vital importance for the bride and groom and their respective families. In a patriarchal society like Syria, it is often argued that no-one is better to serve and preserve the interests of the family than the senior male family members. That is why, in most marriages, the father or the grandfather will act as the legal guardian of the bride (*wali*).[44]

Various legal professionals told me that the commonly held view in contemporary Syria is that when it is a woman's first marriage (i.e. she is considered to be a virgin (*bikr*)), her legal guardian needs to give his consent to the marriage, regardless of her age. The presence of a guardian may thus not be a condition for the validity of the contract (under the law), as he is not a contracting party,[45] but his presence and approval will generally (socially) be preferred to ensure that the interests of the girl and family are protected, especially her financial rights (i.e. the dower). That is why the legal guardian, generally the bride's father, will be present during the marriage contract negotiations and when the contract is officially concluded in the presence of a marriage official or judge.[46]

This social preference or practice tallies with what I discussed earlier, namely the (senior) male family members take a prominent position in the protection of the bride's and the family's interests. The marriage guardian as the representative and protector of the interests of the family is a fine example of the hegemonic patriarchal family model.

The provisions of the SLPS pertaining to the marriage guardian, however, do not give a decisive answer as to whether a mature (i.e. older than 17) bride always needs a legal guardian to marry; the wording of these provisions comes across as rather ambiguous.[47] Articles 20 to 25 seem to imply that the guardian's consent is needed, regardless of the bride's age.

Article 16 SLPS stipulates that the age of capacity for marriage is 18 years for a man and 17 years for a woman. If the betrothed parties are younger than the required age, they need to apply to the judge for permission to marry, and, in addition, if the legal guardian is the father or grandfather, his consent to the marriage is also needed (Art. 18).

Accordingly, when a woman is younger than 17, she needs the consent of her legal guardian. But what if she is older?

If the bride is 17 or older, the guardian's consent is not an absolute prerequisite under the law. Article 20 stipulates that a mature woman (i.e. older than 17) can contract her own marriage but the judge will still ask her guardian for his opinion. If the guardian does not object to the marriage or if his objections are ill-considered, the judge shall give permission for the couple to get married, provided the betrothed parties are of equal social status (*kafa'a*).[48] A court is thus empowered to marry a woman (over 17) against her guardian's will. Still, a woman (over 17) does not have the legal authority to act independently because some form of consent to marry is needed, either from her legal guardian or the judge.

If, however, a mature woman has given herself in marriage, that is, without her guardian's approval, to a husband who appears to be beneath her social standing, her legal guardian may ask the court to nullify the marriage (Art. 27). The SLPS does not, however, define what 'equality of status' (*kafa'a*) entails, whether it refers to the groom's financial situation, his occupation or religious piety, for example.[49] The only direction the law gives is 'the custom of the country' (*'urf al-balad*) (Art. 28), which is an exceptionally 'open norm'. In 1956, the Court of Cassation decided to leave the exact interpretation of the concept *kafa'a* to the discretion of the judge.[50] Upon inquiring with some lawyers, I was told that the key elements of *kafa'a* in marriage today are parity in faith (*iman*) and financial means or wealth (*yasar* or *infaq*) between the two prospective parties. A groom's descent (*nasab*), his occupation or difference in social class is no longer relevant to the court. When, for example, a groom is religious, honourable, pious, and has sufficient financial means, the court cannot reject him as a potential husband.[51]

The requirement that the groom must have sufficient financial means is important in consideration of his ability to pay the mandatory dower and spousal maintenance. A husband's financial obligations are essential for the validity and success of a marriage, as will become evident below.

Dower

A marriage contract (*'aqd al-zawaj*) has to include certain specifications, such as the personal particulars and signatures of the betrothed parties and the witnesses, and the mention of a dower (*mahr*). The dower is a wife's prerogative and a husband's obligation (Arts 53 and 60).

A dower is generally divided into two parts, namely a prompt (*mahr mu'ajjal* or *mahr muqaddam*) and a deferred dower (*mahr mu'ajjal* or *mahr mu'akhkhar*). The prompt dower has to be paid upon conclusion of the marriage contract, whereas the deferred part has to be paid when the marriage is terminated due to an irrevocable divorce or death (Arts 55 and 56). Divorce disputes often revolve around the question of exactly which dower amount (either prompt or deferred) was stipulated, whether or not it was actually paid, whether the wife is entitled to half or the full dower, and so on. In the next chapter the subject of the dower will be discussed in more detail.

The effects of marriage: marital rights and duties

As explained earlier, many studies on Muslim personal status law emphasise the reciprocal nature of the marital bond, in that the husband's main legal obligation is his liability to pay maintenance to his wife and that her main legal obligation, on the other hand, is to be sexually available to her husband. Marriage is a relationship based on exchange of rights and duties: the husband will take care of the wife, in exchange for her co-habitation and obedience.

Financial obligations of the husband

The husband is obliged to pay his wife a (prompt) dower. Once the wife receives the prompt dower, she is obliged to live together with her husband (Art. 66). She may, however, refuse to move in with him if he has not yet paid the prompt dower or if he has not prepared a suitable house for her – a house that meets the legal requirements (a *maskan shar'i*) (Art. 72.2). Providing adequate housing for the wife is one of the obligations falling upon the husband; the SLPS determines the basic rules pertaining to housing in Articles 65 to 70.

Providing a marital home for the wife is only one form of maintenance (*nafaqa*) that needs to be supplied by the husband; there are more. The husband's maintenance obligations include, moreover, the following: clothing, food, medical care, and domestic help – the latter only if this is appropriate to her social standing (Art. 71.1). The level of maintenance to be provided by the husband depends on his financial situation, although a minimal level (*hadd al-kifaya*) has to be met (Art. 76).

If a husband fails to provide maintenance to his wife, she can go to court and file a *nafaqa*-claim against him, forcing him to fulfil his obligations (Art. 71.2). If a claim is brought before the court and the husband denies the allegations, the burden of proof rests upon the wife. If the court decides in her favour and the husband, thereupon, fails to comply with the court-ordered maintenance payment, he can be sentenced to a fine or imprisonment (Article 488 Penal Code). Another option for the wife is to file a judicial divorce claim on the grounds of failure to provide maintenance (Art. 110).

A husband, for his part, is entitled to cease maintenance payments if his wife fails to live up to her end of the bargain, namely obedience to her husband or, to be precise, co-habitation. The financial obligations of the husband are inextricably bound up with her legal obligation to co-habit and obey him.

Obedience of the wife

The issue of co-habitation is closely connected to the concept of disobedience (*nushuz*), for co-habitation implies sexual availability of the wife to her husband, which is an obligation on her side (Arts 66 SLPS, 212 Qadri Pasha). Consummation (*dukhul*) of the marriage plays an essential part in establishing the validity or nullity of a marriage, and in the dissolution thereof, for it is only after sexual intercourse that the judicial and financial consequences of the marriage become effective.

Whether or not sexual relations did in fact occur is occasionally disputed by spouses in the court. In that event the judge will try to establish whether the couple has had the opportunity of consummating the marriage, that is, that 'valid seclusion'[52] (*al-khalwa al-sahiha*) took place. When the court establishes that the couple spent a reasonable amount of time alone together, it is assumed that they had sexual relations. I will elaborate more on this subject in the next chapter, when I discuss legal practices in a *shar'iyya* court.

A wife may forfeit her right to maintenance if she works outside the house without her husband's consent (Art. 73) or if she is considered disobedient (*nashiza*) to her husband. A wife can be considered disobedient if she leaves the conjugal home without a lawful reason or if she prevents her husband from entering the house (Art. 75). Accordingly, if it is established that a wife is disobedient, she loses her right to maintenance, for as long as she is disobedient (Art. 74).

If the husband, however, does not live up to his part of the 'patriarchal bargain' by not paying the prompt dower or if he does not prepare a suitable marital home for her, she may refuse to co-habit with him (Art. 72.2). In that case, she is not considered disobedient and she will not lose her right to maintenance. In short, it may be decided that a wife is considered to be disobedient if the following conditions are fulfilled: (a) there is a suitable house provided by the husband, and (b) the husband has given his wife the full prompt dower. If these conditions are met and the wife has left the 'suitable house' without justification, on her own accord and through no fault of the husband, she will be considered disobedient.[53]

A husband can go to court and claim his wife is disobedient when she refuses to return to the conjugal home. In other words, he can file a so-called *mutaba'a* claim, which (in this context) I translate with the phrase 'marital obedience'.[54] The court may recognise a claim for marital obedience, that is, his claim to be discharged from the requirement to pay, when the wife persistently refuses to 'follow' her husband and return to the marital home.[55]

Dissolution of marriage

The SLPS recognises three types of divorce: (1) unilateral divorce or repudiation by the husband (*talaq*), (2) *mukhala'a* divorce, and (3) judicial divorce (*tafriq*).

*Repudiation (*talaq*) by the husband*

Talaq is a unilateral repudiation of the wife by the husband and is the standard form of divorce. A husband can simply pronounce the formula 'I divorce you' either verbally or in writing (Art. 87.1); this does not mean that the marriage is immediately dissolved. During a period of (more or less) three months, the so-called waiting period (*'idda*), the husband can revoke the divorce and take his wife back. This revocation right is, however, not unlimited. A husband can only repudiate his wife three times (Art. 91); the third *talaq* is irrevocable and thus final (*ba'in*) (Art. 94).

Another distinction that needs to be made is a *talaq* pronounced by or in front of a judge and out-of-court *talaq*, that is, divorce pronounced outside the court, which is then registered at the court. This type of divorce, commonly referred to as 'administrative' *talaq* (*talaq idari*) is quite popular among men; however it leaves many wives in a state of limbo. In the next chapter I will describe a few case studies that deal with these so-called out-of-court *talaq*s.

Divorce by mutual consent (mukhala'a)

Mukhala'a divorce is often referred to as a wife-initiated divorce: it is generally initiated by the wife. Like most Muslim family laws, the SLPS stipulates that, nevertheless, the consent of both spouses is required, in contrast to repudiation (*talaq*), which is the sole prerogative of the husband. This contradicts practice in Egypt and Pakistan, for example, where a woman has the right to initiate a *mukhala'a* divorce without her husband's consent.[56]

In a *mukhala'a* divorce, the spouses sign a contract in which the husband agrees to divorce his wife, in exchange for which the wife agrees to renounce some or all of her financial rights. The wife renounces, at least, her right to any (unpaid) prompt and/or outstanding deferred dower amount, and her right to maintenance (*nafaqa*). In addition, she may agree to return her trousseau (*jihaz*), her gold or household goods, which usually means that some financial compensation would have to be paid.

A *mukhala'a* contract can be drawn up either in court or outside court and then registered *ex post facto*. However, in all events the wife has to be present in court to declare that she is willing to give up her financial rights before the contract can be registered and the divorce can take effect. For the registration of out-of-court *mukhala'a* contracts, it is important that it is evident from the contract that offer and acceptance took place in one session. In addition, it has to be clear that both parties verbally agreed to the agreement: a written agreement or a signature will not be sufficient to validate the contract.[57] In the next chapter I will examine several aspects of the *mukhala'a* divorce in further detail.

Judicial divorce (tafriq)

The SLPS recognises various grounds for judicial divorce (*tafriq*), divided into four types:

(1) *tafriq* on the grounds of disease or defect (*'ilal*), which includes insanity and impotence of the husband (Arts 105–8);
(2) *tafriq* on the grounds of absence or disappearance (*ghayba*), for example due to imprisonment (Art. 109);
(3) *tafriq* on the grounds of non-payment of maintenance (*'adam al-infaq*) (Arts 110–11);
(4) *tafriq* on the grounds of discord between the spouses (*shiqaq bayna al-zawjayn*) (Art. 112).

Only a woman can seek divorce on the first three grounds, while both spouses can bring a judicial divorce petition to court on the grounds of discord. Either one or both can claim that the other is causing so much harm (*darar*) that it impossible to continue their marriage.

Reconciliation and divorce

All the different types of divorce have to go through a reconciliation process. The SLPS stipulates that when a *talaq* or a *mukhala'a* action is brought to court, the judge will defer acting on the case for a month in the hope of reconciliation, in accordance with Article 88. If, after that month, the husband persists in his action for divorce (*talaq*) or the couple persists in their *mukhala'a* request, they will be summoned to court. The judge will try to resolve their differences with the help of their family members or other individuals who might be of assistance. If, despite these attempts, reconciliation cannot be brought about, the judge can register the *talaq* or the *mukhala'a* contract (Art. 88). Whether these prescribed reconciliation procedures are actually followed by the court is different issue.

When one or both of the spouses file for a judicial divorce (*tafriq*) on the grounds of discord, the judge should attempt to reconcile the spouses. If reconciliation cannot be achieved and the plaintiff persists in his or her claim, the judge will appoint two arbiters from the family of the spouses or persons whom the judge considers capable of bringing about reconciliation (Art. 112.3). If the arbiters fail to bring about reconciliation, they will determine the reason for the disagreement and advise the court on how to dissolve the marriage. They will establish the level of culpability ascribed to either the husband or the wife or both, in order to determine if and how much of the remaining dower and (possibly) post-divorce maintenance has to be paid (Arts 114–15). In the next chapter I will pursue the issue of divorce on the grounds of discord, including the court-ordered arbitration procedures, in greater depth.

Legal consequences of divorce: waiting period, unpaid dower and post-divorce maintenance

In the section on *talaq*, we saw that a revocable divorce does not necessarily mean an immediate end to the marriage. A husband may take his wife back during the waiting period (*'idda*) following such a divorce, but if the waiting period expires and the husband has not taken his wife back, the divorce becomes final (Art. 118).

The waiting period is generally three menstrual cycles after the pronunciation of the divorce (Art. 121.1). During the *'idda* period following divorce, annulment of the marriage or death, a woman is not allowed to remarry. For the duration of the waiting period the wife is entitled to post-divorce maintenance (*nafaqat al-'idda*) (Arts 83–84, 125). In addition to the post-divorce maintenance, the wife is also entitled to all of her unpaid dower. The deferred dower becomes payable once the divorce becomes final or after the death of the spouse (Art. 56). Any unpaid part of the dower is usually registered as a debt owed by the husband on the marriage contract (Art. 54.3 and 54.5).[58]

Child custody after divorce

In Chapter 2, the various aspects of child custody were explained; we saw that, in line with classical *fiqh* works, the SLPS makes a distinction between legal guardianship (*wilaya*) and nursing (*hadana*). Legal guardianship is an exclusively male prerogative and therefore belongs to the father (Arts 170–5); the mother, on the other hand, has the obligation and right to nurse her children (*hadana*) (Arts 137–51). If the mother cannot exercise this nursing right, it can be claimed by the child's maternal grandmother or (subsequently) the paternal grandmother, the maternal aunt, and so on (Art. 139).

In the event of separation of the parents, the mother may ask the court to give her the right to nurse (*hadana*) her children until the age of 15 for girls and 13 for boys (Art. 146). When the (divorced) mother obtains the *hadana*-right over her children, the father remains responsible for the cost of nursing (Art. 142); after all he is the legal guardian and therefore remains responsible for the maintenance of this children.

Whether child maintenance is actually paid by the father is another matter. It is therefore important for a mother, who seeks divorce, to know that she can fall back on her family members for financial support, if she intends to take care of the children.[59] Regardless of who physically takes care of the children, the father (as the legal guardian) will always have the final say in the upbringing of his children, in all matters related to their education, property, etc. (Art. 170 ff.). When the *hadana* period ends, the father can demand that the children are 'returned' to his care.

During this nursing period, the father has the right to see his children (*ira'a*). The SLPS (or any other law) does not regulate the actual implementation of visitation rights. The precise visitation arrangements are worked out based on custom (*taqlid*), according to senior lawyer 'Ali.[60]

Finally, a divorcée can also lose her nursing rights. Article 138 stipulates that a Muslim woman loses her right of the nursing of her children when she remarries someone outside the child's immediate family (i.e. a non-*mahram* man).

This brings us to the final sections of this chapter, namely legal regulation of Christian marriage and the dissolution of marriage. Again, the sections on this subject will be brief, especially in comparison with the analysis of the provisions of the SLPS.

Christian marriage and divorce: some general observations

As mentioned earlier, according to estimates, about ten per cent of the population belongs to one of the Christian denominations. The various Christian communities of Syria can be divided into three groups: the Orthodox Christians, the Catholic churches, and the Protestants or Evangelicals. Nearly every denomination or group has its own family law, which include the following: the Greek Orthodox Personal Status Law (2004), the Syriac Orthodox Personal Status Law (2004), the Armenian Orthodox Personal Status Law (n.d.), the Protestant Law of Personal Status (1949)[61] and the Catholic Law of Personal Status (2006).[62] The latter law will be discussed in more detail in Chapter 6, both its content and its practical application in the Catholic courts of Damascus.

Article 308 of the SLPS allows the Christian communities to administer their own religious regulations in certain specified matters of personal status, most importantly betrothal, marriage, marital obedience, wife's and children's maintenance, annulment and dissolution of marriage, nursing, and inheritance. Similar to the analysis of the SLPS provided above, I will confine myself to a discussion of the Christian notions of marriage and divorce, as laid down in the Christian laws of personal status. I will touch briefly on the main characteristics of Eastern Christian family law, as an analysis of all the different Christian laws would be beyond the scope of this book, let alone this chapter.

Christian marriage: marriage as a sacrament

Marriage in the Eastern churches has a different status than it has in Islamic law. The Eastern churches consider marriage a sacrament or a mystery[63] (in Arabic: *sirr al-zawaj*).[64] Tertullian of Carthage, a theologian from the second century, wrote that marriage 'is arranged by the church, confirmed by the oblation (the Eucharist), sealed by the blessing, and inscribed in heaven by the angels'.[65] The Christian churches consider marriage an institution established by God, for '[man] is the image of God, God is love, and man, husband and wife, are recreating love in this life in a concrete expression.'[66]

Furthermore, a marriage can only be considered a sacrament when it constitutes a union between a baptised man and a baptised woman, who voluntarily consent to marry before God. If both or just one spouse is not baptised, the marriage is considered a natural marriage. The church will recognise it as a valid and sacred marriage, also protected by God, but it will not be considered a sacrament.[67]

The theological and canonical position of the Protestant churches on various matters of faith, including marriage, is different from the traditional Eastern churches, because the former come from a different (Western) tradition. The Protestant churches were only established from the nineteenth century onwards, following the arrival of Protestant missionaries from Europe and the United States. Article 21 of the Protestant Personal Status Law describes marriage as a contract between a man and woman and not as a sacrament; the Protestant churches, nevertheless, consider marriage an institution ordained by God and therefore holds great religious significance.

One difference between the Latin (i.e. Western) churches and Eastern (Catholic and non-Catholic) churches with regard to marriage is that the latter require the blessing of a priest. The grace of the sacrament can only come down upon the spouses through the blessing of the priest 'and without this blessing there can be no sacrament'.[68] Whereas the Eastern churches regard the priest as 'the minister of the sacrament of matrimony', the Latin churches, influenced by Roman law, do not require his intercession because they regard marriage as a 'contract' which is concluded by the husband and the wife themselves (and the priest is only a witness).[69] While the Latin church refers to marriage as a 'matrimonial contract', the Eastern churches avoid using the term 'contract', instead they speak of 'matrimonial covenant' and 'celebration of marriage'.[70] Another difference from the Latin church is that the Eastern churches do not consider procreation as the primary aim of marriage, but the central consideration is conjugal love.[71]

This is precisely the argument Christians in Syria invoke, according to Rabo, when they compare themselves to Muslims in regard to marriage. Christians often claim that because Muslim men can divorce their wives or take another wife without any difficulty, their wives are forced into obedience. Rabo quotes a comment she heard from many Syrian clergy who said: 'Muslim men marry not for the companionship between men and women, but only for their own pleasure. Their marriage is not sacred but simply a sexual union.' Furthermore, 'ordinary' Christians also stress the difference in perception of marriage; Rabo quotes a typical Christian comment from Christian men: 'We look for companionship with our wives. A Christian husband and wife spend more time together and the relationship cannot only be based on sex.'[72]

Since marriage is considered an expression of faith, it is celebrated in church, commonly in the church of the husband. In Syria, a marriage is usually celebrated on a Sunday and will be conducted by the local priest in a Eucharistic celebration, that is, a mass. A marriage concluded in a church is recognised by the state as a valid marriage – no additional procedure has to be undertaken by the church's court, for example. After the marriage ceremony the church sends the 'marriage papers' (*mu'amalat al-zawaj*) to the Civil Registry Office.[73]

Christian marital rights and duties

The patriarchal family model is also visible in the various Christian personal status law; for example, the Armenian Orthodox law and the Protestant law state that the husband is the head of the family (Arts 46 and 33, respectively). Similar to the rights and duties pertaining to marriage laid down in the SLPS, the Christian personal status laws also require the husband to provide maintenance for his wife and children.[74] In return, a Christian wife has to be obedient to her husband, which generally means that she is required to live with him and follow him wherever he chooses to live.[75] When, however, the wife is financially well-off (and the husband is not), the duty is on her to support her husband and their children.[76] In a Christian marriage, incidentally, it is common for the family of the bride to pay a dowry (*dutta* or *ba'ina*) to the husband and/or to equip the couple with a trousseau (*jihaz*).[77] The husband does not pay his wife a dower, but he will commonly give his bride gifts, such as gold and other jewellery.

Similar to the SLPS, most Christian laws of personal status stipulate that a Christian husband can be excused from paying maintenance to his wife when the court considers her disobedient.[78] A wife will be considered disobedient if she leaves the marital home without his consent or without informing him and refuses to return. It is therefore important for the court to determine if the wife left the house voluntarily or if she was kicked out by her husband. Based on (witness) statements of the litigants, family members, and neighbours, the court will try to establish a credible narrative so as to determine whether the wife left of her own or her husband's accord, as will be demonstrated in Chapter 6 on Catholic court practices.

Divorce, separation or annulment of marriage?

The Christian marriage bond is deemed exclusive and permanent, after all, Christ himself has reportedly said: 'So then, they are no longer two but one flesh. Therefore what God has joined together, let not man separate.'[79]

In principle, all (Eastern) churches condemn divorce. Because marriage is regarded as a union before God, dissolving such a union is considered problematic. In addition, the problem of divorce is related to the issue of remarriage, since a marriage is an eternal union in Christ which is not broken by death and continues in the afterlife.[80] Broadly speaking, the Orthodox churches take a more lenient stand on divorce and remarriage when compared to the Catholic Church. The Catholic Church does not recognise divorce; it even renounces the very word 'divorce' (*talaq*). A Catholic marriage can, however, be terminated, but only through nullification of a marriage (*butlan al-zawaj*), meaning that the spouses have to prove that the marriage was never valid in the first place; this will only be accepted in exceptional cases.

Generally, the various Christian laws differentiate between legal separation (*hajr*), annulment (*butlan*), and dissolution (*faskh*). The grounds for divorce or separation for each denomination vary. A spouse can, for example, ask for judicial dissolution or annulment of marriage in case:

- the other spouse converted to another religion (Art. 67 sub. A Greek Orthodox Law; Art. 62 sub. D Armenian Orthodox Law; Art. 40 sub. C Protestant Law);
- the other spouse committed adultery (*zina'*) (Art. 68 Greek Orthodox Law; Art. 50.3 Syriac Orthodox Law; Art. 62 sub. A Armenian Orthodox Law; Can. 863 CCEO);
- impotence or sexual dysfunction has been established (Art. 69 sub. E, 70 sub. D Greek Orthodox Law; Art. 51 Armenian Orthodox Law);
- the spouse lacks the sufficient use of reason or the ability to understand the essential obligations of marriage (Can. 818, 819 CCEO).

A husband can file an annulment or divorce petition to the court when he discovers that his wife was not a virgin when he married her (Art. 69 sub a Greek Orthodox Law; Art. 54.1 Syriac Orthodox Law) or when the wife has left the marital home and refuses to return (Art. 69 sub c and d Greek Orthodox Law; Art. 50.5 Syriac Orthodox Law). The wife can seek divorce or annulment when her husband forces her to unnatural sexual acts or adultery (Art. 70 sub a Greek Orthodox Law; art. 50.6 Syriac Orthodox Law).

As stated earlier, the Catholic Church takes a strict stand on divorce and only accepts annulment of marriages in exceptional cases. I was told that the other churches generally have a more liberal approach towards divorce. In my observation, the Greek Orthodox court, when compared to the Catholic court, indeed proceeded more pragmatically in its treatment of divorce cases. The Catholic court took on a much more weighty and formal stand in its handling of annulment petitions. It is my hypothesis that the Catholic judges were also more conservative due to their canonical training in Rome. In Chapter 6, I will expand on this hypothesis in relation to my discussion of the annulment proceedings in a Catholic court of Damascus.

Conclusion

In the first part of this chapter, a description was given of the cultural context in which Syrian law operates. Cultural understandings of family relations and gender roles in the context of personal status law have formed the point of departure. This included an analysis of some key cultural concepts, namely patriarchal family, morality and propriety, family honour and women's sexuality and marriage ideals. These concepts lie at the foundation of Syrian family life and are at the core of the different laws of personal status.

An analysis of the legal rules pertaining to marriage and divorce, as set down in the various personal status laws, demonstrated that the patriarchal supremacy of men over women is securely embodied in these laws. The SLPS and the most important Eastern Christian personal status laws have espoused the patriarchal family model and with that contribute to the preservation and confirmation of that model in the Syrian legal context. The gendered personal status laws prescribe different roles, rights and obligations for men and women, as becomes apparent from the provisions of the different laws.

A man in his gendered role as husband and father is obliged and expected to provide for his wife, children and other family members. A woman in her gendered role as wife and mother is obliged and expected to be obedient to her husband and satisfy the wishes of her husband, their children and her family-in-law. In addition, as a daughter and sibling, she is expected to uphold her family's reputation and honour by living up to the expectations of a dutiful wife and mother. The success or failure of a woman's marriage also reflects on the name and reputation of her own family. Therefore, women in particular are faced with legal and social expectations to adhere to the patriarchal family model.

My main argument in the second part of this book is that shared norms and views on proper or improper gender comportment, marriage and marital roles are emphasised and reinforced time and again in the different personal status courts, both Muslim and Christian. Not just by the judges, litigants, lawyers but by all the participants in the legal arena, thus including witnesses and other 'visitors' to the court. In the time I spent in several personal status courts of Damascus, I observed that, despite their legal and religious differences, the courts were united in their shared cultural understandings of gender, family relations, and social norms and behaviour; this will become evident in the next two chapters. Therefore, the courts can be regarded as sites where norms and expectations are expressed, emphasised and reinforced, not just by the judges but by all those who work on or visit these sites.

CHAPTER 5

THE VERSATILITY OF PERSONAL STATUS LAW: LEGAL PRACTICES IN A *SHAR'IYYA* COURT

This chapter analyses the practical implementation of the SLPS, focusing on different aspects of the judicial process. It describes the legal procedures and practices associated with *shar'iyya* courts in Damascus, including case studies involving marriage, dissolution of marriage, and matters related to children. The connecting thread that runs through the second part of this book is the argument that the diverse personal status courts were united in their shared communal, cultural understandings of marriage, gender and family relations. Throughout this chapter I will argue that (legal and non-legal) shared norms and views on morality, propriety, marital life and gender relations were abundantly present in the *shar'iyya* court of Damascus where I conducted my fieldwork.

I will contextualise the legal rules regarding marriage and marriage dissolution, as expounded in the previous chapter, within the legal procedures and practices in the *shar'iyya* courts. It is important to pay attention to the context in which the law, that is, the SLPS, operates in order to understand its meaning and the effect it has on the lives of individuals. Focusing only on the legal provisions of the SLPS would lead one to miss out on the versatility of Syrian personal status law. It is exactly this versatility or flexibility that is emphasised in this chapter.

The content of the SLPS is more than 60 years old: it dates back to 1953 and was only amended in 1975 and 2003. The SLPS does not always provide clear guidance on how to resolve a particular issue. Syrian society has changed profoundly over the last decades and whether the laws have kept up with the changed realities is open to question. Given the government's rigid stand on change and reform of the SLPS, the question arises: how do legal professionals, that is, *shar'iyya* judges and lawyers, work with(in) the SLPS and its (legal) context? And how do they solve cases when the legal system does not provide a clear answer to the problem at hand?

As explained earlier, the SLPS itself offers a solution, as its provisions are not narrowly defined and leave ample room for interpretation. The substantive provisions of the SLPS are rather brief in many subjects and the 'residual' Article 305 opens the door wide to the rich collection of jurisprudence of the Hanafi school of law, to which judges and lawyers willingly resort. In addition to SLPS' 'open norms', the SLPS also allows for retroactive registration of customary marriage, out-of-court divorce, and proof of paternity. The SLPS and the legal system in which this law operates are thus a rather open, flexible system. This versatility or flexibility of the SLPS and the legal system is, however, not limited to Syria: in legal systems of other contemporary Arab countries, such as Gaza/Palestine, Egypt and Tunisia, we find similar situations.[1]

My data on legal practices include court observations of a Damascus *shar'iyya* court, interviews and recurrent informal interactions with (legal) experts, particularly lawyers. The case studies used in this chapter are summaries of what I observed or of what I was told.[2] The cases presented serve to illustrate different aspects of the judicial process in this particular Damascus *shar'iyya* court.

As explained in the Introduction, the political climate in Syria posed particular challenges in gaining access to the courts, court records, and other relevant material. Possibilities for conducting frequent court observations in the *shar'iyya* courts of Damascus were limited for various reasons, chiefly because I did not have the required clearance from the authorities. Fortunately, through my network of lawyers, I managed to get permission to sit in on the court sessions of one *shar'iyya* judge (hereafter 'Judge Ibrahim'), presiding over one of the six *shar'iyya* courts of Damascus proper.[3] I was allowed to observe court proceedings in Judge Ibrahim's courtroom and I was able to talk to him personally a few times. I sat in his courtroom, and on two occasions in his office (for reconciliation sessions), approximately 20 times (i.e. days), where I observed at least 40 cases. The majority of the cases presented to the court involved divorce cases, most of them initiated by women.

Obviously, I cannot generalise on Judge Ibrahim's way of working, let alone on other Syrian *shar'iyya* judges. However, my time in Judge Ibrahim's court provided me with an opportunity to compare my observations with similar research on court practices, most importantly Carlisle's work on Syria and, in a broader context, research undertaken in other Middle Eastern countries (cf. Buskens (Morocco), Shehada (Gaza), Sonneveld (Egypt), Voorhoeve (Tunisia), Welchman (West Bank)).

Furthermore, my frequent interactions with a number of lawyers provided an interesting perspective on legal practice, as it gave me the opportunity to take a close look behind the scenes of the *shar'iyya* courts. Whereas I found that judges took on a more formal attitude in their interactions with me, the lawyers were often more straightforward. They pointed out that 'theory' often did not correspond with what actually happened in practice. Many lawyers were (generally) not hampered by formalities and were therefore less inclined to give (legally) desirable answers but could give 'honest' answers.[4]

In a Damascus *shar'iyya* court: some general observations

The six *shar'iyya* courts of Damascus proper were housed in Damascus' main courthouse (*al-qasr al-'adli*). The courthouse was a three-storey-building, located right in the city centre at a busy traffic junction, just off the corner of Al-Nasr Street and the entrance to the main shopping street of Damascus (*al-suq al-hamidiyya*). During the courts' working hours (9 a.m. to 3 p.m.), the entrance of the courthouse and the street outside would be bustling with people and activity – even more so inside. Once inside, through the door fitted up with a picture of the former President Hafez al-Assad overlooking the street, one found oneself in a spacious entrance hall, the hot spot of the court building. The six *shar'iyya* courts were located on the ground floor, behind the entrance hall. Next to the *shar'iyya* courts, the *qasr al-'adli* housed numerous other courts, such as criminal and civil courts (both first instance (*mahakim al-bidaya*) and appeal (*mahakim al-isti'naf*), and magistrates' courts (*mahakim al-sulh*).[5]

During my visits to Damascus' main courthouse, the courtrooms, halls and corridors were usually packed with court personnel, lawyers, litigants, witnesses and family members including infants. Judges would go back and forth between the courtrooms and their offices; litigants, witnesses and family members patiently waited their turn, sometimes for hours. Most *shar'iyya* courtrooms opened out to a central hall, where court personnel occupied small offices selling stamps, registering court petitions in their court registry books (*daftars*), and so on.

Each *shar'iyya* court consisted of a single judge (*qadi*) who was assisted by a clerk (*katib*). In the spring of 2009, I attended, for the most part, the court sessions of one particular *shar'iyya* judge (as I have mentioned), Judge Ibrahim. Judge Ibrahim and his clerk were both in their mid to late 40s. There was nothing in the judge's appearance to indicate that he was a judge (he was always in suit and tie), except for his nameplate saying 'Judge [*al-qadi*] Ibrahim'. Together with his clerk he occupied a relatively small courtroom (about 15 m^2). A raised dais running across the width of the room occupied the larger part of the courtroom. The judge and his clerk would sit on the dais, behind piles of files and record books. On one wall there were two closed cupboards, stacked with court files. On the other two sides of the courtroom were simple wooden benches where lawyers, litigants, witnesses and family members would sit and wait. Most lawyers, litigants and witnesses would wait outside in the hall until the judge returned to the courtroom or until they were called in. There was not much else in the room, apart from the furniture and a copy of the Qur'an, wrapped in a cotton bag, used to administer an oath, official stamps, files, registry books, with a calendar used to set new court dates next to the judge's seat.

The court would start around nine o'clock in the morning and would go on until approximately two o'clock in the afternoon. As a rule, Judge Ibrahim was not present in his courtroom on Thursdays, because on Thursday mornings arbitration (*tahkim*) sessions took place in his office. Two appointed arbiters would come to his office and conduct *tahkim* sessions with the judge. On 'regular' court days, Judge Ibrahim did not stay in his courtroom the entire day. He would go back and forth between the courtroom and his office, two doors further down – an office he shared with his colleague next door. The courtroom of the neighbouring judge had a back door leading to this shared, small (approximately 10m^2) office.

During the court's office hours, Judge Ibrahim's courtroom was usually full of activity, with different legal proceedings taking place, often simultaneously. It was not uncommon for Judge Ibrahim to examine a witness while being regularly interrupted by (mostly) lawyers, who came in to ask a question about another case, to make an appointment or simply to greet him. In my view, Judge Ibrahim was a master in multi-tasking. After an interruption, he would just continue from where he had left off, even if it was in the middle of a witness testimony. Testimonies of litigants, witnesses, and/or experts, and all other verbal exchanges were heard in colloquial Arabic. However, court hearings and proceedings were not transcribed verbatim. The presiding judge summarised and dictated to his clerk, in Modern Standard Arabic, what had to be written in the case file. This is not atypical – it happens in all court sessions in Syria;[6] I observed the same procedure in the Catholic and Greek Orthodox personal status courts of Damascus. Similar procedures are followed in other Middle Eastern countries such as the Egyptian family courts and Lebanese courts of personal status. Clarke provides an apt example in his study on kinship and Islamic law in Lebanon: 'The messiness of real life and personal testimony gets converted into crisp legalese. "He's a monster, a tyrant! He beats me, abuses me, my life is unbearable. . ." enters the record as "it emerged that the plaintiff stated that there was strife between her and the defendant, her husband".'[7] It was during witness examinations in particular that patriarchal norms and views on marital life came to the fore.

When the plaintiff (*al-mudda'i*) and the defendant (*al-mudda'i 'alayhi*) were heard by the court, they were required to identify themselves by presenting their goverment-issued identity cards. The clerk copied the personal data of the ID cards into the file, after which the questioning could commence. Witnesses also had to identify themselves by producing their ID cards to the clerk. Before witnesses were questioned by the judge they were also required to swear an oath (*yamin*) on the Qur'an.[8] They had to repeat the following oath after the judge: 'I swear by God, the Almighty, that I will tell the whole truth without adding or omitting anything' (*'uqsim bi-llah al-'azim an aqul al-haqq kullahu dun ziyada aw nuqsan'*). When there were multiple witnesses (a maximum of five), they were instructed to appear, after they were identified by the judge and the clerk, in the courtroom one by one, in accordance with Article 77 paragraphs 1 and 3 of the Law of Evidence. The witnesses had to await their turn in the central hall until the judge finished questioning the preceding witness. Sometimes the 'waiting' witnesses stood too close to the door, then they were told by the judge or clerk to stand back, so that they could not overhear what the other witness was saying. In accordance with Article 12 SLPS, women could only testify in unison in a *shar'iyya* court: a clear example of the gendered nature of this law, as it assigns a different status to men and women. I only saw this happen once: two sisters of a female plaintiff, who had filed a judicial divorce petition, were called in to testify. Not only was the testimony heard simultaneously, but the oath was also administered in unison.

At times, it seemed that lawyers, litigants, and witnesses in the *shar'iyya* courts were fighting to get the judge's attention – this was not the case in the Catholic and Greek Orthodox courts. As we shall see in the next chapter, the Catholic court in particular observes a strict court agenda, with cases processed one at a time. The most obvious reason for this difference in method of working is because of the workload of the *shar'iyya* judges. Most *shar'iyya* judges are faced with an immense workload and a heavy backlog of cases, due to 'cumbersome court procedures, weak administrative capacity and lack of adequate infrastructure'.[9] As a result, litigation is often a slow and tedious process. What is more, the *shar'iyya* judges have to process more cases simply because the majority of Syrians are Muslim (roughly 85 per cent), and because they are the general courts which are competent to hear certain specified cases involving non-Muslims, most notably matters concerning legal guardianship (*wilaya*) and paternity (*nasab*).

According to some of the lawyers I worked with, Judge Ibrahim was quite an exceptional judge. He was considered exceptional because of his humanity and moral standing, and being a true mediator. I was told that Judge Ibrahim was one of the few judges who visited litigants at home to try and resolve disputes between the parties by finding a solution acceptable to all (see section on 'Judicial divorce – *tafriq*' below).[10] That was the reason why some lawyers, when they had a case that deserved special attention, tried to get Judge Ibrahim on the case. Also, I met a few women in Judge Ibrahim's courtroom who had come to see him specifically because others had recommended him because of the characteristics described above.

In the previous chapter, the provisions related to marriage and divorce in the SLPS were examined – in this chapter I describe several aspects of the practical implementation of these provisions and other dimensions of the judicial process in the *shar'iyya* courts. It will become evident that, in addition to the legal rules, other (non-legal) norms and extra-judicial practices related to marriage, divorce and other family relations find their way into the courtroom and, in fact, play an important role in the judicial process.

Marriage

There is no official or reliable data available (at least, not to my knowledge) on the average age for marriage in Syria. According to an article of the national news agency SANA, the Syrian Commission for Family Affairs (SCFA) stated in its second national report on the Syrian Population Status 2010 that the average age for marriage 'rose from 25.9 to 29 years for males and from 20.6 to 25.1 years for females between 1981 and 2000'.[11] Unfortunately, no information is provided about differences between urban and rural areas, the educational and professional background of the contracting parties or the age difference between the spouses. Through my interaction with several legal professionals I learned that custom (*'urf* or *'ada*) continued to play a dominant role in family relations, despite state efforts to regulate them. The prevalence of customary practices provides an explanation as to why the phenomenon of early or child marriages still prevails in Syria, particularly in rural areas, notwithstanding the statutory minimum age required for marriage, that is, 18 for men and 17 for women (Art. 16).

'The age for marriage was set not by law but by practice'; this comment was made by Ms Mouna Ghanem, one of the Syrian delegation members who met with the Committee on the Elimination of Discrimination against Women (CEDAW) in New York to discuss Syria's initial periodic report in May 2007.[12] Her comment confirms the commonly held view that customary practices continue to be applied and often override statutory law provisions. In its initial report, Syria reported that approximately 85 per cent of women from rural areas got married under the age of 20.[13] How many women of this 85 per cent were younger than 17 years (the legal age), remains unclear.[14] As the SLPS allows girls to marry from the age of 13 and boys from the age of 15, provided the marriage guardian gives his consent (Art. 18.1), one could claim that the SLPS itself facilitates early (or child) marriages by providing this opportunity.

According to my sources, marriages are generally concluded by a marriage official (*al-ma'dhun al-shar'i*).[15] By virtue of Article 43 SLPS, marriage officials are (as assistants to the *shar'iyya* court) authorised to conclude a marriage contract, either in court or at the home of one of the spouses, usually the bride. Marriage contracts are generally written up by marriage officials at people's homes after the court's office hours, usually in the evening, in return for a small fee.[16] Before a marriage can be concluded, the marriage official or judge ought to confirm that the marriage application includes all the required documents (Art. 40.1). In addition, a so-called marriage dossier (*musannaf zawaj*) needs to be submitted. This marriage dossier is a six-page pre-printed folder issued by the Ministry of Justice that can be purchased at the court (for 35 SP); it lists the information that is required for the issuance of a marriage contract. All the relevant information can be filled out on dotted lines and checked off in the pre-printed boxes, including the name of the marriage official, the date, hour and place on which the marriage contract was concluded. It also includes a section for the head of the court's registry (*ra'is al-diwan*) to legitimise its authenticity and add a registration number, and a section for the judge for validation of the contract.

Although marriage officials are available, contracting a marriage in court in the presence of a judge is still possible. During my presence in the *shar'iyya* courts, I witnessed a few marriage conclusions; they were usually concluded in an expeditious manner. The marriage company that showed up in court generally consisted of the bride and groom, two witnesses, and often the marriage guardian (*wali*) of the bride. In some cases, one or two other family members would also be present. Here is an example:

> Judge Ibrahim's courtroom was chock-a-block with lawyers, litigants, witnesses and so on, all trying to get the judge's attention. Amidst the boisterous crowd, and tucked away to one side, stood the clerk, at the far end of the dais, with a small crowd squashed together in a corner. I could not hear everything that was being said but I could make out that the small knot of people consisted of the bride and groom, two male witnesses and the marriage guardian. The clerk was reading out the marriage contract. He asked who was acting as the bride's guardian – the

> older man said he was. The judge asked the bride whether she agreed to the marriage – almost shyly (hiding behind the back of the older man), she indicated she did. The two witnesses signed the contract, the clerk stamped and registered it and that was that. Over and done with in a few minutes.[17]

Marriages in court were generally not considered to be a festive event, in that there were no festive elements such as wedding dresses or flowers. The wedding party (*zifaf*) was usually held weeks or months after signing the marriage contract. After the wedding celebration the couple would start living together, meaning that marital life had begun.

As explained earlier, the SLPS describes marriage as a contract between a man and a woman, concluded in the presence of two witnesses. Marriage is considered a contractual relationship, the aim of which is 'to establish a union for a shared life and procreation' (Art. 1). The marriage contract is an essential element in a Muslim marriage, for only a valid contract can generate the legal effects of a marriage, most importantly the rights and duties of the two contracting parties (Art. 49). So what exactly are these marital rights and duties?

Financial obligations of the husband – providing maintenance (*nafaqa*)

As explained in the previous chapter, various studies on Muslim personal status laws have demonstrated that a Muslim marriage was generally viewed along the lines of the maintenance–obedience divide, on both a legal as well as a societal level. This maintenance–obedience divide was laid down (and subsequently changed or abrogated) in several Arab personal status laws in varying degrees. As of late, several states (e.g. Algeria, Morocco, Tunisia) have removed the wife's duty of obedience to her husband from their legislation, while maintaining the husband's maintenance obligation. The Syrian government has not introduced similar changes; the SLPS therefore continues to present marriage as a relationship based on exchange of rights and duties: the husband will take care of the wife, in exchange for her co-habitation and obedience.

According to the SLPS, the husband's 'first' financial obligation is to pay his wife a dower (*mahr*). When a wife receives the prompt dower (*mahr mu'ajjal*), she is obliged to live with her husband, provided he prepares a suitable house for her. Dower amounts vary depending on the financial means of the husband and the social standing of both spouses. In my observation, this amount generally started at a few tens of thousands and went up to hundreds of thousands (or millions) of Syrian pounds (SYP) as a prompt dower; the deferred dower (*mahr mu'ajjal*) was usually either the same or higher. The question of whether or not the husband had actually paid the prompt dower was sometimes disputed, particularly in relation to divorce claims (see below). In addition to the dower, the husband would generally give his wife a trousseau (*jihaz*), often gold and furniture.[18]

Next to paying a dower, the husband has to pay his wife maintenance (*nafaqa*). This maintenance obligation includes, most importantly: a marital home, clothing, food and medical care. The level of maintenance depends on his financial situation, although a minimal level (*hadd al-kifaya*) has to be met. According to one of the lawyers I worked with, the so-called 'minimum maintenance' (*nafaqa kifaya*) amounted to SYP 1,000–1,500 (roughly €15–23) per month.[19] In addition, the husband had to pay maintenance for the children, which was around SYP 800–1,000 per month.[20] The minimum maintenance amount was based on an average Syrian monthly income; for example, a teacher without a university degree made between SYP 6,000–7,000 (€94–110) and a teacher with a university degree made approximately SYP 10,000 (€157) per month. A financially well-off husband ought to pay more maintenance to his wife than the minimum maintenance, but the wife would have to prove that her husband was suitably well-off.[21] This would be not an easy task for most women.

> One day I witnessed a rather peculiar case in Judge Ibrahim's courtroom. A handcuffed man wearing a grey-blue prisoner's suit was brought in by four policemen in the already packed courtroom. The man's handcuffs were removed and he was made to sit down next to me on one of the side benches, where he had to wait until it was his turn. The judge summoned the man, assisted by his lawyer, and a woman who turned out to be his wife to approach the dais. It appeared that the couple had concluded a so-called customary marriage (*zawaj 'urfi*)[22] a few years back. The wife wanted their marriage to be registered officially; she requested a proof of marriage (*tathbit al-zawaj*). She and her lawyer handed

> over the *'urfi* marriage contract, which stated a full dower of SYP 100,000; the dower amount was thus not divided into a prompt and deferred dower. The wife demanded that a new dower would be recorded in the contract; she insisted on getting double the amount. On top of that she demanded that her husband pay her maintenance every month. The judge suggested an amount of SYP 2,000, to which the husband agreed, but this was not to her liking. She demanded more. In the end the contract was adapted and registered by the court. Judge Ibrahim told the wife that if she wanted more maintenance (*nafaqa*) she had to prove to the court that her husband was well-off and she would be entitled to more than the awarded SYP 2,000. Whereupon he dismissed both parties, the husband was handcuffed again and escorted out of the courtroom by the policemen. Almost the entire time the wife was very emotional, arguing with her husband and his lawyer; she was making a dreadful scene. Even after the man was taken away, she kept coming back to plead with the judge to accommodate her wishes.
>
> A few days later I asked Judge Ibrahim why the husband had been brought in handcuffed by the police. According to Judge Ibrahim, the wife had gone to the police, where she had told lies about her husband, as a result of which he was arrested and taken into custody. The judge did not know what he was charged with or whether he had been convicted. Judge Ibrahim was of the opinion that the husband was a good man, in contrast to the wife, who he thought was a morally bad person.[23]

This case raises a number of questions, for example, what were the charges the wife made against her husband; and why did Judge Ibrahim think that the husband was a good man, as opposed to the wife, whom he thought was a morally bad person? I will focus on the latter question, which is in keeping with the 'shared norms' argument that patriarchal views and norms of social propriety and marital behaviour are continuously emphasised and reinforced across the various personal status courts. In that context, the most interesting aspect of this case is the final comment of Judge Ibrahim, uttered in a fleeting moment. The moral qualifications he attributed to the litigants (i.e. 'the husband was a good man, the wife a morally bad person') is a good example of the general appreciation of moral virtues. In my observation, moral views, opinions, expectations of the proper social decorum were commonly expressed in the legal setting, not only by judges but by most participants in the proceedings of the various personal status courts (see, in particular, the next chapter). Critical assessment of spousal or parental behaviour is based on expectations of how a person in one's gender or religion-based role or position (as wife, husband, father or mother) ought to behave.[24] Also, critical assessments of a person's character or personality permeate the courtroom, as became evident in the above-mentioned case. Judge Ibrahim clearly sympathised with the husband and showed himself indifferent to the wife's pleas to impose payment of higher monthly maintenance fees.

The example given above is somewhat extreme in that the husband was detained due to his wife's (false or true) allegations. In any case, if a husband fails to provide maintenance to his wife, she can go to court and file a *nafaqa* claim against him, forcing him to fulfil his obligations. A husband, on the other hand, is entitled to cease maintenance payments if the wife fails to keep her end of the 'patriarchal bargain',[25] namely obedience to him and in particular to co-habit with him. The financial obligations of the husband are inextricably bound up with her legal obligation to co-habit and obey him.

Duty of the wife – marital obedience

It was explained earlier that a wife is obligated to co-habit with and obey her husband. If she is found to be disobedient (*nashiza*) to her husband, she can lose her right to maintenance. Generally, a wife will be considered disobedient if she leaves the conjugal house without a lawful reason or if she works outside the house without her husband's consent.[26]

Article 49 lists the requirement of a wife to 'follow' her husband or, in other words, to practice 'marital obedience' (*wujub al-mutaba'a*[27]) as one of the legal consequences of a valid marriage contract. The SLPS does not include provisions that would allow the courts to (physically) enforce obedience upon a disobedient wife.[28] A Syrian husband can, however, take legal action against his rebellious wife. If a wife remains persistently disobedient to her husband, he can go to court and ask the judge to be suspended from maintenance payments to his wife based on the claim that his wife is disobedient. He can file a claim for 'marital obedience' (*da'wa al-mutaba'a*), requiring his wife to return to the marital home. The deterrent effect of an official court ruling declaring a woman *nashiza* may persuade her to return to the conjugal home or even threatening to file such a claim can already compel a wife to return home.

Sonneveld argues in her book *Khul' Divorce in Egypt* that Cairene husbands often file an obedience (*ta'a*) claim in response to a judicial *khul'* divorce request filed by their wives, as a way of stalling the divorce proceedings or to 'redeem [their] shattered pride'.[29] I have not been able to verify whether Damascene husbands employed the same strategy, that is, to file a claim for 'marital obedience', in response to, for example, a wife's *nafaqa* claim. Although I never came across a case which involved a *mutaba'a* claim during my time in Judge Ibrahim's court, I can imagine that a husband would file such a claim as a strategic manoeuvre in a marital dispute.

Upon inquiry with some lawyers about the composition of a *mutaba'a* petition, I was given a standardised form that is used for these claims. Lawyers generally work with standardised forms for petitions, motions, and other legal proceedings. They purchase these forms (on a DVD-ROM) from, for example, the company SyrianLaw.com or they download them from one of the Syrian Bar Association websites, for example the Damascus Bar Association branch. The form concerning a *mutaba'a* petition (*sighat istid'a' da'wa mutaba'a*) I used here, is taken from the above-mentioned DVD-ROM issued by SyrianLaw.com.

A *mutaba'a* petition is connected to Article 66 SLPS, which concerns the wife's obligation to live with her husband once she has received the prompt dower. For that reason a *mutaba'a* petition should include a description of the house, the household furniture and other relevant amenities, the location of the house and other possible characteristics to prove that the house is a suitable house (a *maskan shar'i*) as prescribed by the law (Arts 65–70 SLPS). In addition, it should state that despite the availability of a suitable house and after mediation of relatives, the wife refuses (without any reasonable reason) to return to the marital home. When the court accepts a *mutaba'a* claim, it will examine (*kashf*) the marital house to investigate whether the house is indeed a suitable house. The wife is obligated to return to the conjugal home when the court concludes, based on the investigation, that the house is suitable.[30] When she refuses to do so, she will be considered disobedient, in accordance with Article 75 SLPS. Consequently, the husband is exempted from paying maintenance to his wife (Art. 74).

Valid seclusion: determining sexual opportunity

The concept of *nushuz* is closely connected to the obligation of the wife to live with her husband; co-habitation implies sexual availability of the wife to her husband. Consummation of the marriage can be a matter of importance in the dissolution of a marriage; in addition to questions regarding the validity and voidability of a marriage. For instance, when a husband claims he has divorced his wife before the marriage was consummated and non-consummation is subsequently established by the court, the husband can be excused from paying his wife the full dower amount.[31] For that reason, Judge Ibrahim normally asked in divorce cases whether or not the marriage was consummated, for example before the *talaq* was pronounced by the husband. In a case where the couple had children this question could obviously be omitted, for children born within a marriage are attributed to the husband by the SLPS. In any event, in the majority of the cases I witnessed, the consummation question was answered in the affirmative.

But what can a judge do in the event that consummation is disputed? It will be difficult to prove that actual consummation has taken place. Often it is simply the husband's word against the wife's. This is where the legal concept of seclusion (*khalwa*) comes into play, meaning that the couple had the opportunity to consummate the marriage. When a couple spent a reasonable amount of time alone together, it is assumed they had sexual intercourse. If the court establishes that valid seclusion (*al-khalwa al-sahiha*) between the couple occurred, the marriage is considered consummated.

A spouse (usually the wife) who claims that he/she had sexual relations with his/her spouse will have to prove that valid seclusion took place. For that purpose, the claimant will present witnesses to the court, regularly close relatives, such as parents and siblings.[32]

> A young woman appeared in Judge Ibrahim's courtroom accompanied by two of her brothers. Her husband claimed that he divorced her before having consummated their marriage. The wife had taken her brothers to court to testify against her

> husband's claim; the alleged husband was present with his lawyer to hear what the opposing party had to say. The judge swore in the two witnesses and began to question them, submitting each of them to a separate interrogation. The judge asked them if private seclusion [*khalwa*] between the spouses had taken place, and if so, to describe the circumstances in which the seclusion took place. Both witnesses were submitted to a lengthy and careful inquiry, in which the judge asked them to describe the house where the seclusion took place in great detail. According to the witnesses, the couple had retreated into the parlour of the bride's family home. Upon which Judge Ibrahim asked them the following questions: What did the house look like? What did the room where the couple allegedly spent four hours together look like? How many doors, windows, entries and exits did the house and the room have? Was it possible for anyone outside to look into the room? Did the room have a balcony? Did they see the couple enter and leave the house and the room? How long were they inside together? According to the second witness, they were together (alone) in the family house a number of times, always for at least two hours, and so on.[33]

This is an example of a case where a dispute over whether or not sexual intercourse had taken place or, more accurate, a dispute over whether the couple had had the opportunity to have sexual intercourse, had been taken to court. The husband in the above-mentioned example wanted to try to extract himself from his dower payment obligation. However, it is also possible for a woman to bring the *khalwa* issue to court, for example if she wants to re-marry without having to take the legally required waiting period (*'idda*) into account.

As we saw in the previous chapter, a woman's sexual propriety is connected to the reputation and honour of her family. Male family members will commonly consider it their responsibility (and are also expected to do so by others) to control and monitor their, in particular, younger female members' (sexual) behaviour. The fact that the institution of valid seclusion exists in the SLPS and legal practice corresponds with the prevailing social norm that non-related men and women should not be together unsupervised or alone in a private setting. It is commonly accepted that this can create an opportunity for possible unlawful (i.e. extra-marital) sexual interactions. This view is (again) a shared norm, shared among Christians and Muslims alike, although in varying degrees.[34]

Unregistered marriages

As explained before, marriages ought to be concluded in or through court. However, marriages concluded outside the court can also be considered valid, provided certain procedures (stipulated by the SLPS) are met. These marriages are often referred to as traditional or customary marriages, in Arabic denoted by the term *zawaj 'urfi* (lit. 'customary marriage'). The phenomenon of *'urfi* marriages in the contemporary Arab world will be discussed in more detail below.

Customary marriages are not always registered at court; there are therefore no statistics or other data available to prove how commonly they occur. Syria's Central Bureau of Statistics only publishes the total number of marriage contracts registered at the Civil Registry of each governorate.[35] In 2009, for example, 241,422 marriages were registered in the country, of which 23,649 marriages were in Damascus proper.[36] However, the type of marriage or where the marriage is contracted, inside or outside the courts, or whether it is a retroactive registration or not, is not specified. In February 2009, I had the opportunity to personally study the notebooks (*daftar*s) used to register cases filed at the Damascus six *shar'iyya* courts. I counted the cases that were filed in January 2009 and a total of 699 cases were filed. The overwhelming majority were divorce cases (474), immediately followed by registration of marriage contracts or 'proof of marriage' (55), so-called *tathbit al-zawaj*. Notwithstanding the lack of statistical data, through observation of court practices and interactions with lawyers and other legal practitioners, it became clear to me that such marriages took place on a regular basis.[37] It appeared that people only decided to register their *'urfi* marriage when there was a legal reason to do so, for instance when children were born from these marriages.[38]

People have different reasons to marry the so-called *'urfi* way. It may be because such marriages are common in the community to which the spouses belong, for example in the rural areas *'urfi* marriages are more common. A man, originally from the area around the city of Deir Atiya (about 90 kilometres north of Damascus), told me once that in the past so-called *al-ihram*[39] marriages were concluded in his village. To perform the pilgrimage (*hajj*) to Mecca, a woman had to be accompanied by her husband or a male family member (*mahram*), as she could not travel unaccompanied.[40] According to my informant, men therefore sometimes married a woman who wanted to go on *hajj*, but could not because she did not have a husband or a close relative to accompany her. Whether these marriages are still contracted today is unknown to me.

There are other reasons for marrying the *'urfi* way, such as: the spouses belong to different (Muslim) sects or the couple marries against the family wishes or because it concerns a polygamous marriage (with or without the first wife's knowledge). It is also possible that the man serves in the army and did not get (or does not want to ask for) permission to marry from the army or because the groom cannot meet the costs of a traditional wedding.[41] Finally, a man can also agree to contract a *'urfi* marriage to make sure the wife's illegitimate child receives a (his) family name. This latter example will be addressed in more detail below.

'Urfi *and other marriage practices*

However, before discussing *'urfi* marriage practices in Syria, I will first address the phenomenon of *'urfi* marriages within a broader Middle Eastern context. First of all, it is important to mention that *'urfi* marriage is an umbrella term employed to denote various (old and new) marriage practices, including traditional or customary marriages, those concluded in conformity with Islamic law, but also those whose Islamic legal status is disputed. As explained earlier, a Muslim marriage is typically defined as a contract between a man and a woman, contracted in the presence of two witnesses and (possibly) a marriage guardian. As long as the basic conditions are met (i.e. offer and acceptance, two witnesses, and a contract including a dower), the marriage will generally be considered valid according to Islamic law. However, for it to be legally valid, according to the statutory laws of most Muslim countries, the marriage contract has to be registered with or drawn up by some official or central state authority. In most countries, the registration requirement only became a necessary legal formality from the late nineteenth century, when governments tried to implement a centralised, uniform civil registry of marriages, births, divorces and deaths.[42] Despite this statutory provision, traditional *'urfi* marriages continue to be concluded, next to the registered ones. In the last decade, however, the *'urfi* marriage seems to have resurged in various guises.

As of late, the *'urfi* marriage phenomenon has been the subject of much debate in many Muslim countries, especially in Egypt.[43] In Saudi Arabia, the approbation by the Grand Mufti of so-called 'ambulant (*misyar*) marriages' in 1996 sparked off debates on informal marriage practices (including *'urfi* marriages), not only in the Kingdom of Saudi Arabia[44] but also in other Middle Eastern countries.[45] The main feature of a *misyar* marriage is that the wife waives her rights to maintenance and housing (i.e. she will agree to continue to live at her parental house), meaning that the husband is excused from his financial obligations.[46] The validity of these marriages is often disputed because they are usually contracted in secret, that is, not registered (and are often polygamous), and preclude, in particular, the financial marital rights of women, despite the fact that they voluntarily waive these rights.[47] What is more, these marriages are often temporary, contracted for a set time period, which also makes them controversial, for temporary (*mut'a*) marriages are only recognised in Shi'i law. According to Sunni law, the institution of *mut'a* marriage is unacceptable; Sunni Muslims commonly consider it a legalised form of prostitution.

The term *'urfi* seems to be blurred with these new types of marriages like *misyar*, but also other types have emerged, for example: *shar'i*[48] (lawful), *misyaf* (summer holiday), *mahatta*[49] (station), *zawaj al-frind* ('friend marriage')[50] and *misfar* (travel). Most of these marriages are temporary and concluded for various reasons, for example enabling a young woman to study abroad.[51] They can be found in various Middle Eastern countries, particularly in the Gulf countries, but also in Syria. So-called 'summer marriages' (*zawaj al-sayf*) are known to be contracted between local women and men from the Gulf visiting Syria during summer holidays.[52] These unions are often temporary, without the legal and financial obligations and duties that are normally associated with marriage, such as spousal maintenance, a marital home, and recognition of children born out these marriages. The outcome of these marriages is not always very rosy; the wife regularly ends up as a divorcee, possibly pregnant or with child. As we saw in the previous chapter, Syrian mothers can generally not pass on their nationality to their children (Art. 3 sub. B Nationality Law).[53] When a marriage is not legally registered and/or the non-Syrian father does not recognise the child according to the law of his home country, the child runs the risk of being without nationality or citizenship. I will elaborate more on the subject in the section 'nameless children'.

Registration of a customary marriage

Now let us return to the subject of the customary or unregistered (*'urfi*) marriage. A *'urfi* marriage concluded outside a Syrian court is eligible for registration, provided the required procedures are met (Art. 40.2). However, in cases where not all requirements all fulfilled, judges tend to agree to register the marriage contract, especially when children are born from the union. When a couple marries the *'urfi* way and a child is born from this union or a pregnancy is apparent, the registration procedure of the marriage and the filiation of the child can be settled promptly.[54] One example:

> A young couple (mid-20s to early 30s) entered Judge Ibrahim's courtroom. The woman appeared to be well into the second trimester of her pregnancy and carried a toddler girl on her arm. As it turned out, the woman was a daughter of a high-ranking official and belonged to the Druze community. The husband, on the other hand, was her father's driver and was Sunni Muslim. They had contracted a *'urfi* marriage and came to court to register their marriage (*tathbit al-zawaj*), in addition to the paternity of their daughter (*tathbit al-nasab*).
>
> Apparently, the wife's father had come to court earlier to state that his daughter never converted to Islam and that she was still Druze. The judge asked the wife if she converted to Islam and, if so, when exactly this had happened. The wife affirmed that she had become a Muslim and that she had converted a year before she got married. To support their claim, the couple had brought two witnesses to the court. Both witnesses (neighbours of the couple) had acted as witnesses to the marriage and had thus been present at the time the marriage contract was signed. The judge asked the two men if they knew whether the wife was Muslim before she signed the marriage contract. They said that she was Muslim before she got married. The judge asked both witnesses who contracted the marriage. They replied by saying that a religious man (*rajul al-din*), studying at the *shari'a* faculty in Damascus, had

> concluded the marriage. The judge accepted the statements of the witnesses and said the marriage would be considered valid and could be registered. The judge issued a decision (*qarar*) by which the marriage contract was legalised and valid, which also entailed recognition of the child being born in wedlock, that is, proof of paternity.[55]

In theory, *'urfi* marriages can be contracted anywhere and by anyone. However, in practice, it is mostly done by a 'religious man' (*rajul al-din*). It should be noted that the 'religious man' who concludes such a marriage without verifying (wittingly or not) all the legal requirements is liable to legal punishment (Arts 469–71 Penal Law). In addition, the spouses, their representatives, and the witnesses are also liable to legal sanction (Art. 472 Penal Law). In legal practice, the couple registering a *'urfi* marriage usually have to pay a fine of 100 SP.[56] This rather insignificant amount does not really have a deterrent effect, as becomes clear from the high frequency and prevalence of these practices.

Carlisle observed that in reality the *shar'iyya* courts tend to turn a blind eye to these practices and will not refer these cases to the criminal courts.[57] This observation corresponds with the attitude of Judge Ibrahim, as described in the case above. Judge Ibrahim did not make any inquiries about the 'religious man' who concluded the marriage. Instead, he was more interested in establishing the exact time and circumstances of the wife's conversion to Islam, whether it had occurred before the spouses signed the marriage contract. The testimony of the spouses and the two witnesses on this point satisfied Judge Ibrahim; he did not make any further inquiry into the matter.

Even though the conversion was dealt with rather matter-of-factly, it raises a number of questions. First of all, why was it necessary for the wife to convert to Islam? After all, the SLPS does not prohibit a Sunni Muslim man from marrying a non-Sunni woman.[58] A Muslim man can marry a woman who belongs to one of the other two monotheistic religions (Art. 120 Qadri Pasha). The likely problem here was that the wife was Druze, and the Druze do not belong to the 'people of the book', that is, Jews and Christians. That being said, there is no consensus among Islamic scholars, nor among the Druze themselves, about whether or not Druze can be considered Muslim. Also, some Druze identify themselves as Muslim, whereas others do not.

What is clear is that interfaith marriages are a highly sensitive issue. Druze personal status law may not explicitly forbid an interfaith marriage, but Druze doctrine does. That is the reason why, according to Bennett, a Sunni–Druze marriage cannot be concluded in a Druze *madhhabiyya* court. [59] It is, however, possible to contract such a marriage in a *shar'iyya* court, as became evident from the example above. The Druze community, like most other religious communities, strongly prefers marriages within its own group. Endogamous marriages are essential for the survival of the Druze community;[60] the more so because one must be born a Druze, one cannot convert to the Druze faith. The chances are that this marriage, validated by Judge Ibrahim, has created problems for the couple. In particular the wife's family would have (in all probability) opposed the marriage and (especially) because she is Druze, she is at risk of being ostracised by her family or, worse, of being killed.[61]

The way in which Judge Ibrahim handled this case was fairly straightforward. Although the circumstances of this union were secretive and complicated, Judge Ibrahim decided to legally recognise the facts as they were presented to him. This recognition was most likely motivated by the need to legalise this union, especially because it was in the best interest of the children, born and unborn. Had he taken a more legalistic stance, the couple and children would have found themselves in an even more difficult position. This is a good example of an advantage of the versatility of Syrian law, for the flexibility of the law allows for a wider discretion of the judge. The possibility of contracting a *'urfi* marriage and the *ex post facto* registration thereof, allows for (in this case) an impossible union to become possible, that is to say, at least, legally possible.

Nameless children: establishing and providing paternity

We saw that in the event of a customary (*'urfi*) marriage, couples do not just register their marriage, but also their born and unborn children.[62] The child's paternity is generally registered simultaneously with the *'urfi* marriage before the court.[63] Once a *'urfi* marriage is registered, it will be considered a legally valid marriage. As a result, the regulations pertaining to paternity of children born during a valid marriage are applicable (Art. 49). In line with the Islamic notion that the child belongs to the marriage bed (*al-walad li-l-firash*), the SLPS considers a child born during a valid marriage attributable to the husband (Art. 128 ff.). Thus, establishing the paternity of children born from a *'urfi* marriage poses no serious problems. But what if there is no proof of marriage (or no marriage at all) and the father has disappeared or is unknown; such cases, although rare, do occur. The child will be considered illegitimate and a child born out of wedlock can only be affiliated to the mother. Since a mother cannot pass on her surname to her child, the child will be without a last name and thus without citizenship. Without a surname, the child cannot get a government-issued identity card (*huwiya*) and will not be able to go to school, travel abroad or own property. This leaves an unwed mother with few options: she can either abandon her child as a foundling (*laqit*), that is, a child of unknown parentage, at an orphanage or, if she wants to keep the child, try to find a man who is willing to marry her and accept to raise the child through fostering (*kafala*).[64]

If she opts for the latter option, the provisions regarding 'proof of paternity' (Arts 134–6) do not apply, because the child is not born from a legitimate union between the mother and the 'new' husband. The 'new' husband/father also cannot legally adopt the child, for the SLPS does not recognise adoption. Adoption (*tabanni*) is prohibited in Islamic law[65] and therefore not recognised by Syrian legislation. It is interesting to note that when Syria ratified the Convention on the Rights of the Child (CRC) on 15 July 1993, it did so with reservations to Articles 14, 20 and 21; the latter article relates to the right of adoption.[66] Syria explained its reservation to Article 21 by stating that the article contravened 'the principles of the Islamic shari'ah which prevail in the country but also with the provisions of national legislation for which Islamic legislation constitutes one of the principal sources'.[67] Interestingly, Syria lifted the reservation to Article 21 (and 20) in 2007.[68] Syria states in its combined *Third and Fourth Periodic Report* that it retains its reservation to Article 14 concerning the right to freedom of thought, conscience and religion in relation to the subject of adoption. It states that

> [t]he reasons for this reservation are related to the religious teachings of Islam. The religion provides for the system of *kafalah* (guardianship) and placement in foster families, on condition that the filiation of the children concerned is not altered to prevent them from enjoying the right to know who their natural

parents are (if their identity subsequently comes to light) and to rejoin them.[69]

Various Christian communities, on the other hand, such as the Catholics and the Greek Orthodox Church, recognise the possibility of adoption. That is to say, adoption regulations are laid down in their substantive laws, but they cannot apply these provisions due to Article 308 SLPS. Article 308 does not list 'adoption' as one of the recognised areas of law in which the Christian and Jewish communities are allowed to apply their own law. The situation was different for the Catholic community from June 2006 until September 2010. During those four years, the Catholics of Syria were solely governed by the provisions of the Catholic Law of Personal Status (CLPS) of 2006, which allowed them to apply provisions which were previously not implementable by the Catholic personal status courts, such as provisions regarding adoption. As explained in Chapter 3, Amendment no. 76 to Article 308 SLPS of 29 September 2010 ended this exceptional legal position for the Catholics, for it stipulated that matters of personal status other than those listed in the revised Article 308 (such as 'adoption') were abrogated by the amendment.

If adoption is not permissible, what options does a newlywed couple have to pass on the father's surname to the 'adoptive' child? Some lawyers find creative ways to provide an illegitimate child with a paternal name and, in consequence, an identity. These lawyers find a man who is willing to be the 'fictitious' father to the child, which means he will agree to sign and register a fabricated *'urfi* marriage contract. As they register the *'urfi* marriage, they simultaneously register the child with the father's last name. Following the registration, the 'husband/father' and mother usually agree upon contracting a *mukhala'a* divorce (see below), which dismisses the 'husband' from any marital or post-divorce financial obligations. Several legal steps thus have to be taken to give mother and child a new chance in life.

I wondered why men were willing to go through such a rigmarole – what was in it for them? My informants said that men were usually willing to co-operate because of philanthropic reasons or because they did not have children of their own. Lawyer Nawal told me of one such example, an arranged marriage between a young man and a young mother with a child born out of wedlock.

> Alaa, a 32-year-old Muslim woman from a poor Damascus suburb, was mother of a four-year-old daughter, Farah. Farah was born from a secret *'urfi* marriage between Alaa and a Lebanese man. At the time, Alaa lived and worked together with her brother in Lebanon to support their family back home in Damascus. In Lebanon she fell victim to sexual abuse by some family members. She eloped with a man and contracted a *'urfi* marriage with him in Beirut. After some time, it turned out that the husband had used a false identity card for the marriage.[70] The husband disappeared, leaving Alaa pregnant and unmarried. She found relief in a women's shelter where she gave birth to Farah. Some people in Damascus, who regularly provide assistance to women like Alaa, arranged a marriage for her with Muhammad, who was three years her junior. They registered a (pre-dated) *'urfi* marriage contract (*tathbit al-zawaj*), as well as the proof of paternity (*tathbit al-nasab*) of Farah in a Damascus *shar'iyya* court.
>
> However, in this particular case Muhammad and Alaa did not divorce. Beyond all expectations, Muhammad and Alaa actually fell in love. The marriage was not just a marriage on paper, for Alaa fell pregnant shortly after the registration process. But Alaa's brother disrupted their marital bliss by instituting legal proceedings against the newlyweds. The brother claimed the marriage and (accordingly) the proof of paternity had to be annulled (*faskh tathbit al-zawaj wa-tathbit al-nasab*). He argued that he was Alaa's legal guardian (*wali*) and that Muhammad was not Farah's real father, which meant he (the brother) was the lawful legal guardian to the girl.[71]

According to lawyer Nawal, the brother's main goal was to get custody over his niece. Her defence was that the brother's claim was inadmissible (*radd al-da'wa*). He was not Alaa's legal guardian and therefore he had no right or legitimate interest (*sifa*) to take legal action against Muhammad and Alaa. I accompanied lawyer Nawal to the *shar'iyya* court (not Judge Ibrahim's court) on the day she was scheduled to submit her defence. Lawyer Nawal was the only one present at the court hearing; the brother (plaintiff) did not appear before the judge. She asked the judge to dismiss the case because the brother did not take the matter seriously. The judge suggested waiting to see whether the plaintiff would make an appearance later that day.[72] If he did not, the court would decide the following day to summon him again or dismiss the case altogether.[73]

Lawyer Nawal told me that the absence of Alaa's brother was beneficial to the case. She had intentionally not submitted her written defence because, if the brother decided to come to court, he would be able to read her defence and know what her defence strategy was. She hoped that Alaa's brother would be half-hearted about pursuing his claim against his sister, which would make the judge more lenient towards Alaa and more likely to dismiss the claim. Besides his claim for annulment of proof of marriage and paternity, the brother considered initiating criminal proceedings against Alaa on the grounds of illicit sexual behaviour (*zina'*).[74] If *zina'* could be proved in court, Farah would be a bastard child (*ghayr shar'i*), as well as Alaa's unborn child. This would of course put Alaa and her daughter in a difficult position. Lawyer Nawal hoped that if the annulment claim were dismissed, the brother would be discouraged to commence criminal charges.

Upon inquiry with lawyer Nawal, a month later, it appeared her strategy and hopes had materialised, for the court had dismissed the brother's claim. However, Alaa heard he had hired a lawyer and wanted to file another claim against her. Lawyer Nawal cautioned Alaa to be careful; she was worried that Alaa would receive a court summons in the near future.[75] I stayed in touch with lawyer Nawal over the course of four months, but the case seemed to have come to a standstill. The brother did not file a new claim.

The possibility of registering customary marriages and establishment of paternity of children born from these marriages (including 'illegitimate' children), is one example of the versatility of Syria's legal system. This versatility also offers the possibility for lawyers and other legal practitioners to find creative solutions, within the legal framework, for women like Alaa, when the existing laws do not provide an adequate or favourable solution. Extra-judicial instruments, such as the possibility of obtaining an *ex post facto* proof of marriage, provide a welcome alternative. Lawyer Nawal took the view that, because of the unfair laws against women and the disadvantaged position of women in general, she is 'forced' to use the existing procedural gaps and legal loopholes (which are many) if this is needed to help her (predominantly female) clients.[76] With the help of connections in the right places, the rules can be circumvented and facts recreated in a manner that they make sense for the purpose at hand.[77]

Obviously, fabricating a marriage contract or proof of paternity is not in accordance with the law. Lawyers who provide legal assistance in these cases knew very well that they were liable to punishment, as the Penal Code forbids any illegal changes in a child's identity, that is, paternity fraud (Art. 479). In addition, the Syrian Bar Association tried to step up against these practices by threatening to impose sanctions on transgressors. For that reason, these lawyers had to be prudent when employing extra-judicial strategies. Even so, I was told that paternity fraud happens with some regularity. One lawyer told me he 'resolved' about 15 cases this way, including an imprisoned single mother and an abandoned Iraqi woman in Damascus, all with the purpose of giving an illegitimate child a last name.

Analogous to Shehada's observations in the Gaza city *shar'iyya* courts concerning the way Gaza's judges handle child custody cases, I would argue here that these Syrian lawyers, litigants, judges and other legal experts involved in the process of legitimising an 'illegitimate' child's descent, exploit the 'gaps of indeterminacy' of the legal order.[78] The legal structure does not provide an adequate solution and therefore the 'good-doers' push the boundaries of the system for the benefit of mother and child.

Dissolution of marriage

> The Prophet (peace be upon him) said: If any woman asks her husband for divorce without some strong reason, the sweet odour of paradise will be forbidden to her.[79]

This *hadith* (tradition of the Prophet Muhammad) was pinned up on one of the cupboards in Judge Ibrahim's courtroom. Apparently the *hadith* did not have the intended effect as I came across numerous women who had come to the *shar'iyya* courts to seek divorce. In particular, so-called *mukhala'a*[80] divorces, often named wife-initiated divorce, appeared to be a popular way to dissolve a marriage. As explained in the previous chapter, *mukhala'a* is one of three types of divorce mentioned in the SLPS, in addition to unilateral divorce or repudiation by the husband (*talaq*) and judicial divorce (*tafriq*).

In the past, according to a senior lawyer, Mr Mulhim, about 75 per cent of family disputes were settled informally, by a *shaykh* or by another respectable, older person. He claimed that nowadays (late 2000s) about 60–70 per cent of family disputes were brought to court. His (probably romanticised) explanation for why the traditional way of dispute settlement had fallen out of fashion was that many *shaykh*s and other religious figures had lost their authority and because many people had moved from the countryside to the cities.[81] The estimates of lawyer Nawal, an experienced family law lawyer, concerning the number of divorce cases taken to court were similar to those of lawyer Mulhim. She estimated that about 70 per cent of all family disputes were taken to court and that approximately 50 divorce cases were filed each day at the Damascus *shar'iyya* courts.[82]

According to the Central Bureau of Statistics website, a total of 29,525 divorce certificates (*shahadat al-talaq*) were registered in Syria (5,292 in Damascus proper) in 2009.[83] During my stay in Damascus, I made copies of the printed edition of the Statistical Yearbook of 2007, which provides more data than the online edition. In 2007, a total of 19,506 divorce certificates (5,080 in Damascus proper) were registered (*shahadat al-talaq al-musajjala*) in Syria.[84] In addition, the yearbook provides the number of divorces issued by the *shar'iyya* courts (*qadaya al-talaq al-sadira 'an al-mahakim al-shar'iyya*), which was a total of 15,916 in Syria, of which 5,430 were issued by the Damascus proper *shar'iyya* courts.[85] The difference between an issued divorce and a registered divorce lies in the fact that the first one is a divorce pronounced by (or before) a judge, whereas a registered divorce is a divorce pronounced by the husband, usually at home, and later (*ex post facto*) registered at court. Similar to the statistics on marriage, the yearbook does not elucidate what exactly is classified under a registered or issued divorce. For example, does a registered divorce also include a divorce pronounced under the terms of a *mukhala'a* contract?

Similar to what has been observed in other Arab personal status courts, the majority of divorce petitions filed at the *shar'iyya* courts are initiated by women.[86] In Syria, petitions for judicial divorce (*tafriq*) and *mukhala'a* are the most common divorce cases (again, the majority of them initiated by women), the former usually on the ground of judicial discord (*shiqaq*). Senior lawyer, Mr Mulhim, commented that these (i.e. *tafriq*) cases often end in *mukhala'a*, a divorce by mutual consent.[87]

Finally, it is important to note, as I was told numerous times, that people generally prefer to settle marital disputes amicably and that only when a dispute cannot be solved informally, will the disputing parties turn to the court. Filing a divorce petition at court is often considered the final step at the end of a long process of reconciliation and mediation by family members and respectable individuals who belong to the spouses' immediate community.[88] The preference to settle disputes through amicable mechanisms (if needed through negotiation with a judge) is another example of a shared norm. In the next chapter, for example, I will demonstrate that the Catholic court also places strong emphasis on reconciliation and restoring social harmony.

That being said, studies on family law practices in the Middle East have also demonstrated that litigation is sometimes used as a strategy to achieve a particular goal, which does not necessarily entail a court ruling. For example, as we saw earlier (in the section on 'Duty of the wife'), a husband can file (or threaten to file) a 'marital obedience' claim to compel his wife to return to the conjugal home. What is more, these studies showed that the majority of filed cases were dropped and never proceeded to trial.[89] According to Sonneveld this suggests that plaintiffs (usually women) were only interested in achieving their particular goal, for example pressuring a husband to fulfil his financial obligations.[90] All of this has to be borne in mind when looking at marital disputes in court, as litigation is only part of the picture.

Divorced or not divorced? Out-of-court talaq

As became evident from the statistical data concerning divorce, the registered (or out-of-court) divorces outnumbered the divorces issued by a judge. Similar to the registration of customary marriages and proofs of paternity, a divorce pronounced outside the court can also be registered at a later date. A unilateral repudiation (*talaq bi-l-irada al-munfarida*) pronounced at home can only be legally validated once it is registered at a *shar'iyya* court. Among legal professionals, this type of divorce was therefore commonly referred to as 'administrative' (*idari*) *talaq*. The husband has to notify the court that he divorced his wife, upon which the court ought to defer acting upon the case for a month in the hope of reconciliation. If, after that month, the husband returns to the court and insists on the divorce, the court will summon the wife to appear in court. If she fails to come, the judge will recognise the divorce and the court will take care of all the required administrative procedures, including sending a notification to the wife to inform her that she is divorced. If, however, she does appear in court and objects to the divorce, the husband's *talaq* is suspended and a process of reconciliation will be initiated.[91] The subject of reconciliation will be dealt with in more detail in below.

Extra-judicial instruments, such as the out-of-court *talaq*, have their advantages. It is cheaper and faster than filing a petition for a judicial divorce and some might consider it beneficial to the already overburdened legal system. However, this male-privileged divorce stands out in stark contrast to the available divorce rights of women, irrespective of the deterrent effect of the financial obligations on the husband following such a divorce. A woman seeking divorce, by contrast, has few options other than waiving her financial rights by agreeing to a *mukhala'a* divorce or filing a judicial divorce petition, which could be a costly and long-winded process. What is more, the legal indeterminacy of out-of-court *talaq*s frequently proves to be troublesome, forcing women to approach the court to establish if they were divorced or not. Some men exercise their divorce rights and then simply disappear or divorce their wives without registering the divorce, sometimes leaving her behind with children and continuing life elsewhere with another wife. Again, the wife is put in a predicament because she will be the one who has to go to court to obtain clarity on her marital status and enforcement of financial payments by the husband.

Obviously, the *talaq* rights of men are not unlimited. The Syrian legislator took measures to prevent (or limit) the occurrence of arbitrary divorces (*talaq ta'assufi*). As explained earlier, the SLPS includes provisions to prevent abuse of *talaq*. Article 117 stipulates that a woman can seek compensation (*ta'wid*) from her former husband when he has divorced her without reasonable cause and she has suffered hardship as a result. Pursuant to this article, the judge can impose maintenance (*nafaqa*) payments for up to three years on the husband, in addition to the 'regular' post-divorce *nafaqa*.[92]

On several occasions, I witnessed women who had come to court to determine whether or not their husbands had in fact divorced them. Either it was not clear how many times the husband divorced his wife or whether the husband had taken her back and if he had done so during the prescribed waiting period (the husband has the right to revoke the divorce and take his wife back, within a set time period; see 'Dissolution of marriage' in Chapter 4). Most women lived with their families from the moment they were repudiated by their husbands for the first, second or third time (a husband can only repudiate his wife three times). Some men left their wives in a state of limbo because they did not register the divorce; as a result these women did not know whether they were divorced or still married. Several women came to court either to claim their deferred dower and post-divorce maintenance or simply to get some formal recognition of the divorce. These women usually brought male family members as witnesses to the court, typically their fathers and/or brothers. The judge would try to establish whether the husband had said to the wife 'you are divorced', where it happened, in which circumstances, how many times, and whether the husband had taken her back. The husband would be summoned to court to tell his side of the story.

> On a morning in April, a young couple in their 20s entered the courtroom. The woman, accompanied by her lawyer, had come to court hoping that Judge Ibrahim could provide some clarity on her marital situation. The wife recounted that she and her husband went to visit her family last July. One night, during this visit her husband divorced her by saying 'I divorce you' three consecutive times. She assumed that he had divorced her and that they were no longer married, but now her husband claimed that he had taken her back, which was not true according to the wife. The judge asked the husband to speak. The husband confirmed that he divorced her while they were at her parents' house, but that (after he said 'I divorce you') she started to cry and pleaded with him to take her back. Two weeks later he told her on the phone and in person that he was willing to take her back. The wife contradicted him and said that he was lying, that was not the way it happened. Her two brothers, who had come with her to court, were sworn in by the judge and questioned one after the other. Both brothers recounted the same story as the wife; they testified that they were both present (as well as their father), when the husband divorced their sister. All they (the brothers and the wife) wanted was that the judge would acknowledge the divorce and register it. Judge Ibrahim sent the couple off with the task of trying to work out

their differences. Then, after a month, if they had not overcome their differences, they could return to court and he would decide on the case.[93]

Judge Ibrahim's decision to defer ruling on the case for a month in hope of reconciliation is in line with the provisions of Article 88. Under this article the judge is required to undertake reconciliation efforts as part of SLPS divorce proceedings. Despite the fact that the SLPS obliges a judge to try to bring about reconciliation in almost all divorce actions, these reconciliation attempts were often conducted in an expeditious manner.

In another case a young woman had come to court claiming that her husband had divorced her and thrown her out of the house, but that he had not met his financial responsibilities associated with divorce. In this particular session the debate revolved around the unpaid (according to the wife) dower.

Both the husband and the wife were present, accompanied by their lawyers. The hearing was a bit chaotic with lawyers constantly interrupting the judge during the testimonies. The husband claimed that he had paid the wife a prompt dower, in addition to gold and a number of household goods. To support his claim he presented three witnesses to the court: his father, a neighbour and a friend. The father gave the first witness testimony.[94] Judge Ibrahim asked the second witness, the neighbour, if he knew what the prompt dower was. He said it was SYP 75,000 (roughly €1,180) and that the husband gave her a trousseau (*jihaz*), including a bedroom suite. The trousseau was worth about SYP 40,000 (€630). The wife interrupted him and said that was not true. The judge asked the witness if he saw the bedroom and, if so, to describe it (the size, the furniture). The witness affirmed that he saw the bedroom but he was unable, despite the judge's repeated questions about the room, to describe it properly, nor could he give an estimated value of the room he claimed he saw. For some reason, Judge Ibrahim was somewhat casual about the regulations concerning the examination of witnesses during this hearing, for all three witnesses were present in the courtroom the entire time. I saw

> witness number one, the father, whispering into the ear of witness number three during the second testimony.
>
> Witness number three was also questioned about the dower. He listed (almost in the same breath) that the prompt dower was SYP 75,000, the deferred dower SYP 35,000 and, furthermore, the husband had also given a trousseau of SYP 40,000. According to the witnesses, the fathers of the spouses had reached an agreement on the dower before the marriage. The judge asked him how he knew about this agreement; he said he heard about it. The wife protested against his statement and claimed that this was not what happened. The judge asked the witness if he knew if the husband actually paid the dower to his wife. He replied that he (the husband) spent it all on the bedroom suite. Upon which the lawyer of the wife mockingly asked the witness if he actually knew what the difference between a prompt and a deferred dower is.[95]

A divorced wife is entitled to her dower; this includes any part of her (unpaid) prompt dower and her deferred dower. The woman in this case tried to prove she never received her prompt or her deferred dower. If Judge Ibrahim decided to rule in her favour, the outstanding dower would be considered an unpaid debt owed by the husband to his wife and would be recorded as such (Arts 54.3 and 54.5).[96]

Similar to what happens in cases concerning customary or unregistered marriages, here too the judge needs to find out what happened based on the statements of the litigants and witnesses. This allows him wide discretion in deciding on an out-of-court divorce case, since he needs to make sense of the often conflicting facts and statements presented to him and decide on what is (or appears to be) the most plausible reality. Especially when claims are disputed, the judge has to reconstruct the events and 'establish a credible narrative' in order to render a fair judgement based on the evidence presented to the court.[97] It is important for the contending parties to present witnesses to the court who can recount the course of events. If the judge finds himself faced with two opposing narratives, he can offer the plaintiff or the defendant the opportunity to take an oath to assert or deny certain facts or their claim entirely. If the plaintiff or defendant agrees to take a decisive oath (*yamin hasima*), the judge will then admit this oath as conclusive evidence upon which he can decide the case.[98]

Mukhala'a *divorce*

In February 2009, I did a personal count from the court's Registry notebooks and counted a total of 699 cases that were taken to the Damascus *shar'iyya* courts. The highest number (264) were *mukhala'a* cases, compared to (for instance) 186 *tafriq* (judicial divorce) cases. These numbers also correspond with what I saw in the courtroom and what I learned from my interactions with lawyers, namely, that *mukhala'a* divorce was a popular way to dissolve a marriage, especially for women.[99]

A *mukhala'a* divorce is generally referred to as divorce by mutual consent or divorce for compensation. In classical *fiqh* and in contemporary literature, divorce by mutual agreement is also denoted as *mubara'a*.[100] The difference between *mukhala'a* (or *khul'*) and *mubara'a* is that the former is generally regarded as divorce on the initiative of the wife in which she gives some form of compensation (i.e. dower and/or marital maintenance) to her husband. *Mubara'a* is a divorce by mutual agreement in which the wife or both parties renounce their financial obligations. Welchman states that most Arab personal status laws use the term *mukhala'a* (or *khul'*) without making a distinction between the different types of divorce; the default type may be denoted as *mukhala'a*, whereas it may technically be a *mubara'a* divorce.[101]

In Syria too, the SLPS uses the term *mukhala'a* as a collective noun and does not differentiate between different types of *mukhala'a*. In legal practice, however, a distinction is made between a *mukhala'a* by agreement and a judicial *mukhala'a*. If the couple jointly agrees to end the marriage through *mukhala'a*, it is denoted as *al-mukhala'a al-rida'iyya*, that is, *mukhala'a* by agreement. This type of divorce bears strong resemblance to the above-mentioned *mubara'a* divorce, although is not denoted as such. If, however, only one of the spouses brings the action to court, it is referred to as a judicial *mukhala'a* (*al-mukhala'a al-qada'iyya*). The latter action is essentially a *talaq* pronounced by a judge (*da'wa al- talaq*).[102]

In Syria, a *mukhala'a* divorce requires the consent of both spouses, contrary to (for example) Egypt and Pakistan, where a woman has the right to initiate a *mukhala'a* divorce without her husband's consent.[103] When a couple agrees to file a *mukhala'a* by agreement (*al-mukhala'a al-rida'iyya*), they will generally draw up a contract outside the court and register it later at the court. Generally, a *mukhala'a* contract will stipulate that the wife compensates her husband, typically by foregoing her outstanding financial rights, in exchange for his *talaq*. The wife relinquishes, at least, her right to any unpaid or outstanding dower amount and her right to the marital maintenance (*nafaqa zawjiyya*).

Mukhala'a contracts are often negotiated by the parties with the help of a lawyer, who submits the contract (on their behalf) for registration by the court.[104] Nevertheless, the wife has to be present in court to register the divorce, because the judge has to verify with her if this is what she really wants. If she accepts the terms of the contract, the *mukhala'a* contract can be registered by the court. Whether or not this consent is always completely voluntary is questionable. Other studies on Muslim divorce practices showed that women are sometimes pressured into a *mukhala'a* divorce, because it can offer a husband a cheap way to obtain a divorce, as he can evade paying post-divorce maintenance and any remaining dower amount that normally come with *talaq*.[105]

On one occasion I accompanied a young trainee lawyer to court; she was assigned to finalise a *mukhala'a* petition file, which her mentor would submit to the court later that day. The trainee needed to collect several documents with the required seals and stamps to certify them. First she had to obtain a copy of the marriage contract from the court's registry office. The second stop was the Civil Registry (*qayd nufus*), located in a building about a 15-minute walk from the courthouse, to obtain a statement about the couple's marital status.[106] The file also included the *mukhala'a* contract (*sakk mukhala'a rida'iyya*), already signed by the husband. Once the trainee was done with all the administrative requirements (which took her about two hours), she called her mentor to come to the court in order to register the file. About half an hour later, the mentor lawyer arrived with the wife, who then signed and fingerprinted the *mukhala'a* contract. The next step was making an appointment with one of the judges, who would then pronounce the divorce.

I was allowed to make a copy of the *mukhala'a* contract; it included the following information:

The wife Lina, a 42-year-old woman, had been married to the husband Mamun (aged 50) for 22 years. The contract read that because marital life became impossible [*wa-nazaran li-istihalat al-hayat al-zawjiyya baynahum*] they agreed to 'divorce by agreement' [*al-mukhala'a al-rida'iyya*]. Mamun agreed to divorce Lina in exchange for being released from any financial obligation (*bara'a dhimma*), including the (paid) prompt dower of SYP 30,000 and the deferred dower (registered as a debt), also SYP 30,000. In addition, Lina could no longer claim any trousseau (*jihaz*), jewellery, gold, marital maintenance (*nafaqat al-zawjiyya*), post-divorce maintenance (*nafaqat al-'idda*) or any other right associated with the marriage contract. The contract had been drawn up eight days before the registration of the agreement at the court. Mamun's exact wording on the contract reads as follows (translation from the author):

> I 'release' you from my marital bond and marriage contract, in exchange for being released from my financial obligation of any dower, trousseau 'goods', gold, jewellery, marital maintenance, post-divorce maintenance, and any other right resulting from the marriage contract, in exchange for [*liqa'*] a divorce [*khul'*] recompense amount of SYP 100, which I pay to you now. In return I release you from all the responsibilities that follow from my marital contract with you.[107]

Upon which the wife immediately answered, saying:

> I accept that you divorced me as you stated it. I received from you a divorce [*khul'*] recompense amount of 100 SYP. I release you from all financial obligations towards me and I accepted your 'release' [from me].[108]

The agreement contract ended with the promise of both parties that they would get the divorce effectuated at the court, and the promise of Lina that she would observe her legal waiting period as of that date (of effectuation).[109]

What is remarkable here is that the husband paid the wife a recompense amount (i.e. *badal al-khul'*) of 100 Syrian pounds (roughly €1.5). In a *mukhala'a* by agreement, according to my informants, it is normal for a husband to pay his wife a symbolic amount (*badal al-khul'*); the couple can agree on a higher amount, but 100 pounds is the minimum amount for a valid *mukhala'a*.[110] It is remarkable because generally, that is, in other Muslim countries[111] and according to Hanafi doctrine,[112] the wife offers or pays the husband a compensation (in exchange for divorce). However, according to Syrian legal practice, the wife not only compensates the husband by foregoing her financial rights, but the husband also pays the wife a (symbolic) recompense amount of 100 Syrian pounds.

A *mukhala'a* by agreement is generally considered an expeditious way to obtain a divorce for both spouses. For the husband it can be an easy and cheap way out because he can terminate the marriage by paying a symbolic amount and, what is more, a *mukhala'a* divorce does not come with the financial obligations of a divorce by *talaq*.[113] The wife, on the other hand, avoids the lengthy litigation procedure that generally comes with a judicial divorce (*tafriq*), where the outcome cannot be guaranteed; or if she filed a judicial *mukhala'a*, the husband might demand additional compensation, that is, in addition to her foregoing her outstanding financial rights.

Lawyers repeatedly told me that *mukhala'a* is the most efficient way for women to obtain a divorce, especially since the amount of maintenance (during the waiting period) awarded in case of judicial divorce is often so low that it is hardly worth filing a petition for judicial divorce in the first place. In contrast to a judicial divorce case, divorce by *mukhala'a* is not about determining fault or blame and the wife is not required to establish grounds for divorce. Though on the other hand, it should be borne in mind, as stated earlier, that women might be pressured to contract a *mukhala'a* divorce. Divorce by mutual consent can thus be advised by lawyers because it is more efficient and expedient than a 'regular' divorce, as will be explained below. Similarly, Carlisle observed that arbiters often advised the couple, during the mandatory arbitration sessions, to resolve their marital dispute by concluding a *mukhala'a* divorce.[114]

Judicial divorce – tafriq

As stated earlier, the SLPS recognises various grounds for judicial divorce (*tafriq*), which include the following: a husband's impotence or insanity, long-term absence or imprisonment of a husband, a husband's failure to provide maintenance, and discord between the spouses. As expected, only the latter reason for divorce can be invoked by both the husband and the wife. When a spouse brings a judicial divorce petition to court on the grounds of discord (*al-tafriq li-l-shiqaq bayna al-zawjayn*), he/she will claim that marital life became impossible on account of the other spouse. Men who cannot afford to repudiate their wives by *talaq*, because they cannot pay the unpaid dower and post-divorce maintenance, can seek divorce on this ground. If it is established that at least part of the harm can be attributed to the wife, the husband may be (partly) excused from his financial obligations under the marriage contract. However, the majority of the claimants are women.

According to Carlisle, judges prefer to settle judicial divorce cases on the grounds of discord, because the other grounds are more susceptible to failure due to their evidence requirements.[115] For example, if a woman invokes the ground of 'non-payment of maintenance' the husband can start (or resume) paying maintenance during the course of the proceedings and/or it may be difficult to prove that maintenance has not been paid. Or if a woman files a petition claiming that her husband is absent, she will be required to put an advertisement in three national newspapers, not once but twice.[116] This is an expensive strategy for a woman to take, especially if the wife is impoverished.

The SLPS stipulates that when a divorce petition on the ground of discord is presented to the court, the judge first has to try to reconcile the disputing parties. Similar to *talaq* and *mukhala'a* procedures, the judge is also required to defer a *tafriq* on the grounds of discord petition for a month in hope of reconciliation (Art. 112.3). However, in contrast to the other two types of divorce, a *tafriq* case on the grounds of discord requires proof of harm (*darar*). If harm cannot be established by the judge and his reconciliation attempt has failed, he has to appoint two professional arbiters who will try and reconcile the spouses during closed reconciliation session, usually conducted outside the court. I will elaborate more on this latter phase in the following sections, but first I will give an example of Judge Ibrahim's own reconciliation attempt in his courtroom.

> An agitated man (a university teacher) and his wife (a doctor) burst into the court of Judge Ibrahim as he was mid-way through the dictation to his clerk of a witness statement he just heard from another case. He told the couple to stay quiet and wait until he had finished. Once the other couple and their witnesses had left the room, they were summoned to the dais by Judge Ibrahim who

> inquired into the reason for their disagreement. The husband said that his wife had left him a year ago and that she wanted a divorce, but he did not agree. He claimed that his wife (in fact) wanted to return to him but that her mother prevented her from returning to the marital home. The judge asked the woman if this was true. She replied that she did not want to return to him because she did not want to upset her family. She claimed that he was very impolite to her mother and that this was the only reason why she had left him. The wife's brother concurred with this statement and added that the husband treated their mother badly, for instance by raising his voice to her. The wife started to cry and said that she did not know what to do. The judge tried to calm everyone down and proposed to accompany them to the mother's house later that day, after the court closed. At the same time, the judge urged the husband to apologise to the mother and told him that they should try to find a solution to this situation. Everyone agreed to act on the judge's advice. Before leaving the court, the husband told the judge that they had a child and that his wife loved him and he loved her, but that pressure was placed upon his wife by her family. The judge reassured him that he would do his utmost to try and help them to resolve their differences.[117]

It should be noted that such an approach is not necessarily common practice amongst the *shar'iyya* judges in Damascus. As I mentioned earlier, Judge Ibrahim was a somewhat exceptional judge, especially when it came to resolving social conflicts. I was told that he was one of the few judges who personally visited litigants at home to try and resolve disputes between the parties and families involved.[118] Whereas most divorce cases were handled swiftly – sometimes a case would be concluded within a few minutes (for example the registration of a *mukhala'a* divorce) – in this particular case Judge Ibrahim was willing to spare no effort to reconcile the spouses. Seeing that the wife's statements about the reason why she left her husband and the reason why she wanted a divorce mostly revolved around her family's interests and interferences (i.e. 'I did not want to upset my family' and 'because he [the husband] was very impolite to my mother'), Judge Ibrahim saw an opportunity for true reconciliation. If he could convince her family, especially her mother, to resolve their differences and to make this marriage work, in particular for the interest of their child, the divorce claim could be dropped.[119] This case study illustrates the importance of family and the influence family members can have on the success or failure of marital life. It calls to mind the case study described by Carlisle (2008) in the article 'Mother Love', where a couple was forced to divorce under pressure of the wife's family.[120] Because marriage is very much a family (i.e. not exclusively a spousal) affair, interference of family members can make or break a marriage. This will also be demonstrated in the next chapter, where I will describe some cases in which relatives had an important influence on the marital relationship of couples who appeared in the Damascus Catholic court.

I once asked Judge Ibrahim about the importance of conciliation (*sulh*) in divorce disputes. In his opinion reconciliation (*musalaha*) is important in all disputes, especially when there are children involved. He maintained that a negotiated solution is always better than a court-ordered ruling, as an amicable divorce settlement can offer parties an opportunity to overcome their past differences and to try and restore their relations. Again, this is especially desirable if a couple has children.[121]

Court-ordered arbitration – **tahkim**

In *tafriq* cases the actual reconciliation sessions are generally undertaken by arbiters appointed by the court. Article 112 paragraph 3 stipulates that these arbiters should be family members of the spouses or persons the judge considers capable of bringing about reconciliation. In actual practice, however, the court usually appoints professional arbiters employed at the court. In 2009, 31 official arbiters were appointed for the six Damascus *shar'iyya* courts; the majority of them were trained lawyers.[122] Judge Ibrahim told me that they did not receive special training in arbitration or dispute settlement; my presumption was that they were selected based on their social skills, character and religious demeanour.

The arbitration sessions are generally conducted outside the court, usually in the arbiters' private offices. But before the case is handed over to the arbiters, the couple first meets with the judge and the appointed arbiters in the judge's office in the court. This first meeting, as well as the subsequent arbitration sessions outside the court, are private; lawyers and family members are not allowed to be present at these sessions.

Judge Ibrahim reserved Thursday mornings for these 'kick-off' meetings. On two occasions I was allowed and able to observe a number of them.[123] The two arbiters I met in Judge Ibrahim's office were two middle-aged men and, similar to Carlisle's description of the arbiters she met, 'well versed in religious ethics'.[124] During the various sessions they frequently quoted *ahadith* (Prophetic traditions) and often tried to reassure the litigants with statements as 'with God's help all will be well', 'God is the only judge', 'through God's guidance, the best solution will present itself'.[125]

The sessions I attended were very brief (five to ten minutes), in contrast to the subsequent sessions which usually lasted for one to two hours, according to one of the arbiters.[126] One by one the couples or, more often, the plaintiff (the defendant often failed to attend) would be called into the office. The judge and arbiters asked the couple or plaintiff to explain why he/she filed the divorce claim and more specifically what (according to him/her) the reason was for the disagreement between them (the spouses). They asked the litigants to 'elaborate' on questions regarding the husband's profession and/or the wife, how much money was made, if there were children (and, if not, why not), if the husband had paid the prompt dower, why the wife had left the marital home, and so on. The questions obviously depended on the nature of the claim. According to the arbiters, the majority of the plaintiffs were female and commonly complained about their husbands failing to provide maintenance for her and the children because he, for example, used alcohol or drugs.[127] In all the cases I saw (about ten in total), the plaintiff was indeed the wife; only in three cases did the husband make an appearance and all of them were against a divorce. The most common accusation against the husbands was that they failed to provide maintenance to their families, just as the arbiters maintained. The husbands, for their part, blamed their wives for, respectively: adultery, being preoccupied with herself and the children, and theft. It turned out that the latter husband had taken a second wife, two months earlier; despite his allegations of theft against her, he said he was ready to reconcile with his first wife.

Judge Ibrahim took notes of each session and wrote them in the file. He concluded each session by officially assigning the two arbiters to the case, which meant that they took an oath to perform their task in equity and honesty (*bi-'adl wa-amana*), in accordance with paragraph 3 of

Article 112.[128] After this 'kick-off' meeting in Judge Ibrahim's office, the arbitration process would be taken over by the arbiters. They are required to conduct a series of reconciliation sessions. If they fail to reach reconciliation, they will need to determine the reason for the disagreement and in the end submit a report to the judge advising the court how to dissolve the marriage (Art. 114).[129]

As mentioned earlier, Carlisle observed that arbiters often advised the spouses to dissolve their marriage by concluding a *mukhala'a* divorce, because it provided spouses with 'an opportunity to settle a case immediately and on known terms'.[130] When the arbiters realised there was no chance of saving the marriage and reconciling the spouses, they offered them an expeditious alternative for dissolving their union. By proposing to resolve the dispute by means of *mukhala'a*, an agreement by mutual consent was reached, which is generally preferred over a court-imposed judgment. Even though it was not the perfect outcome (that would be restoration of the marital bond), it was at best an amicable solution. In addition, a negotiated arbitration outcome was efficient both for the litigants and the judicial system. According to Carlisle, the work of arbiters unburdened the judicial system (i.e. the courts) and, since an arbitration ruling was binding, it was therefore unlikely to be sent to appeal, especially if it was a negotiated outcome. It was also efficient in terms of costs, again both for the litigants and the judicial system; the litigants only paid an arbitration fee of SYP 1,000 and (again) the low likelihood of appeal was beneficial to the judiciary.[131]

Conclusion

This chapter discussed several aspects of the judicial process in the context of the *shar'iyya* courts of Damascus, focusing on procedures and legal practices in one court in particular: the court of Judge Ibrahim. It described the circumstances in which Judge Ibrahim and his colleagues had to work, in particular the tumultuous work environment, the immense workload, and the versatility of the legal system. It was this versatility or flexibility of the SLPS and the legal system that was the focal point of this chapter.

The versatility of Syria's personal status law became most apparent in the discussion on of unregistered *'urfi* marriages and out-of-court divorces. The SLPS allows for registration of proof of marriage, divorce and paternity *ex post facto*, meaning that customary marriages and divorces pronounced or agreed upon outside the courtroom can be registered at a later date at court. The law itself is thus extremely flexible, in the sense that it does not claim regulatory exclusivity on marriage, divorce and paternity. In other words, the Syrian state, similar to other Muslim-majority countries, allows for other 'forms of normative ordering' to work alongside the official legal system. Despite its efforts to discourage traditional practices such as *'urfi* marriages and out-of-court divorces, the state continued to recognise them as valid. Thus, there are several 'forms of normative ordering' at work in the domain of Syrian family law, as the statutory laws are part of only one order among several.

These extra-judicial options proved beneficial to a great variety of people, for example couples who did not wish to marry in court because they married someone against their families' wishes or because the spouses belonged to different (Muslim) sects. Another group that benefited from these extra-judicial possibilities was the judiciary itself. The *ex post facto* registrations of marriages, divorces and proof of paternity unburdened the already overloaded judicial system.

Besides, the versatility of the SLPS proved to offer opportunities for creative legal solutions, in particular to legitimise children born out of wedlock. Because of the possibility of registering proof of paternity *ex post facto*, an illegitimate child could be given a paternal name, even if the name came from a 'fictitious' father. However, extra-judicial instruments also offer ample opportunities for those who are not very strict with the law. It can encourage people to resort to corruptive practices or simply ignore the law; for example, husbands can divorce and abandon their wives, leaving them in a state of legal uncertainty. In that regard, the extra-judicial options only degrade the already poor legal position of women and children, especially in divorce and extra-marital circumstances.

This chapter also argued that the patriarchal family model was not only laid down in the SLPS but also fostered in Syrian society, by participants and visitors to the personal status courts. Women in Judge Ibrahim's court for example often complained that their husbands did not take on their (legal) responsibilities as a husband: they failed to provide maintenance or they spent their money on other things than their families (sometimes drugs or alcohol) or they hit their wives. The SLPS and the *shar'iyya* judiciary could only enforce the patriarchal norms to a certain extent, as its regulatory authority and capacity could not always keep pace with social realities. Unfortunately, social realities did not always correspond with legal and societal values, for there were numerous failing husbands, abandoned wives, mothers and children, marital disputes and children born out of wedlock, as will also be demonstrated in the next chapter.

CHAPTER 6

THE CATHOLIC COURT: GUARDIAN OF ORDER AND SACRAMENTS

This chapter will expound the Catholic personal status law of 2006 and the application thereof by the Catholic judges of the first instance Catholic Damacus court, based on observations in that court. It will focus on marriage nullification proceedings, as they make up the majority of cases brought before this court.

Each personal status court has its own characteristics, routine and distinctive character. This is determined by various factors, including the historical development of Syria's legal system and the position of religious minorities therein, and the influence of the (trans-national) Mother Churches. I contend, however, that the Catholic courts of Damascus are rather remarkable when compared to other courts. The reason for this is, in my opinion, their alliance with the Church of Rome. The Syrian Catholic personal status law is predominately based on canon law issued by Rome and, what is more important, the Catholic judges are trained in this canon law at Pontifical colleges in Rome. Taking this into account, the question arises of whether this alliance with Rome (through legislation and instruction) affects the administration of justice for Catholics in Syria and, if so, how this occurs.

As mentioned before, the argument in the second part of this book is that the presence of, and importance attached to, patriarchal norms and values on marriage and family relations are a common denominator of the various (i.e. *shar'iyya*, Catholic and Greek Orthodox) personal status courts of Damascus. I assert that patriarchal gender roles in marriage and family, which includes matters such as obedience of women and upholding the family honour, were emphasised and reinforced time and again by the different actors involved, that is, judges, lawyers, litigants and witnesses. This attachment to cultural gender norms clearly manifested itself in the extensive examination of litigants and witnesses, as will be demonstrated in the course of this chapter.

Eastern Catholic Churches in Syria

In Syria there are six Catholic denominations that recognise the (judicial) authority of the Pope: Melkite Greeks, Maronites, Armenian Catholics, Syriac Catholics, Latins and Chaldean Catholics. These Eastern Catholic Churches are united in communion with the Bishop of Rome, the Pope. The Catholic Church is made up by 22 *ecclesiae sui iuris* (i.e. 'particular' or 'self-governing' churches), each church *sui iuris* is headed by a patriarch, major archbishop, metropolitan or other hierarch. Worldwide there are 22 *ecclesiae sui iuris*: the Latin (or Western) Church is the biggest 'self-governing' church; the other 21 churches are collectively called the Eastern Catholic churches.[1]

Despite the 'particularity' of the various Eastern Churches, they are collectively governed by one Code, i.e. the Code of Canons of the Eastern Churches, originally published in Latin as the *Codex Canonum Ecclesiarum Orientalium* (hereafter: CCEO).[2] The CCEO was issued by the late Pope John Paul II on 18 October 1990 and came into effect on 1 October 1991. It applies to all members of the Eastern Catholic Churches, which (in addition to Syria) can be found in countries such as Egypt, Lebanon, Jordan, Iran but also Albania, Croatia, Russia, Ukraine, Belarus, India, Ethiopia; in addition to (diasporic) communities in Latin America, the United States, Canada, Australia and Europe. The CCEO governs the ecclesial life of the Eastern Churches and covers various branches of the Church, including the organisation of the Church, the clergy, religious practices such as prayer, celebration of the Eucharist and other sacraments, most importantly (for this study), marriage.

The legal position of Catholics in Syria

As explained earlier, the legislative and judicial autonomy of the Catholic churches, like the other Christian churches, is to a significant extent regulated by the 1953 Syrian Law of Personal Status (the SLPS). Article 306 SLPS provides that: 'The provisions of this law apply to all Syrians except for what is stated in the following two articles.' Article 307 refers to the Druze community; Article 308 is the provision pertaining to Jews and Christians. The latter article is of great importance; in fact, it is the central article concerning the applicability of personal status laws for Christians. It stipulates that Christians and Jews are competent to apply their own religious regulations in certain specified matters, most importantly marriage and divorce.

Furthermore, the SLPS, in relation to non-Muslim family laws and the administration of these laws, has to be considered in conjunction with other statutory laws: first of all, the Law of Judicial Procedures of 1953. Article 535 of this law restricts the exclusive or general jurisdiction of the *shar'iyya* courts (i.e. jurisdiction over all Syrians regardless of their religion) to the matters of personal status listed in this article, such as legal guardianship (*wilaya*), paternity (*nasab*), and maintenance of relatives and children.[3] In other words, the *shar'iyya* courts are the general competent courts to hear cases involving non-Muslims in (these) specified matters. However, in all other personal status matters, the different non-Muslim personal status courts are competent to adjudicate cases involving members of their own denomination, for example in matters pertaining to marriage and marriage dissolution.

The second law that is of importance is the Judicial Authority Law of 1961. Article 36 of this law reads that the religious (*ruhiyya*) courts of the non-Muslims communities continue to be regulated by the 1936 Resolution no. 60/LR, dating back to the French Mandate period. This Resolution, promulgated on 13 March 1936 by the French High Commissioner De Martel, grants specific religious communities the right to draw up their own family laws and courts to adjudicate matters of family law. So, the Catholic communities, like the other Christian communities, have been partially subject to the provisions of the SLPS (pursuant to Art. 308) since 1953. However, the family law position of the Catholics changed significantly in 2006 and then again in 2010.

The 2006 Catholic Law of Personal Status

Chapter 3 described how the Catholic Churches in Syria managed to obtain a new law of personal status (i.e. the CLPS) in June 2006.

The CLPS was considered a revolutionary law because it granted the Catholic courts full jurisdiction in all matters of personal status.[4] Furthermore, the law recognised sensitive rights such as adoption and equal inheritance rights for men and women (these are sensitive in that adoption and equal inheritance are not allowed by Islamic law). The exceptional position of the Catholics vis-à-vis the other Christian groups was subject to criticism. Particularly non-Catholic Christians were discontented that they were put in a false position in relation to the Catholic Churches with regard to the SLPS and the *shar'iyya* courts.

The Catholics' *status aparte* in family law was changed in September 2010, when an amendment was made to Article 308 SLPS. Presidential Decree no. 76, issued on 29 September 2010, amended Article 308 to such an extent that the special jurisdiction of the Christian and Jewish communities over personal status matters also extended to inheritance and bequests (and is still the case now). Before the 2010 amendment, these matters belonged to the competence of the *shar'iyya* courts. With the issuance of the amendment, the government responded to the dissatisfaction prevalent among non-Catholic Christians, who felt that this was a form of discrimination against them. The second article of the amendment is of particular interest to the Catholics of Syria but at their expense. The article states that provisions of the Syriac Orthodox PS Law, Greek Orthodox PS Law, and the Catholic PS Law, pertaining to matters of personal status other than those listed in the revised Article 308, are abrogated by the amendment. As a result, the amendment rendered a substantial part of the CLPS inoperative, which meant that its regulations, for example, adoption, legal guardianship, paternity (or descent), are no longer applicable. Due to this amendment, the Catholics again fall under the scope of Article 308 and thus are back within the competence of the *shar'iyya* courts.[5]

What this amendment means for the current status of the CLPS remains unclear.[6] For example, Article 280 of the CLPS reads that the law can be regarded as an amendment to Article 308 SLPS, meaning that the CLPS 'abrogates' Article 308 SLPS, thereby excluding the Catholics in Syria from application of the SLPS.[7] Article 281 states that all Catholics of Syria are solely governed by the provisions of the SLPS, not by any other laws of personal status and – moreover – that its denominational courts have full jurisdiction over all personal status matters pertaining to Catholics. Clearly, these articles are no longer applicable but what will happen next? Will the Catholics (have to) promulgate a new law or will they be able to use the current one and simply leave parts of it untouched? Also, will all rulings given by the Catholic courts given between 2006 and 2010 contrary to Article 308 SLPS be quashed by the Court of Cassation? These are just a few of many questions that require clarification and remain a subject for further study.

Since I conducted my fieldwork in 2009, I will – in the discussion of the CLPS and its application by the Catholic courts – take the 2009 situation as the point of departure. Besides, the 2010 amendment had no effect on the issues discussed in the remainder of this chapter, namely, the substantial provisions and proceedings pertaining to marriage and nullification of marriage.

The relation between the CLPS and the CCEO

The version of the CLPS I used for this study consists of the full text of Law no. 31/2006 (565 articles in total) *and* the Arabic translation of Title XVI, Chapter VII 'Marriage' of the CCEO in its entirety (i.e. Can. 776–866), as a supplement to the law. The inclusion of this chapter of the CCEO in the CLPS is pursuant to Article 38 of the CLPS, which states that all Catholics are subject to the provisions of the CCEO pertaining to marriage and the dissolution thereof.

As mentioned earlier, a significant part of the CLPS is a direct translation of the CCEO. In addition to Canons 776–866 (Title XVI on sacraments, Chapter IV 'Marriage'), other canons that are of interest to this study, and copied into the CLPS are, most importantly: Can. 1055–356 (Title XXIV and XXV on the ecclesiastical judiciary and its procedures) and Can. 1357–84 (Title XXVI, Chapters 1 and II 'Marriage Processes'). A significant section of these canons is incorporated in its entirety in the CLPS, as becomes evident from the numerous references made to them in the CLPS. Throughout this chapter I will refer, when applicable, to both the CLPS article concerned and the corresponding canon.

Damascus Catholic court: guardian of order and the sacraments

The majority of the cases brought to the Catholic court, similar to the other personal status courts, were nullification of marriage petitions. I deliberately use the word 'nullification' (*butlan*) and not the word 'divorce' (*talaq*), because according to Catholic doctrine a marriage cannot be dissolved due to its sacramental nature. The Church however accepts annulment of marriage but only when it is proven that a marriage was null or invalid from the beginning.

The Damascus Catholic court always reacted fiercely whenever a litigant, witness or lawyer used the word 'divorce' (*talaq*) instead of 'nullification' (*butlan*). This example is illustrative of the strict stand the Catholic court, following church doctrine, took on divorce and it only accepted annulment of marriages in exceptional cases. The proceedings in the Catholic courts and the demeanour of the judges were different, in my observation, from the Greek Orthodox court, for example. The Catholic judges were well-versed in the canonical structures, language and ethics, chiefly – in my opinion – because they received a thorough education in Rome. More examples to support this argument will be given in the following sections.

As mentioned earlier, the second argument of this chapter is that shared patriarchal norms and views on social propriety, marriage and family were emphasised and reinforced by all the participants in the family law arena. Nullification proceedings in the Catholic courts of Damascus were pre-eminently suitable to observe the prevailing or desired standards of acceptable behaviour between spouses. In the next section a description will be given of a Damascus Catholic court in action, which principally concerned nullification proceedings.

Inside a Catholic ruhiyya *court*

The Catholic courts are competent to hear cases involving members belonging to the six Catholic churches in Syria: Greek Melkites, Maronites, Armenian Catholics, Syriac Catholic, Latins and Chaldean Catholics (Art. 1 CLPS).[8] There is a first instance court in every eparchy (i.e. diocese), thus in Damascus, Aleppo, Homs, Lattakia, Bosra, Qamishli and Hassakeh.[9] The Catholic court of appeal of Syria is situated in Damascus. In special circumstances, the Vatican 'Rota' court in Rome can hear appeals from decisions of the Catholic (appellate) courts. However, the Court of Cassation remains the court of last resort.[10]

During my fieldwork, the first instance court of Damascus and the court of appeal were both housed in a building on the premises of the Melkite Greek *Zaytoun* church, tucked away in a calm spot amid the hustle and bustle of the Christian quarter of the old city. The Damascus'

Catholic court premises were a haven of peace, especially compared to its *shar'iyya* counterpart. The courtroom and the neighbouring court's registry, that is, the *diwan*, were located on the ground floor of a building which also served as a centre for educational and religious activities organised by the church. During the court's office hours, lawyers, litigants, and witnesses usually hovered around the courtroom or were waiting in the designated waiting room, chatting and drinking coffee with the clerk in his office (which also served as the court's registry), while waiting their turn to enter the court.

The first instance court and the court of appeal were presided over by two different judges, Father Eliyas and Father Antoun. They operated from the same courtroom but on separate days. The first instance court worked on Monday and Wednesday mornings; Father Eliyas presided over the first instance court on Monday. The Wednesday first instance court, as well as the court of appeal, was presided over by Father Antoun. Because the Wednesday first instance court heard significantly fewer cases than the one on Monday, the court of appeal (after a short intermission) opened its doors immediately following the first instance court sessions. The first instance court occasionally scheduled an extra session on Thursday mornings, if the circumstances so required, for example in order to catch up after a bank holiday. Since I mainly attended sessions of the Catholic first instance court, I will refer only to the first instance court proceedings in the remainder of this chapter.

Over the course of four months, during my presence in the Catholic first instance courts of Damascus, I counted a total of 213 cases.[11] I calculated that the first instance court heard about 15 cases on average on Mondays (the busiest court day) and about eight cases on Wednesdays. Again, the vast majority of them concerned nullification of marriage petitions. The cases ranged from cause-list sittings where lawyers handed in documents (*mudhakkirat*) or just came in to make an appointment for a next session, but also cases that involved lengthy witness testimonies, for example. What struck me, especially in comparison with the court proceedings at the *shar'iyya* courts, was that the judges were very strict in their observance of the court's agenda. For example, lawyers were required to make appointments for future sessions before 10 a.m. If they appeared in court past 10 a.m. to make an appointment, they would be reprimanded by the judges. Indeed, court sessions at the Catholic courts were generally very orderly, with cases processed one at a time. In my opinion, the Catholic judges distinguished themselves by their procedural tenacity.

One could argue that Catholic judges, and other Christian judges or judges belonging to another minority, could afford the luxury of being meticulous, contrary to their colleagues working at the *shar'iyya* courts, who had to handle a considerably heavier workload. The Christian judges had to handle a considerably lower number of cases compared to their Muslim counterparts, if only because the (total) number of Christians in Syria is much smaller (10 per cent of the total population, vs roughly 85 per cent Muslims).

Be that as it may, in none of the other personal status courts I visited were the judges as rule-conscious and orderly as they were in the Catholic courts (or at least they did not appear to be). The judges belonging to the biggest Christian 'group', that is, the Greek Orthodox (503,000 souls vs 204,600 Catholics), were also confronted with considerably fewer cases. Nevertheless, they were much more relaxed and informal during the court proceedings than their Catholic colleagues, who took on a much more weighty and formal stand in their handling of annulment petitions. The Catholic nullification proceedings were generally lengthy and complicated, whereas the Greek Orthodox divorce proceedings were not. This can partially be explained by the fact that the Greek Orthodox Church does accept divorce; it is possible that – because of its more tolerant stand on divorce – the Greek Orthodox judges proceeded more pragmatically in their treatment of divorce cases.[12] Their way of working and their interaction with lawyers, litigants and witnesses bore, in my opinion, more resemblance to what happened in the court of Judge Ibrahim (see previous chapter).

That being said, I believe there is another reason why the Catholic judges were very strict when it came to procedures, compared to their colleagues of the *shar'iyya* and the Greek Orthodox courts. My explanation for this finding lies in the fact that they received their canonical training in Rome. If a Catholic priest wants to work as a clerical judge, he is required to obtain a licence in Oriental canon law from the Pontifical Oriental Institute in Rome.[13] During this thorough three-year training in canon law the candidate judges are educated in the Eastern Codex, including the extensive regular procedures that need to be followed in any ecclesiastical trial. To verify the hypothesis that the evident procedural attitude of Catholic judges has its origin in their training in Rome would require further research, possibly involving comparative research on other Catholic courts in Syria or the Middle East and research on the place of training, that is, the Faculty of Oriental Canon Law in Rome.

A truly ecclesiastical court?

In accordance with the regulations of the CCEO, the Catholic first instance court of Damascus consisted of three judges,[14] a scribe (*katib*), the 'promoter of justice'[15] (*wakil al-'adl*), and the 'defender of the marital bond' (*al-muhami 'an al-withaq*).[16] As a rule, the 'defender of the marital bond', sitting on the right-hand side of the presiding judge, objected to a nullification request presented to the court, as it was his task to preserve and defend the marital bond.[17] The 'promoter of justice', on the other hand, was responsible for the common good (*al-khayr al-'amm*) and had the authority to ask the court for nullification of a marriage if he thought it was better for a couple to 'divorce' (Arts 313–15, 542 CLPS; Can. 1094–6, 1360 CCEO). For example, when it is established that a husband and wife are in fact brother and sister, it is the responsibility of the 'promoter of justice' to ask for nullification of the marriage. One of the two first instance judges at the Damascus Catholic court, Father Antoun, informed me that in the 15 years that he had been a judge, the 'promoter of justice' had never filed a nullification request to the court.[18] In other words, *butlan* petitions were always filed by a husband or a wife, the litigants.

To recapitulate, the Damascus first instance Catholic court consisted, at least in theory, of six persons. From what I saw, however, the court was only complete when a *butlan* petition was brought before the court for the first time, given that the 'defender of the bond' has to have the opportunity to object to a *butlan* request. The court was also fully staffed when a *butlan* was announced (*i'lan*) and at sessions when the court of appeal gave the final decision (*hukm*) on *butlan* (more on these procedural differences below). During regular sessions, which were the majority of the sessions, the court was never fully staffed; usually only two judges and the scribe would be present.

The court sat on a raised dais behind a long, skirted table (*qaws al-mahkama*). The litigants, for their part, sat behind a table facing the court. Each party had its designated place: the petitioner was seated on the right-hand side of the court, the respondent on the left-hand side, both usually accompanied by their lawyers. As we saw in the previous chapter, the situation in the *shar'iyya* courts was quite different, where lawyers, litigants and witnesses often seemed to be caught up in a fight to try to get the judge's attention.

The rest of the courtroom was occupied by wooden benches on which family members, lawyers, litigants, witnesses and others awaited their turn. The bare white-washed walls were decorated only with a picture of the Syrian President, Bashar al-Assad and a simple wooden crucifix. Each court day commenced with a community prayer led by the presiding judge, facing the crucifix hanging over the court table. Once the court seated itself, everyone else followed suit.

The community prayer was a small but significant example of the specific environment in which the Catholic court operated. The Catholic court came across as a truly ecclesiastical court. There were a number of factors contributing to this observation. First, the fact that the court was situated on the church premises. Second, the judges themselves: in a Catholic court, as in all Christian courts, the judge is a priest. The Catholic judges received their training outside Syria; they were required to obtain a degree in Oriental canon law in Rome. Furthermore, the judges' and court personnel's attire was quite distinctive: the judges were dressed in a cassock (clerical robe), the other court personnel usually wore a clerical collar. Also, whereas a *shar'iyya* judge would be addressed as '*ustadh*' (polite form of address for an educated, respectable person), a Catholic judge preferred to be addressed as '*abuna*' (i.e. 'father'). In fact, litigants or lawyers would be corrected by the judges or the scribe if they used the word '*ustadh*' by mistake. These are just some examples of the external characteristics of the court; when one looks at the substantive aspects of the proceedings and the applicable law, the ecclesiastical nature of the court becomes even more apparent.

The indissolubility of a sacramental marriage

We saw earlier that a Muslim marriage is a contract between the bride and groom, and therefore considered a contractual relationship. A Christian marriage is different from a Muslim one in many ways, most importantly because an Eastern Christian marriage is considered a sacrament (in Arabic: *sirr al-zawaj*). The Code of Canons for the Eastern Churches defines marriage as follows:

> By the marriage covenant [*'ahd al-zawaj*], founded by the Creator and ordered by His laws, a man and woman by irrevocable personal consent establish between themselves a partnership of the whole of life; this covenant is by its very nature ordered to the good of the spouses and to the procreation and education of children. (Can. 776 §1 CCEO)

and:

> By Christ's institution, a valid marriage between baptised persons is by that very fact a sacrament in which the spouses are united by God. (Can. 776 § 2 CCEO)

The fact that marriage is considered a union before God is an essential property of a Christian marriage, therefore dissolving such a union is deemed problematic. Paragraph 3 of Canon 776 explicitly cites 'indissolubility' as another essential property of marriage. Although the Church strongly condemns and discourages it, in reality a marriage can be dissolved but never by divorce. The Catholic Church even renounces the very word 'divorce' (*talaq*) and only acknowledges nullification of a marriage (*butlan al-zawaj*), meaning that the spouses have to prove that the marriage was unsound from the very beginning. Through annulment, a marriage can be terminated but only those marriages that were never valid in the first place because of lack or absence of matrimonial consensus (Can. 817–27 CCEO). In the eyes of the Church such a marriage never legally existed.[19]

It should be noted, however, that the Catholic Church does recognise 'legal separation' (*infisal*),[20] in the event of adultery and mental or physical danger (Can. 863–6 CCEO). It means that an 'innocent spouse' has a right to separation (i.e. he/she will no longer be required to continue conjugal co-habitation) but it will not dissolve the marital bond.

The fact that 'divorce' is a difficult concept in the Catholic Church also becomes apparent from the lengthy proceedings of a *butlan* case. Marriage nullification cases took a long time before a settlement was reached, which might provide an additional discouragement for a couple looking to divorce. The CCEO stipulates that every *butlan* ruling issued by a first instance court has to be affirmed by an appellate tribunal (Can. 1368). Therefore, when the Damascus first instance court concluded that a marriage could be nullified, it 'announced' the nullification. After this announcement (*i'lan*), the nullity decision was transferred to the appellate tribunal for review (Art. 550 CLPS, Can. 1368 CCEO). This court reviewed the case again and when it concluded that indeed the marriage was void, the appeal court would give a *butlan* ruling (*hukm*); only then was the marriage annulled.[21] That is why it generally took at least a year and a half to conclude a case.

The procedure of a *butlan* announcement, as well as a ruling, was accompanied with considerable ceremony. The court was present with its full complement: three judges, the 'promoter of justice', the 'defender of the marital bond', and the scribe. Everyone present in the courtroom (the litigants themselves did not have to be present) stood up when the *butlan* announcement was read out loud. The presiding judge read out the decision: saying 'in the name of the Father, the Son and the Holy Spirit, the court has decided that the marriage between [. . .] is declared void, because [. . .]', thereby stating the reasons for the nullification of the marriage in question. The announcement ended with everyone making the sign of the cross.

Butlan al-zawaj*: nullification of a marriage*

Petitions for nullification of a marriage (*butlan al-zawaj*) made up, by far, the majority of the cases at the Catholic court in Damascus. When husbands filed a case for *butlan*, they commonly presented arguments such as: 'My wife left the marital home to stay with her family without informing me' or 'She does not fulfil her marital or household duties because she is always out of the house.' When a wife leaves the marital home without her husband's consent and this claim is accepted by the court, she will lose her right to maintenance (*nafaqa*). As we saw in the previous chapters, this maintenance–obedience equation is a shared patriarchal norm and laid down in the SLPS as well as Christian personal status laws. In the Catholic court, abandonment by the wife was one of the most commonly heard claims filed by men. Female petitioners, for their part, often presented arguments along the lines of: 'My husband avoids his marital duties because he does not support me financially', 'My husband threw me out of the house and took my money and gold' or 'My husband beats me.'

Strikingly, the petitioners[22] were predominantly male. Of the 86 cases in which I was able to determine the gender of the petitioner/

respondent, the petitioner was male in 54 cases, and 32 times the petitioner was female. This was different from the *shar'iyya* courts and the Greek Orthodox court of Damascus where the majority of the petitioners were female. I can, however, not support this claim with substantive quantitative evidence. This observation is based on personal calculations, from cases I was able to observe while present in the courts, sometimes aided by the clerks of the respective courts, who would fill me in on who the petitioner was in a case that was on trial. The observation that it was predominantly women who brought judicial divorce cases to the *shar'iyya* courts was also supported by lawyers with whom I became acquainted, based on their experience of working in these courts. I have no explanation as to why more men than women filed a *butlan* petition. Possibly it was a question of money, as *butlan* proceedings are long and complicated. Litigants need a lawyer to assist and guide them through the lengthy and complex proceedings. Bearing in mind that the division of labour in Syrian households is generally patriarchal, also among Christians, it means that a husband is usually the breadwinner and a wife the (unpaid) housewife. For that reason it might be difficult for a wife to start (and continue) a *butlan* case, having to pay lawyers' fees that accumulate during the course of the proceedings.

The nullification process began with establishing whether the court accepted a petition for nullification. Then, if the court accepted the petition, it would investigate whether the validity of the marriage was rightfully challenged. Several facts had to be established. To begin with, whether there was indeed – if so alleged by the petitioner – a diriment impediment that rendered the marriage null and void. Canon 790 § 1 reads as follows: 'A diriment impediment renders a person unqualified to celebrate marriage validly', which means that the impediment remains and thus no valid marriage came about. Examples of diriment impediments are: impotence, marriage with a non-baptised person, consanguinity, and affinity (Can. 801, 803, 808, 809 respectively).[23]

The most common ground for contesting the validity of a marriage investigated by the court of Damascus was the claim that there was a defect of matrimonial consent (Can. 817–27). A defective consent implies that one or both parties do not have the necessary knowledge to choose marriage and understand the obligations resulting from the marriage consent. First of all, both parties should be of age and of sound mind upon entering marriage. In addition, they have to have the ability to understand and foresee, and the willingness to take on the essential obligations resulting from a marriage.[24] A couple entering marriage has to understand 'that marriage is an enduring, permanent relationship between a man and a woman, ordered to the procreation of children through some sexual cooperation' (Can. 819). Furthermore, when a person was coerced into marriage or when a marriage is based on a condition, for instance excluding an essential element of marriage such as producing children, this renders a marriage invalid (Can. 825–6). The court also needs to investigate whether the proper form for the celebration of marriage was observed (Can. 828–42), meaning that, for example, an Eastern Catholic marriage has to be celebrated in church in public, not secretly (see below), in the presence of a priest who is authorised to validly bless the marriage, in addition to at least two witnesses.

Reconciliation: return to marital life

In the Catholic court the judges considered it their spiritual duty to seek reconciliation (*musalaha*) between the spouses in order to avoid nullification of a marriage. The Church's focus on reconciliation is a natural one, for marriage is considered a sacrament. As explained earlier, according to the Church, divorce or dissolution contradicts the sacramental nature of marriage and is accordingly difficult to obtain.

Before one or both spouses could file a claim for nullification of the marriage, the couple first had to turn to the local priest (*khuri*) to try to reconcile their differences. Only when no reconciliation could be reached were they able to refer to the court. At every stage of the case, the court would try to reach reconciliation between the spouses,[25] or in the words of a Catholic judge: 'The door to reconciliation remains always open!' ('*bab al-musalahat da'iman maftuh*!')[26]

Canon 1362 CCEO reads:

> Before accepting a case and whenever there seems to be hope of a favorable outcome, a judge is to use pastoral means to induce the spouses, if possible, to convalidate the marriage and restore the partnership of conjugal life.

This duty imposed on the judge is, however, not absolute. When there is no hope of success or when, for example, a permanent psychological defect is the cause for the defective consent, an attempt to save the marriage 'no matter what' would be pointless.[27] Cox in his commentary on the identical Latin canon (Can. 1676) admits that '[n]ormally, when a petition reaches a tribunal, there is little or no reasonable hope of reconciliation.'[28]

Before accepting a *butlan* case, a judge is thus obliged to use pastoral means to persuade the disputing spouses to settle their differences. In the Damascus court, this meant that when a claim for *butlan* was submitted to the court the couple were usually given one to two months to try to reach a reconciliation. If after that period they still had not settled their differences and persisted in their refusal to continue the marriage, the spouses were invited before the court for a reconciliation session. At a *musalaha* session in court, the lawyers, and anyone else present in the courtroom, had to step outside while the court talked to the disputing couple. Fortunately, I was allowed to stay and thus witnessed several *musalaha* sessions being held in the courtroom. For example, I witnessed the following case:

> A young couple entered the courtroom. The wife, Michelle, who appeared to be in her late 20s, had filed a case for nullification of her marriage. Since this was their first appearance in court, the judge wanted to talk to the couple alone without the lawyers present. The couple had been married for somewhat over a year and lived in France until recently. Michelle said that it had become impossible to live together because her husband, Yusuf, only married her to take advantage of her, more precisely her French nationality. Yusuf did not work and depended on her. Yusuf, on the other hand, claimed that Michelle did not want to have children and that there was no marital life to speak of. The judge asked Michelle whether this was true, whether she wanted to have children or not. She replied that she wanted to have children but not with him. Michelle refused reconciliation, she thought that it was impossible to continue this marriage and she said that continuation would be unfair to both parties. This answer upset the judge and he asked her angrily, 'Do you think marriage is a game? You married in a Catholic church, under God's eyes, in His house.' The judge reminded her that there had to be an 'essential' reason for *butlan*, otherwise the court could not and would not

> nullify the marriage. Therefore it was better for them to reconcile their differences and make the marriage work; the judge told them to 'invoke the Lord and reconcile!' Michelle and Yusuf, however, persisted in their claim. The lawyers were summoned back to the courtroom and the judge informed them that the court had tried to persuade the couple to drop their claim, but to no avail.[29]

Musalaha sessions in the courtroom generally did not last very long, usually around ten minutes. If the court saw an opportunity for actual reconciliation the couple was told to go (back) to their priest and try to settle their differences with his help and the help of family and friends. The court seemed to really put their backs into it when it concerned young couples. When young couples appeared in the courtroom, the judges tended to speak to them in a moralistic preachy tone. They would, for example, remind the spouses they got married in a church, in God's House, as we saw in the reconciliation session of Michelle and Yusuf. If the court got the impression the couple had not tried hard enough to make the marriage work, they would be told to seek counselling with their local priest first and try to get their marriage back on track. Occasionally, the court suggested conducting additional (one-on-one or joint) reconciliation outside the court office hours; a couple (or separately) would then meet with the judges in the judge's office on another day.

As we saw in the previous chapter, many marital disputes in Syria have increasingly been taken to court, among all religious groups.[30] Despite the principle of the indissolubility of marriage, marriage nullity cases form the vast majority of Catholic court trials, not only in Syria but worldwide.[31] During my time in Damascus, I was told that the number of couples seeking divorce or annulment had gone up in the last decades, both in the Orthodox and Catholic communities. I observed that nowadays couples filing for divorce are primarily young, which appears to be a widespread phenomenon in many personal status courts. While this observation cannot be supported by quantitative evidence, the trend was also observed by various legal practitioners with whom I interacted during my fieldwork in Damascus. For instance, during one of Michelle and Yusuf's interrogation sessions I had to wait in the court's registry (the *diwan*). Earlier I had been told that the number of *butlan* petitions increased rapidly over the last decade. I asked the Registrar what he thought the reason was for the recent increase in *butlan* cases. He explained that nowadays many wives have a job and no longer depended on their husbands. Besides, he added, these days newlyweds did not try hard enough to make the marriage work: 'Many women are not like our mothers who stayed at home and were more tolerant towards their husbands.'[32] A senior female lawyer had told me earlier that the families of the spouses are equally to blame, because they often worsened the disagreements between the husband and the wife (see examples below).[33]

During the various stages of Michelle and Yusuf's case, as in all cases presented in the Damascus Catholic court, the court repeatedly emphasised the importance of preserving or restoring the marital bond. One could argue that the lengthy procedures kept this hope of reconciliation alive. However, when the court tried but could not see any hope for reconciliation, the petition would be accepted, provided a ground for nullity had been established. Once the petition was accepted, the nullification process was taken to the next level.

Collection of proof

When the petition (*'arida*) was accepted by the court, the petitioner would have to bring forth proof establishing his/her claim of nullity. However, it is also the court's task to gather and assess evidence to investigate whether the assertion of nullity is a fact.[34] First of all, the Damascus court would interrogate both spouses on the facts of the case in a joint session (*jalsat istijwab*).[35] The court questioned them on how they met, about their engagement period, how they got married, about their marital life and, most importantly, what the reasons were for their disagreement (*khilaf*).

In Michelle and Yusuf's case (see above), the questioning of spouses took place shortly after the reconciliation session in court.

> Four days later, Michelle and Yusuf were back for questioning by the court. Both took an oath on the Bible before the court started with the actual questioning. Michelle (being the petitioner) was the first party to be interrogated. The judge asked her how they met and about their engagement. She answered that they met in church and that they got married after seven months. When the

judge asked about the reason for the disagreement between them, she said that Yusuf was very jealous and a trouble-maker. Michelle stated that he hit her, called her names, kicked her out of their house, and asked her father to pay for several household goods, such as a washing machine and a refrigerator. She was afraid of Yusuf and said he always caused trouble; for example, he went to her workplace and created problems there with his jealous behaviour. At this point Michelle indicated to the court that she would like to continue without any outsiders present in the courtroom, therefore a trainee lawyer and I were asked to leave the courtroom. The session continued for about an hour.[36]

Some four weeks later, Michelle and Yusuf were back in court and the questioning continued. This time I was allowed to remain during the questioning. Michelle's main complaint was that Yusuf did not work and that he squandered her own and her father's money. She said that, in retrospect, they married too fast because she had to travel back to France, where she lived at the time. Yusuf joined her in France but never made a serious attempt to settle down there. After a month he went back to Syria. She followed him back to Syria, meaning she had to give up her job in France.

Yusuf, when questioned, said that they did not have a good marriage, partly because of the influence of his father-in-law. Indeed, a month later while being questioned as a witness, Michelle's father acknowledged that he had been against the marriage from the very beginning, fearing that Yusuf was only interested in his daughter's French nationality and her (family's) money, and that he did not want to work. Yusuf, when asked by the court, admitted that the main reason why he married Michelle was because of her French nationality and the fact that she had a job in France. Both spouses declared that there was no hope of reconciliation between them. Although the court continued throughout each session to underline the importance of reconciliation, it appeared in this case to have acknowledged that there was no more hope of saving this marriage (i.e. its validity was rightfully challenged). The judge warned Yusuf not to make the same mistake again, that is, to get married for the wrong reasons.[37]

Another example of an interrogation of spouses in a joint session:

> Samir, a young man in his 30s, filed a case requesting the court to nullify his marriage because his wife, Muna, concealed her illness from him before they got married. In this session both spouses were heard by the court. After both spouses were sworn in, Samir (being the petitioner) was the first being questioned by the court. The court started by asking what his denomination was and if he went to church to pray. The husband answered he was Catholic and that he went to church almost every Sunday. Asked what kind of profession he had, he answered he worked in a restaurant in Lebanon. The judge asked him where he had met Muna and when he had proposed to her. Samir answered that he met Muna in her father's shop in the countryside. He asked her to marry him after three months, but they were never engaged because they had married secretly. When the judge asked about the reason for the disagreement between them, he said that Muna never stayed home. She always went out and she was sick, she had epilepsy and this influenced her mind. Samir had stated in his petition that Muna lied to him before the marriage because she concealed her disease from him. The judge asked him to elucidate on the allegations before the court. Samir explained that she did not tell him about the disease before the marriage. He only discovered it later on when they travelled to Lebanon and he saw her medications. He then took her to a doctor who told him Muna was epileptic. The judge concluded his questioning by asking if there was still hope for reconciliation; Samir said there was not. Samir's lawyer was allowed to question his client. He asked how many times they had met before the marriage; Samir answered that they had met three or four times, and that Muna's father had objected to the marriage. His lawyer asked if her disease affected her household duties. Samir reacted strongly, saying: 'Of course! The illness has an effect on her duties, because she is very slow. If she wants to make *tabbouleh*,[38] she needs three hours! If I would have known she was sick, I would not have married her.' The judge finally asked him where they used to meet before they got married; he said that they used to meet each other in her grandmother's house. The grandmother had only

> told him indirectly about Muna's illness by telling him to be patient with her.
>
> The line of questioning of Muna was more or less the same. The differences in her answers lay in the reason of their disagreement. Muna claimed that Samir did not give her any money, just SYP 1,000 (roughly €15) per month, and that he did not buy her the medication she needed for her illness. She added that he did not provide a good marital house to live in and that he took her gold and sold it. She denied Samir's allegations that she hid her disease from him. Muna stated that her sister and her friends informed him about her disease and that she could support her claim by bringing witnesses to the court. She said that Samir told her before they married that he wanted to marry her even if she was sick, even if she had cancer he still wanted to marry her. Like Samir, Muna saw no possibility of reconciliation.[39]

In addition to their own statements, the parties are required to deliver evidence to the court to support their claims. The court or parties may seek assistance from a professional expert, a *khabir*, such as doctors and psychiatrists.[40] In the above-mentioned case Muna was examined by two doctors appointed by the court to determine the severity of her illness.[41] The petitioner had to cover the costs of a medical expert's opinion (3,000 SP).

The most important source of information for the court, however, was witness statements. The petitioner was required to produce witnesses to support his/her case; the respondent could do the same but was not obliged to do so. The court prefer to hear witnesses who know (and knew) the parties well, particularly during their courtship, betrothal and the wedding day itself. For instance in the above-mentioned case, Samir and Muna had to bring witnesses to the court to prove that Samir was (or was not) informed about Muna's illness.[42] As I mentioned earlier, it is during these witness examinations that the attachment to patriarchal gender norms clearly manifested itself. In the following paragraphs, several cases will be described demonstrating that shared patriarchal norms and views on social propriety, marriage and family, such as the obedience of women and upholding the family honour, are greatly valued, also in the Catholic courtroom.

Witness statements

In what is known as a witness hearing (*jalsat istima' li-l-shuhud*), the court tried to get an idea of the seriousness of the disagreement between the spouses, the circumstances leading up to the marriage (i.e. the circumstances and length of courtship and betrothal), the wedding day, marital life itself, and so on. The line of questioning was, by and large, always the same. The hearing focused on the reason for the disagreement (*khilaf*). The witnesses were asked to share their thoughts and opinions on this issue with the court, preferably illustrated by examples. In a case where the wife was accused of not being a good housewife, the court asked whether she fulfilled her household duties and whether the witness could attest to her negligence (or diligence). For example, did the house look clean when the witness visited the house? Did the wife serve him/her coffee? Besides the more trivial questions, the court also asked more personal/intimate questions regarding the couple's life. For example, why did they not have any children? Was it because he/she did not want them or was there perhaps a physical problem? And if there was a medical problem, had they seen a doctor?

Anyone questioned by the court had first to identify him or herself. A litigant/witness gave his/her ID card to the scribe, who copied the personal particulars into the file. Subsequently, the judge asked the interviewee for his/her name, religion, denomination, profession and – in the case of a witness – his/her relation to the petitioner/respondent, and whether he/she was involved in a lawsuit with one of the litigants. It is interesting to note that the Catholic court always asked the litigants and witnesses to which religious denomination (*ta'ifa*) they belonged and if they went to church to pray, regardless of their religion, that is, Christians and Muslims (witnesses) alike. I never observed a *shar'iyya* or Greek Orthodox judge who took any profound interest in someone's denomination, church attendance or prayer habits, in relation to being a witness.

Anyone being heard by the court was sworn in before testifying by taking an oath on the Bible or the Qur'an, depending on their respective religion.[43] No difference was made between litigants or witnesses – they both had to take the oath, unlike the *shar'iyya* courts where only witnesses were required to swear an oath.[44] On a few occasions I saw Muslim witnesses taking the stand, usually neighbours, colleagues or friends of either the petitioner or the respondent. However, the majority were Christian, generally family members: fathers, mothers, siblings, grandparents, aunts and uncles, cousins, but also neighbours, colleagues and friends. For instance, in the case of Michelle and Yusuf, Michelle (petitioner) presented five witnesses to support her claim.

> The first witness she presented to the court was her father. As mentioned earlier, he said he had been against the marriage from the very beginning, fearing that Yusuf was only interested in his daughter's French nationality and her (family's) money, and that Yusuf did not want to work. In addition, he testified that the relationship was good before they got married but that as soon as they married Yusuf changed completely. The second witness was a friend of Yusuf, who attested to the court that Yusuf told him he only wanted to marry Michelle because he was interested in travelling and obtaining French citizenship. The third witness was a friend of Michelle; she also stated that the relationship between the couple changed as soon as they got married. She told the court that Yusuf changed his behaviour shortly after the wedding. According to the witness, it was clear from the beginning that the spouses were socially very different. Witness number four was a young Muslim woman, a friend of Michelle. Her testimony corresponded to the previous three witnesses; she also testified that everything was fine before the wedding and that Yusuf changed afterwards. She said he did not work, that he was lazy and did not do anything in the house, instead he slept most of the day. The final witness was a young woman, also a friend of Michelle, who testified that she had heard that Yusuf had told a friend that he did not love Michelle (even before the wedding) and that he only married her because of her French nationality and because she came from a wealthy family.[45]

When there were several witnesses taking the stand in the same case, only one witness was allowed in the courtroom; other witnesses had to wait their turn outside.[46] The procedures concerning witness examinations correspond to what we saw in the previous chapter, namely the proceedings in the *shar'iyya* courts. This makes sense as all personal status court follow the same national procedural and evidence law.

According to the CCEO, the spouses cannot be present at the questioning of witnesses, unless the judge allows them to be present (Art. 425 CLPS, Can. 1240 CCEO).[47] Nevertheless, sometimes one or both spouses would be present, in addition to their lawyers who were always present. More than that, occasionally the spouses would comment on the witness testimonies, sometimes leading to heated discussions or emotional outbursts, either by the spouses or the witnesses, as in this example where a husband (petitioner) undermined the statements of the witnesses he presented to the court to support his claim.

> The wife (respondent) was accused of having left the house, without her husband's permission, to stay with her family. In addition, he alleged, she did not want to have children and had taken precautions to avoid pregnancy. The witnesses were unable to back the husband's allegations with strong evidence. After the witnesses had their say in the matter, the wife got the opportunity to ask them questions. The judge insisted she asked her questions via the judge, not directly to the witnesses.[48] She then asked the first witness (related to the husband *and* the wife) whether he knew that her husband hit her. The witness, a middle-aged man in his 50s, said he did not know. She asked him 'Don't you remember when we met in the street and my face was bruised and I had a blue eye?' Again he said he did not remember. Whereupon the husband responded in an irritated tone: 'Yes, I beat her!', as if he wanted to get it over and done with.[49]

Marital rights and duties

In the various Syrian communities, similar to other Middle Eastern communities, the family and marital structures are generally patriarchal (see Chapter 4). As a rule, the husband is the breadwinner and the wife stays at home to take care of the house and children, whether she has a job or not. Patriarchal gender roles, values and expectations of what is right and proper spousal behaviour were constantly expressed, acknowledged and reinforced in the Catholic courts. Furthermore, witnesses presented to court by the litigants often stressed the moral character of the plaintiff/defendant, for example whether he/she is a good man/woman, husband/wife, father/mother, and so on. However, it is important to bear in mind that the witnesses' – and with that the court's – assessment of the litigants' performance as husband or wife was often also strategically guided by their lawyers. They prepared their litigants and witnesses before they were interrogated by the court, making sure their clients came across as a good wife or husband.

In the examination of witnesses, considerable attention was given to the marital roles at stake. An example of a case in which views on what constituted (im)proper spousal behaviour on account of the wife was clearly expressed in the following witness statements. In this court session, three witnesses were presented to the court by the petitioner (the husband, hereafter called Michel), who was in his late 30s. Michel was married to Sawsan, who was about 15 years his junior.

> The first witness was the mother of Michel, an elderly woman originally from Iraq. The court's first question (as usual) was what the witness thought the reason for the disagreement between the spouses was. The witness said the problems started shortly after the marriage; Sawsan did not fulfil her household duties or her marital duties (*wajibat manziliyya wa wajibat zawjiyya*) and she always quarrelled in a loud voice, in the presence of the neighbours. The judge asked what the witness meant by marital duties, whether she referred to sexual relations between the spouses. She simply responded by saying that she (Sawsan) was not close to him. As for her household duties, the witness explained that the couple lived with them, his parents. Therefore she knew for a fact that Sawsan did not cook and that she refused to learn how. The court asked whether the wife had left the house without informing her husband. The witness answered in the affirmative and said that Sawsan occasionally left the house at 9 a.m. only to return around midnight. She went on to say: 'Once she left the house and locked the door. When my son returned from work, he could not enter his house. He had to sleep at our [his parents'] house [the couple's residence was the upstairs part of the house; the parents lived downstairs in the same building]. When I asked her why she had done that, she replied "It is my house!" While he pays everything for her! She just buys many things, we do not know where she gets the money from.' The witness continued by saying that the last time Sawsan left, she went with her father and

youngest brother and took all her gold with her. The judge asked where the wife was at the moment; the witness said she was with her family. The judge asked the witness whether she knew if the wife wanted to return to the conjugal home; she replied that there had been several reconciliation sessions in church and in court. After the last reconciliation in court, Sawsan called the police[50] in the evening and told Michel she wanted to divorce him.

The second witness was an elderly man, the father of Michel. The court asked him for the reason for the disagreement. He answered that during the first 20 days of the marriage Sawsan's behaviour had been exemplary but that then she had started to spread bad rumours about Michel and his family. According to the witness, Sawsan had absolutely no respect for her husband. Michel (his son) was a good man, a person with high moral character. She, on the other hand, was the opposite: she was an ill-natured woman. The lawyer of the husband agreed with the witness and added: 'He really is a very kind man, everyone likes Michel!' The judge continued to question the witness and asked if the wife fulfilled her household duties. He answered that she did not, because she did not cook nor clean: 'She does not know how to be a good wife – she serves cold coffee!' The judge asked who did the grocery shopping. The witness said his wife and his daughter usually did it; Sawsan rarely helped around the house. The court pursued the question of abandonment by the wife and asked whether she had left the house of her own accord. The witness replied in an ironic tone: 'Ah! She is a woman of importance!' After which he told the same story as his wife (the first witness), about how Sawsan had left the house, locked it (thereby shutting her husband out of the house) and forcing him to spend the night with his parents. The judge asked about the last time she had left the house; the witness explained how Sawsan left the house with her mother and sisters, taking all of her gold with her. The court asked whether there was a possibility of reconciliation (*musalaha*). The witness did not think there was much hope because Sawsan always said 'I do not want to return.' She wanted to divorce him; she already started saying this after two and a half months of marriage. Michel's lawyer asked the witness whether any reconciliation attempts had taken place. He answered that a priest had come to their house with some other people to try and reconcile the couple: 'We have tried *musalaha* but we failed.' The lawyer asked what else happened on that day, the witness related how in the evening Sawsan came back with the police; they came to collect her belongings. Finally, Sawsan's lawyer asked the witness about their engagement period, and the witness explained that Michel's family had made inquiries about Sawsan before the wedding among her family members, in particular her mother and siblings. Everything seemed perfectly normal; she changed about ten days after the wedding.

The third witness was a woman in her 40s; she was Michel's sister. Broadly speaking, she told the same story as her parents. Sawsan did not fulfil her household duties; she did not cook or clean. According to the sister, Sawsan was lazy; when she was at home she watched TV, and she refused to help around the house.[51]

When a wife was accused of not fulfilling her marital duties, the witness' questioning usually focused on her role as a housewife. What did the witness see when he/she visited the marital house? Examples of domestic negligence heard in the Damascus court included the following: 'The house was not clean', 'She is always out', 'She does not cook, she buys food from the market', 'She does not serve coffee or tea' or 'She serves cold coffee'. When a husband allegedly failed to fulfil his marital duties, the accusations were usually more serious: 'He beats his wife', 'He expelled her from the marital home', 'He has a (unlawful) relationship with another woman', 'He refuses to financially support her' or 'After she had an operation in hospital, he never inquired after her health and simply ignored her'. This latter statement was given by a witness in a case where the husband (hereafter called Firas) had filed a *butlan* case claiming his wife, Miryam, had left the house without his permission. In this session the respondent, Miryam, presented her witnesses to the court, five in total; they were all family members, including siblings and her mother. Miryam was present the entire time.

All witnesses stressed that Miryam was an exemplary wife, as opposed to Firas who they all depicted as a bad person who treated

> his wife badly. They stated that when they visited the couple the house always looked clean, as Miryam kept the house clean, she did the grocery shopping, prepared food, and did all that is expected of a wife. It appeared that Miryam had some medical problems and had to go to hospital because she needed surgical treatment for a prolapsed uterus. After the surgery she went to stay with her family and – to make matters worse – Firas had told Miryam's mother he did not want her daughter as a wife. Miryam stayed with her family for more than a month and not once did he ask how she was. Miryam's sister-in-law testified she met Firas in the *servees* (minibus) after she had returned to the marital home and she asked him how Miryam was doing; he said he did not know. The sister-in-law went to see Miryam the same day to help her in the house and Firas just sat there, completely indifferent, doing nothing. Besides, he refused to give her money, money she needed for the household, but also money to pay for her medical expenses. According to one of Miryam's sisters, Firas had told her (the sister) last time she saw him in court that he was not going to give Miryam any money.

That was why Miryam's lawyer asked the court to impose alimony obligations on Firas during the pendency of the *butlan* proceedings, what is known as interim maintenance (*nafaqa musta'jala*). A petition for interim maintenance could be decided upon immediately and would become payable from the date the *butlan* case was presented to court. Interim maintenance may include: child support, payment of school fees, spousal support, housekeeping allowance, and so on.[52] As a matter of fact, both husband and wife can file a petition for *nafaqa* to the court, depending on who the petitioner is, and the litigants' financial and other relevant circumstances.[53]

Miryam's lawyer asked the court to impose an overdue *nafaqa* payment of 20,000 SP, to be paid by Firas a week later. Firas' lawyer objected, but to no avail, for the court granted Miryam's request. What was remarkable in this case was that the presiding judge made no secret of his opinion. After the witnesses' statements he said 'This is not normal, he did not visit her after the surgery at her family's house. She is his wife. Three months she stayed with her family and he did not inquire after her – that is just unheard of! [*ma bisir*!]'[54]

Spousal maintenance versus obedience of the wife

Chapter 4 described the regulation of marital rights and duties according to the SLPS and the main Christian laws of personal status. When we look at Catholic canon law, we see that the maintenance–obedience equation is also clearly laid down in the CLPS.

Article 38 of the CLPS states that all Eastern Catholics are subject to the provisions of the CCEO pertaining to marriage and the dissolution thereof. According to the CCEO, the marriage covenant 'is by its very nature ordered to the good of the spouses and to the procreation and education of children' (Can. 776). Canon 777 reads '[o]ut of marriage arise equal rights and obligations between the spouses regarding what pertains to the partnership of conjugal life.' But what exactly are these rights and obligations?

The CCEO does not provide a definition of 'spousal rights and obligations'. According to Pospishil, they are determined by doctrinal writings and canonical jurisprudence.[55] Although the CLPS, similar to the CCEO, does not elaborate on the concept of marital obligations in general, it does pay considerable attention to the issue of maintenance between the spouses (Arts 121–33). The husband has to provide financially for his wife and family from the time a valid marriage is concluded (Art. 121). The maintenance (*nafaqa*) obligation includes food, clothing, housing and medical care (Arts 107–8 CLPS). The wife, for her part, is obliged to co-habit with her husband in the marital house (Art. 125).[56] If, however, she leaves the marital house without a valid reason, she is considered disobedient (*nashiza*) and she consequently loses her right to maintenance (Art. 127). She is also considered disobedient when she prevents her husband from entering her house or when she refuses to move with him to a new house, provided she does so without any valid reason (Art. 127.2). A wife who has been found guilty of marital disobedience or abandonment cannot claim maintenance for as long as the period of abandonment continues (Art. 128 CLPS). In exceptional cases, a disobedient wife can be ordered to pay maintenance to her husband to compensate for damages she caused by leaving the conjugal house, but only when the wife is well-off (Art. 129 CLPS). Thus, similarly to the SLPS and other Christian personal status laws, the wife's right to marital maintenance is made conditional upon her behaviour and co-habitation.

Similarly, the concept of marital obedience, that is, the obedience of the wife, is found in Muslim and Christian communities and laws alike.

Akin to the SLPS, the Catholic law also 'punishes' a wife for leaving the marital home of her own accord: for when she leaves the house, she loses her right to *nafaqa* (Art. 74 SLPS, Art. 127 CLPS). Similar to proceedings at the *shar'iyya* courts, a Catholic husband can go to court to file a claim requiring the wife to return to the marital home, that is, a claim for marital obedience (*da'wa al-mutaba'a*) (see also the case study below). When the court receives such a claim, it will have to investigate whether the wife has in fact left the house and what the reasons for the abandonment are.[57] Questions that need answering are: Did the wife leave the house on her own initiative or was she ejected from the house by her husband? Was and/or is she willing to return to the house voluntarily? If not, why does she refuse to return to her husband's house?

To determine whether the wife was really disobedient, witness statements (again) were crucial, preferably coming from relatives and others who knew and interacted with the spouses regularly, for example neighbours. An example: on a hot day in June, George presented three witnesses to the court to support his claim that his wife Hind was disobedient. The three witnesses were all male and appeared to be somewhere between the ages of 35 and 45. Besides the litigants' lawyers, Hind was also present. However, she had to step outside the courtroom as soon as the witness examinations began.

> The court asked the first witness, a friend of George, to give his account of the reason why the couple was in disagreement with each other. He explained they were often at variance with each other and that Hind had left the conjugal house. The witness said George told him that his wife was disobedient (*nashiza*). He went on telling a tangled story about Hind being a woman of questionable morals. The judge was visibly annoyed with this garrulous witness; he cut him short and dictated to the clerk: 'There are several reasons for the disagreement between the spouses but I do not know what the main reason is.' The court asked whether the wife left the house of her own accord or whether the husband expelled her from the conjugal house. The witnesses related that Hind left the house and went to the village of Marmarita to stay with her family. The judge asked him who had told him this. He explained that he happened to be at their house when Hind phoned her husband to tell him she had gone

to her family in Marmarita. Later she returned to the marital home, accompanied by a friend, to collect her belongings and other goods, such as cooking utensils. The judge inquired whether the wife fulfilled her marital duties [*wajibat zawjiyya*]. The witness started rattling away about Hind and failed to give a direct answer to the court. Again the judge cut him short and asked him: 'He said she does not want children, is that true?' The witness answered by saying he did not know, George did not tell him anything about that. The questioning by the court continued but the answers did not seem to satisfy the court or the lawyers. Occasionally, the lawyers objected to the statements of the witness, leading to counter-objections against each other, much to the anger of the judge: 'I am in charge here, you talk to me, not to each other!'

The second witness, a neighbour and friend of George, was able to give a more satisfying statement. The witness told the court that Hind had no respect for her husband. In answer to the court's question of whether she had deserted the conjugal house alone or with her husband, he replied that George told him that Hind had left the house alone. The judge asked whether he thought she wanted to continue with the marriage, he answered in the negative: 'No, of course not'. He added that her behaviour as a married woman was generally disrespectful. One evening he saw Hind out on the street with another man. He said that it was inappropriate for a married woman to be seen with another man in public. Furthermore, whenever George and Hind had an argument, she would leave the house, not to go her family but to outsiders. Again, the witness thought this was inappropriate because she should go to her family instead, who would help her to reconcile with her husband. He said he visited the couple only once; however, he saw her often – that is to say – he saw her out on the street. He was therefore not surprised to hear that George managed to obtain a performance claim for marital obedience [*tanfidh al-mutaba'a*]. Finally, the judge asked whether – to his knowledge – the wife wanted to have children. The witness said she already had a child from a previous marriage. He thought she did not want to have more children. According to the witness, George tried to reconcile with Hind but she refused.

> The third witness was also a neighbor; he lived in the same district [*hara*]. He gave a rather brief testimony, mainly because he either could not answer the questions of the court or because his knowledge was only based on hearsay.[58]

Earlier, I discussed the concepts of 'morality', 'propriety' and 'family honour and women's sexuality' in relation to (in particular) spousal and parental behaviour of litigants. The case described above is a good example of expression of norms and views on (im)proper spousal behaviour: ideas about improper spousal behaviour on account of the wife were clearly expressed by the witnesses, especially by the second witness. His moral assessment of Hind's conduct was clear: a married woman should not interact with unrelated men in public; when a couple has an argument, they should turn to their families for help in resolving their differences, and so on. Here we see that the assessment of a person's character and/or behaviour is indeed based on daily interactions. Hind did not live up to the domestic ideal of a housewife because she deserted her husband and the conjugal house, and she 'mixed and mingled' with men in public. As explained earlier, a woman's sexuality is closely connected to the good name and reputation of her family. As marriage is considered the only place for licit sexual relations, a wife's sexuality is obviously directly connected to that of her husband. Muslim and Christian women alike are expected to keep in line with social decorum and behave modestly and self-effacingly and not embarrass their husbands and families by mingling with men in public.

Unconventional marriage practices

One day I witnessed a rather peculiar case, as the husband claimed that he discovered (six months into the marriage) that his wife had been married before. But what made the case so peculiar was that he heard his wife had 'contracted' a so-called *zawaj 'urfi masihi*. Marrying the *'urfi* way (i.e. informal or traditional) meant – in this case – that the marriage was not celebrated in the church and therefore also not registered at the Church or the Civil Registry. The judges were visibly surprised when they heard the husband's claims. Their reaction of amazement is understandable since the Church does not recognise such marriages.

A valid Christian marriage has to be publicly celebrated in a church, blessed by a priest (Can. 828, 838 CCEO).[59]

The phenomenon of *'urfi* marriage was already discussed in the previous chapter in relation to Muslim marriage practices. What is striking here is that the phenomenon also seems to occur among Christians, which is unusual because it is contrary to Christian doctrine. A possible explanation is that Christian communities in Syria and Lebanon have become acquainted with Muslim *'urfi* marriage practices, especially in those areas where Christians and Muslims live together, but whether these practices are actually copied by Christians is questionable. However, since the wife in this case was a Lebanese Christian from Shtura, a city close to the Syrian–Lebanese border in the Beqaa' valley, where the majority of the population is mostly Shi'ite and Christian, her alleged marriage might have been the outcome of interactions between the various religious communities. Whether or not she actually had been married and to whom, remained unclear.

In the session I witnessed, the couple (a young couple who lived in Lebanon) had come to court for a *musalaha* session. Interestingly, the reconciliation session lasted for about five minutes with lawyers still present in the courtroom; afterwards the court took a short break and went straight on with the cross-examination of the spouses.

> According to the husband, after he pressed his wife for an explanation, she admitted to him that she had concluded a *zawaj 'urfi masihi* with a man called Ibrahim. The husband said that after the discovery she left the house and took all her belongings, including her gold, and went to her family. The wife's lawyer asked the husband – with due suspicion – who had told him about this marriage, what was the religion of these individuals? He said he did not know. When questioned by the court, the wife strongly denied all allegations. She swore on the Bible, in the name of God and Jesus, that it was not true. Upon which the judge warned her not to use these words lightly because in the end she had to answer to God, not to them (i.e. the court). In her view, his family constantly gossiped about her, from the first day of their marriage they started spreading rumours about her. She said she loved her husband, that he was a good man but that his family was toxic.

Despite the fact that she loved him, she also believed that reconciliation was no longer possible.[60]

During my time in the Catholic court I heard of one other case where a man claimed he married his second wife the *'urfi* way, a marriage he wanted to have annulled. When I asked his lawyer about this case, he told me not to take his client seriously. According to him, his client did not know what he was talking about, because being married to two women at the same time is not possible for Christians. Besides, the lawyer added, the husband had filed a *butlan* petition, yet now regretted it and wanted his wife back.[61]

Such alleged wedding practices are, admittedly, probably rare. Unfortunately, I have not had the opportunity to follow up on this matter. It would be interesting to find out if such informal marriages are in fact contracted (or 'celebrated') among Christians and, more likely, between Christians and Muslims. The examples described above aim to demonstrate that the various communities do not live in a vacuum but that they cross-pollinate with each other. The Muslim and Christian communities are different in many ways but also have a shared historical and cultural heritage, from which the shared patriarchal norms and values (and possibly practices) emerge.

Conclusion

The peculiarities of each (religious) group, each with their own personal status law and court, is what makes the Syrian plural legal landscape so fascinating. This chapter was aimed at revealing some of the particularities of a Catholic court in Damascus. Due to their strong relationship with Rome, the Catholic courts were quite distinctive, when compared to the other personal status courts. The first part of this chapter sought to demonstrate that it is exactly this alliance to Rome that distinguished the Catholic court from the other courts.

The Syrian Catholic personal status law is predominantly based on Oriental canon law issued by Rome. The Catholic view on marriage and divorce is different from other (also Christian) laws. The Catholic Church does not accept divorce because it considers marriage a sacrament, which cannot be dissolved by men. A marriage can be annulled but only when it is proven that it was null or invalid from the very beginning. Furthermore, the Catholic judges of Damascus received their training in canon law at Pontifical colleges in Rome. Catholic priests who want to work as clerical judges are required to go through an intensive three years of training in (Eastern) canon law and the extensive regular procedures that need to be followed at any ecclesiastical trial. It was argued that, because of their canonical training in Rome, the judges of the Catholic court of Damascus took a much weightier and more formal stand in their handling of annulment petitions than their colleagues of the other personal status courts. In my view, the court proceedings I observed in Damascus were affected by both the canonical legislation and educational background of the judges.

The Catholic courts might have been different from their Christian and Muslim counterparts in some regards; they also shared some key similarities with other personal status courts, namely the prevalence of patriarchal family norms and values. This chapter has demonstrated that views on traditional marital roles, marital rights and duties were repeatedly emphasised and reinforced by the different actors appearing in the legal arena. The argument that patriarchal views and norms of social propriety, marriage and family were continuously emphasised and reinforced in the personal status courts became especially apparent in the marriage nullification (*butlan*) proceedings. During these proceedings in the Catholic courts of Damascus, the marital roles in question were thoroughly examined, relying on (in particular) oral statements from the litigants themselves but also witnesses. It was during witness examinations in particular that patriarchal norms and views on marital life came to the fore.

CONCLUSIONS

This book focused on the various manifestations of legal plurality that characterised – both historical and contemporary – family or personal status law in Syria. This research has not only demonstrated that Syrian family law was characterised by its inherent legal plurality, as the legal system allowed for a multiplicity of religiously based personal status laws and courts to operate simultaneously, but has also shown that Syrian family relations were – in addition to statutory laws – also governed by other (i.e. non-state) 'forms of normative ordering'.[1] One example of another 'form of normative ordering' was, as the example of the young couple in the Greek Orthodox court of Damascus (with which the introduction of this book started) showed, the patriarchal norms and values on gender, family and marital relations that were shared across the different religious communities. In my view, these shared norms were as salient a feature of Syria's family law as legal plurality.

Syrian communities that were united in their attachment to shared patriarchal norms and values may sound, given the violent civil war that has ravaged the country since 2011, like a utopia of the past. However, even though the situation in Syria has changed dramatically since this research was carried out (2007–12), this study has made a substantial contribution to understanding the historical, socio-political and religious complexities that have not only shaped Syria's personal status law, but also marked the present situation in which Syria finds itself. How this historical and socio-political context has shaped the plural landscape of Syria's personal status law will, amongst others, be described in what follows.

Syria's pluralistic personal status law: the origins

Legal plurality has always been present in Syria. It was partly inherited from earlier, predecessor dynasties and rulers; in particular, the political and legal system of the Ottomans was foundational to Syria's legal system. The Islamic Ottoman Empire, like Syria today, was a multi-religious state, with Muslim and non-Muslim citizens. Non-Muslim Ottoman citizens were guaranteed certain privileges under the so-called *millet* system, meaning that the religious or confessional communities (*millets*) enjoyed the right to apply their own religious laws in matters of personal status, most importantly marriage and divorce. From the late 1800s onwards the Ottoman political and legal system underwent a series of significant reforms (*Tanzimat*), heavily influenced by European political and legal traditions. However, the separate status of Muslims and non-Muslims in family law continued to exist. The Ottoman *millet* system laid the foundation for Syria's contemporary plural legal system, which is characterised by a mix of Ottoman, Egyptian, European-styled civil laws (mostly French in origin), and a broad variety of religious – or religiously based – laws.

This plural legal system was maintained and reinforced by the French during the Mandate period (1920–46) as part of their divide-and-rule politics. The subsequent post-independence Syrian governments, including the al-Asad regime, also kept the system in place, often dictated by political motives. Inspired by the then popular ideologies of secularism, socialism and Arab nationalism, the latter governments tried to nationalise and centralise the legal system but they failed to do so in the field of family law due to conservative religious opposition. Secularism and religious diversity were important ideologies for the regime to support, yet difficult to uphold due to its contested political legitimacy. The government has been engaged in a delicate balancing act of, on the one hand, upholding its official secular discourse and policies, and on the other hand, maintaining the status quo and appeasing, most importantly, a significant segment of its conservative Sunni Muslim citizens.

The politics of legal plurality

From its coming to power in 1963, Syria's Ba'th Party has had a troublesome relationship with Islam, in particular with some segments of the Sunni population. The political and religious legitimacy of the 'Alawi-dominated minority regime has been challenged from the very beginning, which forced the regime to try continuously to find a balance between religion and politics. The government's secular ideology proved difficult to uphold; such difficulty included the area of family law. History showed that both the Sunni majority and the various Christian minorities were often ill-disposed towards far-reaching government interference in the domain of family affairs.

During the last decade (2000–10), several proposed changes and reforms in the domain of family law were also, similar to Ottoman and French times, met with significant controversy, primarily because government interference in personal status matters was considered an infringement on (the already limited) sovereignty of the different religious groups. The post-independence state had maintained the Ottoman-inherited family legal system, delegating part of its legislative and judicial power in the area of family law to patriarchal religious clerics and with that family matters entered 'into the domain of non-negotiable sacred religion'.[2] The religious establishments, for their part, supported this legal plurality because it allowed them – within the boundaries of the state – to administer their own affairs in their respective communities.

Furthermore, the Syrian government, being a 'secular' minority regime, presented itself as the best (or only) possible safeguard for the various religious minorities against Sunni dominance. The partnership between the state and religious minority groups (most notably Christians) therefore also contributed to the preservation of the plural family law system: it served the religious minorities because it granted them some degree of legislative and judicial autonomy in personal status affairs in return for support and legitimisation of the government. In this regard, the family law system had become a convenient tool for the state to use for its own political objectives, in particular to keep the sectarian and religious division intact in order to sustain its political survival.

During the last decade, several efforts were made by the Syrian government and civil society groups to introduce changes to the personal status laws, most importantly Syria's main family law: the SLPS. Recent modifications to the SLPS and controversial family (draft) laws caused quite a stir in the heterogeneous Syrian society and reverberated on the already tensed relations between the Sunni majority population and the religious minority groups.

At the same time, conservative Muslim scholars were given ample opportunity to put forward family law proposals based on strict interpretations of Islamic law. This leeway for conservative Sunni scholars has been explained as an attempt by the government to channel religious opinions through state organs, and with that to circumvent public debates about family law and prevent strong religious opposition against law reforms. Plurality in family law was thus utilised as a political instrument by both the Syrian government and religious groups, as both have something to lose if the system were to collapse.

The government under Bashar al-Asad (r. 2000–present) appeared to be unwilling to undertake any serious large-scale reforms, not just regarding personal status laws, but any law in general. Instead, the government employed a 'patchwork approach', which consisted of minor modifications to various laws without really improving the existing situation. The reason for this reluctance was, most likely, that the government feared that any serious family law reform, or law reform in general, would have incited calls for other legal and political reforms.

An exception to this political strategy was the promulgation of the CLPS in 2006. This law was considered revolutionary because it meant that all Catholics of Syria were solely governed by the provisions of the CLPS, which included sensitive rights such as adoption and equal inheritance rights for men and women. However, this exceptional legal position for the Catholics only lasted four years, for in 2010 an amendment to the SLPS effectively rendered a substantial part of the CLPS inoperative.

Asymmetrical plurality

It has to be noted here that, despite the raging civil war, Syria's legal system has not been disbanded and still appears to function, at least in the government-controlled areas. For that reason, this study considered the official legal system, including its laws and institutions, as currently in force, hence the use of the present tense.

The current mosaic of Syria's legal plurality in family law presents a wide variety of personal status laws and courts that regulate matters of personal status, including marriage, dower, dissolution of marriage, maintenance, child custody and succession. The main law in Syria that governs family relations is the 1953 Syrian Law of Personal Status; it is the general law and applies to all Syrians, irrespective of their religion. Nevertheless, the SLPS grants the Druze, Jewish and Christian communities limited legislative and judicial autonomy in certain personal status matters, most importantly marriage and divorce. This legal plurality, however, does not entail equality between the different jurisdictions. The SLPS is the general, overriding law in matters of personal status; the non-Muslim laws are exemptions to and subordinate to the SLPS. Similarly, the *shar'iyya* courts, which implement the SLPS, function as national state courts and have full jurisdiction over all personal status matters involving Muslims and limited exclusive jurisdiction with regard to proof of paternity and legal guardianship over all Syrians, irrespective of their religion. Syria's plurality in family law is thus an unbalanced or asymmetrical plurality because the SLPS and the *shar'iyya* courts clearly enjoy the upper hand over the other laws and courts. This affects in particular non-Muslim minorities, most notably Christians, especially when these jurisdictions intersect, for example in the event of interdenominational or interreligious marriages or when one of the (Christian) spouses converts to Islam, for example in order to obtain a divorce. When a spouse coverts to Islam (the other way around is not possible), the SLPS becomes the applicable law and the *shar'iyya* courts are considered the competent courts. This also means that when a non-Muslim father or mother converts to Islam, the religious identity of the converted parent automatically devolves upon the children. Consequently, the converted Muslim parent can demand full custody over the children and the *shar'iyya* courts have generally granted such requests in favour of the Muslim parent. The supremacy of the Muslim faith over other faiths, and with that the supremacy of the SLPS and the *shar'iyya* courts over other laws and courts, are a manifestation of the asymmetrical plurality in Syria's family law.

The laws of patriarchy

The different manifestations of legal plurality discussed above are directly associated with the state. However, not only statutory laws of personal status governed family relations in Syria but other 'forms of normative ordering' were also found in addition to and within the official state system. Patriarchal and other social, cultural or religious norms formed often just as powerful a force in family law. This did not mean that state law norms were necessarily different from those non-statutory norms, for in fact some of these latter norms were also laid down in the various personal status laws, Muslim and non-Muslim alike.

I have demonstrated that Syria's personal status laws, like most Arab family laws, in varying degrees, reflected the patriarchal family model. The laws privileged men, in particular men from the patrilineal line, in numerous ways: in child custody, inheritance, divorce, choice of marriage partner, passing on religious identity to children (and with that, citizenship), household division of labour, and authority and obedience in marriage. Certain matters were typically associated with Muslim family law (e.g. the dower and polygamy) or, on the contrary, Christian family law (e.g. the sacramental marriage and the prohibition of divorce), but the underlying structures were generally the same. The patriarchal family model has been enshrined in all laws of personal status, Muslim and Christian alike, and with that contributed to the preservation and confirmation of that model in the Syrian legal context – despite reform attempts by those who challenged that very model. In my view, it was this family model that determined the gender roles in society; it was more powerful than legal or religious norms, specific to the different ethnic and religious communities.

A plurality of norms and legal practices

The SLPS and the *shar'iyya* courts operated in a fairly open, flexible system. The provisions of the SLPS were not narrowly defined and thus left ample room for interpretation by the *shar'iyya* courts. This versatility of the SLPS also revealed itself in the fact that it authorised registration of proof of marriage, divorce and paternity *ex post facto*. This meant that customary marriages and divorces pronounced or agreed upon outside the courtroom could be registered at a later date at court. These extra-judicial options proved beneficial to a great variety of people, for example couples who did not wish to marry in court because they married someone against their families' wishes or because the spouses belonged to different (Muslim) sects. Another group that benefited from these extra-judicial possibilities was the judiciary itself. The *ex post facto* registrations of marriages, divorces and proof of paternity unburdened the already overloaded judicial system. Besides, the versatility of the SLPS has proved to offer opportunities for creative legal solutions, in particular to legitimise children born out of wedlock. Because of the possibility to register proof of paternity *ex post facto*, an illegitimate child could be given a paternal name, even if the name came from a 'fictitious' father.

The SLPS itself is thus extremely flexible, in a sense that it does not claim regulatory exclusivity on marriage, divorce and paternity. In other words, the Syrian government, similar to other Muslim-majority countries, allowed for other 'forms of normative ordering' (in this case customary law) to work alongside the legal system of the state. Despite its efforts to discourage traditional practices such as *'urfi* marriages and out-of-court divorces, the state continued to recognise them. Thus, there were several 'forms of normative ordering' at work in the domain of Syrian family law: the statutory laws were part of only one order among several.

Syria's plural legal system also allowed for Christian Churches to regulate their family relations according to their own canon laws. In the case of the Catholics of Syria, it permitted the import of Eastern Catholic canon law issued by the Bishop of Rome, the Pope. Moreover, the Catholic judges in Syria have all been educated in Rome: if a Catholic priest wanted to work as a clerical judge, he was required to go through a thorough three-year training in Eastern canon law, which included the extensive regular procedures that need to be followed in any ecclesiastical trial. Thus, in the Catholic courts we found 'foreign' legal rules and procedures from Rome fused with Syrian national procedural laws. This is another example of how the Syrian government allowed for other 'forms of normative ordering', in this case (supranational) canon law, to work within the family legal system.

The Catholic personal status courts were different from their Christian and Muslim counterparts in several regards, mostly due to their alliance with the Church of Rome. However, they also shared some key similarities with other personal status courts, namely the prevalence of patriarchal family norms and values. During my fieldwork I had observed that the Christian and Muslim communities of Syria shared many common cultural values and traditions, in particular views on marriage, family, gender and sexual propriety. Throughout my time in a *shar'iyya*, a Catholic, and a Greek Orthodox personal status court (all in Damascus), I had noticed that the same themes were constantly addressed: the ideal of marriage, the proper role of women – wives in particular – the husband as the provider and head of the household, upholding the family honour, and so on. The attachment to these patriarchal norms and views was of great importance in the various personal status courtrooms, regardless of their legal and religious differences, which brought me to the conclusion that these courts were united in their shared cultural understandings of gender, family relations, social norms and behaviour.

The interaction between various social, legal and religious norms (codified and uncodified) in the field of family law cannot be underestimated. Ideas about proper gender comportment in family and marital relationships (public and private) shaped and influenced legal discourses and practices. In my observation, they were continuously expressed by individuals in the different courtrooms and played a role in, most importantly, the assessment of spousal or parental behaviour of the parties involved. The narratives presented to the courts by the litigants, their lawyers and witnesses influenced the outcome of a case, as judges took social (and not necessarily legal) norms and values into account. Therefore, the courts could be regarded as sites where norms and expectations were expressed, emphasised and reinforced, not just by the judges but by all those who work on or visit these sites.

Syria's plural family law – what will the future hold?

This book has demonstrated that it is important, if not essential, to understand Syria's plural family law in its historical and socio-political context. This historical and socio-political context has not only shaped Syria's contemporary family law but also informs us about the the ongoing Syrian crisis that started in March 2011. In the first chapter, I stated that I believe that the way in which the (future) government of Syria – and the same applies to other Arab multi-ethnic and multi-religious states, especially those in transition – deals with the plurality of the personal status law, will be indicative for the (future) position of minorities in the country, not only their position within the legal system but also their position in society. We have seen that family law has been used as a political instrument for governance and negotiation by various governments as well as the various religious groups within the country.

In the present conflict, the government has continued to play the 'secular card', claiming that only a secular, minority regime can protect the interests of the minorities against a Sunni majority. The government felt empowered in its propaganda by the emergence of several jihadi militant groups, whose members have indeed attacked and killed non-Sunni civilians. Yet, at the same time, the government has used, especially at the start of the conflict, these events to stir up sectarian divisions and strife amongst its population, in order to legitimise its rule and secure the support of the minority groups. Now that the conflict has escalated into a full-scale civil war that has claimed thousands of lives, turned millions of Syrians into refugees and has torn the country apart, we can only hope that a future Syria will be successful in overcoming – however difficult that will be – the sectarian challenges and divisions, by following the path of national, communal reconciliation and transitional justice, which will, it is hoped, pave the way for a Syria where there is a place for diversity, equality and justice.

APPENDIX

MARRIAGE AND DIVORCE ACCORDING TO THE SYRIAN LAW OF PERSONAL STATUS

I. Marriage: legal requirements and consequences

Article 1 of the Syrian Law of Personal Status (SLPS) defines marriage as:

> Marriage is a contract between a man and a woman, who is lawfully permitted to him, with the aim to establish a bond for a joint life and procreation.

i. Offer and acceptance, witnesses, majority and compos mentis

A marriage involves an offer (*ijab*) by one contracting party and acceptance (*qabul*) by the other (Art. 5). Both parties have to hear and understand the offer and acceptance, and need to understand what the purpose of this contract is, namely marriage (Art. 11.1). The offer and acceptance ought to take place in one session, clearly and audibly expressed in the presence of witnesses (Arts 11–12).

The witnesses can be either two men or one man and two women, all of whom should be 'of age', Muslim, and *compos mentis* (Art. 12). The betrothed parties, like the witnesses, ought to be 'of age' (*bulugh*) and *compos mentis* (*'aql*) (Art. 15.1). Paragraph two of the same article states that the judge may permit a 'lunatic' (*majnun*) or a 'feeble-minded' person (*ma'tuh*) to marry if a group of psychiatrists establishes that the marriage will benefit his recuperation.

ii. Age of capacity

The age of capacity for marriage is 18 years for a young man (*fatan*) and 17 years for a young woman (*fatah*) (Art. 16).

If the betrothed parties are younger than the required age, they can apply to the judge for permission to get married, provided they are (physically) mature or, as Article 18.1 reads:

> When an adolescent boy [*murahiq*] claims to be physically mature [i.e. *bulugh*] after attaining the age of 15 or an adolescent girl [*murahiqa*] after attaining the age of 13, the judge may allow the boy or girl to be wed, if he deems the petition to be sincere and they are physically capable [i.e. to have sexual relations].

Article 18.2 stipulates that if the legal guardian (*wali*) of the (minor) bride is her father or grandfather, the couple will need his consent to the marriage.

A judge may withhold permission for a marriage if he finds the betrothed parties show a disparity in age, and if he can see no benefit in the marriage (Art. 19).

*iii. Marriage guardian (*wali*)*

Article 20 stipulates that when a mature girl (*kabira*), who has reached the age of 17, approaches the court with a marriage request, the judge will first ask her legal guardian for his opinion. The guardian is required to respond to this request within a set time period. If her guardian does not object to the marriage or if his objections are ill-considered, the judge shall give permission for the couple to get married, provided the betrothed parties are of equal social status.

In general, the father or the grandfather will act as the legal guardian to the marriage. If either one is not available or suitable, another male agnate, in the order of inheritance, can act as the marriage guardian, provided he is in a degree of consanguinity precluding marriage (*mahram*) (Art. 21). Articles 33–5 define exactly who is forbidden in marriage due to consanguinity and/or foster relationships. If the future bride or groom does not have any paternal family members who can act as the legal guardian, the judge will act as the guardian (Art. 24).

In addition to the SLPS provisions, reference is also made to Article 34 of the Qadri Pasha, Code;[1] this article reads as follows:

> The *wali* is a condition for the validity of the marriage of a minor boy and a minor girl,[2] and adults who lack full legal capacity [*ghayr mukallaf*]. The *wali* is not a condition for the validity of the marriage of free, sane, mature [i.e. past puberty] men and women – rather, their marriage is executed without a *wali*.[3]

In his commentary on the Syrian laws of personal status, Shaqfa writes that when a bride (the same accounts for the groom) has reached the age of puberty, that is, she is 'of age' (*baligha*), and she is *compos mentis* (*'aqila*), she can contract a marriage by herself, without her legal guardian.[4] Nevertheless, he continues, it is recommended for a mature and sane woman to delegate the authority of executing her marriage to a guardian since he has more experience in life than she does.[5]

*iv. Suitability of the groom (*kafa'a*)*

The suitability of the husband receives considerable attention in the SLPS and is dealt with in a separate section entitled *kafa'a* (Arts 26–32). Article 20 (concerning legal capacity) already mentioned the concept of *kafa'a*, meaning that the betrothed parties ought to be of equal social status, regardless of their age.

Article 26 reads that a marriage can only be valid if the husband is of equal social status to the wife. The other way around, that is, a man marrying a woman beneath his social standing, is not considered problematic (see Art. 62 Qadri Pasha). Article 28 states that the custom of the country (*'urf al-balad*) will determine what can be designated as 'equality of status'.

The requirement of social parity is the exclusive right that belongs to the bride and her guardian (Art. 29).[6] The legal guardian may file a petition to the court for annulment of the marriage (*faskh al-nikah*) when his female (mature) ward has given herself in marriage – without his approval – to a husband who appears to be beneath her social standing (Art. 27).

When, however, the wife is pregnant or the decline in social status occurred during the marriage, the bride and her guardian lose the right to ask for an annulment of the marriage (Arts 30–1). If, after the conclusion of the marriage contract, it turns out that the husband has lied about his social standing, both the wife and her guardian may file a petition for annulment of the marriage contract (Art. 32).

v. Marriage registration

Article 40 paragraph 1 stipulates that a couple needs to submit a marriage petition to a *shar'iyya* district judge (*qadi al-mantiqa*), which should include the following documents:

i. a certificate issued by the local official (i.e. *mukhtar*[7]) stating the name, age, and place of residence of both parties, the name of the marriage guardian, and a statement that there is no lawful impediment to the marriage (Art. 40.1 sub A);
ii. a certified extract from the Civil Registry (*qayd nufus*) certifying the betrothed parties' civil status (Art. 40.1 sub B);
iii. proof of a premarital medical examination attesting that there are no medical impediments to their marriage (Art. 40.1 sub C);
iv. permission for marriage for those who serve in the army or those who are subject to military service (Art. 40.1 sub D);
v. permission from the Security Department when one of the spouses is a foreigner (Art. 40.1 sub E).[8]

The SLPS also allows for the registration of customary or traditional marriages (i.e. *'urfi* marriages) *ex post facto* under Article 40 paragraph 2. This article stipulates that a customary marriage can be registered once the required legal procedures are met. If, however, a child is born or a pregnancy is apparent, the marriage will be recognised without the required procedures.

All marriages need to be registered in the court's registry, after which the court sends a copy of the marriage certificate (*sakk al-zawaj*) within ten days to the Department of Civil Affairs (*da'irat al-ahwal al-madaniyya*) (Art. 45.1).

The same registration procedure applies to the certification of marriages (*tathbit al-zawaj*), unilateral divorce by the husband (*talaq*, i.e. the 'administrative' or registered *talaq*), proof of paternity (*nasab*), and death of a missing person (Art. 45.3).

vi. Valid, irregular and invalid marriages

If all the required conditions and procedures stipulated by the SLPS are met, the marriage shall be considered valid (*sahih*) (Art. 47).

In the event that some conditions are not fulfilled, the marriage is considered irregular (*fasid*), meaning it is subject to annulment by a judge (Art. 48.1). Examples of irregular marriages are, amongst others, a marriage contracted under duress (*ikrah*), a marriage contracted without witnesses or when the betrothed parties or the witnesses did not have the competence to act.

Some marriages cannot be repaired and are considered invalid or void (*batil*) from the very beginning. The only example of a void marriage explicitly mentioned in the SLPS is a marriage between a Muslim woman and a non-Muslim man (Art. 48.2). An invalid marriage is considered non-existent under the law, even if the purported marriage was consummated (Art. 50).

vii. Legal effects of a consummated, irregular marriage

An irregular marriage that has not yet been consummated shall be considered invalid and will not produce any legal effects associated with a valid marriage (Art. 51.1). However, consummation (*dukhul*) of an irregular marriage does entail certain legal effects, namely:

- a portion of the dower has to be paid (either the proper dower or, if the dower was specified, the specified dower, whichever is the smaller (Arts 51.2 sub A and 63 SLPS);
- children born from such a marriage shall receive the father's family name (Art. 51.2 sub B in conjunction with Art. 133 SLPS);
- impediment to marriage due to affinity (*musahara*) (Art. 51.2 sub C);
- the rules pertaining to payment of
    i. post-divorce maintenance (*'idda nafaqa*) following the separation by or death of the husband, and
    ii. maintenance following divorce during the waiting (*'idda*) period, will come into effect;

- rules regarding hereditary succession between the spouses, however, do not apply (Art. 51.2 sub D).

A wife who entered into an irregular marriage in good faith shall be entitled to marital maintenance (*nafaqa zawjiyya*), as long as she is unaware of the defective nature of the marriage (Art. 51.3).

II. The effects of marriage: marital rights and duties

Part IV of the SLPS deals with 'the effects of marriage' and is subdivided into three sections: dower, housing and maintenance, all of which are financial obligations falling upon the husband, in return for certain obligations falling upon the wife.

viii. Dower

The stipulation of a dower (*mahr*) is a vital condition for a valid marriage, whether it is specified in the contract or denied (Art. 53). The dower is a wife's prerogative and a husband's obligation (Arts 53 and 60). In fact, an unpaid dower is considered a debt (*dayn*) of the husband to his wife (Art. 54.3 and 54.5).

The SLPS stipulates that the amount of the dower may vary, in that there is no upper or lower limit to it (Art. 41.1 and 41.2). However, distinction is made between the proper dower (*mahr al-mithl*) and the specified dower (*mahr al-musamma*). When the dower is not specified in the contract or when the specified dower is irregular, a proper dower will be determined based on what is considered equal to that of her peers (Art. 61.1). To determine a suitable dower amount commensurate with that of her peers, the judge shall follow the local custom (*'urf*) (Art. 55).

A dower is generally divided into two parts, namely a prompt dower (*mahr mu'ajjal*) and a deferred dower (*mahr mu'ajjal*). The prompt dower ought to be paid upon conclusion of the marriage contract (Art. 55); the deferred part has to be paid when the marriage is terminated due to an irrevocable divorce or death (Art. 56).

ix. Payment of the dower and consummation of marriage

When a husband divorces his wife before the marriage was consummated or before the couple had the opportunity to consummate the marriage, that is, valid seclusion (*al-khalwa al-sahiha*), the husband has to pay half of the dower to his wife (Art. 58).

If, however, in the event of an irrevocable divorce, the husband can prove it is his wife's fault that they are irrevocably divorced, his obligation to pay the dower expires (Art. 59).

x. Maintenance obligations of the husband

The husband's maintenance (*nafaqa*) obligations include the following: housing, clothing, food, medical care and domestic help; the latter only if this is appropriate to her social standing (Art. 71.1). The husband's obligation to provide a marital home for the wife is addressed in in Articles 65–7 (a separate section of the SLPS).

The husband ought to provide his wife with a house that is suitable to her social standing (Art. 65). In case of polygamy, the first wife needs to consent to sharing the marital home with a co-wife (Art. 67), and he needs to provide equal housing to all his wives (Art. 68). A husband cannot house his wife with his relatives if it is established that co-habitation with them would damage her; however, if he happens to have a minor child, who has not yet reached the age of discretion (*ghayr al-mumayyiz*), she will have to accept the child into their household (Art. 69).

The level of maintenance to be provided by the husband depends on his financial situation, although a minimal level (*hadd al-kifaya*) has to be met (Art. 76). The amount of maintenance may be increased or decreased due to inflation, deflation or a change in the financial situation of the husband; a claim for an increase or decrease of maintenance can be backdated to a maximum of six months (Art. 77).

xi. Obedience of the wife

After the wife has received the prompt dower, she is obliged to live together with her husband (Art. 66). The issue of co-habitation is closely connected to the concept of disobedience (*nushuz*). Article 74 stipulates that if a wife is disobedient (*nashiza*) to her husband, she loses her right to maintenance, for as long as she is disobedient.

A wife will be considered disobedient if she leaves the conjugal house without a lawful reason or if she prevents her husband from entering her house before asking him to be moved to another house (Art. 75). A wife may also forfeit her maintenance right if she works outside the house without her husband's consent (Art. 73).

If the husband, however, failed to pay the prompt dower or did not provide a suitable marital home – a house that meets the legal requirements (*maskan shar'i*) – for her, she may refuse to co-habit with him (Art. 72.2).

III. Dissolution of marriage: types, requirements and consequences

xii. Repudiation (talaq) *by the husband*

Talaq is a unilateral repudiation of a wife by the husband. It is the standard form of divorce and is regulated in Articles 85–94.

Article 85.1 stipulates that a man of 18 years or older has the legal capacity to divorce his wife by *talaq*. A married man who has not yet attained the age of 18, but who is considered legally mature (*bulugh*), has two options to divorce: (i) a judge will pronounce the *talaq* (*tatliq*) or (ii) the young man's own *talaq* will be authorised by the judge if the judge finds some benefit (*maslaha*) in it (Art. 85.2).

A husband can simply pronounce the formula 'I divorce you' either verbally or in writing (Art. 87.1). A husband can also delegate his *talaq* right to someone else, that is, divorce by proxy, including his own wife (Art. 87.2). A delegated *talaq* right to the wife (a *tafwid al-talaq*) has to be laid down in the marriage contract.[9] If such a clause is inserted into the contract, the wife is allowed to divorce herself from her husband when, for example, he marries another wife.

Each *talaq* has to be pronounced in a separate session. The SLPS does not recognise a so-called 'triple *talaq*', that is, the formula 'I divorce you' said three times in a row (Art. 92). A 'triple *talaq*' is considered a single *talaq*, thereby giving the couple the opportunity to reconcile.[10]

The SLPS considers a repudiation pronounced by a man who is intoxicated, under duress or overwhelmed by anger, and therefore does not know what he is saying, to be without legal effect (Art. 89). If a repudiation is intended only as a threat, to induce some action or as an oath, it is also subject to nullification (Art. 90).

xiii. Revocable and irrevocable talaqs

A distinction has to be made between a revocable (*raj'i*) and an irrevocable (*ba'in*) *talaq*. A revocable *talaq* means that the husband may revoke the divorce by taking his wife back during the waiting period (*'idda*) (Art. 118.1).

However, this revocation right is not unlimited; the maximum number of revocable *talaqs* is two (Art. 91); after the third *talaq* the divorce becomes irrevocable and thus final (*ba'in*) (Art. 94).

Other types of final, irrevocable *talaq*s are:

- *talaq* pronounced before the marriage was consummated or valid seclusion occurred;
- 'divorce for compensation' (*al-talaq 'ala badal*) or (*mukhala'a*) divorce;
- judicial divorce on the grounds of a defect of the husband that prevents consummation of the marriage;
- divorce on the grounds of discord between the spouses (Arts 94, 108).[11]

In the event that the husband does not revoke a *talaq* during the waiting period, the marriage will be considered dissolved once the waiting period has elapsed (Art. 118.2). If the couple wants to be re-united, they would have to renew their marriage, thus entering a new contract, which should also include a new dower (Art. 119).[12]

A husband who pronounced three *talaq*s, after which the divorce has become final, can only re-marry his wife after she first marries and divorces another man. Only then she can enter into a new marriage with her former husband (Arts 120 and 36).

*xiv. Arbitrary divorce (*talaq al-ta'assuf*)*

Article 116 stipulates that when a man pronounces an irrevocable *talaq* while he is suffering from a deadly disease or is in a bad state and subsequently dies because of his disease or condition during the waiting period of the woman, her right to inherit from her deceased husband will not be forfeited, provided she has the legal capacity to inherit from him in the period from the pronouncement of the *talaq* until his death.

Article 117 enables the court to honour a woman's claim for compensation from her ex-husband when it is apparent to the court that the husband acted arbitrarily and divorced her without reasonable cause (*sabab ma'qul*). If as a result of this she suffers hardship and poverty, the court may impose compensation payments on the ex-husband, taking his circumstances and the degree of the arbitrariness into account.

The husband can be forced to pay maintenance (*nafaqa*) for up to three years, in addition to the regular post-divorce maintenance (*'idda nafaqa*). Finally, the article reads that the judge may, depending on the circumstances, impose either a lump sum payment or payment in monthly instalments. There is no prescriptive period for filing a compensation claim based on arbitrary divorce.[13]

The husband has to prove he had a lawful reason (*sabab mashru'*) to divorce her;[14] while the wife has to prove she is impoverished.[15] However, a husband who arbitrarily divorces his wife shall not be obliged to pay compensation when there are others, for example relatives, who can financially support her.[16]

xv. Mukhala'a *divorce*

Mukhala'a divorce proceedings are regulated in Articles 95–104. In a *mukhala'a* divorce, the spouses sign a divorce contract in which the husband agrees to divorce his wife, in exchange for which the wife agrees to renounce some or all of her financial rights.

A *mukhala'a* contract has to meet the following requirements: a valid marriage, both parties must have legal capacity (Arts 85 and 95); agreement of both parties through exchange of offer and acceptance (Art. 96), and it should include a compensation payment.[17] However, a wife who has not yet reached the age of majority (*sinn al-rushd*) cannot be obliged to pay the compensation payment without the consent of her financial guardian (*wali al-mal*) (Art. 95.2).

There has to be a compensation payment (*badal al-khul'*), that is, a recompense or consideration that the wife offers to the husband in exchange for divorce, for a *mukhala'a* divorce to take effect. Without a compensation payment the divorce would not be considered a *mukhala'a* divorce, but a regular revocable *talaq* (Art. 100).

The contracting parties are free to decide on the amount or value of the compensation (Art. 97). If another payment besides the dower and marital maintenance is stipulated in the contract or when nothing is stipulated in the contract, all rights connected to the dower and the marital maintenance will be forfeited (Art. 98 and 99).

If a divorcing couple stipulates that the husband will be dismissed, in exchange for divorce, from paying nursing fees to the wife (mother) or when it is agreed that the child will stay with the wife (mother) for a specified period, and if the wife then remarries or when she leaves the child, the ex-husband may claim the equivalent amount for the nursing fees or the child maintenance for the remaining period (Art. 102.1). However the husband cannot take a child into his care while the child is of an age where he or she is entitled to stay with his or her mother, – during the nursing (*hadana*) period (Art. 103).

xvi. Reconciliation before registration of talaq *and* mukhala'a

When a *talaq* or a *mukhala'a* action is taken to court, the judge must defer action on the case for one month in the hope of reconciliation between the spouses (Art. 88.1).

Once that month has passed, both parties will be called to appear in court if the husband persists in his action for divorce (*talaq*) or if the couple persists in their *mukhala'a* request. The judge will listen to their disagreement and has a legal duty to try to resolve their differences. To this end the judge will involve the families of the spouses and any other person capable of resolving those differences (Art. 88.2).

If the reconciliation attempts fail, the judge can allow registration of the *talaq* or the *mukhala'a* contract (Art. 88.3).

If neither spouse follows up on the divorce action within three months after the filing of the request, that is, does not (re)appear in court to take action, the request will be considered dropped (Art. 88.4).

*xvii. Judicial divorce (*tafriq*)*

The SLPS recognises various grounds for judicial divorce (*tafriq*); these are divided into four types:

I. *tafriq* on the grounds of disease or defect (*'ilal*), which include:

i. a husband's defect which prevents consummation of the marriage, provided the wife does not suffer from the same defect (Art. 105.1);
ii. a husband who has become insane after the marriage conclusion (Art. 105.2);
iii. a husband's impotence (Art. 106.2).

A wife cannot seek divorce on the grounds of her husband's defect under Article 105 if she knew about it before the marriage conclusion or agreed to accept it (Art. 106). The judge will determine whether the disease or defect is curable or not – if it is incurable he will dissolve the marriage. If, however, there is a possibility for a cure, the judge should defer the claim for a maximum period of one year in the hope of recovery; if the husband is not cured, the judge may dissolve the marriage (Art. 107). A divorce issued on one of the grounds listed above will be a final divorce (*talaq ba'in*) (Art. 108).

II. *tafriq* on the grounds of absence or disappearance (*ghayba*)

When a husband is absent or missing without reasonable justification or when he is sentenced to more than three years in prison, the wife can, after one year of his absence or imprisonment, file a petition for divorce, even if the husband has the financial means of supporting her (Art. 109.1). A divorce on this ground is revocable, for if the husband reappears or is released from prison during the waiting period, he can take his wife back (Art. 109.2).

III. *tafriq* on the grounds of non-payment of maintenance (*'adam al-infaq*)

A wife may seek divorce when her husband abstains from paying maintenance to her, when he is capable of doing so and his inability to pay cannot be proven (Art. 110.1). If the husband is absent or he proves his inability to pay, the judge may give him time (not more than three months) to mend his ways; if he fails to do so, the judge will pronounce the divorce (Art. 110.2). A divorce on this ground is also revocable, for the husband can take his wife back during the waiting period provided he proves he has sufficient financial means and is prepared to pay maintenance (Art. 111).

IV. *tafriq* on the grounds of discord between the spouses (*shiqaq bayna al-zawjayn*)

Both spouses can bring a judicial divorce petition to court on the grounds of discord, claiming that the other is causing so much harm (*darar*) that it impossible to continue their marriage (Art. 112.1). If harm can be proved and the judge fails to reconcile the spouses, he can divorce them; this divorce will be considered an irrevocable divorce (Art. 112.2). If harm cannot be proved, the judge will postpone the proceedings for at least a month in the hope of reconciliation (Art. 112.3).

xviii. Judicial divorce and court-ordered arbitration

Article 112 paragraph 3 stipulates that if the plaintiff persists in his or her claim and reconciliation cannot be achieved, the court will appoint two arbiters from the family of the spouses or persons who the judge considers capable of bringing about reconciliation.

If the arbiters' reconciliation efforts fail and harm is established and it has been established that discord is caused by 'wrongdoing' (*isa'a*) of the husband, the arbitrators will decide upon an irrevocable divorce (Art. 114.1).

If the wife is to blame for the greater part of the discord or caused equally by both parties, the arbiters shall decide on judicial divorce on condition that the wife returns part or the full amount of the dower, as is deemed appropriate considering the degree of the 'wrongdoing' (Art. 114.2).

If the arbiters find no fault with either of the spouses, they may propose dissolving the marriage by a *mukhala'a* divorce, but only if the wife agrees to give up her financial rights in exchange for divorce. This latter option is only possible when the arbiters are convinced that discord between the spouses is deep-rooted and cannot be solved (Art. 114.3).

When the two appointed arbitrators complete the arbitration procedure, they submit a report to the judge (Art. 115). If the judge rejects the arbiters' report he can appoint two other arbiters or he can add a third one (Art. 114.4). A third arbiter has to side with one of the dissenting arbiter's advice – as he cannot deliver his own independent advice.[18]

xix. Waiting period and post-divorce maintenance

The waiting period is generally three complete menstrual cycles after the pronunciation of the divorce for a menstruating non-pregnant woman (Art. 121.1). The duration of the *'idda* for a widow is four months and ten days (Art. 123), for pregnant women until she gives birth or miscarries (Art. 124), for women who have had no menstruation for an extended period it is one complete year (Art. 121.2), and three months for those who are in their menopause (Art. 121.3).

During the *'idda* period following divorce, annulment of the marriage or death, a woman is not allowed to remarry.

When the marriage is not consummated or when it is established that they did not have the opportunity to consummate the marriage, the compulsory waiting period (*'idda*) does not have to be observed (Art. 126).

Article 83 (in conjunction with Art. 125) stipulates that a husband is obliged to pay his ex-wife post-divorce maintenance (*nafaqat al-'idda*) for the period that she is serving the waiting period, following *talaq*, judicial divorce (*tafriq*), annulment (*faskh*) or death.

NOTES

Introduction

1. Therefore note the use of the present tense when referring to the legal system, its laws and institutions.
2. Central Intelligence Agency, *The World Fact Book* (online edition, 2013–14). Available online at https://www.cia.gov/library/publications/the-world-fact-book/geos/sy.html (accessed 23 August 2015); United States Department of State, *2013 International Religious Freedom Report – Syria*. Available online at http://www.state.gov/j/drl/rls/irf/religiousfreedom/index.htm?year = 2013&-dlid = 222313#wrapper (accessed 23 August 2015).
3. Personal status law is also commonly referred to as 'family law'; for that reason I use the terms 'family law' and 'personal status law' interchangeably. The term 'statut personnel' originates from Medieval Europe and was used to denote rules and regulations concerning the status and capacity of persons, vis-à-vis the term 'statut réel', which referred to matters connected to property (see Wyndham A. Bewes, 'The Theory of the Statutes', *Journal of Comparative Legislation and International Law* 4/3 (1922), pp. 97–103). The term 'personal status' (in Arabic: *ahwal al-shakhsiyya*) was only introduced in Arab legal writings in the late nineteenth century, most notably by Muhammad Qadri Pasha in Egypt (see Jamal J. Nasir, *The Islamic Law of Personal Status* (The Hague, Kluwer Law International, 2002) p. 34 ff.; Amira E.A. Sonbol, '"The woman follows the nationality of her husband": Guardianship, citizenship and gender', *Hawwa: Journal of Women of the Middle East and the Islamic World* 1 (2003), pp. 89–90).
4. The rationale behind the choice to leave the adjective *shar'iyya* untranslated is explained in the section 'Family law in the Middle East and North Africa' (Introduction).
5. In international private law this intersection of jurisdictions, which follows from the co-existence of different laws for different groups within one country, is commonly referred to as 'interpersonal conflict of laws'. For an overview of the

various forms of interpersonal conflict of laws, see Kurt Lipstein and István Szászy, Chapter 10: 'Interpersonal conflict of laws', in K. Lipstein (ed.), *International Encyclopedia of Comparative Law*, Vol. III Part 1 (Private International Law) (Tübingen: Mohr Siebeck; Leiden, Martinus Nijhoff Publishers, 2011), pp. 1–35.

6. Sally E. Merry, 'Legal Pluralism', *Law and Society Review* 22/5 (1988), p. 870.
7. The concept of legal pluralism has been the subject of much debate, particularly amongst scholars of anthropology and other social sciences. The idea of legal pluralism challenges the assumed monopoly of the state over law and the legal system. There is a wide, complex – and at times contradictory – debate about what legal pluralism is or entails; see for example (amongst others), John Griffiths, 'What is legal pluralism?', *Journal of Legal Pluralism* 24 (1986), pp. 1–55; Merry, 'Legal Pluralism'; Brian Z. Tamanaha 'The folly of the "social scientific" concept of legal pluralism', *Journal of Law and Society* 20/2 (1993), pp. 192–217; Boaventura de Sousa Santos, 'Law: A map of misreading: Toward a postmodern conception of law', *Journal of Law and Society* 14/3 (1987), pp. 279–302; for an overview, see for example, Baudouin Dupret, 'Legal pluralism, plurality of laws, and legal practices: theories, critiques, and praxiological re-specification', *European Journal of Legal Studies* 1 (2007a). Available at http://www.ejls.eu/1/14UK.pdf (accessed 9 September 2015) and Brian Z. Tamanaha, 'Understanding legal pluralism: past to present, local to global', *Sydney Law Review* 30 (2008), pp. 375–411.
8. For a similar situation in Egypt, see Dupret, 'Legal Pluralism'.
9. An analysis of the 'patriarchal family model' (cf. Léon Buskens, 'Recent debates on family law reform in Morocco: Islamic law as politics in an emerging public sphere', *Islamic Law and Society* 10/1 (2003), pp. 70–131), meaning that (senior) men are the head of the family with women and younger family members in a more subordinate role, will be given in Chapter 4.
10. Léon Buskens, *Islamitisch recht en familiebetrekkingen in Marokko* (Amsterdam, Bulaaq, 1999); Ziba Mir-Hosseini, *Marriage on Trial: Islamic Family Law in Iran and Morocco* (London, I.B.Tauris, 2000); Annelies Moors, *Women, Property and Islam: Palestinian Experiences, 1920–1990* (Cambridge, Cambridge University Press, 1995); Lynn Welchman, *Beyond the Code: Muslim Family Law and the Shari'a Judiciary in the Palestinian West Bank* (The Hague, Kluwer Law International, 2000); Nahda Shehada, *Justice without Drama: Enacting Family Law in Gaza City Sharī'a Court* (Maastricht, Shaker Publishing, 2005).
11. Jessica Carlisle, *Rules, Negotiation, Claims and Counter Claims: Judicial Discretion in a Damascus Shari'a Court* (unpublished PhD thesis, University of London, 2007c); Nadia Sonneveld, *Khul' Divorce in Egypt: Public Debates, Judicial Practices, and Everyday Life* (Cairo, American University of Cairo Press, 2012a); Maaike Voorhoeve, *Gender and Divorce Law in North Africa: Sharia, Custom and the Personal Status Code in Tunisia* (London, I.B.Tauris, 2014).
12. Annelies Moors, 'Introduction: Public Debates on Family Law Reform. Participants, Positions, and Styles of Argumentation in the 1990s', *Islamic Law*

and Society 10/1 (2003), pp. 1–11; Léon Buskens, 'Recent Debates on Family Law Reform in Morocco: Islamic Law as Politics in an Emerging Public Sphere', *Islamic Law and Society* 10/1 (2003), pp. 70–131; Nadia Sonneveld, *Khul' Divorce in Egypt: Public Debates, Judicial Practices, and Everyday Life* (Cairo, American University of Cairo Press, 2012a).

13. Baudouin Dupret, 'What is Islamic Law? A Praxiological Answer and an Egyptian Case Study', *Theory, Culture & Society* 24/2 (2007b), p. 97. In this article Dupret focuses on personal status law in Egypt.
14. Ibid., p. 82.
15. See also Marie-Aimée Hélie-Lucas, 'The preferential symbol for Islamic identity: women in Muslim personal laws', in V.M. Moghadam (ed.), *Identity Politics and Women. Cultural Reassertions and Feminisms in International Perspective* (Boulder, Westview Press, 1994), pp. 391–407.
16. Lynn Welchman, *Women and Muslim Family Laws in Arab States: A Comparative Overview of Textual Development and Advocacy* (Amsterdam, Amsterdam University Press, 2007), p. 16.
17. Knut S. Vikør, *Between God and the Sultan: A History of Islamic Law* (London, Hurst & Company, 2005), p. 1.
18. Joseph Schacht, *An Introduction to Islamic Law* (Oxford, Clarendon Press, 1982), p. 1. See also Léon Buskens and Baudouin Dupret, 'De l'invention du droit musulman à la pratique juridique contemporaine', in B. Dupret (ed.), *La charia aujourd'hui: Usages de la référence au droit islamique* (Paris, La Découverte, 2012), pp. 9–17.
19. N. Calder, 'Sharī'a', in C.E. Bosworth et al. (eds), *Encyclopaedia of Islam,* Vol. XI, 2nd edn (Leiden, Brill, 1997), p. 321.
20. Baudouin Dupret, 'What is Islamic Law? A Praxiological Answer and an Egyptian Case Study', *Theory, Culture & Society* 24/2 (2007b), p. 81.
21. Mariz Tadros, 'The non-Muslim "other": gender and contestations of hierarchy or rights', *Hawwa: Journal of Women of the Middle East and the Islamic World* 7 (2009), p. 111.
22. J.N.D. Anderson, 'The Syrian Law of Personal Status', *Bulletin of the School of Oriental and African Studies* 17/1 (1955), pp. 34–49; Maurits S. Berger, 'The legal system of family law in Syria', *Bulletin d'Études Orientales* 49 (Damascus, Institut Français de Damas, 1997), pp. 115–27.
23. The commentary of legal scholar and lawyer, Muhammed Fihr Shaqfa, on Syrian personal status law is an example of secondary literature in Arabic on this topic (see Muhammad Fihr Shaqfa, *sharh ahkam al-ahwal al-shakhsiyya: li-l-muslimin wa-l-nasara wa-l-yahud* [*Explaining the Law of Personal Status: Muslims, Christians, and Jews*] (Damascus, Mu'assasat Al-Nuri, 1998)).
24. Nevertheless, I always presented myself as a doctoral student, which I was at the time, in my interactions with experts and interviewees and I always informed them that I was pursuing a PhD in the field of Syrian family law.
25. For example, court *mores* prescribed that you could not sit with your legs crossed in the presence of a judge, a habit which proved difficult for me to break.

26. Compare with Dupret and Sonneveld, who both underlined the orientation of Egyptian judges towards procedural correctness in their rulings and interactions with litigants and lawyers (Baudouin Dupret, 'The Practice of Judging: The Egyptian Judiciary at Work in a Personal Status Case', in Muhammad K. Masud et al. (eds), *Dispensing Justice in Islam. Qadis and their Judgements* (Leiden, Brill, 2006), pp. 150–7); Nadia Sonneveld, 'Khul' Divorce in Egypt: How Family Courts Are Providing a "Dialogue" between Husband and Wife', *Anthropology in the Middle East* 5/2 (2010), pp. 106–8, respectively).
27. Just before I finalised my research plans in the spring of 2007, the Minister of Justice had issued a regulation denying foreigners access to Syrian courtrooms.
28. In Syria, court sessions are generally open to public.
29. Mainly due to conflicting court schedules; on one occasion the court was closed for no apparent reason, or sometimes the witnesses did not appear on the scheduled hearing date, which meant the hearing had to be postponed.
30. On seven occasions (i.e. days) I was able to attend 26 court hearings.
31. Taking notes meant a limitation to my data collection, as I could not note everything down verbatim. Instead I wrote summaries of the events and/or my observations. The observations were thus my own interpretation of the events and interactions.
32. Panagiotis Geros, 'Doing Fieldwork within Fear and Silences', in Heidi Armbruster and Anna Lærke, *Taking Sides: Ethics, Politics and Fieldwork in Anthropology* (New York, Berghahn Books, 2010), p. 94.
33. Ibid., p. 95 ff.
34. Initially, I considered applying for permission from the Ministry of Justice to visit the *shar'iyya* courts but several of my informants advised against it, because they considered the chance of acquiring permission to be close to zero. Besides, it would only draw the attention of the authorities to my presence in the court and my research – a risk that would be better avoided.

Chapter 1 Law, Politics and Religion in Syria: Past and Present

1. Apart from a short intermission from 1831 to 1833, when the Egyptian viceroy, Muhammad 'Ali Pasha, conquered Syria, together with Palestine and Lebanon.
2. There are four established Sunni schools of law, namely the Hanafi, Maliki, Shafi'i and the Hanbali school of law.
3. See C.V. Findley, 'Maḥkama. ii. The reform era (ca. 1789–1922)', in C.E. Bosworth et al. (eds), *Encyclopaedia of Islam*, Vol. VI, 2nd edn (Leiden, Brill, 1991a), pp. 5–11; Halil İnalcık 'Ḳānūn. iii. Financial and Public Administration', in E. van Donzel et al. (eds), *Encyclopaedia of Islam*, Vol. IV, 2nd edn (Leiden, Brill, 1978), pp. 558–62.

4. See, for example, Anh Nga Longva, 'From the *Dhimma* to the Capitulations: Memory and Experience of Protection in Lebanon', in A.N. Longva and A.S. Roald (eds), *Religious Minorities in the Middle East: Domination, Self-Empowerment, Accommodation* (Leiden, Brill, 2012), pp. 47–69.
5. For an analysis of the concept 'millet' (including the *millet* system), see Maurits H. van den Boogert, 'Millets: Past and Present', in A.N. Longva and A.S. Roald (eds), *Religious Minorities in the Middle East: Domination, Self-Empowerment, Accommodation* (Leiden, Brill, 2012), pp. 27–45.
6. Anh Nga Longva, 'From the *Dhimma* to the Capitulations: Memory and Experience of Protection in Lebanon', in A.N. Longva and A.S. Roald (eds), *Religious Minorities in the Middle East: Domination, Self-Empowerment, Accommodation* (Leiden, Brill, 2012), p. 49.
7. Cf. Najwa al-Qattan, 'Dhimmis in the Muslim Court: Legal Autonomy and Religious Discrimination', *International Journal of Middle East Studies* 31/3 (1999), pp. 429–44; Ronald C. Jennings, 'Zimmis (non-Muslims) in Early 17th Century Ottoman Judicial Records: The Sharia Court of Anatolian Kayseri', *Journal of the Economic and Social History of the Orient* 21/3 (1978), pp. 225–93; Bruce Masters, *Christians and Jews in the Ottoman Arab World. The Roots of Sectarianism* (Cambridge, Cambridge University Press, 2001), amongst many others.
8. Najwa al-Qattan, 'Dhimmis in the Muslim Court: Legal Autonomy and Religious Discrimination', *International Journal of Middle East Studies* 31/3 (1999), p. 433.
9. Ibid., pp. 433–5.
10. David D. Grafton, *The Christians of Lebanon: Political Rights in Islamic Law* (London, I.B.Tauris, 2003), pp. 74–5.
11. However, the formal nationality law was only passed in 1869 (see Kemal H. Karpat, 'Millets and Nationality: The Roots of the Incongruity of Nation and State in the Post-Ottoman Era', in B. Braude and B. Lewis (eds), *Christians and Jews in the Ottoman Empire: The Functioning of a Plural Society* (New York, Holmes & Meier Publishers, 1982), pp. 162–3).
12. Grafton, *The Christians of Lebanon*, p. 75; R.H. Davidson, 'Tanẓīmāt', in P. Bearman et al. (eds), *Encyclopaedia of Islam*, Vol. X, 2nd edn (Leiden, Brill, 2000), pp. 201–9.
13. Maurits H. van den Boogert, 'Millets: Past and Present', in A.N. Longva and A.S. Roald (eds), *Religious Minorities in the Middle East: Domination, Self-Empowerment, Accommodation* (Leiden, Brill, 2012), p. 35.
14. Boogert, 'Millets', p. 39; Mariz Tadros, 'The Non-Muslim 'Other': Gender and Contestations of Hierarchy or Rights', *Hawwa: Journal of Women of the Middle East and the Islamic World* 7 (2009), p. 115.
15. Longva, 'From the Dhimma', pp. 51–3.
16. The new laws were primarily based on European, especially French, models, such as the 1850 Commercial Code, the 1858 Penal Code and the 1861 Code of Commercial Procedure.

17. Elizabeth Thompson, *Colonial Citizens. Republican Rights, Paternal Privilege, and Gender in French Syria and Lebanon* (New York, Columbia University Press, 2000), p. 114.
18. Avi Rubin, 'Legal borrowing and its impact on Ottoman legal culture in the late nineteenth century', *Continuity and Change* 22/2 (2007), pp. 279–80.
19. The *nizamiyya* courts were modelled after the French judiciary structure: a three-tier court system was introduced, including first-instance courts, courts of appeal, and a Court of Cassation in Istanbul. The courts were divided into commercial, criminal and civil sectors. The codes of procedure which dictated the judicial proceedings at these courts were largely a direct translation of French law codes (ibid., pp. 283–4).
20. C.V. Findley, 'Medjelle', in C.E. Bosworth et al. (eds), *Encyclopaedia of Islam*, Vol. VI, 2nd edn (Leiden, Brill, 1991b), pp. 971–2.
21. Some scholars argue that the whole process of codification and legislation itself is completely alien to classical Islamic legal theory, see, for example, Aharon Layish, 'The Transformation of the *Shari'a* from Jurists' Law to Statutory Law in the Contemporary Muslim World', *Die Welt des Islams* 44/1 (2004), pp. 85–113.
22. J.N.D. Anderson, 'Law as a Social Force in Islamic Culture and History', *Bulletin of the School of Oriental and African Studies*, University of London 20-1/3 (1957), p. 24; Dora G. Nadolski, 'Ottoman and Secular Civil Law', *International Journal of Middle East Studies* 8/4 (1977), p. 524.
23. In Turkey, the *Mecelle* was abrogated in 1926 and replaced for the (translated to Turkish) Swiss Civil Code. In Syria, the *Mecelle* remained applicable during the French Mandate period until it was replaced by the Syrian Civil Code in 1949 (Findley, 'Medjelle').
24. Anderson, 'Law as a Social Force', p. 24.
25. Ibid., p. 27.
26. B.F. Stowasser and Z. Abul-Magd, 'Legal Codes and Contemporary Fatawa: Muslim Women and Contesting Paradigms', *Hawwa: Journal of Women of the Middle East and the Islamic World* 6 (2008), p. 41.
27. Lynn Welchman, *Beyond the Code: Muslim Family Law and the Shari'a Judiciary in the Palestinian West Bank* (The Hague, Kluwer Law International, 2000), p. 10.
28. Stowasser and Abul-Magd, 'Legal Codes', p. 41.
29. Amira E.A Sonbol, 'Shari'ah and State Formation: Historical Perspective', *Chicago Journal of International Law* 8/1 (2007), p. 75.
30. In addition, a law on *shari'a* court procedure was issued in 1917; see Findley, 'Maḥkama. ii. The reform era', pp. 5–11.
31. Comprising modern-day Lebanon, Syria, Jordan, and part of Palestine.
32. However, its radius of authority never really extended beyond the cities of Damascus, Aleppo, Hama and Homs (see P.S. Khoury, *Syria and the French Mandate: The Politics of Arab Nationalism, 1920–1945* (Princeton, Princeton University Press, 1987), p. 19).

33. B. Botiveau, 'Le movement de rationalisation du droit en syrie au cours de la première moitié du XXe siècle', *Bulletin d'Études Orientales* 35 (Damascus, Institut Français de Damas, 1983), pp. 130, 133.
34. Albert Hourani, *A History of the Arab Peoples* (New York, Grand Central Publishing, 1991), p. 318.
35. P.S. Khoury, *Syria and the French Mandate: The Politics of Arab Nationalism, 1920–1945* (Princeton, Princeton University Press, 1987), pp. 58–9.
36. Ibid., p. 152 ff.
37. Ibid., p. 248–51.
38. Ibid., p. 300.
39. Ibid., p. 340.
40. Ibid., p. 340–1, 348.
41. Botiveau, 'Le movement de rationalisation', p. 129.
42. Martin Kramer, 'Syria's Alawis and Shi'ism', in M. Kramer (ed.), *Shi'ism, Resistance, and Revolution* (Boulder, Westview Press, 1987), p. 240.
43. Ibid., pp. 243–4.
44. Thompson, *Colonial Citizens*, p. 113.
45. Grafton, *The Christians of Lebanon*, p. 94.
46. Thompson, *Colonial Citizens*, p. 114.
47. Botiveau, 'Le movement de rationalisation', p. 131.
48. In contrast to Turkey, where the first President of the new republic (est. 1923), Mustafa Kemal Atatürk, abolished Islamic laws and religious courts altogether (Thompson, *Colonial Citizens*, p. 114).
49. Ibid., p. 115.
50. Grafton, *The Christians of Lebanon*, p. 96.
51. Thompson, *Colonial Citizens*, p. 152.
52. Suad Joseph, *Gender and Citizenship in the Middle East. Contemporary Issues in the Middle East* (edited by S. Joseph) (Syracuse, NY, Syracuse University Press, 2000), p. 130.
53. Grafton, *The Christians of Lebanon*, p. 97.
54. Also known as the 'Law of Communities' (*nizam* or *qanun al-tawa'if*), see Thomas Pierret, *Religion and State in Syria: the Sunni Ulama from Coup to Revolution* (Cambridge, Cambridge University Press, 2013), p. 168.
55. Ibid.
56. Thompson, *Colonial Citizens*, p. 152.
57. Benjamin T. White, 'Addressing the State: The Syrian "Ulama" Protest Personal Status Law Reform, 1939', *International Journal Middle Eastern Studies* 42 (2010), p. 11.
58. Jacques el-Hakim, 'Syria', in *Yearbook of Islamic and Middle Eastern Law* Vol. 1 (1994) (London, Kluwer Law International, 1995), p. 148.
59. William L. Cleveland, *A History of the Modern Middle East* (Boulder, Westview Press, 2000), pp. 212–3.
60. R. Roded, 'Lessons by a Syrian Islamist from the Life of the Prophet Muhammad', *Middle Eastern Studies* 42/6 (2006), p. 861.

61. J.N.D. Anderson, 'Modern Trends in Islam: Legal Reform and Modernisation in the Middle East', *International and Comparative Law Quarterly* 20/1 (1971), p. 12.
62. Nabil Saleh, 'Civil Codes of Arab Countries: The Sanhuri Codes', *Arab Law Quarterly* 8/2 (1993), pp. 162–3.
63. English translation taken from G.M. Badr, 'The New Egyptian Civil Code and the Unification of the laws of the Arab Countries', *Tulane Law Review* 30 (1955–56), p. 302.
64. Guy Bechor, *The Sanhuri Code, and the Emergence of Modern Arab Civil Law (1932 to 1949)* (Leiden, Brill, 2007), p. 57.
65. Badr, 'The New Egyptian Civil Code', p. 302.
66. Joshua Landis, 'Shishakli and the Druzes: Integration and Intransigence', in T. Philipp and B. Schäbler (eds), *The Syrian Land: Processes of Integration and Fragmentation* (Stuttgart, Franz Steiner Verlag, 1998), p. 369.
67. 'Aflaq and Al-Bitar belonged to the Damascene middle-class, they were both school teacher and graduates from Sorbonne University in Paris, where they studied in the early 1930s (see Nikolaos van Dam, *The Struggle for Power in Syria: Politics and Society under Asad and the Ba'th Party*, 4th edn (London, I.B.Tauris, 2011).
68. Nikolaos van Dam, *The Struggle for Power in Syria: Politics and Society under Asad and the Ba'th Party*, 4th edn (London, I.B.Tauris, 2011), p. 15.
69. Khoury, *Syria and the French mandate*, pp. 605–6.
70. Line Khatib, *Islamic Revivalism in Syria: The Rise and Fall of Ba'thist Secularism* (London, Routledge, 2011), p. 24.
71. Khoury, *Syria and the French mandate*, p. 606.
72. P. Seale, *Asad of Syria: The Struggle for the Middle East* (Berkeley, University of California Press, 1990), pp. 76–7.
73. Umar F. Abd-Allah, *The Islamic Struggle in Syria* (Berkeley, Mizan Press, 1983), pp. 53–4.
74. Mariam Cooke, *Dissident Syria: Making Oppositional Arts Official* (Durham, Duke University Press, 2007), p. 7.
75. Cf. Raymond Hinnebusch, 'The Ba'th Party in Post-Ba'thist Syria: President, Party and the Struggle for "Reform"', *Middle East Critique* 20/2 (2011), 109–25; Dam, *The Struggle for Power.*
76. Abd-Allah, *The Islamic Struggle*, p. 17.
77. See, for example, Dam, *The Struggle for Power*, p. 111; Seale, *Asad of Syria*, p. 334.
78. Annika Rabo, 'Conviviality and Conflict in Contemporary Aleppo', in A.N. Longva and A.S. Roald (eds), *Religious Minorities in the Middle East: Domination, Self-Empowerment, Accommodation* (Leiden, Brill, 2012a), p. 131.
79. Ibid.
80. Annika Rabo, 'Gender, State and Civil Society in Jordan and Syria', in C. Hann and E. Dunn (eds), *Civil Society. Challenging Western Models* (London, Routledge, 1996), pp. 168–70. See also Khatib, *Islamic Revivalism*, p. 102.

81. Rabo, 'Gender, State', p. 170.
82. The Constitution was amended to lower the minimum age allowing for a president to take office, from the age of 40 to 34 (Dam, *The Struggle for Power*, pp. 132–3).
83. The presidential election was only held in territories controlled by the government, excluding the areas that were under rebel control; according to the Supreme Constitutional Court the turnout was 73.42 per cent. See *The Guardian* (4 June 2014), 'Bashar al-Assad wins re-election in Syria as uprising against him rages on'. Available at: http://www.theguardian.com/world/2014/jun/04/bashar-al-assad-winds-reelection-in-landslide-victory (accessed 4 September 2014).
84. Cooke, *Dissident Syria*, pp. 160–1. Following the assassination of the Lebanese Prime Minister Rafiq Hariri and Syria's subsequent withdrawal of Syrian armed troops from Lebanon in 2005, several Syrian opposition figures and groups, including human rights advocates, Communists, Kurdish Nationalists and the Muslim Brotherhood, issued a joint document – 'Damascus Declaration for Democratic and National Change' (October 2005) – establishing a united platform for democratic change. In the years that followed, a number of signatories were arrested and sentenced to imprisonment (Pace and Landis 2009, p. 128 ff.).
85. The state of emergency was declared by a legislative decree in December 1962 by the Shakisly-regime. The Ba'th regime, after seizing power on 8 March 1963, re-issued the state of emergency by a military command on the day it came to power, formalising it the next day as Legislative Decree No. 1. The State of Emergency Law gave extraordinary powers to members of the government and the judiciary; it authorised the restriction of freedom of movement and assembly, and the arrest of anyone suspected of endangering state security and public order, disturbing public confidence, and other similar offences (see Alan George, *Syria: Neither Bread nor Freedom* (London, Zed Books, 2003). p. 108).
86. BBC News website (7 April 2011), 'Syria's Assad grants nationality to Hasaka Kurds'. Available at http://www.bbc.co.uk/news/world-middle-east-12995174 (accessed 8 September 2014).
87. Anyone who could not prove he/she was a Syrian citizen or who was not at home at the time of the census or refused to participate in the census had his/her Syrian citizenship removed, and was listed as a 'foreigner' or 'unrecorded' (interview Sawsan Zakzak, Syrian Women League and independent researcher, Damascus, 13 April 2008).
88. Zahra Albarazi, 'The Stateless Syrians', Tilburg Law School Research Paper No. 011/2013 (32 pp.), p. 16.
89. See, for example: http://www.reuters.com/article/2012/02/27/us-syria-referendum-idUSTRE81Q1CZ20120227 (accessed 14 March 2012).
90. Translation taken from the Syrian Arab News Agency (SANA) website: http://www.sana.sy/en/?page_id = 1489 (accessed 26 September 2014).

91. See Jörg Michael Dostal, 'Analyzing the domestic and international conflict in Syria: Are there lessons from political science?', in J.M. Dostal and O. Imady (eds), *Syria Studies* 6/1 (Fife, University of St Andrews Centre for Syrian Studies, 2014), p. 52.
92. BBC News website (7 May 2012), 'Syrians vote for new parliament amid boycott calls'. Available at http://www.bbc.com/news/world-middle-east-17980342 (accessed 26 September 2014).
93. Provided candidates receive the support of at least 35 members of Parliament (Art. 85.3).
94. Also referred to as ISIL, ISIS or Da'ish (the Arabic acronym).
95. Al-Jazeera website (23 September 2014), 'US and allies strike ISIL targets in Syria'. Available at http://www.aljazeera.com/news/middleeast/2014/09/us-begins-bombing-isil-positions-syria-201492313622252650.html (accessed 16 October 2014).
96. Translation taken from the Syrian Arab News Agency (SANA) website: http://www.sana.sy/en/?page_id = 1489 (accessed 26 September 2014).
97. Earlier constitutions stated that *fiqh* was *the* main source of legislation (Khatib, *Islamic Revivalism*, p. 19).
98. English translation taken from S.H. Amin, *Middle East Legal Systems* (Glasgow, Royston Limited, 1985), p. 359.
99. This third paragraph is a contraction of the two paragraphs of Article 35 of the 1973 Constitution; the English translation (of the 1973 Constitution) is taken from the International Constitutional Law (ICL) Project. Available at http://www.servat.unibe.ch/icl/sy00000_.html (accessed 15 March 2012).
100. However, a similar provision was included in the Constitutions of 1950, 1953 and 1962 (Maurits S. Berger, 'The legal system of family law in Syria', *Bulletin d'Études Orientales* 49 (Damascus, Institut Français de Damas, 1997), p. 117 n. 6).
101. Seale, *Asad of Syria*, p. 173.
102. A. Böttcher, *Official Sunni and Shi'i Islam in Syria* (EUI Working Paper RSC No. 2002/3) (Florence, European University Institute, 2002), p. 15.
103. Kramer, 'Syria's Alawis', pp. 247–8.
104. Seale, *Asad of Syria*, p. 173.
105. Khatib, *Islamic Revivalism*, p. 88 ff.
106. Böttcher, *Official Sunni*, pp. 5–7.
107. Ibid., p. 15.
108. Elham Manea, *The Arab State and Women's Rights: The Trap of Authoritarian Governance* (London, Routledge, 2011), pp. 182–3.
109. Pierret, *Religion and State*, p. 76 ff. In addition, the Grand Mufti or other recognised Islamic authority rarely issues *fatwa*'s on social or political issues (see Pierret 2009, pp. 78–9). For an elaborate study of contemporary state-*'ulama'* relations in Syria, see Pierret, *Religion and State*.
110. Paulo G. Pinto, '"Oh Syria, God Protects You": Islam as Cultural Idiom under Bashar al-Asad', *Middle East Critique* 20/2 (2011), p. 192.

111. Until 2012 (when the 2012 Constitution introduced a multi-party system), the National Progressive Front (established in 1972), headed by the President of Syria, was guaranteed two-thirds of the 250 seats in the People's Assembly. The Front is a coalition of the Ba'th Party and a number of smaller left-wing political parties. From 1990–2012, the remaining seats were open to independent pro-government candidates, including prominent Islamic figures (Khatib, *Islamic Revivalism*, pp. 93, 117–18).
112. Pinto, 'Oh Syria', p. 193; Khatib, *Islamic Revivalism*, p. 90 ff.
113. Pinto, 'Oh Syria', p. 191.
114. Ibid., p. 194.
115. Ibid., p. 191.
116. B. Botiveau, 'The Law of the Nation-State and the Status of Non-Muslims in Egypt and Syria', in A. Pacini (ed.), *Christian Communities in the Arab Middle East: The Challenge of the Future* (Oxford, Clarendon Press, 1998), p. 118.
117. For a similar situation in Egypt, see Maurits S. Berger, *Sharia and Public Policy in Egyptian Family Law* (Groningen, Hephaestus Publishers, 2005), p. 27 ff. In Morocco, Algeria, and Tunisia, on the other hand, this plurality in the legal system was abrogated (Elizabeth A. Mayer, 'Reform of Personal Status Laws in North Africa: A Problem of Islamic or Mediterranean laws?' *Middle East Journal* 49/3 (1995), p. 433).
118. Cf. Maurits S. Berger, *Sharia and Public Policy in Egyptian Family Law* (Groningen, Hephaestus Publishers, 2005); Nael Georges, *Le droit des minorités: Le cas de chrétiens en Orient arabe* (Aix-en-Provence, Presses Universitaires d'Aix-Marseille, 2012); Mariz Tadros, 'The Non-Muslim "Other": Gender and Contestations of Hierarchy or Rights', *Hawwa: Journal of Women of the Middle East and the Islamic World* 7 (2009), pp. 111–43. For a similar situation with regard to (Islamic) education in Syria, that is, the dominance of Sunni Islamic orthodoxy in Syria's education system, see Joshua Landis, 'Syria: Secularism, Arabism, and Sunni Orthodoxy', in E.A. Doumato and G. Starrett (eds), *Teaching Islam. Textbooks and Religion in the Middle East* (Boulder, Lynne Riener Publishers, 2007), pp. 177–96.
119. Botiveau calls this an 'imperfect citizenship'; in Egypt's and Syria's case this means that citizenship is not only linked to a territory but also to religion (see Botiveau, 'The Law of the Nation-State', pp. 122–3).
120. Annika Rabo, 'Syrian Transnational Families and Family Law', in A. Hellum et al. (eds), *From Transnational Relations to Transnational Laws: Northern European Laws at the Crossroads* (Farnham, Ashgate Publishers, 2011), p. 80.
121. Rania Maktabi, 'Gender, family law and citizenship in Syria', *Citizenship Studies* 14/5 (2010), p. 568.
122. Maktabi, 'Gender, family law', p. 565.
123. Paul S. Rowe, 'Neo-millet Systems and Transnational Religious Movements: The Humayun Decrees and Church Construction in Egypt', *Journal of Church and State* 49 (2007), p. 331.
124. Ibid.

125. Damascus is home to three patriarchates.
126. Fiona McCallum, 'Religious institutions and authoritarian states: church–state relations in the Middle East', *Third World Quarterly* 33/1 (2012), pp. 121–2.
127. Tadros, 'The Non-Muslim "Other"', p. 119.

Chapter 2 Mapping the Plurality of Jurisdictions: The Laws of Personal Status

1. Maurits S. Berger, *Sharia and Public Policy in Egyptian Family Law* (Groningen, Hephaestus Publishers, 2005), p. 46.
2. Central Intelligence Agency, *The World Fact Book*; *2013 International Religious Freedom Report – Syria*. In addition, I have not been able to obtain any information on the Yazidi community in Syria; I assume they fall under the general jurisdiction of the SLPS and the *shar'iyya* courts.
3. J.N.D. Anderson, 'The Syrian Law of Personal Status', *Bulletin of the School of Oriental and African Studies* 17/1 (1955), p. 34.
4. Ibid., p. 35. In his analysis of the SLPS, Anderson compares the SLPS with the 1917 Ottoman Law of Family Rights, Egyptian laws, and the Jordanian Personal Status Law of 1951.
5. Ibid., p. 35. In Arabic: *yakhtaru min al-aqwal akthariha mawafaqat li-l-'urf wa-mutabiqat li-l-maslahat al-zamaniyya* (see Mamduh 'Atari (ed.), *qanun al-ahwal al-shakhsiyya* (Law of Personal Status) (Damascus, mu'assasat al-nuri, 2006), p. 6).
6. For an explanation of the various legal devices used by twentieth-century law-makers, see Wael B. Hallaq, *Sharī'a: Theory, Practice, Transformations* (New York, Cambridge University Press, 2008), pp. 447–9.
7. An example of a provision which has, according to Anderson, a base in Ja'fari *fiqh*, i.e. the Twelver Shi'i school of law, is Article 90, which deals with a repudiation pronounced intended only as a threat, to induce some action or as an oath (Anderson, 'The Syrian Law', p. 39 n. 3). This type of repudiation is subject to nullification, see Appendix (xii).
8. See Explanatory Memorandum to the SLPS.
9. Anderson, 'The Syrian Law', p. 35.
10. J.N.D. Anderson, 'Law as a Social Force in Islamic Culture and History', *Bulletin of the School of Oriental and African Studies*, University of London 20-1/3 (1957), p. 31.
11. Aharon Layish, 'The Contribution of the Modernists to the Secularization of Islamic Law', *Middle Eastern Studies* 14/3 (1978), p. 270).
12. The principle of *siyasa shar'iyya* refers to the discretionary authority of the ruler to promulgate legislation as long as it is in accordance with and supplements *shari'a* (Hallaq, *Sharī'a: Theory*, 2008), p. 200 ff.
13. 'Atari, *qanun al-ahwal al-shakhsiyya* (Law of Personal Status), p. 8.
14. A good number of countries followed suit and included a similar provision in their personal status laws, including Morocco (1958), Iraq (1959), Jordan (1976), Egypt (1985), and Yemen (1992); see Lynn Welchman,

Women and Muslim Family Laws in Arab States: A Comparative Overview of Textual Development and Advocacy (Amsterdam, Amsterdam University Press, 2007), pp. 126, 217 n. 92.

15. 'Atari, *qanun al-ahwal al-shakhsiyya*, p. 10.
16. Anderson, 'The Syrian Law of Personal Status', p. 41; Layish, 'The Contribution of the Modernists', p. 271. The Explanatory Memorandum refers to works of the Hanafi jurists Ibn Najim and Ibn 'Abidin as sources of reference for Article 117; see 'Atari, *qanun al-ahwal al-shakhsiyya*, p. 10.
17. Zouhair Ghazzal, 'Droit et société', in B. Dupret et al. (eds), *La Syrie au présent: Reflets d'une société* (Arles, Actes Sud, 2007a), p. 653. The SLPS classifies the major topics in books (sg. *kitab*), sub-topics in chapters (sg. *bab*), which are, in turn, broken down into 'sections' (sg. *fasl*).
18. Welchman, *Women and Muslim Family Laws*, pp. 45–6.
19. Jessica Carlisle, *Rules, Negotiation, Claims and Counter Claims: Judicial Discretion in a Damascus Shari'a Court* (unpublished PhD thesis, University of London, 2007c), p. 68.
20. In Arabic: *kitab al-ahkam al-shar'iyyat fi al-ahwal al-shakhsiyyat 'ala madhhab al-imam abi hanifa al-nu'man* [*Book of Legal Rulings in Personal Status according to the School of Imam Abi Hanifa*].
21. Nahda Shehada, 'House of Obedience: Social Norms, Individual Agency and Historical Contingency', *Journal of Middle Eastern Women's Studies* 5/10 (2009a), pp. 30 and 46 n. 15. Likewise, Dupret asserts that Egyptian judges make use of the Qadri Pasha Code (Baudouin Dupret, 'The Practice of Judging: The Egyptian Judiciary at Work in a Personal Status Case', in Muhammad K. Masud et al. (eds), *Dispensing Justice in Islam: Qadis and their Judgements* (Leiden, Brill, 2006), p. 150).
22. Nahda Shehada, 'Negotiating Custody Rights in Islamic Family Law', in T. Kirsch and B. Turner (eds), *Permutations of Order: Religion and Law as Contested Sovereignties* (Farnham, Ashgate, 2009c), p. 250.
23. Cf. Shehada, 'Negotiating Custody Rights'; Maaike Voorhoeve, 'Judicial Discretion in Tunisian Personal Status Law', in M. Voorhoeve (ed.), *Family Law in Islam. Divorce, Marriage and Women in the Muslim World* (London, I.B. Tauris, 2012).
24. Anderson, 'The Syrian Law of Personal Status', p. 34. For example, Syria was the first post-independent Arab country to restrict polygamous marriages. The text of the 1953 SLPS stipulated that a husband has to prove he can support more than one wife, before a judge can give permission for a second marriage.
25. Voorhoeve, 'Judicial Discretion', p. 199.
26. Interestingly, Syrian and Tunisian legal experts were involved in the South Yemeni family law drafting process in the early 1970s. The South Yemeni law, promulgated in 1974, included some progressive provisions that were clearly inspired by the personal status laws of Tunisia and Syria (Maxine Molyneux, 'Women's Rights and Political Contingency: The Case of Yemen, 1990–1994', *Middle East Journal* 49/3 (1995), pp. 421–2).

27. Muhammad Fihr Shaqfa, *sharh ahkam al-ahwal al-shakhsiyya: li-l-muslimin wa-l-nasara wa-l-yahud* [*Explaining the Law of Personal Status: Muslims, Christians, and Jews*] (Damascus, Mu'assasat Al-Nuri, 1998), p. 19.
28. According to Layish, the SLPS is, at least in theory, also applicable to matrimonial matters in the Druze court on the Israeli-occupied Golan Heights (Aharon Layish, *Marriage, Divorce and Succession in the Druze Family: A Study based on decisions of Druze arbitrators and religious courts in Israel and the Golan Heights* (Leiden, Brill, 1982) p. 12).
29. Mariz Tadros, 'The Non-Muslim 'Other': Gender and Contestations of Hierarchy or Rights', *Hawwa: Journal of Women of the Middle East and the Islamic World* 7 (2009), p. 114.
30. Maurits S. Berger, 'The legal system of family law in Syria', *Bulletin d'Études Orientales* 49 (Damascus, Institut Français de Damas, 1997), p. 126; Dina C. Feller, *La garde (Ḥaḍanah) en droit musulman et dans les droits égyptien, syrien et tunisien* (Geneve, Librairie Droz, 1996), p. 36.
31. Berger, *Sharia and public policy*, pp. 28–9.
32. B. Botiveau, 'The Law of the Nation-State and the Status of Non-Muslims in Egypt and Syria', in A. Pacini (ed.), *Christian Communities in the Arab Middle East: The Challenge of the Future* (Oxford, Clarendon Press, 1998), p. 119 n. 14.
33. Ghazzal, 'Droit et société', p. 262.
34. Monique C. Cardinal, 'Why Aren't Women Sharīʿa Court judges? The Case of Syria', *Islamic Law and Society* 17 (2010), pp. 213–14).
35. See also Berger, 'The legal system', p. 121.
36. Moreover, if one or both parties is/are Muslim, the case ought to be referred to a civil court (Berger, 'The legal system', p. 126).
37. Cardinal, 'Why Aren't Women', p. 201 n. 40.
38. Monique C. Cardinal, 'Islamic Legal Theory Curriculum: Are the Classics Taught Today?', Islamic Law and Society 12/2 (2005), p. 229 n. 10.
39. Cardinal, 'Why Aren't Women', pp. 186–7, 206.
40. Cardinal, 'Islamic Legal Theory Curriculum', pp. 189–90. For an elaborate analysis of this line of reasoning, please refer to this article written by Cardinal.
41. Cardinal notes that the identical university textbook on personal status law is used at the Faculty of Law *and* the Faculty of Shariʿa of Damascus University (Cardinal, 'Why Aren't Women', p. 193 n. 20).
42. Annika Rabo, 'We are Christians and we are equal citizens': perspectives on particularity and pluralism in contemporary Syria', *Islam and Christian–Muslim Relations* 23/1 (2012b), p. 84.
43. B. Botiveau, *Loi islamique et droit dans les sociétés arabes. Mutations de systèmes juridiques du Moyen-Orient* (Paris, Karthala, 1993), pp. 180–1.
44. Cardinal, 'Why Aren't Women', p. 206.
45. Ibid., p. 207.
46. Interview, 26 March 2009, Damascus.
47. Cardinal, 'Why Aren't Women', p. 205.

48. More than that, in my observation, several senior lawyers also had limited knowledge on other personal status laws. For example, one of the senior lawyers working in Mr Mulhim's office claimed that there was no such thing as a separate Druze personal status law (visit 1 April 2008).
49. Interview with Mr Mulhim, lawyer and member of the Board of the Damascus Bar Association, Damascus, 13 April 2009.
50. Mr Mulhim's law office numbered six senior lawyers, including himself, who were responsible for the training of around 20 lawyer trainees (visit 6 April 2009).
51. In the end, we only gave two mini-lectures on a Monday morning; on the two occasions (6 and 16 April 2009) there were about five to eight trainees present. We focused on the Catholic personal status law and the Catholic court procedures. Mr Mulhim commented and drew comparisons with the SLPS on various topics, such as the duty of the wife to be obedient to her husband. The Catholic personal status law, analogous to the provisions of the SLPS, stipulates that a woman who is disobedient to her husband, for example by leaving the house of her own accord, loses her right to maintenance.
52. Estimates of the number of Druze residing in Syria vary greatly, the number mentioned here is based on figures presented on the website of the American Druze Heritage, which lists various numbers and sources, without claiming to know the exact number of Druze worldwide (see http://americandruze.com/Druze%20Population.html, accessed 16 May 2012). There are also considerable communities in Lebanon, Israel, and Jordan.
53. M.G.S. Hodgson, 'Durūz', in B. Lewis et al. (eds), *Encyclopaedia of Islam*, Vol. II, 2nd edn (Leiden, Brill, 1965), pp. 631–4.
54. Joshua Landis, 'Syria: Secularism, Arabism, and Sunni Orthodoxy', in E.A. Doumato and G. Starrett (eds), *Teaching Islam: Textbooks and Religion in the Middle East* (Boulder, Lynne Riener Publishers, 2007), p. 188). It remained unclear to me whether they regard or present themselves as Muslims, by means of *taqiyya* ('simulation'). My interactions with members of the Druze community were limited; besides, I did not investigate the matter closely.
55. Aharon Layish, 'The status of Islamic law in the Druze family in a non-Muslim state as reflected in judicial practice', in K. Kehl-Bodrogi et al. (eds), *Syncretistic Religious Communities in the Near East* (Leiden, Brill, 1997), p. 143.
56. Layish, 'The status of Islamic law', p. 139.
57. Landis, 'Syria', p. 188.
58. Interview with judge of the Druze court, Ma'moun Barjas Al-'Afif, 19 May 2009, Suwayda. In addition, Article 35.3 Judicial Authority Law makes note of this abolished appeal court.
59. Aharon Layish, *Marriage, Divorce and Succession in the Druze Family: A Study Based on Decisions of Druze Arbitrators and Religious Courts in Israel and the Golan Heights* (Leiden, Brill, 1982), p. 287.
60. During my visit to the court, an employee of the court registry presented the court's registry book (*daftar*). He counted a total of 30 divorce cases in April

2009; 257 in 2006, 259 in 2007, and 312 in 2008, which included the three types of divorces recognised by the SLPS (i.e. *talaq*, *mukhala'a*, and *tafriq*).

61. The adjective 'Syriac' refers to the liturgical language used in these churches, namely classical Syriac, an Eastern Aramaic language, the language of the early Christians (Sebastian Brock, *An Introduction to Syriac Studies* (Piscataway, NJ, Gorgias Press, 2006) p. 20).
62. Cf. Anthony O'Mahony (ed.), *Christianity in the Middle East: Studies in Modern History, Theology and Politics* (London, Melisende, 2008); Anthony O'Mahony and Emma Loosley (eds), *Eastern Christianity in the Modern Middle East* (London, Routledge, 2010); Ken Parry (ed.), *The Blackwell Companion to Eastern Christianity* (Malden, Blackwell Publishing, 2007).
63. See the website of the Middle East Council of Churches (MECC). Available at www.mec-churches.org/member_churches/member_churches.htm (accessed 17 May 2012).
64. Central Intelligence Agency, *The World Fact Book*; *2013 International Religious Freedom Report* 2012.
65. Habib Moussalli, 'The Christians of Syria', in Andrea Pacini (ed.), *Christian Communities in the Arab Middle East: The Challenge of the Future* (Oxford, Clarendon Press, 1998), p. 287.
66. These churches follow the so-called Byzantine rite, which originates in the Greek city of Antioch and later developed in Byzantium or Constantinople. The adjective 'Greek' (in Arabic: *rum*) refers to the Byzantine rite and has no reference to the Hellenic ethnicity or nationality.
67. Youssef Courbage and Philippe Fargues, *Christians and Jews under Islam* (London, I.B.Tauris, 1998), p. 209. All the figures related to Christians cited in this chapter date back to 1995 and are cited this book by Courbage and Fargues.
68. For centuries, the Patriarch of Antioch resided in southeast Turkey, due to the political situation; in the first half of the twentieth century the Patriarchal See was forced to move, first to Homs in 1933, later to Damascus in 1959 (Heleen Murre-Van den Berg, 'Syriac Christianity', in K. Parry (ed.), *The Blackwell Companion to Eastern Christianity* (Malden, Blackwell Publishing, 2007), p. 259).
69. The Latins are also designated as Roman Catholics, meaning they follow the Western rite.
70. According to the minister and judge of the Damascus Evangelical court, Boutrus Za'our, a relatively new group in Syria, originally from Sudan (interview 26 March 2009, Damascus).
71. The Catholicos-Patriarch of the Assyrian Church of the East, Mar Dinkha IV, remains in exile in Chicago (Heleen Murre-Van den Berg, 'Syriac Christianity', in K. Parry (ed.), *The Blackwell Companion to Eastern Christianity* (Malden, Blackwell Publishing, 2007), p. 260).
72. See Damascus Bar Association website at: http://www.damascusbar.org/AlMuntada/showthread.php?t = 12413 (accessed 17 May 2012).

73. Berger, 'The legal system', p. 119. Interestingly, according to Rose, it is only in the Muslim-dominated countries that Christians have consciously developed and codified their own community laws (1982, pp. 160, 174).
74. Cardinal, 'Why Aren't Women', p. 201.
75. The Catholics in Lebanon, for example, are also governed by Eastern canon law, but in Lebanon the Catholic law never reached the official status of statutory law. In 1951, Christian and Jewish national laws were issued, but they were never ratified by the Lebanese government; they thus operate as 'quasi law' (interview with judge Fr Antoun of the Catholic court in Damascus, 25 April 2008; Lamia R. Shehadeh 'Gender-Relevant Legal Change in Lebanon', *Feminist Formations* 22/3 (2010), p. 211.
76. Interview with minister and judge of the Damascus Evangelical court, Boutrus Za'our, 26 March 2009, Damascus.
77. Ibid.
78. See Robert Tuttle, 'The Jews of Syria', on *SyriaComment.com* (24 October 2005). Available at http://faculty-staff.ou.edu/L/Joshua.M.Landis-1/syria-blog/2005/10/jews-of-syria-by-robert-tuttle.htm (accessed 18 May 2012); Mark Klingman, 'Diaspora Communities. 6. Syria/Lebanon', in Norman A. Stillman et al. (eds), *Encyclopedia of Jews in the Islamic World*, Vol. II (Leiden, Brill, 2010),
79. See also Berger's article, in which he refers to examples of Court of Cassation rulings in this regard ('The legal system', p. 120).
80. This gender imparity only exists in personal status cases, in civil and criminal law a woman's testimony is equal to that of a man (Zakaria Taha, 'Régimes arabes laïcs et politique du genre: La condition de la femme à travers le Code du statut personnel: le cas de la Syrie', *Cahiers de la Méditerranée* 81 (2010), p. 312 n. 47).
81. Cardinal, 'Why Aren't Women', p. 191.
82. See: http://www.syrianlaw.com/?page = news_read&threadid = 593 (accessed 16 July 2012).
83. Jacques el-Hakim, 'Syria', in *Yearbook of Islamic and Middle Eastern Law* Vol. 12 (2005–06) (London, Kluwer Law International, 2007), p. 280).
84. This requirement was abolished in 1949, under the rule of colonel Al-Za'im (B. Botiveau, The Law of the Nation-State and the Status of Non-Muslims in Egypt and Syria', in A. Pacini (ed.), *Christian Communities in the Arab Middle East: The Challenge of the Future* (Oxford, Clarendon Press, 1998), p. 115).
85. Cf. Maurits S. Berger, *Sharia and Public Policy in Egyptian Family Law* (Groningen, Hephaestus Publishers, 2005); Mariz Tadros, 'The Non-Muslim "Other": Gender and Contestations of Hierarchy or Rights', *Hawwa: Journal of Women of the Middle East and the Islamic World* 7 (2009).
86. Berger, 'The legal system', p. 122; interview with lawyer Hala Barbara, Damascus, 25 March 2008.

87. Berger uses the term 'interreligious law' to refer to the situation when more than one religious family law applies to a single case (2005, p. 102).
88. The Egyptian and Jordanian personal status laws, for example, also contain a similar provision to Article 48.2 SLPS (Anne F. Weber, 'Briser et suivre le norms: les couples islamo-chrétiens au Liban', in B. Drieskens (ed.), *Les métamorphoses du mariage au Moyen-Orient* (Beirut, Institut Français du Proche-Orient (IFPO) 2008), p. 28.
89. Ibid.
90. See, for example, Yüksel Sezgin, *Human Rights under State-Enforced Religious Family Laws in Israel, Egypt and India* (Cambridge, Cambridge University Press, 2013) p. 106; Lubna Tarabey, *Family Law in Lebanon: Marriage and Divorce among the Druze* (London, I.B.Tauris, 2013) p. 100.
91. Cf. Najwa Al-Qattan, 'Dhimmis in the Muslim Court: Legal Autonomy and Religious Discrimination', *International Journal of Middle East Studies* 31/3 (1999); Aznan Hasan, 'Granting Khul for a Non-Muslim Couple in Egyptian Personal Status Law: Generosity or Laxity?', *Arab Law Quarterly* 18/1 (2003); Richard B. Rose, 'Islam and the Development of Personal Status Laws Among Christian Dhimmis: Motives, Sources, Consequences', *The Muslim World* 72/3-4 (1982), pp. 159–79; Ron Shaham, 'Jews and the Sharī'a Courts in Modern Egypt', *Studia Islamica* 82 (1995), Shopping for legal forums: Christians and family law in modern Egypt', in Khaled Masud et al. (eds), *Dispensing justice in Islam: Qadis and their judgments* (Leiden, Brill, 2006).
92. Rania Maktabi, 'Gender, family law and citizenship in Syria', *Citizenship Studies* 14/5 (2010), p. 562).
93. Personal communication with a senior Christian lawyer, November 2008, Damascus.
94. Berger, 'The legal system', p. 124–5.
95. Nael Georges, *Le droit des minorités. Le cas de chrétiens en Orient arabe* (Aix-en-Provence, Presses Universitaires d'Aix-Marseille, 2012), p. 294.
96. Cardinal, 'Why Aren't Women', p. 191.
97. See Tadros for a similar situation in Egypt ('The Non-Muslim 'Other'', p. 126 ff.); Georges observes similar legislative and legal practices in most Arab countries, with the exception of Lebanon (*Le droit des minorités*, pp. 289–92).
98. Georges, *Le droit des minorités*, p. 289.
99. The Syrian Court of Cassation ruled in 1981 that, based on Article 381 Qadri Pasha, a *shar'iyya* judge can investigate allegations of negative influence of a non-Muslim parent on the child's religion (Georges, *Le droit des minorités*, p. 289).
100. It should be added that this provision only concerns children who reside in a Muslim country, i.e. outside the 'house of Islam' (*dar al-islam*).
101. Feller, *La garde (Ḥaḥanah)*, p. 216.
102. Berger, 'The legal system', p. 125.
103. Nael Georges, 'Les chrétiens dans le monde arabe et la question de l'apostasie en islam', *Maghreb-Machrek* 209 (2011), pp. 118–9.

104. Georges does not give any further information on where or how the marriage was contracted, I suspect it was a so-called *'urfi* marriage (see Chapter 5 for a detailed discussion of these types of marriages).
105. Georges, *Le droit des minorités*, p. 294.
106. Tadros, 'The Non-Muslim "Other"', p. 130.
107. Ibid., p. 132.

Chapter 3 Debating and Changing Family Law

1. Alexis de Tocqueville, *L'Ancien régime et la Révolution* (Paris, Calmann Lévy, 1887), p. 259.
2. Léon Buskens, 'Recent Debates on Family Law Reform in Morocco: Islamic Law as Politics in an Emerging Public Sphere', *Islamic Law and Society* 10/1 (2003), p. 7; cf. Mariz Tadros 'The Non-Muslim "Other": Gender and Contestations of Hierarchy or Rights', *Hawwa: Journal of Women of the Middle East and the Islamic World* 7 (2009), p. 119.
3. Buskens, 'Recent Debates', p. 122.
4. Ibid., p. 71; cf. Marie-Aimée Hélie-Lucas, 'The Preferential Symbol for Islamic Identity: Women in Muslim Personal Laws', in V.M. Moghadam (ed.), *Identity Politics and Women. Cultural Reassertions and Feminisms in International Perspective* (Boulder, Westview Press, 1994).
5. Buskens, 'Recent Debates', pp. 79–83.
6. The sources that are used for this chapter are, most importantly: interviews with some of the most important participants of the recent debates, such as initiators of the 2003 petition, members of civil society groups, members of Parliament, lawyers, scholars, and religious figures. In addition, reference will be made to some of the draft law projects that were published, which are in the possession of the author.
7. Nikolaos van Dam, *The Struggle for Power in Syria: Politics and Society under Asad and the Ba'th Party*, 4th edn (London, I.B.Tauris, 2011), p. 17.
8. Annika Rabo, 'Secularism: Arab States (excepting North Africa and the Gulf)', in S. Joseph (ed.), *Encyclopedia of Women in Islamic Cultures II* (Leiden, Brill, 2005c), p. 726.
9. Sara Lei Sparre, 'Educated Women in Syria: Servants of the State, or Nurturers of the Family?', *Critique: Critical Middle Eastern Studies* 17/1 (2008), p. 11.
10. Annika Rabo, 'Conviviality and Conflict in Contemporary Aleppo', in A.N. Longva and A.S. Roald (eds), *Religious Minorities in the Middle East: Domination, Self-Empowerment, Accommodation* (Leiden, Brill, 2012a), p. 131.
11. Paulo G. Pinto, '"Oh Syria, God Protects You": Islam as Cultural Idiom under Bashar al-Asad', *Middle East Critique* 20/2 (2011), p. 192.
12. See Annika Rabo, 'Gender, State and civil society in Jordan and Syria', in C. Hann and E. Dunn (eds), *Civil Society: Challenging Western Models* (London, Routledge, 1996), 'Syrian Transnational Families and Family Law', in A. Hellum et al. (eds), *From Transnational Relations to Transnational Laws:*

Northern European Laws at the Crossroads (Farnham, Ashgate Publishers, 2011); Sara Lei Sparre 'Educated Women in Syria: Servants of the State, or Nurturers of the Family?', *Critique: Critical Middle Eastern Studies* 17/1 (2008). On the position of women in relation to nation state building projects in the Middle East, see Mounira M. Charrad, *States and Women's Rights: The Making of Postcolonial Tunisia, Algeria, and Morocco* (Berkeley, University of California Press, 2001); Deniz Kandiyoti, *Women, Islam and the State* (edited by D. Kandiyoti) (London, Macmillan Press, 1991).

13. Rabo, 'Gender, State', p. 162; Sparre, 'Educated Women', p. 7.
14. In Syria, education is compulsory for both boys and girls until the age of 12 (Bouthaina Sha'aban, 'The Status of Women in Syria', in S. Sabbagh (ed.), *Arab Women. Between Defiance and Restraint* (New York, Olive Branch Press, 2003), p. 56).
15. Rabo, 'Gender, State', p. 167. Therefore, according to Khatib, 'the uncontrolled private sector mirrored better the prevailing gender bias in Syrian society' (Line Khatib, *Islamic Revivalism in Syria: The Rise and Fall of Ba'thist Secularism* (London, Routledge, 2011), p. 99).
16. Rabo, 'Gender, State', p. 162.
17. Sparre, 'Educated Women', p. 9.
18. Ibid., p. 13.
19. Translation taken from the Syrian Arab News Agency (SANA) website: http://sana.sy/en/?page_id = 1489 (accessed 16 October 2015).
20. Maktabi describes this 'legal incongruence between constitutional laws, which maintain that citizens are equal before the law, and gendered state laws' as 'gendered citizenship' (Maktabi 2013, p. 281 n. 6).
21. Syria's Nationality Act (Law no. 276, 24 November 1969, amended in 1972) stipulates that – as a rule – a child acquires nationality through the father (Art. 3 sub a). In exceptional cases, however, for example when a child is born to a Syrian national mother and the father is unknown, the mother can pass on her nationality to the child, provided the child was born on Syrian soil (Art. 3 sub b).
22. Bouthaina Sha'aban was the Minister of Expatriates from 2003 to 2008. Since 2008, she has been the political and media advisor to President Bashar al-Asad. Before she became a state official, she was a professor in literature at Damascus University.
23. Bouthaina Sha'aban, 'The Status of Women in Syria', in S. Sabbagh (ed.), *Arab Women. Between Defiance and Restraint* (New York, Olive Branch Press, 2003), pp. 60–1.
24. Cf. Khatib, *Islamic Revivalism in Syria*, p. 98 ff.
25. Elizabeth A. Mayer, 'Reform of Personal Status Laws in North Africa: A Problem of Islamic or Mediterranean laws?', *Middle East Journal* 49/3 (1995), p. 446.
26. Mamduh 'Atari (ed.), *qanun al-ahwal al-shakhsiyya* (Law of Personal Status) (Damascus, mu'assasat al-nuri, 2006), p. 13.

27. One of the amendments concerned Article 17, the provision pertaining to polygamous marriages. As of 1975, the article stipulates that a judge may refuse permission for a second marriage, unless the husband can prove that (1) he is capable of supporting two (or more) wives, and (2) he has a lawful justification (*musawwigh shar'i*) to marry a second wife. The latter condition was added in 1975.
28. See Lynn Welchman, *Women and Muslim Family Laws in Arab States: A Comparative Overview of Textual Development and Advocacy* (Amsterdam, Amsterdam University Press, 2007); on codifications and reform policies in various Arab states, and for individual country studies see, for example: Nadia Sonneveld, *Khul' Divorce in Egypt: Public Debates, Judicial Practices, and Everyday Life* (Cairo, American University of Cairo Press, 2012a) (Egypt); Léon Buskens, *Islamitisch recht en familiebetrekkingen in Marokko* (Amsterdam, Bulaaq, 1999) (Morocco); Maaike Voorhoeve, *Gender and Divorce Law in North Africa: Sharia, Custom and the Personal Status Code in Tunisia* (London, I.B.Tauris, 2014) (Tunisia).
29. Syria made reservations to Arts 2; 9 par. 2; 15 par. 4; 16 par. 1 sub c, d, f, g; 16 par. 2; and 29 par. 1 CEDAW (source: www.bayefsky.com).
30. This draft law (2006) included provisions dealing with nursing (*hadana*), child care, and the right to see family members following a divorce (interview with the director of the Syrian Commission of Family Affairs, Dr Farouk al-Basha, Damascus, 16 April 2009).
31. Rania Maktabi, 'Gender, family law and citizenship in Syria', *Citizenship Studies* 14/5 (2010), p. 566.
32. Dr Muhammad al-Habash is also the founding director of the Centre of Islamic Studies in Damascus, established in the 1980s, which advocates religious renewal and religious dialogue.
33. Interview with Dr Muhammad al-Habash, Damascus, 22 April 2008. Furthermore, it may be interesting to note that the Grand Mufti of Syria, Ahmad Hassoun, made the same conclusions as al-Habash with regard to the reservations to CEDAW (Maktabi 'Gender, family law', p. 567).
34. Interview with Sawsan Zakzak, Syrian Women League and independent researcher, Damascus, 13 April 2008; interview with Daad Musa, women's rights activist and lawyer, Damascus, 17 November 2008.
35. Interview with Hanaan Najmeh, Damascus, 2 April 2008.
36. Interview with Sabah Hallaq, Syrian Women League and independent consultant, Damascus, 25 April 2008. For the sake of readability, I will refer to the different drafts as 'the government draft' and 'the NGO draft', respectively.
37. This divorce compensation should be awarded in addition to the post-divorce maintenance (*nafaqat al-'idda*), which generally covers the period of three menstrual cycles after the divorce, and any unpaid dower amount.
38. Egypt's Personal Status Law (revised in 2000) makes it possible for a woman to initiate a *khul'* divorce without her husband's consent (cf. Nadia Sonneveld,

Khul' Divorce in Egypt: Public Debates, Judicial Practices, and Everyday Life (Cairo, American University of Cairo Press, 2012a).

39. Until 2003, when these age limits were raised, a divorced mother could nurse her son until the age of 11 and her daughter until the age of 13.
40. Interviews with Hanaan Najmeh, Sabah Hallaq. The family court system was introduced in Egypt in 2004 (Sonneveld, *Khul' Divorce*, pp. 108–9).
41. Interview with Sawsan Reslan, (dissolved) Association for the Social Initiative, Damascus, 24 April 2008.
42. Rania Maktabi, 'State, Law and Religion – Gendered Debates on Family Law in Syria and Lebanon' (unpublished paper presented at the 15th Norwegian Conference in Political Science, Trondheim, January 2007), pp. 18–9.
43. Interview with Hanaan Najmeh, 2 April 2008.
44. Annika Rabo, 'Family law in multicultural and multireligious Syria', in G. Collste (ed.), *Possibilities of Religious Pluralism* (Linköping, Linköping University Electronic Press, 2005b), pp. 85–6).
45. Souhaïl Belhadj and Baudouin Dupret, 'La religion à toutes fins parlementaires pratiques: comment l'islam est thématisé à l'Assemblée du Peuple syrienne', *Maghreb-Machrek* 198 (2009), pp. 33–4.
46. Furthermore, there are some radical Muslims, but, according to al-Habash, their number is negligible (interview with Dr Muhammad al-Habash, 22 April 2008).
47. For an elaborate discussion on Muhammad al-Habash as a leading figure in the religious renewal movement in Syria see the article written by Paul Heck, 'Religious renewal in Syria: the case of Muhammad al-Habash', *Islam and Christian-Muslim Relations* 15/2 (2004), pp. 185–207.
48. Interview with Dr Muhammad al-Habash, 22 April 2008.
49. Interview with Sawsan Reslan, 24 April 2008.
50. In Arabic: *istitla' ra'y hawla darurat taghyir al-qawanin al-mujhifat bi-haqq al-mar'a*; see Kareem Abu Halawa, *Survey on the need to change laws prejudicial to women* (*istitla' ra'i hawla dururat taghyir al-qawanin al-mujhat bi-haqq al-mar'a*) (in English and Arabic) (Damascus, Karama, 2006).
51. Abu Halawa, *Survey on the need*, p. 5.
52. Ibid., pp. 44–7.
53. Maktabi, 'Gender, family law', pp. 563–4.
54. Interview with Sawsan Reslan, 24 April 2008.
55. The GUSW is a semi-governmental organisation, established in 1976, dominated by Ba'th Party members. For an analysis of the organisation see Mayyah El-Rahabi's study, *Assessment of National Women's Machineries in Syria* (Cairo, Euromed Role of Women in Economic Life Programme, 2006) p. 14 ff.
56. The results of this field study were published in 2006 and are available online, see: http://www.unifem.org/attachments/stories/currents_200606_Syria-VAWstudyKeyFindings.pdf (accessed 9 April 2012).
57. Penal Law (*qanun al-'uqubat*), Law No. 148/1949, with amendments.

58. See http://www.thara-sy.com/TharaEnglish/modules/news/article.php?storyid = 62 (accessed 9 April 2012). Also available at http://web.archive.org/web/20110106000849/http://www.thara-sy.com/TharaEnglish/modules/news/article.php?storyid = 62 (accessed 16 October 2015).
59. There are still several disputed articles that remained unchanged: Articles 192 and 240–2 allow a judge to reduce punishment if the crime was committed in rage or due to extenuating circumstances. In addition, Articles 473–5 stipulate different punishments to male and female adulterers, so women are subject to double the penalty compared to men. For example, a man can be acquitted of punishment for rape if he marries his victim (Art. 475). Finally, Article 489 permits marital rape (Euromed, 'Role of Women in Economic Life Programme,' *Analysis of the Economic Situation of Women in Syria* (Cairo, Euromed Role of Women in Economic Life Programme, 2006), pp. 22–3.
60. The Syrian Women League also coordinated and published the NGO's CEDAW shadow report (2007), in addition to the NGO's report on Beijing +10 Declaration and Platform for Action.
61. As mentioned earlier, in exceptional cases, for example when a child is born to a Syrian national mother and the father is unknown, the mother can pass on her nationality to the child, provided the child was born on Syrian soil (Art. 3 sub B Nationality Law).
62. Most notably: interview with lawyer and independent consultant, Hala Barbara, Damascus, 25 March 2008; interview with Sawsan Zakzak, Syrian Women League and independent researcher, Damascus, 13 April 2008.
63. Interview with Sawsan Zakzak.
64. Conversely, other Arab states have changed their nationality laws, enabling women to pass their nationality to their children, such as: Morocco in 2006 (Fatima Sadiqi, 'Facing Challenges and Pioneering Feminist and Gender Studies: Women in Post-colonial and Today's Maghrib', *African and Asian Studies* 7 (2008) p. 461; Egypt in 2004 (Sonneveld, *Khul' Divorce*, p. 51); Tunisia in 1993 (Voorhoeve, *Gender and Divorce*, p. 54).
65. The title archimandrite is an honorary title used in the Melkite Church; the title is equivalent to the title of *Monsignor* used in the Latin Church (Edward Faulk, *101 Questions and Answers on Eastern Catholic Churches* (New York, Paulist Press, 2007), p. 52).
66. The Arabic translation (of the original Latin text) was conducted by a committee established by the late Coptic Catholic Patriarch of Alexandria (Egypt), Stephanos II Ghattas (d. 2005), in 1995.
67. Interview with Fr Antoun, judge in the first instance and appeal of the Catholic court in Damascus, Damascus, 25 April 2008; Anton Moslih, 'La legge sullo statuto personale delle confessioni cattoliche', *Il Regno Attualità* 4 (2008), p. 138.
68. Moslih, 'La legge sullo statuto' p. 138. Law no. 31/2006 was published in the Official Gazette Issue 26, on 5 July 2006.
69. Adoption (*tabanni*) is prohibited in Islam, and therefore not recognised by Syrian law.

70. Anton Moslih, 'Code du Statut Personnel des Catholiques en Syrie: Etude' (unpublished document, n.d.), p. 7.
71. Annika Rabo, 'To reform or not to reform? Elusive family law debates in Syria' (unpublished paper presented at conference 'Re-imagining the Shari'a: Theory, Practice and Muslim Pluralism at Play', Venice, 13–16 September 2009), p. 7.
72. Annika Rabo, '"We are Christians and we are equal citizens": perspectives on particularity and pluralism in contemporary Syria', *Islam and Christian–Muslim Relations* 23/1 (2012b), p. 92 n. 20.
73. Furthermore, Rabo observed that some lawyers complained about the wording of the law and 'claimed it had not passed the critical assessment of legal experts' (Rabo, 'We are Christians', p. 86).
74. Monique C. Cardinal, 'Why Aren't Women Sharīʿa Court judges? The Case of Syria', *Islamic Law and Society* 17 (2010), p. 208.
75. For example, a campaign against the draft was launched through the website of the organisation *Syrian Women Observatory* (*Nesasy*), www.nesasy.org.
76. Fay Ferguson and Nadia Muhanna, 'Personal Status Matters', *Syria Today* (online edition), August 2009. Available at http://www.syria-today.com/index.php/august-2009/377-society/2443-personal-status-matters (accessed 17 March 2012). Buskens' states that similar reactions were expressed on government plans to reform the family law in Morocco in the early 2000 ('Recent Debates', pp. 100–3).
77. This proposal brings to mind the Egyptian *hisba*-procedure, which allows a Muslim to file a *hisba*-petition against a fellow Muslim at a civil court invoking the defence of Islamic public order (Bernard-Maugiron 2004, pp. 333–9). The case of Nasr Abu Zayd is probably the most famous case in which such a petition was accepted (cf. Berger 2005, pp. 89–101).
78. Fay Ferguson and Nadia Muhanna, 'Personal Status Matters', *Syria Today* (online edition), August 2009. Available at http://web.archive.org/web/20101224001431/http://syria-today.com/index.php/august-2009/377-society/2443-personal-status-matters (accessed 16 October 2015); Cardinal 'Why aren't Women', p. 209 n. 65.
79. The oaths of sexual abstention (*ila'* and *zihar*) are believed to date back to pre-Islamic times.
80. See also Rabo, 'We are Christians', p. 79.
81. Yahya al-Aws, 'The Ministry of Endowments – Where is it Going?' (translated by Susanna Ferguson), 30 January 2010. Available at http://www.thara-sy.com/TharaEnglish/modules/news/article.php?storyid = 204 (accessed 17 March 2012).
82. Apparently, the Ministry of Religious Endowments has also been instrumental in dismissing the calls from civil society groups to lift the reservations to the CEDAW Convention.
83. The SCFA operates under the umbrella of the Ministry of Labour and Social Affairs.

84. The Minister of Labour and Social Affairs is, amongst other things, responsible for the emancipation of women. One interviewee commented to me that the suitability of the then (i.e. 2008–09) Minister, Mrs Diala Al Hajj Aref, was questionable, particularly knowing that she (allegedly) married as a second wife to her husband.
85. Rabo, 'We are Christians', p. 84.
86. See also Bisan al-Bunni, '*suriyya: ta'dil li-l-ahwal al-shakhsiyyat yatatawalu al-irth wa-l-wasiyya wa-l-ikhtisasat al-tawa'if*' in: *Al-Hayat* newspaper, 21 October 2010. Available online http://international.daralhayat.com/internationalarticle/194022 (accessed 17 June 2011).
87. Due to the revolution in Syria, which started in March 2011, I have not been able to return to Damascus and have therefore not been able to follow up on this issue.
88. Suad Joseph, 'The Public/Private: The Imagined Boundary in the Imagined Nation/State/Community: The Lebanese Case', *Feminist Review* 57 (1997), p. 81. In this article Suad Joseph argues that 'patriarchal connectivity' is linked to the Lebanese nation/state-building enterprise.
89. Rania Maktabi, 'Female Citizenship in the Middle East: Comparing family law reform in Morocco, Egypt, Syria and Lebanon', *Middle East Law and Governance* 5 (2013), p. 303.
90. Ibid., p. 301.
91. Ibid., p. 302.
92. Gema M. Muñoz, 'Feminism in the Arab World. The Silent Revolution' (online article at Qantara.de), 17 April 2012. Available at http://en.qantara.de/wcsite.php?wc_c = 18942&wc_id = 19849 (accessed 26 July 2012).
93. Ibid.
94. Cf. Hisham Sharabi, *Neopatriarchy: A Theory of Distorted Change in the Arab World* (New York, Oxford University Press, 1992). See Lisa Wedeen, *Ambiguities of Domination: Politics, Rhetoric, and Symbols in Contemporary Syria* (Chicago, The University of Chicago Press, 1999), pp. 49–65 for an analysis of the use of the familial metaphor and the Asad cult in Syrian state rhetoric.
95. Valentine M. Moghadam, *Modernizing Women: Gender and Social Change in the Middle East* (Boulder, Lynne Rienner Publishers, 2003a), p. 11.
96. Ibid., pp. 129–30.
97. Elham Manea, *The Arab State and Women's Rights: The Trap of Authoritarian Governance* (London, Routledge, 2011), p. 169.
98. Ibid., pp. 168–9. The Nasser regime adopted the same strategy in Egypt (Lisa Moghadam, 'Engendering Citizenship, Feminizing Civil Society: The Case of the Middle East and North Africa', *Women & Politics* 25–1/2 (2003b), p. 71.
99. Manea, *The Arab State*, p. 171.
100. Catherine Warrick, *Law in the Service of Legitimacy: Gender and Politics in Jordan* (Farnham, Ashgate, 2009), pp. 42–3.
101. Al-Aws, 'The Ministry of Endowments'; cf. Maktabi 'State, Law and Religion', pp. 27–8.

102. Thomas Pierret, *Religion and State in Syria: the Sunni Ulama from Coup to Revolution* (Cambridge, Cambridge University Press, 2013), pp. 194–204, 214–5. For example, in 2010, the niqab (face-covering veil) was banned from universities and thousands of niqab-wearing primary school teachers were transferred to administrative jobs (ibid., p. 215).
103. See also Al-Thara online article 'Mending the Personal Status Law' (translated by Anna Jozwik, 6 November 2011). Available at http://web.archive.org/web/20110105151913/http://www.thara-sy.com/TharaEnglish/modules/news/article.php?storyid = 298 (accessed 16 October 2015).

Chapter 4 Patriarchy, Religion and Legal Rules

1. The wording of Article 44 of the 1973 Constitution was nearly the same; it read: 'The family is the fundamental nucleus of society and is protected by the state.'
2. For example, Halim Barakat, 'The Arab Family and the Challenge of Social Transformation', in E.W. Fernea (ed.), *Women and the Family in the Middle East: New Voices of Change* (Austin, University of Texas Press, 1985); Halim Barakat, *The Arab World: Society, Culture, and State* (Berkeley, University of California Press, 1993); Beshara Doumani (ed.), *Family History in the Middle East: Household, Property, and Gender* (Albany, State University of New York Press, 2003); Suad Joseph, *Gender and Citizenship in the Middle East: Contemporary Issues in the Middle East* (Syracuse, NY, Syracuse University Press, 2000); Elizabeth W. Fernea (ed.), *Women and the Family in the Middle East: New Voices of Change* (Austin, University of Texas Press, 1985).
3. For example, Kenneth M. Cuno and Manisha Desai (eds), *Family, Gender, and Law in a Globalizing Middle East and South Asia* (Syracuse, NY, University Press, 2009); Doumani, *Family History*; Dale F. Eickelman, *The Middle East and Central Asia: An Anthropological Approach* (Upper Saddle River, NJ, Prentice-Hall, 1998); Suad Joseph, *Gender and Citizenship in the Middle East: Contemporary Issues in the Middle East* (edited by S. Joseph) (Syracuse, NY, Syracuse University Press, 2000); Annelies Moors, *Women, Property and Islam: Palestinian Experiences, 1920–1990* (Cambridge, Cambridge University Press, 1995); Judith E. Tucker *Women, Family, and Gender in Islamic Law* (New York, Cambridge University Press, 2008); Lynn Welchman, *Women and Muslim Family Laws in Arab States: A Comparative Overview of Textual Development and Advocacy* (Amsterdam, Amsterdam University Press, 2007) and many more. I will not discuss the various analyses and discussions about the concept of 'family' as it is beyond the scope of these introductory paragraphs.
4. In Syria different words are used to refer to 'family', most importantly, *'a'ila*, *ahl* or *usra*, depending on the context.
5. Léon Buskens, 'Recent Debates on Family Law Reform in Morocco: Islamic Law as Politics in an Emerging Public Sphere', *Islamic Law and Society* 10/1 (2003), p. 75 n. 5.

6. Lisa Wedeen, *Ambiguities of Domination: Politics, Rhetoric, and Symbols in Contemporary Syria* (Chicago, The University of Chicago Press, 1999), p. 51.
7. Cf. Valentine M. Moghadam, 'Patriarchy in Transition: Women and the Changing Family in the Middle East', *Journal of Comparative Family Studies* 35/2 (2004), p. 145; Tucker, *Women, Family, and Gender*, pp. 73–4; Lynn Welchman, 'A Husband's Authority: Emerging Formulations in Muslim Family Laws', *International Journal of Law, Policy and the Family* 25/1 (2011), pp. 10–11; Welchman, *Women and Muslim Family Laws*, pp. 93–9. For detailed discussions on the historical and state ideological analyses of the patriarchal nature of the Arab family laws, see Mounira M. Charrad, *States and Women's Rights: The Making of Postcolonial Tunisia, Algeria, and Morocco* (Berkeley, University of California Press, 2001); Deniz Kandiyoti, *Women, Islam and the State* (edited by D. Kandiyoti) (London, Macmillan Press, 1991); Sharabi Hisham, *Neopatriarchy: A Theory of Distorted Change in the Arab World* (New York, Oxford University Press, 1992).
8. Suad Joseph distinguishes 'patriarchy' into various kinds, including 'social patriarchy', 'economic patriarchy', 'political patriarchy', and 'religious patriarchy' (1996, pp. 14–18).
9. See for example, Léon Buskens, *Islamitisch recht en familiebetrekkingen in Marokko* (Amsterdam, Bulaaq, 1999); Jessica Carlisle, '*Asbab li-l-darb ktir basita*: the legality of claims of violence during judicial divorce cases in Damascus', *Hawwa: Journal of Women of the Middle East and the Islamic World* 5 (2007a); Carlisle, 'Mother Love: A Forced Divorce in Damascus', *Anthropology of the Middle East* 2/1 (2007b); Carlisle, *Rules, Negotiation, Claims and Counter Claims: Judicial Discretion in a Damascus Shari'a Court* (unpublished PhD thesis, University of London, 2007c); Jessica Carlisle, 'From Behind the Door: A Damascus Court copes with an alleged out of Court marriage', in B. Drieskens (ed.), *Les métamorphoses du mariage au Moyen-Orient* (Beirut, Institut Français du Proche-Orient (IFPO) 2008); Lawrence Rosen, *The Anthropology of Justice: Law as Culture in Islamic Society* (Cambridge, Cambridge University Press, 1989); Nahda Shehada, 'House of Obedience: Social Norms, Individual Agency and Historical Contingency', *Journal of Middle Eastern Women's Studies* 5/10 (2009a); Nahda Shehada, 'Flexibility versus Rigidity in the Practice of Islamic Family Law', *PoLAR: Political and Legal Anthropology Review* 32/1 (2009b); 'Negotiating Custody Rights in Islamic Family Law', in T. Kirsch and B. Turner (eds), *Permutations of Order: Religion and Law as Contested Sovereignties* (Farnham, Ashgate, 2009c); Nadia Sonneveld, *Khul' Divorce in Egypt: Public Debates, Judicial Practices, and Everyday Life* (Cairo, American University of Cairo Press, 2012a).
10. Susanne Dahlgren, *Contesting Realities: The Public Sphere and Morality in Southern Yemen* (Syracuse, NY, Syracuse University Press, 2010), p. 88–9.
11. Ibid., p. 127.
12. Ibid., p. 10.
13. I am aware that my use of the general concept 'morality' does not do justice to the broad range of literature available on the topic; see, for example, Dahlgren,

Contesting Realities for a discussion of some of the principal anthropological studies of Islam in relation to 'morality'.

14. Cf. Anne Meneley, *Tournaments of Value: Sociability and Hierarchy in a Yemeni Town* (Toronto, University of Toronto Press, 1996).
15. In 2009, it was estimated that almost 200 people, mainly women, are killed every year by a family member because the family honour was considered to be tarnished (http://www.hrw.org/news/2009/07/28/syria-no-exceptions-honor-killings, accessed 22 February 2012).
16. Mary Elaine Hegland, 'Gossip', in S. Joseph (ed.), *Encyclopedia of Women in Islamic Cultures* II (Leiden, Brill, 2005), p. 211.
17. Annika Rabo, *A Shop of One's Own: Independence and Reputation among Traders in Aleppo* (London, I.B.Tauris, 2005a), p. 82.
18. Cf. Annika Rabo, *Change on the Euphrates: Villagers, Townsmen and Employees in Northeast Syria* (Stockholm, Studies in Social Anthropology, 1986); Halim Barakat, *The Arab World: Society, Culture, and State* (Berkeley, University of California Press, 1993); Noriko Sato, *Memory and Social Identity among Syrian Orthodox Christians* (unpublished PhD thesis, University of Durham, 2001).
19. Joseph emphasises that the brother/sister relationship takes up a central role in the reproduction of Arab patriarchy, in particular in relation to the honour/shame complex: Suad Joseph, 'Brother/Sister Relationships: Connectivity, Love, and Power in the Reproduction of Patriarchy in Lebanon', *American Ethnologist* 21/1 (1994), pp. 50–73.
20. Annika Rabo, 'We are Christians and we are equal citizens': perspectives on particularity and pluralism in contemporary Syria', *Islam and Christian–Muslim Relations* 23/1 (2012b), p. 90.
21. Sato, *Memory and Social Identity*, pp. 118–19.
22. Ibid., pp. 118–20.
23. Case A, Damascus Greek Orthodox court, 9 April 2009.
24. Sato, *Memory and Social Identity*, p. 120.
25. Rabo, *A Shop of One's Own*, p. 88.
26. Ibid., pp. 86–7.
27. Judith E. Tucker, *In the House of the Law: Gender and Islamic Law in Ottoman Syria and Palestine* (Berkeley, University of California Press, 1998), p. 42.
28. See, for example, Barakat, *The Arab World*, p. 107; Marjorie A. Bennet, *Reincarnation, Marriage, and Memory: Negotiating Sectarian Identity among the Druze of Syria* (unpublished PhD thesis, University of Arizona, 1999), p. 159; Rabo, *A Shop of One's Own*, p. 89 ff.
29. Cf. Barbara Drieskens, 'Changing Perceptions of Marriage in Contemporary Beirut', in B. Drieskens (ed.), *Les métamorphoses du mariage au Moyen-Orient* (Beirut, Institut Français du Proche-Orient (IFPO) 2008); Rabo, *A Shop of One's Own*.
30. Rabo, *A Shop of One's Own*, p. 90.
31. See Carlisle, 'Mother Love'.
32. Anne F. Weber maintains that interreligious marriages are also rare in Lebanon ('Briser et suivre le norms: les couples islamo-chrétiens au Liban', in

B. Drieskens (ed.), *Les métamorphoses du mariage au Moyen-Orient* (Beirut, Institut Français du Proche-Orient (IFPO) 2008), p. 15.

33. Interview, 26 March 2009, Damascus.
34. In their case, most importantly a neighbourhood that was not predominantly Christian.
35. See Weber's article on Muslim–Christian couples in Lebanon; she concludes that families' objections to a mixed union are usually socially motivated instead of religiously motivated ('Briser et suivre', p. 27).
36. See, for example, Wael B. Hallaq, *Sharīʿa: Theory, Practice, Transformations* (New York, Cambridge University Press, 2008 p. 129; Yvon Linant de Bellefonds, *Traité de droit musulman comparé. Tome II: Le mariage, la dissolution du mariage* (Paris, Mouton & Co, 1965), p. 23; Ziba Mir-Hosseini, 'Towards gender equality: Muslim family laws and the Shari'ah', in Z. Anwar (ed.), *Wanted: Equality and Justice in the Muslim Family* (Kuala Lumpur, Sisters in Islam and Musawah, 2009), p. 28; Tucker, *Women, Family, and Gender*, p. 41.
37. Tucker, *Women, Family, and Gender* p. 42.
38. Cf. Wael B. Hallaq, *Sharīʿa: Theory, Practice, Transformations* (New York, Cambridge University Press, 2008), pp. 271–2; Linant de Bellefonds, *Traité de droit musulman*, pp. 26–8.
39. See, for example, Buskens, *Islamitisch recht*, pp. 185–90; Mir-Hosseini, 'Towards gender equality', p. 31; Shehada, 'House of Obedience', p. 28 ff.; Sonneveld, *Khulʿ Divorce*, p. 17 ff.; Tucker, *Women, Family, and Gender*, pp. 50–6; Welchman, *Women and Muslim Family*, pp. 93–9; Welchman, 'A Husband's Authority'.
40. Lama Abu-Odeh, 'Modern Family Law, 1800–Present: Arab States', in S. Joseph (ed.), *Encyclopedia of Women in Islamic Cultures* II (Leiden, Brill, 2005), p. 460.
41. Lynn Welchman, *Women and Muslim Family Laws*, pp. 94–7. The People's Democratic Republic of Yemen was the first Arab state to drop the wife's duty of obedience from its statutory law in 1974 (Welchman, 'A Husband's Authority', pp. 11–12).
42. Translation taken from J.N.D. Anderson, 'The Syrian Law of Personal Status', *Bulletin of the School of Oriental and African Studies* 17/1 (1955), p. 49.
43. The Jordanian (1951) and Iraqi (1959) personal status law give a definition of marriage that is practically the same as the Syrian one (Jamal J. Nasir, *The Islamic Law of Personal Status* (The Hague, Kluwer Law International, 2002), p. 44).
44. It is important to note that the SLPS distinguishes between different types of guardianship (*wilaya*), namely guardianship in marriage (*wilayat al-zawaj*); guardianship of property (*wilayat 'ala al-mal*); and guardianship over a person, such as minors and insane persons (*wilayat 'ala al-nafs*).
45. Court of Cassation, *sharʿiyya* chamber, decision dated 19 November 1956, see Mamduh 'Atari (ed.), *qanun al-ahwal al-shakhsiyya* (Law of Personal Status) (Damascus, mu'assasat al-nuri, 2006), pp. 120–1.

46. Email correspondence with lawyer Yusuf, 10 February 2012.
47. The same goes for the 1976 Jordanian personal status law; see the elaborate analysis of Welchman on the subject in her study, *Beyond the Code: Muslim Family Law and the Shari'a Judiciary in the Palestinian West Bank* (The Hague, Kluwer Law International, 2000), pp. 121–33.
48. The role of the marriage guardian needs to be understood in conjunction with the doctrine on concept of equal social status (*kafa'a*), which was particularly developed by the Hanafi school of law (Yvon Linant de Bellefonds, *Traité de droit musulman comparé. Tome II: Le mariage, la dissolution du mariage* (Paris, Mouton & Co, 1965), p. 171 ff.). According to Linant de Bellefonds, Hanafi scholars attributed great importance to *kafa'a* because this school allows an adult woman to conclude her own marriage (without her guardian), it is for that reason that *kafa'a* serves to secure the interests of the bride and her family (Linant de Bellefonds, 'kafā'a', in E. van Donzel et al. (eds), *Encyclopaedia of Islam*, Vol. IV, 2nd edn (Leiden, Brill, 1978), p. 404).
49. Unlike the 1976 Jordanian Law of Personal Status, which limited it to 'the groom's ability to pay the prompt dower and the wife's maintenance' (Welchman, *Beyond the Code*, p. 99).
50. Court of Cassation, *shar'iyya* chamber, Decision No. 325, 19 November 1956.
51. Email correspondence with lawyer Yusuf, 10 February 2012.
52. Translation taken from Welchman, *Women and Muslim Family Laws*, p. 184.
53. Muhammad Fihr Shaqfa, *sharh ahkam al-ahwal al-shakhsiyya: li-l-muslimin wa-l-nasara wa-l-yahud* [*Explaining the Law of Personal Status: Muslims, Christians, and Jews*] (Damascus, Mu'assasat Al-Nuri, 1998), pp. 314–15.
54. Although more literally it would come closer to the meaning of 'to follow', meaning that a wife has to 'follow' her husband.
55. Shaqfa, *sharh ahkam al-ahwal al-shakhsiyya*, pp. 314–15. It is important to note here that the issue of *mutaba'a* is mentioned in Article 308 SLPS as one of the specified matters falling under the jurisdiction of the Christian and Jewish judges.
56. See, for example, Sonneveld, *Khul' Divorce in Egypt* and Kruiniger, respectively (Pauline Kruiniger, 'Repudiated by husband and Europe?', in M.C. Foblets and N. Yassari (eds), *Cultural Diversity* (The Series of Centre for Studies and Research in International Law and International Relations of the Hague Academy of International Law) (Leiden, Martinus Nijhoff Publishers, 2013), pp. 464–520.
57. Court of Cassation, *shar'iyya* chamber, Decision No. 388/385, 21 April 1976, see 'Atari, *qanun al-ahwal al-shakhsiyya*, p. 123.
58. See also Carlisle, *Rules, Negotiation, Claims and Counter Claims*, p. 194.
59. See also Carlisle, 'Mother Love', p. 96.
60. Personal communication with lawyer Mr Mulhim, 26 January 2009.
61. Promulgated by law in Syria in 1952 and amended in 1962.
62. I understand that the Assyrian Church of the East also has its own personal status law, but unfortunately I have not yet been able to obtain a copy of this law

or information of the date of promulgation (if it was ever officially promulgated), its exact title, and so on.

63. The apostle Paul described marriage as 'a great mystery in Christ and in the Church' (Ephesians 5: 32). In Greek the word 'sacrament' and 'mystery' are the same (John Meyendorff, *Marriage: An Orthodox Perspective* (Crestwood, NY, St Vladimir's Seminary Press, 1984), p. 19).
64. Art. 11 Greek Orthodox PS Law; Art. 40 Armenian Orthodox PS Law; Can. 776 CCEO (pertaining to Catholics). The Syriac Orthodox PS Law does not define marriage as a sacrament but as a contract; that being said, Article 18 stipulates that there can be no valid marriage contract unless it is concluded by a priest of the Syrian Orthodox Church.
65. Quotation taken from Meyendorff, *Marriage: An Orthodox Perspective*, p. 21. He states that an Orthodox marriage has to be understood in the context of the Eucharist, for 'it is the Eucharist which gives to marriage its specifically Christian meaning' (ibid.).
66. Victor J. Pospishil, *Eastern Catholic Marriage Law: According to the Code of Canons of the Eastern Churches* (Brooklyn NY, Saint Maron Publications, 1991), p. 123.
67. Victor J. Pospishil, 'The Problem of Divorce in the Catholic Church', *Journal of Family Law* 7/4 (1968), p. 602.
68. Clarence Gallagher, 'Marriage in Eastern and Western Canon Law', *Law & Justice. The Christian Law Review* 157 (2006), p. 10.
69. Meyendorff, *Marriage: An Orthodox Perspective*, p. 23.
70. John D. Faris, 'An Overview of the Code of Canons of the Eastern Churches', in John P. Beal et al. (eds), *New Commentary on the Code of Canon Law*, commissioned by the Canon Law Society of America (New York, Paulist Press, 2000), p. 38.
71. Clarence Gallagher, 'Marriage in the Revised Canon Law for the Eastern Catholic Churches', *Studia Canonica* 24 (1990), p. 85.
72. Rabo, 'We are Christians', p. 89.
73. Interview with judge of the first instance and appeal Catholic court Fr Antoun, 26 March 2009, Damascus.
74. Arts 33–5 Greek Orthodox PS Law; Art. 34 Syriac Orthodox PS Law; Art. 121 Catholic PS Law; Art. 31 Protestant PS Law.
75. Art. 22 Greek Orthodox PS Law; Arts 47–48 Armenian Orthodox PS Law; Art. 33 Syriac Orthodox PS Law; Art. 125 Catholic PS Law; Art. 32 Protestant PS Law.
76. Art. 32 Greek Orthodox PS Law; Art. 35 Syriac Orthodox PS Law; Art. 123 Catholic PS Law.
77. Arts 42 ff. Greek Orthodox PS Law; Arts 79, 90, 92–93 Armenian Orthodox PS Law; Arts 42 ff. Syriac Orthodox PS Law; Art. 40 Catholic PS Law.
78. Art. 37 Greek Orthodox PS Law; Arts 49–51 Syriac Orthodox PS Law; Art. 127 Catholic PS Law.
79. Matthew 19:6; *New King James Version*, 1982.
80. Meyendorff, *Marriage: An Orthodox Perspective*, p. 54.

Chapter 5 The Versatility of Personal Status Law: Legal Practices in a *Shar'iyya* Court

1. Cf. Nahda Shehada, 'Flexibility versus Rigidity in the Practice of Islamic Family Law', *PoLAR: Political and Legal Anthropology Review* 32/1 (2009b), pp. 28–46; Nahda Shehada, 'Negotiating Custody Rights in Islamic Family Law', in T. Kirsch and B. Turner (eds), *Permutations of Order: Religion and Law as Contested Sovereignties* (Farnham, Ashgate, 2009c), pp. 247–62; Nadia Sonneveld, *Khul' Divorce in Egypt: Public Debates, Judicial Practices, and Everyday Life* (Cairo, American University of Cairo Press, 2012a); Maaike Voorhoeve, 'Judicial Discretion in Tunisian Personal Status Law', in M. Voorhoeve (ed.), *Family Law in Islam: Divorce, Marriage and Women in the Muslim World* (London, I.B.Tauris, 2012), pp. 199–229.
2. As mentioned earlier, all the names used in these case studies are fictitious.
3. However, I could not copy files or other documents, until I received the required clearance, which I never obtained in the end.
4. Cf. Baudouin Dupret, 'The Practice of Judging: The Egyptian Judiciary at Work in a Personal Status Case', in Muhammad K. Masud et al. (eds), *Dispensing Justice in Islam. Qadis and their Judgements* (Leiden, Brill, 2006), pp. 150–7; and Nadia Sonneveld, 'Khul' Divorce in Egypt: How Family Courts Are Providing a "Dialogue" between Husband and Wife', *Anthropology in the Middle East* 5/2 (2010), pp. 106–8) with regard to Egyptian judges.
5. Magistrates' courts are first instance courts which have limited jurisdiction over certain types of criminal and civil cases.
6. See also Monique C. Cardinal, 'Women and the judiciary in Syria: appointments process, training and career paths', *International Journal of the Legal Profession* 15/1–2 (2008), pp. 123–39; Zouhair Ghazzal, 'Violence and Legal Responsibility: Crime-in-Action in Contemporary Syria' (2007b). Available online at http://ssrn.com/abstract=997374 (accessed 22 December 2011).
7. Morgan Clarke, *Islam and New Kinship: Reproductive Technology and the Shariah in Lebanon* (New York, Berghahn Books, 2009), p. 60.
8. Apparently, there were also copies of the Old and New Testament present in the *shar'iyya* courtrooms, for Jews and Christians witnesses respectively. During my time in the courtrooms, however, I never saw a Jewish or Christian witness in the court.
9. United Nations Development Programme (UNDP), *Modernization of the Justice Sector in Syria*, UNDP Project Syria (SYR/06/010) (2006), p. 9. Personal communication with lawyers Ahmed, Nawal and others.
10. Personal communication with lawyer Ahmed, 26 February 2009.
11. The primary source, i.e. the report of the Syrian Commission for Family Affairs (SCFA), could not be found in order to verify the information provided in the article.

12. Committee on the Elimination of Discrimination against Women (CEDAW), *Summary record of the 785th meeting*, 18 July 2007, UN Doc. CEDAW/C/SR.785, para. 54.
13. Committee on the Elimination of Discrimination against Women (CEDAW), *Initial Report: Syrian Arab Republic*, 29 August 2005, UN Doc. CEDAW/C/SYR/1, pp. 69–70.
14. Rabo writes in her study on the province of Raqqa (conducted in the late 1970s to early 1980s) that villagers in Raqqa's countryside married their children before the legal age. Also, they did not register marriages, births and deaths with the authorities. According to Rabo, the villagers played fast and loose with the state-promulgated laws and procedures (Annika Rabo, *Change on the Euphrates: Villagers, Townsmen and Employees in Northeast Syria* (Stockholm, Studies in Social Anthropology, 1986, p. 88).
15. The marriage officials are generally 'regular' employees of the Ministry of Justice. However, one can only be a marriage official if one has applied for and obtained special permission from the Ministry to draw up marriage contracts. Damascus' main courthouse has at least 25 marriage officials at its disposal (personal communication with lawyer Ahmed, 15 January 2012).
16. The amount of the fee is not fixed; people can decide at their own discretion. The average amount lies somewhere between SYP 1,000 and 2,000 (personal communication with lawyer Ahmed, 15 January 2012).
17. Case A, Damascus *shar'iyya* court, 31 March 2009.
18. When a betrothal ends, the wife will have to return the received dower and trousseau (Art. 4); besides this article (and Art. 307 pertaining to the Druze community), no further mention is made of the trousseau in the SLPS.
19. The converted Euro amounts are based on the exchange rate of 1 Syrian pound (SYR) to €0.015 (the average exchange rate in spring 2009).
20. Personal communication with lawyer Ahmed, 15 February 2009.
21. Ibid.
22. See section 'Unregistered marriages' below for a more detailed discussion on *'urfi* marriages.
23. Case A, Damascus *shar'iyya* court, 22 March 2009.
24. Cf. Jessica Carlisle, *Rules, Negotiation, Claims and Counter Claims: Judicial Discretion in a Damascus Shari'a Court* (unpublished PhD thesis, University of London, 2007c), p. 255 ff.
25. Deniz Kandiyoti, 'Bargaining with Patriarchy', *Gender and Society* 2/3 (1988), pp. 274–90.
26. Vincent-Grosso shows in her study on judicial practices in Tunisia, where similar legal provisions on the subject of co-habitation apply, that it is very difficult for a Tunisian husband to prove his wife abandoned the marital home 'without justification', as the judges tend to give the wives the benefit of the doubt in these cases (Sarah Vincent-Grosso, 'Maktub: An Ethnography of Evidence in a Tunisian Divorce Court', in M. Voorhoeve (ed.), *Family Law in*

Islam: Divorce, Marriage and Women in the Muslim World (London, I.B.Tauris, 2012), pp. 189–91).

27. See Chapter 4 for an explanation as to why I translate the term *mutaba'a* with 'marital obedience'.
28. For example, the institution of 'house of obedience' (*bayt al-ta'a*), as existed in Egypt, cannot be found in Syria. This legal institution enabled an Egyptian husband to obtain a 'house of obedience' ruling against his disobedient wife, upon which she could then be forced, with help of the police, to return to the marital home (Judith E. Tucker, *Women, Family, and Gender in Islamic Law* (New York, Cambridge University Press, 2008, p. 74). For an interesting perspective on the origins of the institution of 'house of obedience', see Amira E.A. Sonbol, '"The woman follows the nationality of her husband": Guardianship, citizenship and gender', *Hawwa: Journal of Women of the Middle East and the Islamic World* 1 (2003), pp. 86–117; Amira E.A. Sonbol, 'Shari'ah and State Formation: Historical Perspective', *Chicago Journal of International Law* 8/1 (2007), pp. 59–83. She argues that the institution of *bayt al-ta'a* was modelled on the European legal doctrine of 'coverture', i.e. 'coerced incarceration of wives at the will of the husband enforced by the state through its courts and police' ('The woman follows the nationality of her husband', p. 112).
29. Nadia Sonneveld, *Khul' Divorce in Egypt*, pp. 125–8.
30. Email correspondence with lawyer Yusuf, 3 November 2011.
31. See Appendix.
32. See also Jessica Carlisle, 'From Behind the Door: A Damascus Court copes with an alleged out of Court marriage', in B. Drieskens (ed.), *Les métamorphoses du mariage au Moyen-Orient* (Beirut, Institut Français du Proche-Orient (IFPO) 2008), p. 64.
33. Case J, Damascus *shar'iyya* court, 12 May 2009.
34. For Christians, interaction between non-related men and women is slightly more acceptable, but Christian girls can also be looked down upon when they are seen in public with a man to whom they are not related, especially in conservative Christian-majority communities (see Chapter 4).
35. It should be noted, however, that the accuracy and reliability of the statistical data published by the Central Bureau of Statistics is disputed by many.
36. Central Bureau of Statistics, *Statistical Yearbook 2010*, issue 63. Available online at http://cbssyr.org/yearbook/2010/Data-Chapter2/TAB-15-2-2010.htm (accessed 9 December 2011).
37. Cf. Carlisle, 'From Behind the Door'; Annika Rabo, 'Syrian Transnational Families and Family Law', in A. Hellum et al. (eds), *From Transnational Relations to Transnational Laws: Northern European Laws at the Crossroads* (Farnham, Ashgate Publishers, 2011), pp. 34–5.
38. The same practice was observed by Rabo in the late 1970s–early 1980s in the Raqqa governorate (*Change on the Euphrates*, p. 55 n. 6).

39. The word *ihram* refers to the 'state of ritual consecration of the Mecca pilgrim' (Hans Wehr, *A Dictionary of Modern Written Arabic (Arabic–English)*, 4th edn, edited by J.M. Cowan (Ithaca, NY, 1994), p. 202.
40. According to Tucker, this requirement was prescribed by most Hanafi jurists (*Women, Family, and Gender*, p. 181).
41. Cf. Carlisle, 'From Behind the Door'; Frances S. Hasso, *Consuming Desires: Family Crisis and the State in the Middle East* (Stanford, Stanford University Press, 2011); Nadia Sonneveld, 'Rethinking the Difference Between Formal and Informal Marriages in Egypt', in M. Voorhoeve (ed.), *Family Law in Islam: Divorce, Marriage and Women in the Muslim World* (London, I.B.Tauris, 2012b).
42. See, for example, Joseph Schacht, 'Nikāḥ. I. In Classical Islamic Law', in C.E. Bosworth et al. (eds), *Encyclopaedia of Islam*, Vol. VIII, 2nd edn (Leiden, Brill, 1995); Lynn Welchman, *Women and Muslim Family Laws in Arab States: A Comparative Overview of Textual Development and Advocacy* (Amsterdam, Amsterdam University Press, 2007), p. 53 ff.
43. Cf. Sonneveld, 'Rethinking the Difference'.
44. Yamani contends that the increase in wealth of many Saudis, due to oil revenues, and the promotion of polygamy by the Saudi government and *'ulama'* led to an increase in polygamous practices, including *misyar* marriages (M.A.Z Yamani, *Polygamy and Law in Contemporary Saudi Arabia* (Reading, Ithaca Press, 2008), pp. 47–53, 215).
45. Most notably, Shaykh Yusuf al-Qaradawi, an influential Sunni scholar from Egypt, declared *misyar* marriages religiously valid (Hasso, *Consuming Desires*, p. 92).
46. O. Arabi, *Studies in Modern Islamic Law and Jurisprudence* (The Hague, Kluwer Law International, 2001), p. 147 ff.
47. See Sonneveld, 'Rethinking the Difference'.
48. Léon Buskens, *Islamitisch recht en familiebetrekkingen in Marokko* (Amsterdam, Bulaaq, 1999), p. 449 (Morocco).
49. Yamani, *Polygamy and Law*, p. 105.
50. Sonneveld, 'Rethinking the Difference', p. 85.
51. See for example: http://www.islamwomen.org/EngIw/NwsDetails.aspx?id=1334 (accessed 15 December 2011).
52. See, for instance, Nadia Muhanna, 'Marriages of Convenience', Syria Today (online edition), February 2011. Available at http://www.syria-today.com/index.php/life/14365-marriages-of-convenience (accessed 15 June 2011).
53. In addition, Syria entered a reservation to Article 9, paragraph 2 CEDAW on granting children the nationality of their mother, because the CEDAW article was considered incompatible with *shari'a* (CEDAW 2005, p. 43).
54. Carlisle, 'From Behind the Door', p. 67. Carlisle concluded that only when 'proof of marriage' is disputed, would the court examine whether all legal criteria had been fulfilled (ibid.).
55. Case A, Damascus *shar'iyya* court, 26 February 2009.
56. Personal communication, lawyer Ahmed, 26 February 2009.

57. Carlisle, 'From Behind the Door', p. 62.
58. The only marriage which the SLPS considers invalid (*batil*) is a marriage between a Muslim woman and a non-Muslim man (Art. 48.2)
59. Marjorie A. Bennet, *Reincarnation, Marriage, and Memory: Negotiating Sectarian Identity among the Druze of Syria* (unpublished PhD thesis, University of Arizona, 1999), p. 134; Aharon Layish, *Marriage, Divorce and Succession in the Druze Family: A Study based on Decisions of Druze Arbitrators and Religious Courts in Israel and the Golan Heights* (Leiden, Brill, 1982), pp. 108–110.
60. Cf. Barbara Drieskens, 'Changing Perceptions of Marriage in Contemporary Beirut', in B. Drieskens (ed.), *Les Métamorphoses du Mariage au Moyen-Orient* (Beirut, Institut Français du Proche-Orient (IFPO) 2008), p. 101.
61. See Drieskens, 'Changing Perceptions', p. 102; Refugee Review Tribunal Australia, *RRT Research Response No. LBN30136*, Country: Lebanon, 6 June 2006. Available online http://www.unhcr.org/refworld/pdfid/4b6fe27e0.pdf (accessed 15 December 2011).
62. It should be noted that the Syrian government discourages these practices. For example, in 2007, an amendment (by Decree no. 26 of 12 April 2007) was made to the Law of Civil Status (*qanun al-ahwal al-madaniyya*), Law no. 376 of 2 April 1957, which obligates parents to register all children at birth (CRC 2009, par. 119).
63. In 2009, a total of 670,793 children were born and registered. An additional 50,794 children, who born before 2009, were registered during that year. One may assume that the latter number refers to *ex post facto* proofs of paternity. Source: Central Bureau of Statistics, *Statistical Yearbook 2010*, issue 63. Also available online at http://cbssyr.org/yearbook/2010/Data-Chapter2/TAB-13-2-2010.htm (accessed 9 December 2011).
64. This brings to mind a famous paternity case between two Egyptian celebrities, Hind al-Hinnawy and Ahmad al-Fishawy, who had secretly contracted a *'urfi* marriage and conceived a child. Al-Fishawy denied he had married al-Hinnawy and refused to recognise the child as his own. In 2004, al-Hinnawy filed a case against him and requested he be compelled to submit to a DNA test; in 2006, an appeal court decided in her favour, recognising the marriage and the child as al-Fishawy's legitimate daughter (Hasso, *Consuming Desires*, pp. 1–2).
65. The prohibition is based on two verses of the Qur'an (33: 5 and 37), which state that giving one's name to someone 'who does not belong within his "natural" descendance' is forbidden (E. Chaumont, 'Tabann(in)', in P. Bearman et al. (eds), *Encyclopaedia of Islam*, Vol. XII Suppl., 2nd edn (Leiden, Brill, 2004)). Having an adopted child in the family is deemed problematic because it might infringe on the inheritance rights of the 'natural' family members and it might lead to moral corruption because the adopted child is not (religiously) prohibited against marriage with his or her close family members (Morgan Clarke, *Islam and New Kinship: Reproductive Technology and the Shariah in Lebanon* (New York, Berghahn Books, 2009), pp. 72–3).

66. Article 14 relates to 'freedom of thought, conscience and religion'; Article 20 relates to 'children deprived of their family environment'.
67. Committee on the Rights of Children (CRC), *Initial Report: Syrian Arab Republic*, 22 September 1995, UN Doc. CRC/C/28/Add.2, par. 124.
68. Decree No. 12 of February 2007 (CRC 2009, par. 171).
69. Committee on the Rights of Children (CRC), *Third and Fourth Periodic Report: Syrian Arab Republic*, 4 March 2009, UN Doc. CRC/C/SYR/3-4, par. 171. The position of foundlings (or children of unknown parentage) and the connected system of fostering (*kafala*) are regulated by a separate law, i.e. the Law of Custody of Foundlings (*qanun ri'aya al-luqata'*), Law No. 107 of 4 May 1970.
70. Lawyer Nawal assumed that the Lebanese husband was non-Muslim, because he used a false identity card, which belonged to a Sunni Muslim.
71. Personal communication with lawyer Nawal, 18 February 2009.
72. A writ of summons (*tabligh*) only specifies the day, not an exact time.
73. Damascus *shar'iyya* court, 10 March 2009.
74. In other words, sexual intercourse between a man and a woman who are not legally married to each other.
75. Personal communication with lawyer Nawal, 6 April 2009.
76. Personal communication with lawyer Nawal, 10 March 2009.
77. For an adoption case in Syria, in which similar extra-judicial instruments are employed, see 'Ahmed's story' recounted by Clarke (*Islam and New Kinship*, pp. 21–5). Bargach states in her study on abandoned children in Morocco that similar practices occurred in Morocco (Jamila Bargach, *Orphans of Islam: Family, Abandonment, and Secret Adoption in Morocco* (Lanham, Rowman & Littlefield Publishers, 2002), pp. 110–111, 116). Likewise, Voorhoeve states that Tunisian family judges are willing to manoeuvre around the rules to establish legal paternity of an illegitimate child (Maaike Voorhoeve, 'Judicial Discretion in Tunisian Personal Status Law', in M. Voorhoeve (ed.), *Family Law in Islam: Divorce, Marriage and Women in the Muslim World* (London, I.B. Tauris, 2012), pp. 220–1).
78. Shehada, 'Negotiating Custody Rights', p. 248.
79. This *hadith* is said to be narrated by Thawban and can be found in the *Sunan* of Abu Dawud (*kitab al-talaq*, book 12, *hadith* 2218).
80. Also commonly referred to as *khul'* divorce; the SLPS, however, uses the term *mukhala'a*.
81. Interview with Mr Mulhim, lawyer and member of the Board of the Syrian Bar Association, Damascus, 13 April 2008.
82. Interview with lawyer Nawal, 15 April 2008, Damascus.
83. Central Bureau of Statistics, *Statistical Yearbook 2010*, issue 63. Available online at http://cbssyr.org/yearbook/2010/Data-Chapter2/TAB-15-2-2010.htm (accessed 9 December 2011).
84. Central Bureau of Statistics, *Statistical Yearbook 2008*, issue 61 (Damascus, Syrian Arab Republic Office of Prime Minister, 2008), p. 73. In comparison, a

total of 237,592 marriage certificates (26,135 in Damascus proper) were registered in Syria in 2007 (ibid.).

85. Ibid., p. 408.
86. Cf. Buskens, *Islamitisch recht en familiebetrekkingen in Marokko*; Jessica Carlisle, 'Mother Love: A Forced Divorce in Damascus', *Anthropology of the Middle East* 2/1 (2007b); Nahda Shehada, 'House of Obedience: Social Norms, Individual Agency and Historical Contingency', *Journal of Middle Eastern Women's Studies* 5/10 (2009a), pp. 24–49; Sonneveld, *Khul' Divorce in Egypt*; Lynn Welchman, *Beyond the Code: Muslim Family Law and the Shari'a Judiciary in the Palestinian West Bank* (The Hague, Kluwer Law International, 2000).
87. Interview with lawyer Mr Mulhim, Damascus, 13 April 2008. His claim corresponds with Carlisle's findings (*Rules, Negotiation, Claims*), who observed that *tafriq* petitions on the grounds of discord often end in a *mukhala'a* divorce.
88. See, for example, Carlisle, 'Mother Love', p. 95; Nahda Shehada, 'House of Obedience: Social Norms, Individual Agency and Historical Contingency', *Journal of Middle Eastern Women's Studies* 5/10 (2009a), p. 27.
89. See, for example, Shehada, 'House of Obedience', p. 27; Sonneveld, *Khul' Divorce in Egypt* 2012a, p. 128.
90. Sonneveld, *Khul' Divorce in Egypt*, pp. 127–8.
91. Shaqfa, *sharh ahkam al-ahwal al-shakhsiyya*, pp. 412–13.
92. This post-divorce maintenance generally covers the period of three menstrual cycles after the dissolution of the marriage (Art. 121).
93. Case A, Damascus *shar'iyya* court, 7 April 2009.
94. Due to the constant interruptions and noise I missed parts of his testimony.
95. Case H, Damascus *shar'iyya* court, 12 May 2009.
96. Unfortunately, I do not know how Judge Ibrahim settled this case.
97. Carlisle, 'From Behind the Door', p. 60.
98. Articles 112–120 Law of Evidence; see also Carlisle, *Rules, Negotiation, Claims*, pp. 52, 135–44.
99. Studies on other Muslim-majority countries in the region also showed that divorce by mutual consent was very popular amongst women, see for example: Aharon Layish, *Women and Islamic Law in a Non-Muslim State* (Jerusalem, Israel University Press, 1975) (Israel); Ziba Mir-Hosseini, *Marriage on Trial: Islamic Family Law in Iran and Morocco* (London, I.B.Tauris, 2000) (Iran and Morocco); Annelies Moors, *Women, Property and Islam: Palestinian experiences, 1920–1990* (Cambridge, Cambridge University Press, 1995); Lynn Welchman, *Beyond the Code* (Palestine); Sonneveld, *Khul' Divorce in Egypt* (Egypt).
100. See, for example, Linant de Bellefonds for references to classical *fiqh* (Yvon Linant de Bellefonds, *Traité de Droit Musulman Comparé. Tome II: Le Mariage, La Dissolution du Mariage* (Paris, Mouton & Co, 1965), p. 421 n.1). For contemporary studies, see, for example, John L. Esposito, *Women in Muslim Family Law* (Syracuse, NY, Syracuse University Press, 2001), p. 32; Mir-Hosseini, *Marriage on Trial*, pp. 38–9; Jamal J. Nasir, *The Islamic Law of Personal Status* (The Hague, Kluwer Law International, 2002), p. 115;

Welchman, *Women and Muslim Family Laws*, p. 112. Divorce by agreement has also been described as *talaq 'ala mal* (divorce for money or 'divorce in exchange for a consideration'; Linant de Bellefonds, *Traité de Droit Musulman*, p. 446 or *talaq muqabil ibra'* ('divorce in return for renunciation') or simply as *ibra'* (release or renunciation) in the West Bank and Egypt (Welchman, *Beyond the Code*, p. 347; Sonneveld, *Khul' Divorce in Egypt*, p. 33, respectively).

101. Welchman, *Women and Muslim Family Laws*, p. 211 n. 2. For example, the Moroccan family law makes a distinction between divorce by mutual consent and *khul'*, but does not attribute the term *mubara'a* to the former. Pakistani divorce law, on the other hand, does make a distinction between *khul'* and *mubara'a* divorce (see Pauline Kruiniger, 'Repudiated by husband and Europe?', in M.C. Foblets and N. Yassari (eds), *Cultural Diversity* (The Series of Centre for Studies and Research in International Law and International Relations of the Hague Academy of International Law) (Leiden, Martinus Nijhoff Publishers, 2013)).
102. Email correspondence with lawyer Yusuf, 10 February 2012.
103. Welchman states that other Arab states (e.g. Jordan, Algeria, Qatar) have also introduced (or attempts were undertaken) this Egyptian-styled *khul'* divorce (i.e. without the husband's consent) (*Women and Muslim Family Laws*, pp. 116–22).
104. See also Jessica Carlisle, '*Asbab li-l-darb ktir basita*: the legality of claims of violence during judicial divorce cases in Damascus', *Hawwa: Journal of Women of the Middle East and the Islamic World* 5 (2007a), p. 242.
105. See, for example, Moors, *Women, Property and Islam*, p. 141; Sonneveld, *Khul' Divorce in Egypt*, pp. 125–7; Welchman, *Beyond the Code*, pp. 353–4.
106. This was written down on the back of the marriage contract and certified with seals and stamps.
107. "خلعتك من عصمتي وعقد نكاحي لقاء براءة ذمتي من المهرين والأشياء الجهازية والمصاغ والحلي والنفقة الزوجية ونفقة العدة وأي حق آخر ناشئ عن عقد الزواج لقاء بدل الخلع البالغ مائة ليرة سورية أدفعها لك الآن وبالمقابل أبرئ ذمتك من كل حق ناشئ عن عقد زواجي بك"
108. "قبلت منك مخالعتك لي على ما ذكرت وقبضت منك بدل الخلع البالغ مائة ليرة سورية وأبرأت ذمتك تجاهي وقبلت إبراءك لي"
109. Damascus *shar'iyya* court, 28 April 2009.
110. Personal communication with lawyer Ahmed, 11 February 2009; and lawyer Yusuf, 10 February 2012.
111. See, for example, Sonneveld, *Khul' Divorce in Egypt* (Egypt); Moors, *Women, Property and Islam,* and Welchman, *Beyond the Code* (Palestine); Buskens, *Islamitisch recht en familiebetrekkingen in Marokko* (Morocco).
112. See, for example, Mida R. Zantout, 'Khul': Between Past and Present', *Islamic Law and Law of the Muslim World Research Paper Series*, No. 08–14 (New York Law School, 2006).
113. See also Judith E. Tucker, *In the House of the Law: Gender and Islamic Law in Ottoman Syria and Palestine* (Berkeley, University of California Press, 1998), p. 99; Sonneveld, *Khul' Divorce in Egypt*, pp. 125–7.

114. See Carlisle, '*Asbab li-l-darb ktir basita*: the legality of claims', and Carlisle, *Rules, Negotiation, Claims*; Sonneveld observed that the same practice was employed by mediators in the family courts of Egypt (*Khul' Divorce in Egypt*, p. 130).
115. Carlisle, *Rules, Negotiation, Claims*, p. 157.
116. Personal communication with lawyer Ahmed, 11 February 2009.
117. Case B, Damascus *shar'iyya* court, 26 February 2009.
118. Personal communication with lawyer Ahmed, 26 February 2009.
119. I was not able to find out what the grounds for divorce were nor do I know whether a divorce petition had already been filed with the court.
120. Carlisle, 'Mother Love', pp. 89–102.
121. Personal communication with *shar'iyya* Judge Ibrahim, 21 May 2009, Damascus.
122. Personal communication with *shar'iyya* Judge Ibrahim, 21 May 2009, Damascus.
123. The reason I did not attend more of these 'kick-off' sessions is because they coincided with the Greek Orthodox court sessions, also on Thursday mornings, which I tried to attend as often as I could.
124. Carlisle, 'Mother Love', p. 93.
125. See Carlisle for similar observations (ibid., pp. 94–5).
126. Office Judge Ibrahim, Damascus *shar'iyya* court, 21 May 2009.
127. Ibid.
128. Interestingly enough, the judge and arbiters all took this oath, but not on the Qur'an. Instead, they stood up and placed their right hand over their hearts and took the oath simultaneously.
129. Since I did not attend any of these arbitration sessions, i.e. those conducted in the arbiter's private offices, I cannot report on how they were carried out. In 2005–06, during her fieldwork, Carlisle observed several arbitration sessions; I therefore refer to her PhD thesis for a detailed description of these sessions, conducted in arbiters' offices in Damascus (see Carlisle *Rules, Negotiation, Claims* (in particular Chapters 5–8), as well as Carlisle, 'Mother Love').
130. Carlisle, *Rules, Negotiation, Claims*, pp. 189, 202–6. See also Carlisle, '*Asbab li-l-darb ktir basita*: the legality of claims', pp. 251, 258. Likewise, Sonneveld asserts that similar strategies are employed by Egyptian mediators working for the family courts (*Khul' Divorce in Egypt*, p. 130).
131. Carlisle, *Rules, Negotiation, Claims*, p. 209.

Chapter 6 The Catholic Court: Guardian of Order and Sacraments

1. John D. Faris, 'An Overview of the Code of Canons of the Eastern Churches', in John P. Beal et al. (eds), *New Commentary on the Code of Canon Law*, commissioned by the Canon Law Society of America (New York, Paulist Press, 2000), p. 32.

2. It has to be noted that Catholics who belong to the Latin Church are officially governed by the Latin Codex (the Code of Canon Law or *Codex Iuris Canonici* of 1983), see Can. 1 CCEO and 38 CLPS. Article 1 CLPS stipulates that the Catholic courts in Syria can also hear cases of Latin Catholics but, with regard to marriage and nullifications, they are subject to the Canons 1055–1165 (Title VII 'Marriage') of the Latin Codex (see Art. 38).
3. See also Anton Moslih, 'La legge sullo statuto personale delle confessioni cattoliche', *Il Regno Attualità* 4 (2008), p. 135.
4. Fortunately, my fieldwork in the Catholic court of Damascus (February–July 2009) fell within this exceptional period (2006–10). However, I did not observe any court cases involving adoption or inheritance.
5. See also al-Bunni 2010.
6. Due to the revolution in Syria, which started in March 2011, I have not been able to return to Damascus and have therefore not been able to follow up on this issue.
7. Anton Moslih, 'Code du Statut Personnel des Catholiques en Syrie. Etude' (unpublished document, n.d.), p. 7.
8. That is to say, the provisions of the CLPS apply only to those who are baptised or received into the Catholic Church (Arts 10 and 29 CLPS and Can. 8 and 29).
9. Information taken from the following website: http://www.catholic-hierarchy.org/diocese/qview6.html#sy (accessed 18 May 2011).
10. Jacques El-Hakim, 'Syria', in *Yearbook of Islamic and Middle Eastern Law* Vol. 1 (1994) (London, Kluwer Law International, 1995), p. 149.
11. This number (213) is based on personal calculations and by no means an exhaustive number. In addition, the majority of the 213 'cases' include reappearing cases, meaning that I saw several cases at different stages of the proceedings.
12. Rabo writes that the Orthodox communities have become more liberal in granting divorce since the 1970s and 1980s (Annika Rabo, '"We are Christians and we are equal citizens": perspectives on particularity and pluralism in contemporary Syria', *Islam and Christian–Muslim Relations* 23/1 2012b, p. 87).
13. For more information on the Pontifical Oriental Institute, please refer to their website: http://www.unipio.org.
14. On the competence of collegiate tribunal (three judges), see Article 303 par. 1 sub b CLPS and Can. 1084 par. 1 CCEO.
15. The English translations of the CCEO used in this study are taken from the *Code of Canons of the Eastern Churches, Latin-English Edition, New English Translation*, prepared under the auspices of the Canon Law Society of America (2001).
16. On the composition of an ecclesiastical tribunal and the required qualifications for the officers of the tribunal, see Articles 305–20 CLPS and Canons 1086–1101 CCEO; interview with judge of the first instance and appeal Catholic court Fr Antoun, 26 March 2009, Damascus.
17. Interview with judge in the first instance and appeal Catholic court Fr Antoun, 26 March 2009, Damascus.

18. Ibid.
19. See Victor J. Pospishil, 'The Problem of Divorce in the Catholic Church', *Journal of Family Law* 7/4 (1968), p. 604. Although children born during such a marriage are recognised by the Church and remain legitimate (Victor J. Pospishil, *Eastern Catholic Marriage Law: According to the Code of Canons of the Eastern Churches* (Brooklyn NY, Saint Maron Publications, 1991), p. 490).
20. Also known in 'divorce of bed and board' or as 'séperation de corps' (in French).
21. Interview with judge in the first instance and appeal Catholic court Fr Antoun, 26 March 2009, Damascus.
22. The CCEO speaks of 'petitioner' and 'respondent', see for example Canon 1134 ff. Therefore I will employ these terms when discussing Catholic personal status cases, instead of the terms 'plaintiff' and 'defendant' as used in Chapter 5. In Arabic no such distinction is made; in the Syrian different personal status laws and courts, the terminology is one and the same, i.e. *al-mudda'i*, meaning plaintiff or petitioner, and *al-mudda'i 'alayhi*, meaning defendant or respondent.
23. Whether or not such impediments exist ought to be investigated by a priest before the marriage is celebrated (Can. 785).
24. Victor J., Pospishil, *Eastern Catholic Marriage Law: According to the Code of Canons of the Eastern Churches* (Brooklyn NY, Saint Maron Publications, 1991), pp. 337–9.
25. Article 322 CLPS and Canon 1103 § 2 CCEO regarding trials in general; Article 544 CLPS and Canon 1362 CCEO regarding nullification processes.
26. Interview with Fr Eliyas, judge in the Catholic first instance, Damascus, 12 March 2009.
27. See Pospishil, *Eastern Catholic Marriage Law*, pp. 448–9.
28. Craig A. Cox, 'Part III. Certain Special Processes [cc. 1671–1716]', in John P. Beal et al. (eds), *New Commentary on the Code of Canon Law*, commissioned by the Canon Law Society of America (New York, Paulist Press, 2000), p. 1769.
29. Case E, Catholic first instance court, 12 March 2009, Damascus.
30. Unfortunately, there are no detailed statistics on divorce available, for any of the religious groups (see also Chapter 5).
31. Cox, 'Part III', p. 1760.
32. Personal communication, 16 March 2009, Damascus.
33. Personal communication with lawyer Hanan, 26 November 2008, Damascus. See also Jessica Carlisle, 'From Behind the Door: A Damascus Court copes with an alleged out of Court marriage', in B. Drieskens (ed.), *Les métamorphoses du mariage au Moyen-Orient* (Beirut, Institut Français du Proche-Orient (IFPO) 2008).
34. Canon 1207 ff. on 'proofs'; on 'witnesses and testimonies' (Can. 1228 ff.); specific or additional regulations on 'proofs' in a marriage nullity case, see Canons 1364–7. See also Pospishil, *Eastern Catholic Marriage Law*, p. 501.
35. On one occasion I observed that the interrogation of the spouses did not take place in a joint session in court, this was due to the fact that the husband lived in the United States of America. The husband was questioned by a priest in the

USA, the report was subsequently sent to the Catholic court in Damascus, which used this document as evidence in the case.

36. Case N, Catholic first instance court, 16 March 2009, Damascus.
37. Since this case was still in its early stages and my fieldwork ended a month later, I could not follow up on this case (Case T, Catholic first instance court, 20 April 2009, Damascus).
38. A traditional salad, popular in Syria and Lebanon.
39. Case L, Catholic first instance court, 23 March 2009, Damascus.
40. See Articles 440–7, 548 CLPS and Canons 1255–1262, 1366 CCEO.
41. Unfortunately, I was unable to attend the session in which the doctors presented their medical reports.
42. My fieldwork period had come to an end by the time these witness hearings were scheduled, for that reason I do not know how this case developed over time. However, I got the impression that, based on the way the judges communicated with the wife, they seemed to sympathise with her, especially as she could not afford a lawyer and was forced to manage her own legal affairs.
43. A copy of the Bible was placed on a bookstand on the litigants' table; a copy of the Qur'an lay behind the bookstand.
44. The oath was the same as in the *shar'iyya* courts, namely: 'I swear by God, the Almighty, that I will tell the whole truth without adding or omitting anything' (*'uqsim bi-llah al-'azim an aqul al-haqq kullahu dun ziyada aw nuqsan'*).
45. Case O, Catholic first instance court, 18 May 2009, Damascus.
46. Article 77.1 Law of Evidence. In addition, separate examination of witnesses is also prescribed by the CCEO in Canon 1241.
47. On 'Witnesses and Testimonies' see Articles 413 ff. CLPS and Canons 1228 ff. CCEO.
48. Article 427 CLPS and Canon 1242 CCEO.
49. Case C, Catholic first instance court, 2 March 2009, Damascus.
50. I do not know the reason why Sawsan called the police.
51. This latter witness statement was wrapped up rather quickly, most likely because her statements corresponded with the former two. Case S, Catholic first instance court, 4 May 2009, Damascus.
52. Personal communication with Fr Eliyas, judge in the Catholic first instance, Damascus, 12 March 2009.
53. Ibid.
54. Case A, Catholic first instance court, 25 May 2009, Damascus.
55. Pospishil, *Eastern Catholic Marriage Law*, p. 197.
56. A wife can, however, not be forced to live with her in-laws or children from a previous marriage (Art. 126 CLPS).
57. Anton Moslih, 'La legge sullo statuto personale delle confessioni cattoliche', *Il Regno Attualità* 4 (2008), p. 138 n. 1.
58. Case P, Catholic first instance court, 15 June 2009, Damascus.
59. The CCEO does, however, accept exceptions for exceptional circumstances, for instance when there is no competent priest available (see Can. 832 and 834).

Besides, the Catholic Church also acknowledges 'secretly celebrated' marriages but, again, only in exceptional circumstances. These 'secret' marriages are 'to be recorded only in the special register that is to be kept in the secret archive of the eparchial curia' (Can. 840).

60. Case J, Catholic first instance court, 11 May 2009, Damascus.
61. Personal communication, 8 June 2009, Damascus.

Conclusions

1. Cf. Sally E. Merry, 'Legal Pluralism', *Law and Society Review* 22/5 (1988), pp. 869–96.
2. Suad Joseph, 'The Public/Private: The Imagined Boundary in the Imagined Nation/State/Community: The Lebanese Case', *Feminist Review* 57 (1997), p. 81.

Appendix Marriage and Divorce according to the Syrian Law of Personal Status

1. Muhammad Fihr Shaqfa, *sharh ahkam al-ahwal al-shakhsiyya: li-l-muslimin wa-l-nasara wa-l-yahud* [*Explaining the Law of Personal Status: Muslims, Christians, and Jews*] (Damascus, Mu'assasat Al-Nuri, 1998), p. 191.
2. Whether the (minor) bride is a virgin (*bikr*), that is, not previously married, or a non-virgin girl (*thayyib*), that is, widow or divorcée, is irrelevant (Shaqfa, *sharh ahkam al-ahwal al-shakhsiyya*, p. 199).
3. The translation is taken from Welchman and slightly adapted by the author (see Lynn Welchman, *Beyond the Code: Muslim Family Law and the Shari'a Judiciary in the Palestinian West Bank* (The Hague, Kluwer Law International, 2000), p. 125).
4. Shaqfa, *sharh ahkam al-ahwal al-shakhsiyya*, p. 199.
5. Ibid.
6. Lynn Welchman, *Women and Muslim Family Laws in Arab States: A Comparative Overview of Textual Development and Advocacy* (Amsterdam, Amsterdam University Press, 2007), p. 73.
7. A *mukhtar* (lit. 'chosen person') is the chief or headman of a village or a city district who is responsible for, amongst other things, keeping record of births and deaths of the population of his village or district. It is an administrative position created by the Ottomans in the nineteenth century, which continues to exist in Syria today (C.V. Findley, 'Mukhtār', in C.E. Bosworth et al. (eds), *Encyclopaedia of Islam*, Vol. VII, 2nd edn (Leiden, Brill, 1993)).
8. See also Article 1 of Legislative Decree No. 272 ('Conditions regarding Marriage of Syrians and Palestinians to Non-Arab Women') of 4 November 1969. A foreign spouse needs to submit additional documents, including certified documents regarding the spouse's civil status and religion issued through the Embassy, and proof of an HIV test (see website of the Damascus Bar

Association: http://www.damascusbar.org/english/LL%20Eng%20S%20marriage%20with%20foreigners.htm (accessed 25 June 2013).

9. Shaqfa, *sharh ahkam al-ahwal al-shakhsiyya*, pp. 381–2.
10. Liyakat Takim, 'Law: The Four Sunnī Schools of Law', in S. Joseph (ed.), *Encyclopedia of Women in Islamic Cultures* II (Leiden, Brill, 2005), p. 443.
11. Shaqfa, *sharh ahkam al-ahwal al-shakhsiyya*, p. 403.
12. Ibid.
13. Court of Cassation, *shar'iyya* chamber, 20 November 1960 (no case number mentioned), see Mamduh 'Atari (ed.), *qanun al-ahwal al-shakhsiyya* (Law of Personal Status) (Damascus, mu'assasat al-nuri, 2006), p. 121.
14. Court of Cassation, *shar'iyya* chamber, 16 March 1963 (no case number mentioned), see 'Atari, *qanun al-ahwal al-shakhsiyya*, p. 121; Shaqfa, *sharh ahkam al-ahwal al-shakhsiyya*, p. 434.
15. Shaqfa, *sharh ahkam al-ahwal al-shakhsiyya*, p. 435.
16. Court of Cassation, *shar'iyya* chamber, decision number 647/693, 28 September 1981, see 'Atari, *qanun al-ahwal al-shakhsiyya*, p. 121; Welchman, *Women and Muslim Family Laws*, p. 127.
17. Shaqfa, *sharh ahkam al-ahwal al-shakhsiyya*, pp. 446–53.
18. Personal communication with senior lawyer Mr Mulhim, Damascus, 13 April 2008.

BIBLIOGRAPHY

Laws (in Arabic)

Al-Malki, Khalid 'A. (ed.), *qanun al-sultat al-qada'iyya* (Judicial Authority Law), in Khalid 'A. Al-Malki (ed.), *adwa' 'ala qanun al-sultat al-qada'iyya* (Insights into the Judicial Authority Law) (Damascus, mu'assasat al-nuri, 2006).

Al-Zawahira Al-Sa'igh, Nabil (ed.), *qawanin al-ahwal al-shakhsiyyat al-urthudhuk-siyyat fi suriyya wa-lubnan* (Orthodox Laws of Personal Status in Syria and Lebanon) (Damascus, dar kiwan, 2004).

'Atari, Mamduh (ed.), *qanun al-ahwal al-shakhsiyya* (Law of Personal Status) (Damascus, mu'assasat al-nuri, 2006).

—— *qanun usul al-mahakimat* (Law of Judicial Procedures) (Damascus, mu'assasat al-nuri, 2007).

—— *qanun al-'uqubat* (Penal Code) (Damascus, mu'assasat al-nuri, 2008).

—— *qanun al-madani* (Civil Code) (Damascus, mu'assasat al-nuri, 2008).

—— *qanun al-bayyinat* (Law of Evidence) (Damascus, mu'assasat al-nuri, 2010).

Damascus Bar Association (far' niqabat al-muhamin fi Dimashq) (ed.), *qanun al-ahwal al-shakhsiyya* (Law of Personal Status) (Damascus, manshurat far' niqabat al-muhamin fi Dimashq, 2006).

Pasha, Qadri 'kitab al-ahkam al-shar'iyyat fi al-ahwal al-shakhsiyyat 'ala madhhab al-imam abi hanifa al-nu'man' (Book of Legal Rulings in Personal Status according to the School of Imam Abi Hanifa), in Damascus Bar Association (ed.), *qanun al-ahwal al-shakhsiyya* (Damascus, manshurat far' niqabat al-muhamin fi Dimashq, 2006).

qanun al-ahwal al-shakhsiyyat li-l-tawa'if al-kathulikiyya (Personal Status Law for the Catholic Communities) (Damascus, mu'assasat al-nuri, 2007).

Books, articles and other sources

Abd-Allah, Umar F., *The Islamic Struggle in Syria* (Berkeley, Mizan Press, 1983).

Abu Halawa, Kareem, *Survey on the need to change laws prejudicial to women* (*istitla' ra'i hawla dururat taghyir al-qawanin al-mujhat bi-haqq al-mar'a*) (in English and Arabic) (Damascus, Karama, 2006).

Abu-Odeh, Lama, 'Modern Family Law, 1800–Present: Arab States', in S. Joseph (ed.), *Encyclopedia of Women in Islamic Cultures II* (Leiden, Brill, 2005), pp. 459–63.

Al-Aws, Yahya, 'The Ministry of Endowments – Where is it Going?' (translated by Susanna Ferguson), 30 January 2010. Available at http://www.thara-sy.com/TharaEnglish/modules/news/article.php?storyid=204 (accessed 17 March 2012).

Albarazi, Zahra, 'The Stateless Syrians', Tilburg Law School Research Paper No. 011/2013 (32 pp).

Al-Habash, Mohammad, *dirasat fiqhiyyat li-l-tahaffuzat allati wada'aha al-marsum al-tashri'i 330 li-'am 2002 'ala ittifaqiyya mukafaha kull ashkal al-tamyiz didd al-mar'a, sidaw* (*Islamic jurisprudence study on the reservations, based on legislative decree 330 of 2002, to the Convention on the Elimination of All Forms of Discrimination Against Women, CEDAW*) (Damascus, Syrian Commission for Family Affairs and the Islamic Studies Centre, 2005).

—— *Jurisprudence Study: Reservation on the Legislative decree No. 330 of 2002 on the Convention on the Elimination of All Forms of Discrimination against Women, CEDAW* (Damascus, Syrian Commission for Family Affairs and the Islamic Studies Centre, 2006).

Al-Qattan, Najwa, 'Dhimmis in the Muslim Court: Legal Autonomy and Religious Discrimination', *International Journal of Middle East Studies* 31/3 (1999), pp. 429–44.

Amin, S.H., *Middle East Legal Systems* (Glasgow, Royston Limited, 1985).

Anderson, J.N.D., 'The Syrian Law of Personal Status', *Bulletin of the School of Oriental and African Studies* 17/1 (1955), pp. 34–49.

—— 'Law as a Social Force in Islamic Culture and History', *Bulletin of the School of Oriental and African Studies, University of London* 20–1/3 (1957), pp. 13–40.

—— 'Modern Trends in Islam: Legal Reform and Modernisation in the Middle East', *International and Comparative Law Quarterly* 20/1 (1971), pp. 1–21.

Arabi, O., *Studies in Modern Islamic law and Jurisprudence* (The Hague, Kluwer Law International, 2001).

Badr, G.M., 'The New Egyptian Civil Code and the Unification of the Laws of the Arab Countries', *Tulane Law Review* 30 (1955–56), pp. 299–304.

Barakat, Halim, 'The Arab Family and the Challenge of Social Transformation', in E.W. Fernea (ed.), *Women and the Family in the Middle East: New Voices of Change* (Austin, University of Texas Press, 1985), pp. 27–48.

—— *The Arab World: Society, Culture, and State* (Berkeley, University of California Press, 1993).

Bargach, Jamila, *Orphans of Islam: Family, Abandonment, and Secret Adoption in Morocco* (Lanham, Rowman & Littlefield Publishers, 2002).

Bechor, Guy, *The Sanhuri Code, and the Emergence of Modern Arab Civil Law (1932 to 1949)* (Leiden, Brill, 2007).

Belhadj, Souhaïl and Dupret, Baudouin, 'La religion à toutes fins parlementaires pratiques: comment l'islam est thématisé à l'Assemblée du Peuple syrienne', *Maghreb-Machrek* 198 (2009), pp. 31–41.

Bennet, Marjorie A., *Reincarnation, Marriage, and Memory: Negotiating Sectarian Identity among the Druze of Syria* (unpublished PhD thesis, University of Arizona, 1999).

Berger, Maurits S., 'The legal system of family law in Syria', *Bulletin d'Études Orientales* 49 (1997), pp. 115–27.

—— *Sharia and Public Policy in Egyptian Family Law* (Groningen, Hephaestus Publishers, 2005).

Bernard-Maugiron, Nathalie, 'Can *Hisba* be "Modernised"? The Individual and the Protection of the General Interest before Egyptian Courts', in B. Dupret (ed.), *Standing Trial: Law and the Person in the Modern Middle East* (London, I.B.Tauris, 2004), pp. 318–44.

Bewes, Wyndham A., 'The Theory of the Statutes', *Journal of Comparative Legislation and International Law* 4/3 (1922), pp. 97–103.

Boogert, Maurits H. van den, 'Millets: Past and Present', in A.N. Longva and A.S. Roald (eds), *Religious Minorities in the Middle East: Domination, Self-Empowerment, Accommodation* (Leiden, Brill, 2012), pp. 27–45.

Botiveau, B., 'Le movement de rationalisation du droit en syrie au cours de la première moitié du XXe siècle', *Bulletin d'Études Orientales* 35 (1983), pp. 123–35.

—— *Loi islamique et droit dans les sociétés arabes: Mutations de systèmes juridiques du Moyen-Orient* (Paris, Karthala, 1993).

—— 'The Law of the Nation-State and the Status of Non-Muslims in Egypt and Syria', in A. Pacini (ed.), *Christian Communities in the Arab Middle East: The Challenge of the Future* (Oxford, Clarendon Press, 1998), pp. 111–26.

Böttcher, A., *Official Sunni and Shi'i Islam in Syria* (EUI Working Paper RSC No. 2002/3) (Florence, European University Institute, 2002).

Brock, Sebastian, *An Introduction to Syriac Studies* (Piscataway, NJ, Gorgias Press, 2006).

Buskens, Léon, *Islamitisch recht en familiebetrekkingen in Marokko* (Amsterdam, Bulaaq, 1999).

—— 'Recent Debates on Family Law Reform in Morocco: Islamic Law as Politics in an Emerging Public Sphere', *Islamic Law and Society* 10/1 (2003), pp. 70–131.

Buskens, Léon and Dupret, Baudouin, 'De l'invention du droit musulman à la pratique juridique contemporaine', in B. Dupret (ed.), *La charia aujourd'hui: Usages de la référence au droit islamique* (Paris, La Découverte, 2012), pp. 9–17.

Calder, N., 'Sharī'a', in C.E. Bosworth et al. (eds), *Encyclopaedia of Islam*, Vol. XI, 2nd edn (Leiden, Brill, 1997), pp. 321–26.

Canon Law Society of America, *Code of Canons of the Eastern Churches, Latin–English Edition, New English Translation* (Washington DC, Canon Law Society of America, 2001).

Cardinal, Monique C., 'Islamic Legal Theory Curriculum: Are the Classics Taught Today?', *Islamic Law and Society* 12/2 (2005), pp. 224–72.

—— 'Women and the Judiciary in Syria: Appointments Process, Training and Career Paths', *International Journal of the Legal Profession* 15/1-2 (2008), pp. 123–39.

—— 'Why Aren't Women Sharī'a Court judges? The Case of Syria', *Islamic Law and Society* 17 (2010), pp. 185–214.

Carlisle, Jessica, '*Asbab li-l-darb ktir basita*: the Legality of Claims of Violence during Judicial Divorce cases in Damascus', *Hawwa: Journal of Women of the Middle East and the Islamic World* 5 (2007a), pp. 239–61.

—— 'Mother Love: A Forced Divorce in Damascus', *Anthropology of the Middle East* 2/1 (2007b), pp. 89–102.

—— *Rules, Negotiation, Claims and Counter Claims: Judicial Discretion in a Damascus Shari'a Court* (unpublished PhD thesis, University of London, 2007c).

—— 'From Behind the Door: A Damascus Court copes with an alleged out of Court marriage', in B. Drieskens (ed.), *Les métamorphoses du mariage au Moyen-Orient* (Beirut, Institut Français du Proche-Orient (IFPO), 2008), pp. 59–74.

Central Bureau of Statistics, *Statistical Yearbook 2008*, issue 61 (Damascus, Syrian Arab Republic Office of Prime Minister, 2008).

Charrad, Mounira M., *States and Women's Rights: The making of Postcolonial Tunisia, Algeria, and Morocco* (Berkeley, University of California Press, 2001).

Chaumont, E., 'Tabann(in)', in P. Bearman et al. (eds), *Encyclopaedia of Islam*, Vol. XII Suppl., 2nd edn (Leiden, Brill, 2004), pp. 768–69.

Central Intelligence Agency, *The World Fact Book* (online edition, 2013–14). Available online at https://www.cia.gov/library/publications/the-world-factbook/geos/sy.html (accessed 23 August 2015).

Clarke, Morgan, *Islam and New Kinship: Reproductive Technology and the Shariah in Lebanon* (New York, Berghahn Books, 2009).

Cleveland, William L., *A History of the Modern Middle East* (Boulder, Westview Press, 2000).

Committee on the Elimination of Discrimination against Women (CEDAW), *Initial Report: Syrian Arab Republic*, 29 August 2005, UN Doc. CEDAW/C/SYR/1.

—— *Summary record of the 785th meeting*, 18 July 2007, UN Doc. CEDAW/C/SR.785.

Committee on the Rights of Children (CRC), *Initial Report: Syrian Arab Republic*, 22 September 1995, UN Doc. CRC/C/28/Add.2.

—— *Third and Fourth Periodic Report: Syrian Arab Republic*, 4 March 2009, UN Doc. CRC/C/SYR/3-4.

Cooke, Miriam, *Dissident Syria: Making Oppositional Arts Official* (Durham, Duke University Press, 2007).

Courbage, Youssef and Fargues, Philippe, *Christians and Jews under Islam* (London, I.B.Tauris, 1998).

Cox, Craig A., 'Part III. Certain Special Processes [cc. 1671–1716]', in John P. Beal et al. (eds), *New Commentary on the Code of Canon Law*, commissioned by the Canon Law Society of America (New York, Paulist Press, 2000), pp. 1760–89.

Cuno, Kenneth M. and Desai, Manisha (eds), *Family, Gender, and Law in a Globalizing Middle East and South Asia* (Syracuse, NY, University Press, 2009).

Dahlgren, Susanne, *Contesting Realities: The Public Sphere and Morality in Southern Yemen* (Syracuse, NY, Syracuse University Press, 2010).

Dam, Nikolaos van, *The Struggle for Power in Syria: Politics and Society under Asad and the Ba'th Party*, 4th edn (London, I.B.Tauris, 2011).

Davidson, R.H., 'Tanẓīmāt', in P. Bearman et al. (eds), *Encyclopaedia of Islam*, Vol. X, 2nd edn (Leiden, Brill, 2000), pp. 201–09.

Dostal, Jörg Michael, 'Analyzing the Domestic and International Conflict in Syria: Are there Lessons from Political Science?', in J.M. Dostal and O. Imady (eds), *Syria Studies* 6/1 (Fife, University of St Andrews Centre for Syrian Studies, 2014), pp. 1–80.

Doumani, Beshara (ed.), *Family History in the Middle East. Household, Property, and Gender* (Albany, State University of New York Press, 2003).

Drieskens, Barbara, 'Changing Perceptions of Marriage in Contemporary Beirut', in B. Drieskens (ed.), *Les métamorphoses du mariage au Moyen-Orient* (Beirut, Institut Français du Proche-Orient (IFPO) 2008), pp. 97–118.

Dupret, Baudouin, 'The Practice of Judging: The Egyptian Judiciary at Work in a Personal Status Case', in Muhammad K. Masud et al. (eds), *Dispensing Justice in Islam: Qadis and their Judgements* (Leiden, Brill, 2006), pp. 143–68.

—— 'Legal Pluralism, Plurality of Laws, and Legal Practices: Theories, Critiques, and Praxiological Re-specification', *European Journal of Legal Studies* 1 (2007a). Available at http://www.ejls.eu/1/14UK.pdf (accessed 9 September 2015).

—— 'What is Islamic Law? A Praxiological Answer and an Egyptian Case Study', *Theory, Culture & Society* 24/2 (2007b), pp. 79–100.

Dupret, Baudouin, Berger, Maurits and Al-Zwaini, Laila (eds), *Legal Pluralism in the Arab World* (The Hague, Kluwer Law International, 1999).

Eickelman, Dale F., *The Middle East and Central Asia: An Anthropological Approach* (Upper Saddle River, NJ, Prentice-Hall, 1998).

El-Alami, Dawoud S. and Hinchcliffe, Doreen, *Islamic Marriage and Divorce Laws of the Arab World* (London, Kluwer Law International, 1996).

El-Hakim, Jacques, 'Syria', in *Yearbook of Islamic and Middle Eastern Law* Vol. 1 (1994) (London, Kluwer Law International, 1995), pp. 142–55.

—— 'Syria', in *Yearbook of Islamic and Middle Eastern Law* Vol. 12 (2005–06) (London, Kluwer Law International, 2007), pp. 269–80.

El-Rahabi, Mayyah, *Assessment of National Women's Machineries in Syria* (Cairo, Euromed Role of Women in Economic Life Programme, 2006).

Esposito, John L., *Women in Muslim Family Law* (Syracuse, NY, Syracuse University Press, 2001).

Euromed Role of Women in Economic Life Programme, *Analysis of the Economic Situation of Women in Syria* (Cairo, Euromed Role of Women in Economic Life Programme, 2006).

Faris, John D., 'An Overview of the Code of Canons of the Eastern Churches', in John P. Beal et al. (eds), *New Commentary on the Code of Canon Law*, commissioned by the Canon Law Society of America (New York, Paulist Press, 2000), pp. 27–44.

Faulk, Edward, *101 Questions and Answers on Eastern Catholic Churches* (New York, Paulist Press, 2007).

Feller, Dina C., *La garde (Ḥaḍanah) en droit musulman et dans les droits égyptien, syrien et tunisien* (Geneve, Librairie Droz, 1996).

Fernea, Elizabeth W. (ed.), *Women and the Family in the Middle East: New voices of change* (Austin, University of Texas Press, 1985).

Findley, C.V., 'Maḥkama. ii. The reform era (ca. 1789–1922)', in C.E. Bosworth et al. (eds), *Encyclopaedia of Islam*, Vol. VI, 2nd edn (Leiden, Brill, 1991a), pp. 5–11.

—— 'Medjelle', in C.E. Bosworth et al. (eds), *Encyclopaedia of Islam*, Vol. VI, 2nd edn (Leiden, Brill, 1991b), pp. 971–2.

—— 'Mukhtār', in C.E. Bosworth et al. (eds), *Encyclopaedia of Islam*, Vol. VII, 2nd edn (Leiden, Brill, 1993), pp. 519–21.

Ferguson, Fay and Muhanna, Nadia, 'Personal Status Matters', *Syria Today* (online edition), August 2009. Available at http://www.syria-today.com/index.php/august-2009/377-society/2443-personal-status-matters (accessed 17 March 2012).

Gallagher, Clarence, 'Marriage in the Revised Canon Law for the Eastern Catholic Churches', *Studia Canonica* 24 (1990), pp. 69–90.

—— 'Marriage in Eastern and Western Canon Law', *Law & Justice. The Christian Law Review* 157 (2006), pp. 7–16.

George, Alan, *Syria: Neither Bread nor Freedom* (London, Zed Books, 2003).

Georges, Nael, 'Les chrétiens dans le monde arabe et la question de l'apostasie en islam', *Maghreb-Machrek* 209 (2011), pp. 110–19.

—— *Le droit des minorités. Le cas de chrétiens en Orient arabe* (Aix-en-Provence, Presses Universitaires d'Aix-Marseille, 2012).

Geros, Panagiotis, 'Doing Fieldwork within Fear and Silences', in Heidi Armbruster and Anna Lærke, *Taking Sides: Ethics, Politics and Fieldwork in Anthropology* (New York, Berghahn Books, 2010), pp. 89–118.

Ghazzal, Zouhair, 'Droit et société', in B. Dupret et al. (eds), *La Syrie au présent: Reflets d'une société* (Arles, Actes Sud, 2007a), pp. 625–59.

—— 'Violence and Legal Responsibility: Crime-in-Action in Contemporary Syria' (2007b). Available online at http://ssrn.com/abstract=997374 (accessed 22 December 2011).

Grafton, David D., *The Christians of Lebanon: Political Rights in Islamic Law* (London, I.B.Tauris, 2003).

Griffiths, John, 'What is Legal Pluralism?', *Journal of Legal Pluralism* 24 (1986), pp. 1–55.

Haidar, Dalia, 'Just Challenges', *Syria Today* (online edition), July 2009. Available at http://www.syria-today.com/index.php/july-2009/363-focus/1997-just-challenges (accessed 8 September 2009).

Hallaq, Wael B., *Sharīʿa: Theory, Practice, Transformations* (New York, Cambridge University Press, 2008).

Hasan, Aznan, 'Granting Khul for a Non-Muslim Couple in Egyptian Personal Status Law: Generosity or Laxity?', *Arab Law Quarterly* 18/1 (2003), pp. 81–9.

Hasso, Frances S., *Consuming Desires: Family Crisis and the State in the Middle East* (Stanford, Stanford University Press, 2011).

Heck, Paul L., 'Religious renewal in Syria: the case of Muhammad al-Habash', *Islam and Christian-Muslim Relations* 15/2 (2004), pp. 185–207.

Hegland, Mary Elaine, 'Gossip', in S. Joseph (ed.), *Encyclopedia of Women in Islamic Cultures* II (Leiden, Brill, 2005), pp. 210–14.

Hélie-Lucas, Marie-Aimée, 'The Preferential Symbol for Islamic Identity: Women in Muslim Personal Laws', in V.M. Moghadam (ed.), *Identity Politics and Women. Cultural Reassertions and Feminisms in International Perspective* (Boulder, Westview Press, 1994), pp. 391–407.

Hinnebusch, Raymond, 'The Baʿth Party in Post-Baʿthist Syria: President, Party and the Struggle for "Reform"', *Middle East Critique* 20/2 (2011), pp. 109–25.

Hodgson, M.G.S, 'Durūz', in B. Lewis et al. (eds), *Encyclopaedia of Islam*, Vol. II, 2nd edn (Leiden, Brill, 1965), pp. 631–4.

Hourani, Albert, *A History of the Arab Peoples* (New York, Grand Central Publishing, 1991).

İnalcik, Halil, 'Ḳānūn. iii. Financial and Public Administration', in E. van Donzel et al. (eds), *Encyclopaedia of Islam*, Vol. IV, 2nd edn (Leiden, Brill, 1978), pp. 558–62.

Jennings, Ronald C., 'Zimmis (non-Muslims) in Early 17th Century Ottoman Judicial Records: The Sharia Court of Anatolian Kayseri', *Journal of the Economic and Social History of the Orient* 21/3 (1978), pp. 225–93.

Joseph, Suad, 'Brother/Sister Relationships: Connectivity, Love, and Power in the Reproduction of Patriarchy in Lebanon', *American Ethnologist* 21/1 (1994), pp. 50–73.

—— 'Patriarchy and development in the Arab world', *Gender and Development* 4/2 (1996), pp. 14–19.

—— 'The Public/Private: The Imagined Boundary in the Imagined Nation/State/ Community: The Lebanese Case', *Feminist Review* 57 (1997), pp. 73–92.

—— *Gender and Citizenship in the Middle East: Contemporary Issues in the Middle East* (edited by S. Joseph) (Syracuse, NY, Syracuse University Press, 2000).

Kandiyoti, Deniz, 'Bargaining with Patriarchy', *Gender and Society* 2/3 (1988), pp. 274–90.

—— *Women, Islam and the State* (edited by D. Kandiyoti) (London, Macmillan Press, 1991).

Karpat, Kemal H., 'Millets and Nationality: The Roots of the Incongruity of Nation and State in the Post-Ottoman Era', in B. Braude and B. Lewis (eds), *Christians and Jews in the Ottoman Empire. The Functioning of a Plural Society* (New York, Holmes & Meier Publishers, 1982), pp. 141–69.

Khatib, Line, *Islamic Revivalism in Syria: The Rise and Fall of Ba'thist Secularism* (London, Routledge, 2011).

Khoury, P.S., *Syria and the French Mandate: The Politics of Arab Nationalism, 1920–1945* (Princeton, Princeton University Press, 1987).

Klingman, Mark, 'Diaspora Communities. 6. Syria/Lebanon', in Norman A. Stillman et al. (eds), *Encyclopedia of Jews in the Islamic World*, Vol. II (Leiden, Brill, 2010), pp. 77–81.

Kramer, Martin, 'Syria's Alawis and Shi'ism', in M. Kramer (ed.), *Shi'ism, Resistance, and Revolution* (Boulder, Westview Press, 1987), pp. 237–54.

Kruiniger, Pauline, 'Repudiated by husband and Europe?', in M.C. Foblets and N. Yassari (eds), *Cultural Diversity* (The Series of Centre for Studies and Research in International Law and International Relations of the Hague Academy of International Law) (Leiden, Martinus Nijhoff Publishers, 2013), pp. 464–520.

Landis, Joshua, 'Shishakli and the Druzes: Integration and Intransigence', in T. Philipp and B. Schäbler (eds), *The Syrian Land: Processes of Integration and Fragmentation* (Stuttgart, Franz Steiner Verlag, 1998), pp. 369–96.

—— 'Syria: Secularism, Arabism, and Sunni Orthodoxy', in E.A. Doumato and G. Starrett (eds), *Teaching Islam. Textbooks and Religion in the Middle East* (Boulder, Lynne Riener Publishers, 2007), pp. 177–96.

Lapidus, Ira M., *A History of Islamic Societies* (Cambridge, Cambridge University Press, 2002).

Layish, Aharon, *Women and Islamic Law in a Non-Muslim State* (Jerusalem, Israel University Press, 1975).

—— 'The Contribution of the Modernists to the Secularization of Islamic Law', *Middle Eastern Studies* 14/3 (1978), pp. 263–77.

—— *Marriage, Divorce and Succession in the Druze Family: A Study based on decisions of Druze arbitrators and religious courts in Israel and the Golan Heights* (Leiden, Brill, 1982).

—— 'The status of Islamic law in the Druze family in a non-Muslim state as reflected in judicial practice', in K. Kehl-Bodrogi et al. (eds), *Syncretistic Religious Communities in the Near East* (Leiden, Brill, 1997), pp. 139–53.

—— 'Ṭalāḳ. II. Reforms in the modern Middle East and North Africa', in P.J Bearman et al. (eds), *Encyclopaedia of Islam*, Vol. X, 2nd edn (Leiden, Brill, 2000), pp. 155–7.

—— 'The Transformation of the *Shari'a* from Jurists' Law to Statutory Law in the Contemporary Muslim World', *Die Welt des Islams* 44/1 (2004), pp. 85–113.

Linant de Bellefonds, Yvon, *Traité de droit musulman comparé. Tome II: Le mariage, la dissolution du mariage* (Paris, Mouton & Co, 1965).
—— 'kafā'a', in E. van Donzel et al. (eds), *Encyclopaedia of Islam*, Vol. IV, 2nd edn (Leiden, Brill, 1978), p. 404.
Lipstein, Kurt and Szászy, István, 'Chapter 10: Interpersonal conflict of laws', in K. Lipstein (ed.), *International Encyclopedia of Comparative Law*, Vol. III Part 1 (Private International Law) (Tübingen: Mohr Siebeck; Leiden, Martinus Nijhoff Publishers, 2011), pp. 1–35.
Longva, Anh Nga, 'From the *Dhimma* to the Capitulations: Memory and Experience of Protection in Lebanon', in A.N. Longva and A.S. Roald (eds), *Religious Minorities in the Middle East: Domination, Self-Empowerment, Accommodation* (Leiden, Brill, 2012), pp. 47–69.
Maktabi, Rania, 'State, Law and Religion – Gendered Debates on Family Law in Syria and Lebanon' (unpublished paper presented at the 15th Norwegian Conference in Political Science, Trondheim, January 2007), pp. 1–34.
—— 'Family Law and Gendered Citizenship in the Middle East' (unpublished paper presented at the World Bank/Yale workshop 'Societal Transformation and the Challenges of Governance in Africa and the Middle East', Yale University, 31 January–1 February 2009), pp. 1–27.
—— 'Gender, family law and citizenship in Syria', *Citizenship Studies* 14/5 (2010), pp. 557–72.
—— 'Female Citizenship in the Middle East: Comparing family law reform in Morocco, Egypt, Syria and Lebanon', *Middle East Law and Governance* 5 (2013), pp. 280–307.
Manea, Elham, *The Arab State and Women's Rights: The Trap of Authoritarian Governance* (London, Routledge, 2011).
Masters, Bruce, *Christians and Jews in the Ottoman Arab World. The Roots of Sectarianism* (Cambridge, Cambridge University Press, 2001).
Mayer, Elizabeth A., 'Reform of Personal Status Laws in North Africa: A Problem of Islamic or Mediterranean laws?', *Middle East Journal* 49/3 (1995), pp. 432–46.
McCallum, Fiona, 'Religious Institutions and Authoritarian States: church–state relations in the Middle East', *Third World Quarterly* 33/1 (2012), pp. 109–24.
Meneley, Anne, *Tournaments of Value: Sociability and Hierarchy in a Yemeni Town* (Toronto, University of Toronto Press, 1996).
Merry, Sally E., 'Legal Pluralism', *Law and Society Review* 22/5 (1988), pp. 869–96.
Meyendorff, John, *Marriage: An Orthodox Perspective* (Crestwood, NY, St Vladimir's Seminary Press, 1984).
Mir-Hosseini, Ziba, *Marriage on Trial. Islamic Family Law in Iran and Morocco* (London, I.B.Tauris, 2000).
—— 'Towards gender equality: Muslim family laws and the Shari'ah', in Z. Anwar (ed.), *Wanted: Equality and Justice in the Muslim Family* (Kuala Lumpur, Sisters in Islam and Musawah, 2009), pp. 25–63.
Moghadam, Valentine M., *Women, work and economic reform in the Middle East and North Africa* (Boulder, Lynne Rienner Publishers, 1998).
—— *Modernizing Women: Gender and Social Change in the Middle East* (Boulder, Lynne Rienner Publishers, 2003a).
—— 'Engendering Citizenship, Feminizing Civil Society: The Case of the Middle East and North Africa', *Women & Politics* 25-1/2 (2003b), pp. 63–87.

—— 'Patriarchy in Transition: Women and the Changing Family in the Middle East', *Journal of Comparative Family Studies* 35/2 (2004), pp. 137–62.

Molyneux, Maxine, 'Women's Rights and Political Contingency: The Case of Yemen, 1990–1994', *Middle East Journal* 49/3 (1995), pp. 418–31.

Moors, Annelies, *Women, property and Islam: Palestinian experiences, 1920–1990* (Cambridge, Cambridge University Press, 1995).

—— 'Introduction: Public Debates on Family Law Reform. Participants, Positions, and styles of argumentation in the 1990s', *Islamic Law and Society* 10/1 (2003), pp. 1–11.

Moslih, Anton, 'Code du Statut Personnel des Catholiques en Syrie : Etude' (unpublished document, n.d.), pp. 1–7.

—— 'La legge sullo statuto personale delle confessioni cattoliche', *Il Regno Attualità* 4 (2008), pp. 135–38.

Mouawad, Ray J., 'Syria and Iraq – Repression. Disappearing Christians of the Middle East', *Middle East Quarterly* (2001), pp. 51–60,

Moussalli, Habib, 'The Christians of Syria', in Andrea Pacini (ed.), *Christian Communities in the Arab Middle East: The Challenge of the Future* (Oxford, Clarendon Press, 1998), pp. 286–93.

Muhanna, Nadia, 'Marriages of Convenience', *Syria Today* (online edition), February 2011. Available at http://www.syria-today.com/index.php/life/14365-marriages-of-convenience (accessed 15 June 2011).

Muñoz, Gema M., 'Feminism in the Arab World. The Silent Revolution' (online article at Qantara.de), 17 April 2012. Available at http://en.qantara.de/wcsite.php?wc_c=18942&wc_id=19849 (accessed 26 July 2012).

Murre-Van den Berg, Heleen, 'Syriac Christianity', in K. Parry (ed.), *The Blackwell Companion to Eastern Christianity* (Malden, Blackwell Publishing, 2007), pp. 249–68.

Nadolski, Dora G., 'Ottoman and Secular Civil Law', *International Journal of Middle East Studies* 8/4 (1977), pp. 517–43.

Nasir, Jamal J., *The Islamic Law of Personal Status* (The Hague, Kluwer Law International, 2002).

O'Mahony, Anthony (ed.), *Christianity in the Middle East: Studies in Modern History, Theology and Politics* (London, Melisende, 2008).

O'Mahony, Anthony and Loosley, Emma (eds), *Eastern Christianity in the Modern Middle East* (London, Routledge, 2010).

Otto, Jan Michiel, *Sharia Incorporated: A Comparative Overview of the Legal Systems of Twelve Muslim Countries in Past and Present* (Leiden, Leiden University Press, 2010).

Pace, Joe and Landis, Joshua, 'The Syrian Opposition: The struggle for unity and relevance, 2003–2008', in F.H. Lawson (ed.), *Demystifying Syria* (London, Saqi Books, 2009), pp. 120–43.

Parry, Ken (ed.), *The Blackwell Companion to Eastern Christianity* (Malden, Blackwell Publishing, 2007).

Peletz, Micheal G., *Islamic Modern: Religious Courts and Cultural Politics in Malaysia* (Princeton, Princeton University Press, 2002).

Pierret, Thomas, 'Sunni Clergy Politics in the Cities of Ba'thi Syria', in F.H. Lawson (ed.), *Demystifying Syria* (London, Saqi Books, 2009), pp. 70–84.

—— *Religion and State in Syria: the Sunni Ulama from Coup to Revolution* (Cambridge, Cambridge University Press, 2013).

Pinto, Paulo G., '"Oh Syria, God Protects You": Islam as Cultural Idiom under Bashar al-Asad', *Middle East Critique* 20/2 (2011), pp. 189–205.

Pospishil, Victor J., 'The Problem of Divorce in the Catholic Church', *Journal of Family Law* 7/4 (1968), pp. 595–612.

—— *Eastern Catholic Marriage Law: According to the Code of Canons of the Eastern Churches* (Brooklyn NY, Saint Maron Publications, 1991).

Rabo, Annika, *Change on the Euphrates: Villagers, Townsmen and Employees in Northeast Syria* (Stockholm, Studies in Social Anthropology, 1986).

—— 'Gender, State and civil society in Jordan and Syria', in C. Hann and E. Dunn (eds), *Civil Society. Challenging Western Models* (London, Routledge, 1996), pp. 155–77.

—— *A Shop of One's Own: Independence and Reputation among Traders in Aleppo* (London, I.B.Tauris, 2005a).

—— 'Family law in multicultural and multireligious Syria', in G. Collste (ed.), *Possibilities of Religious Pluralism* (Linköping, Linköping University Electronic Press, 2005b), pp. 71–87.

—— 'Secularism. Arab States (excepting North Africa and the Gulf)', in S. Joseph (ed.), *Encyclopedia of Women in Islamic Cultures II* (Leiden, Brill, 2005c), pp. 725–6.

—— 'To reform or not to reform? Elusive family law debates in Syria' (unpublished paper presented at conference 'Re-imagining the Shari'a: Theory, Practice and Muslim Pluralism at Play', Venice, 13–16 September 2009).

—— 'Syrian Transnational Families and Family Law', in A. Hellum et al. (eds), *From Transnational Relations to Transnational Laws: Northern European Laws at the Crossroads* (Farnham, Ashgate Publishers, 2011), pp. 29–49.

—— 'Conviviality and Conflict in Contemporary Aleppo', in A.N. Longva and A.S. Roald (eds), *Religious Minorities in the Middle East: Domination, Self-Empowerment, Accommodation* (Leiden, Brill, 2012a), pp. 123–47.

—— '"We are Christians and we are equal citizens": perspectives on particularity and pluralism in contemporary Syria', *Islam and Christian–Muslim Relations* 23/1 (2012b), pp. 79–93.

Refugee Review Tribunal Australia, *RRT Research Response No. LBN30136*, Country: Lebanon, 6 June 2006. Available online http://www.unhcr.org/refworld/pdfid/4b6fe27e0.pdf (accessed 15 December 2011).

Roded, R., 'Lessons by a Syrian Islamist from the Life of the Prophet Muhammad', *Middle Eastern Studies* 42/6 (2006), pp. 855–72.

Rose, Richard B., 'Islam and the Development of Personal Status Laws Among Christian Dhimmis: Motives, Sources, Consequences', *The Muslim World* 72/3–4 (1982), pp. 159–79.

Rosen, Lawrence, *The Anthropology of Justice: Law as Culture in Islamic Society* (Cambridge, Cambridge University Press, 1989).

Rowe, Paul S., 'Neo-millet Systems and Transnational Religious Movements: The Humayun Decrees and Church Construction in Egypt', *Journal of Church and State* 49 (2007), pp. 329–50.

Rubin, Avi, 'Legal borrowing and its impact on Ottoman legal culture in the late nineteenth century', *Continuity and Change* 22/2 (2007), pp. 279–303.

Sadiqi, Fatima, 'Facing Challenges and Pioneering Feminist and Gender Studies: Women in Post-colonial and Today's Maghrib', *African and Asian Studies* 7 (2008), pp. 447-70.

Saleh, Nabil, 'Civil Codes of Arab Countries: The Sanhuri Codes', *Arab Law Quarterly* 8/2 (1993), pp. 161–7.
Sato, Noriko, *Memory and Social Identity among Syrian Orthodox Christians* (unpublished PhD thesis, University of Durham, 2001).
Schacht, Joseph, *An Introduction to Islamic Law* (Oxford, Clarendon Press, 1982).
—— 'Nikāḥ. I. In Classical Islamic Law', in C.E. Bosworth et al. (eds), *Encyclopaedia of Islam*, Vol. VIII, 2nd edn (Leiden, Brill, 1995), pp. 26–9.
Seale, P., *Asad of Syria: The Struggle for the Middle East* (Berkeley, University of California Press, 1990).
Sezgin, Yüksel, *Human Rights under State-Enforced Religious Family Laws in Israel, Egypt and India* (Cambridge, Cambridge University Press, 2013).
Sha'aban, Bouthaina, 'The Status of Women in Syria', in S. Sabbagh (ed.), *Arab Women. Between Defiance and Restraint* (New York, Olive Branch Press, 2003), pp. 54–61.
Shaham, Ron, 'Jews and the Sharī'a Courts in Modern Egypt', *Studia Islamica* 82 (1995), pp. 113–36.
—— 'Shopping for legal forums: Christians and family law in modern Egypt', in Khaled Masud et al. (eds), *Dispensing Justice in Islam: Qadis and their Judgments* (Leiden, Brill, 2006), pp. 451–72.
Shaqfa, Muhammad Fihr, *sharh ahkam al-ahwal al-shakhsiyya: li-l-muslimin wa-l-nasara wa-l-yahud* (*Explaining the Law of Personal Status: Muslims, Christians, and Jews*) (Damascus, Mu'assasat Al-Nuri, 1998).
Sharabi, Hisham, *Neopatriarchy: A Theory of Distorted Change in the Arab World* (New York, Oxford University Press, 1992).
Shehada, Nahda, *Justice without Drama: Enacting Family Law in Gaza City Sharī'a Court* (Maastricht, Shaker Publishing, 2005).
—— 'House of Obedience: Social Norms, Individual Agency and Historical Contingency', *Journal of Middle Eastern Women's Studies* 5/10 (2009a), pp. 24–49.
—— 'Flexibility versus Rigidity in the Practice of Islamic Family Law', *PoLAR: Political and Legal Anthropology Review* 32/1 (2009b), pp. 28–46.
—— 'Negotiating Custody Rights in Islamic Family Law', in T. Kirsch and B. Turner (eds), *Permutations of Order: Religion and Law as Contested Sovereignties* (Farnham, Ashgate, 2009c), pp. 247–62.
Shehadeh, Lamia R., 'Gender-Relevant Legal Change in Lebanon', *Feminist Formations* 22/3 (2010), pp. 210–28.
Sonbol, Amira E.A., '"The woman follows the nationality of her husband": Guardianship, citizenship and gender', *Hawwa: Journal of Women of the Middle East and the Islamic World* 1 (2003), pp. 86–117.
—— 'Shari'ah and State Formation: Historical Perspective', *Chicago Journal of International Law* 8/1 (2007), pp. 59–83.
Sonneveld, Nadia, 'Khul' Divorce in Egypt: How Family Courts Are Providing a "Dialogue" between Husband and Wife', *Anthropology in the Middle East* 5/2 (2010), pp. 100–20.
—— *Khul' Divorce in Egypt: Public Debates, Judicial Practices, and Everyday Life* (Cairo, American University of Cairo Press, 2012a).
—— 'Rethinking the Difference Between Formal and Informal Marriages in Egypt', in M. Voorhoeve (ed.), *Family Law in Islam. Divorce, Marriage and Women in the Muslim World* (London, I.B.Tauris, 2012b), pp. 77–107.

Sousa Santos, B. de, 'Law: A Map of Misreading. Toward a Postmodern Conception of Law', *Journal of Law and Society* 14/3 (1987), pp. 279–302.

Sparre, Sara Lei, 'Educated Women in Syria: Servants of the State, or Nurturers of the Family?', *Critique: Critical Middle Eastern Studies* 17/1 (2008), pp. 3–20.

Stowasser, B.F. and Abul-Magd, Z., 'Legal Codes and Contemporary Fatawa: Muslim Women and Contesting Paradigms', *Hawwa: Journal of Women of the Middle East and the Islamic World* 6 (2008), pp. 32–51.

Syrian Arab News Agency (SANA), 'Second National Report on Syrian Population Status 2010 ... Syrian Population Set to Double in Next Four Decades' (online article), 16 December 2011. Available at http://sana.sy/eng/21/2011/12/16/388614.htm (accessed 13 February 2012).

Tadros, Mariz, 'The Non-Muslim "Other": Gender and Contestations of Hierarchy or Rights', *Hawwa: Journal of Women of the Middle East and the Islamic World* 7 (2009), pp. 111–43.

Taha, Zakaria, 'Régimes arabes laïcs et politique du genre: La condition de la femme à travers le Code du statut personnel: le cas de la Syrie', *Cahiers de la Méditerranée* 81 (2010), pp. 305–17.

Takim, Liyakat, 'Law: The Four Sunnī Schools of Law', in S. Joseph (ed.), *Encyclopedia of Women in Islamic Cultures* II (Leiden, Brill, 2005), pp. 440–5.

Tamanaha, Brian Z., 'The Folly of the "Social Scientific" Concept of Legal Pluralism', *Journal of Law and Society* 20/2 (1993), pp. 192–217.

—— 'Understanding Legal Pluralism: Past to Present, Local to Global', *Sydney Law Review* 30 (2008), pp. 375–411

Tarabey, Lubna, *Family Law in Lebanon: Marriage and Divorce among the Druze* (London, I.B.Tauris, 2013).

Thompson, Elizabeth, *Colonial citizens. Republican rights, paternal privilege, and gender in French Syria and Lebanon* (New York, Columbia University Press, 2000).

Tocqueville, Alexis de, *L'Ancien régime et la Révolution* (Paris, Calmann Lévy, 1887).

Tucker, Judith E., *In the House of the Law: Gender and Islamic Law in Ottoman Syria and Palestine* (Berkeley, University of California Press, 1998).

—— *Women, Family, and Gender in Islamic Law* (New York, Cambridge University Press, 2008).

Tuttle, Robert, 'The Jews of Syria', on *SyriaComment.com* (24 October 2005). Available at http://faculty-staff.ou.edu/L/Joshua.M.Landis-1/syriablog/2005/10/jews-of-syria-by-robert-tuttle.htm (accessed 18 May 2012).

United Nations Development Programme (UNDP), *Modernization of the Justice Sector in Syria*, UNDP Project Syria (SYR/06/010) (2006).

United States Department of State, *2013 International Religious Freedom Report – Syria*. Available online at http://www.state.gov/j/drl/rls/irf/religiousfreedom/index.htm?year=2013&dlid=222313#wrapper (accessed 23 August 2015).

Vikør, Knut S., *Between God and the Sultan. A History of Islamic Law* (London, Hurst & Company, 2005).

Vincent-Grosso, Sarah, 'Maktub: An Ethnography of Evidence in a Tunisian Divorce Court', in M. Voorhoeve (ed.), *Family Law in Islam: Divorce, Marriage and Women in the Muslim World* (London, I.B.Tauris, 2012), pp. 171–98.

Voorhoeve, Maaike, 'Judicial Discretion in Tunisian Personal Status Law', in M. Voorhoeve (ed.), *Family Law in Islam. Divorce, Marriage and Women in the Muslim World* (London, I.B.Tauris, 2012), pp. 199–229.

—— *Gender and Divorce Law in North Africa: Sharia, Custom and the Personal Status Code in Tunisia* (London, I.B.Tauris, 2014).

Warrick, Catherine, *Law in the Service of Legitimacy: Gender and Politics in Jordan* (Farnham, Ashgate, 2009).

Weber, Anne F., 'Briser et suivre le norms: les couples islamo-chrétiens au Liban', in B. Drieskens (ed.), *Les métamorphoses du mariage au Moyen-Orient* (Beirut, Institut Français du Proche-Orient (IFPO) 2008), pp. 13–31.

Wedeen, Lisa, *Ambiguities of Domination: Politics, Rhetoric, and Symbols in Contemporary Syria* (Chicago, The University of Chicago Press, 1999).

Wehr, Hans, *A Dictionary of Modern Written Arabic (Arabic-English)*, 4th edn, edited by J.M. Cowan (Ithaca, NY, 1994).

Welchman, Lynn, *Beyond the Code: Muslim Family Law and the Shari'a Judiciary in the Palestinian West Bank* (The Hague, Kluwer Law International, 2000).

—— *Women and Muslim Family Laws in Arab States: A Comparative Overview of Textual Development and Advocacy* (Amsterdam, Amsterdam University Press, 2007).

—— 'A Husband's Authority: Emerging Formulations in Muslim Family Laws', *International Journal of Law, Policy and the Family* 25/1 (2011), pp. 1–23.

White, Benjamin T., 'Addressing the State: The Syrian "Ulama" Protest Personal Status Law Reform, 1939', *International Journal Middle Eastern Studies* 42 (2010), pp. 10–12.

Yamani, M.A.Z, *Polygamy and Law in Contemporary Saudi Arabia* (Reading, Ithaca Press, 2008).

Zantout, Mida R., 'Khul': Between Past and Present', *Islamic Law and Law of the Muslim World Research Paper Series*, No. 08–14 (New York Law School, 2006), pp. 1–47.

Zisser, Eyal, 'Where Is Bashar al-Assad Heading?', *Middle East Quarterly* 15/1 (2008), pp. 35–40.

INDEX

www.ingramcontent.com/pod-product-compliance
Ingram Content Group UK Ltd.
Pitfield, Milton Keynes, MK11 3LW, UK
UKHW021905150926
475560UK00003B/191

9 781784 533342